SHAKESPEARE

A Life in Drama

Also by Stanley Wells

Literature and Drama
Royal Shakespeare:
Four Major Productions at Stratford-upon-Avon
Shakespeare: An Illustrated Dictionary
Shakespeare: The Writer and his Work
Modernizing Shakespeare's Spelling
(with 'Three Studies in the Text of *Henry V*', by Gary Taylor)
Re-Editing Shakespeare for the Modern Reader
William Shakespeare: A Textual Companion
(with Gary Taylor, John Jowett, and William Montgomery)

EDITED WORKS
Shakespeare: *A Midsummer Night's Dream*
(New Penguin Shakespeare)
Shakespeare: *The Comedy of Errors*
(New Penguin Shakespeare)
Shakespeare: *Richard II* (New Penguin Shakespeare)
Thomas Dekker: *The Shoemaker's Holiday*
(Revels Plays; with R.L. Smallwood)
Nineteenth Century Shakespeare Burlesques
William Shakespeare: A Bibliographical Guide
English Drama: A Bibliographical Guide
The Cambridge Companion to Shakespeare Studies
Shakespeare's Sonnets
William Shakespeare: *The Complete Works*
(with Gary Taylor, John Jowett, and William Montgomery)
An Oxford Anthology of Shakespeare

SHAKESPEARE

A Life in Drama

STANLEY WELLS

W·W·NORTON & COMPANY
New York   London

Printed in the United States of America

Manufacturing by the Maple-Vail Manufacturing Group, Inc.

ISBN 0-393-03765-7

W. W. Norton & Company, Inc., 500 Fifth Avenue, New York, N.Y. 10110
W. W. Norton & Company Ltd., 10 Coptic Street, London WC1A 1PU

1 2 3 4 5 6 7 8 9 0

For
JESSICA

Contents

Acknowledgements

I am grateful to my wife, Susan Hill, for suggesting that I write a book explaining why I think Shakespeare can still speak to modern readers and theatregoers, and to Christopher Sinclair-Stevenson both for agreeing to publish it and for welcome encouragement along the way. A term's study leave from the University of Birmingham was of great help in making a start. I have received valuable assistance from Dr Susan Brock, librarian of the Shakespeare Institute, from its secretaries, Daphne Ingram and Etta Mahon, and from the library staff of the Shakespeare Centre, Stratford-upon-Avon. Christine Buckley read the typescript with characteristically scrupulous care. Douglas Matthews supplied the index.

January, 1994

S.W.W.

References

I have not thought it desirable in a book of this nature to provide full documentation of well-known facts. Short references are used as listed below for works repeatedly cited; place of publication is London unless stated otherwise. Quotations from Shakespeare are from the Oxford *Complete Works*, General Editors Stanley Wells and Gary Taylor, with John Jowett and William Montgomery (Oxford, 1986; Compact Edition 1981, etc.)

Bullough   Geoffrey Bullough, ed., *Narrative and Dramatic Sources of Shakespeare,* 8 vols (1957–75)

Chambers   E.K. Chambers, *The Elizabethan Stage,* 4 vols (Oxford, 1923)

Hazlitt, *Characters*   William Hazlitt, *Characters of Shakespeare's Plays* (1817; World's Classics, 1916, etc.)

Hazlitt on Theatre   Hazlitt on Theatre, ed. William Archer and Robert Lowe (1895; repr. New York, n.d.)

Johnson, Samuel   *Samuel Johnson on Shakespeare,* ed. H.R. Woudhuysen, New Penguin Shakespeare Library (1989)

Odell   G.C.D. Odell, *Shakespeare from Betterton to Irving,* 2 vols (New York, 1920; repr. London, 1963)

Schoenbaum, *Compact Documentary Life*   S. Schoenbaum, *William Shakespeare: A Compact Documentary Life* (Oxford, 1977; paperback, 1978)

Schoenbaum, *Shakespeare's Lives*   S. Schoenbaum, *Shakespeare's Lives* (Oxford, 1970; revised 1991)

Shaw on Shakespeare   Shaw on Shakespeare, ed. Edwin Wilson (1962)

Textual Companion   William Shakespeare: A Textual Companion, by

Stanley Wells and Gary Taylor, with John Jowett and
William Montgomery (Oxford, 1987)
Vickers   Brian Vickers, ed., *Shakespeare: The Critical Heritage*,
6 vols (1974–81)

Note At a few points I draw, usually with extensive revision, on previously published work of my own. The principal instances are:

'Shakespeare and Human Evil', *En Torno A Shakespeare*, ed. M.A. Conejero (Valencia, 1980), pp. 67–91 (for *Othello* and *King Lear*)
'Shakespeare and Romance', *Later Shakespeare*, ed. J.R. Brown and B. Harris, Stratford-upon-Avon Studies 8 (1966), pp. 48–79 (for *The Comedy of Errors, Twelfth Night, The Winter's Tale,* and *The Tempest*)
'Shakespeare Performances in London and Stratford-upon-Avon, 1986–7', *Shakespeare Survey 41* (Cambridge, 1989), pp. 159–81 (for *Titus Andronicus*)
'*The Taming of the Shrew* and *King Lear*: A Structural Comparison', *Shakespeare Survey 33* (1981), pp. 55–66

ONE

Who is Shakespeare?

Shakespeare is all around us, as both a source of pleasure and an instrument of education. His plays are central to the theatrical repertoire not only in English-speaking countries but in many others too. They form the basis of innumerable films, operas, ballets, and musical scores. Poets, novelists, and dramatists play variations on their narratives, characters, and ideas. Some of their characters have acquired the status of mythic figures: we can speak of a Shylock, a Romeo, or a Hamlet, as of an Adonis, a Don Juan or a Scrooge without implying reference to the works in which they occur. Shakespeare has had an ineradicable influence on the English language, so that we often quote him without knowing that we are doing so. Even at a time when the established canon of English literature is under attack, Shakespeare's plays continue to form the basis of a literary education. They are taught at every level, from the primary to the postgraduate. They stand at the centre of a huge academic industry, manifesting itself in a plethora of books, theses, new editions, and learned papers; of conferences and summer schools; of courses, lectures, and lessons; of exhibitions, workshops, and educational visits.

During the centuries since they were written the plays have accumulated a range of meanings that can never have occurred to their author. It is in the nature of plays to be different every time they are performed, whether because of textual adaptation or, more simply, because every performance of a play is necessarily a work of collaboration between the person who has written the words that are spoken and those who project the text in performance, all of whom make their own contribution to its meanings and effect, which must vary too along with the composition of the audiences before whom they perform. As time passes, and indeed as place changes (both playing place and geographical location), plays change in significance, and are reshaped according to the preoccupations of their interpreters and beholders. *Measure for Measure* would have had a quite different significance for the Victorians, if they had been allowed to see it, than it does for us; and *The Merchant of Venice* is a play whose reception has been greatly affected by the passage of time, and which arouses very different feelings according to where it is performed.

In a sense, then, plays have no stable identity: the text the author pens is not the play because it can mean only through performance; and any individual performance is not the play the author wrote but, rather, one of an infinite number of events to which the original text can give rise. In our own time Shakespeare's plays have been claimed by conservative forces as part of a national heritage, as bulwarks of orthodoxy, and by radicals as a potent source of subversion, as works through which, even in totalitarian regimes, the voice of rebellion has been able to make itself heard; one of many possible examples is the Romanian production of *Hamlet*, first given in 1985, in which Claudius and Gertrude took on the likeness of Ceauşescu and his wife. Intellectual criticism has laboured to deconstruct traditional interpretations, to force a rethinking of relationships among individual parts of the texts, even to insist that, as Terence Hawkes puts it, 'Shakespeare doesn't mean: *we* mean *by* Shakespeare'.[1]

This statement is itself open to interpretation. If the plays were merely blank screens on to which any set of meanings could be projected, there would be no point in invoking Shakespeare at all. On the other hand, it would seem self-evident that if there is to be any justification for the incessant stream of publications about Shakespeare, and for the constant reinterpretation of his plays in our theatres, this must be because of a fruitful interaction between the texts written centuries ago and the minds and imaginations of those who have gone on reading and performing them, an interaction that can both draw meanings from the texts and impose meanings upon them. Some readers of the present day still believe that the plays enshrine essential meanings that can be squarely ascribed to the dramatist himself. Others – the New Historicists – see the plays as products of the age as much as, or rather than, the creations of an individual mind, and labour hard to recapture meanings that they may have had for audiences in their own time, whether or not these meanings were designed by, or even apparent to, Shakespeare himself. Still others, avowedly indifferent to authorial intention or historical circumstance, read these old texts purely in the light of their personal intellectual, political, and emotional preoccupations.

All the readings produced by readers of these persuasions, and of all the intervening ones, have validity for those who hold them, and may be disputed by those who do not. But whatever may be our critical stance on the relation between the author and his work, it would be hard to deny the material fact that the scripts that have given rise to the phenomenon we now know, in all its various manifestations, as Shakespeare, were penned long ago by a person – possibly writing sometimes in collaboration with others – known to his contemporaries as William Shakespeare.

In this book I shall concern myself mainly with the plays and poems ascribed to this writer, not as historical texts but as works that have within them an abiding capacity to engage the minds and hearts of readers and theatregoers. I shall also try to suggest some of the reasons why I, as just one of these readers and playgoers, but one whose career has to an exceptional degree been bound up with these texts, think they continue to be worth our attention.

Anyone who speaks to non-specialist audiences about Shakespeare is likely to be asked whether he or she believes that Shakespeare really wrote Shakespeare. And any professional Shakespearian suffers the occupational hazard of receiving frequent, unsolicited brown envelopes postmarked 'Sussex Coast' emanating from the Shakespeare Authorship Information Centre and containing photocopied quotations from books and newspapers supposed to support the claim that Shakespeare did not write Shakespeare and that almost anyone else did. Many attempts have been made to demonstrate that the works ascribed to William Shakespeare of Stratford-upon-Avon were in fact written by someone else – Francis Bacon, or Christopher Marlowe, or the Earl of Oxford, or Queen Elizabeth I, or even Daniel Defoe. As will become apparent, I do believe that the author was William Shakespeare of Stratford-upon-Avon; and I think that attempts to disprove this are usually the result of snobbery – reluctance to believe that works of genius can be produced by a person of relatively humble birth or by one who did not enjoy a university education – or of the desire for self-publicity, or of both.

Questioners who become impatient of attempts to demonstrate Shakespeare's authorship are liable to go on to ask whether it matters who wrote the plays anyway. In one sense the answer is no, it doesn't matter – or at any rate it wouldn't if their author were someone who had no independent reputation; if, for example, William Shakespeare turned out to be a pen-name for his townsmen Thomas Quiney or Philip Rogers, or for some other relatively undistinguished Elizabethan. Likewise, someone who believed absolutely that the meaning of each individual work is constructed simply by the work itself would not care what name was attached to them.

But my own view is that it does matter that they were all written by one person, whatever that person was called, because I think the links between plays as different as *The Comedy of Errors* and *King Lear*, or *Love's Labour's Lost* and *The Winter's Tale*, and the fact that these plays could all proceed from the same imagination, tell us something about the capacity of the human mind. T.S. Eliot put it rather hyperbolically: 'The whole of Shakespeare's work is *one* poem; and it is the poetry of it in this sense, not the poetry of isolated lines and passages or the poetry of the single figures which he created, that matters most'; the work is 'united by one significant, consistent, and developing personality'.[2] It is for this reason that, rather than discussing each work on its own in a random fashion, or in a purely generic sequence, I adopt a partly chronological scheme, tracing Shakespeare's career sometimes through related groups of plays, while devoting full chapters to those that have most preoccupied later ages. And because I think there is a real relationship between the writer and his work, I want to precede my discussion of the works with one chapter on the writer himself, and a second on his professional career as a man of the theatre.

Though it is often said that we know very little about Shakespeare's life, it would be closer to the truth to say that we know quite a lot, but that what we know includes very little of what we should most like to know. We have virtually no direct information about his private life, no accounts of his childhood or of his relationship with members of his family or with colleagues, no love-letters – no manuscript letters indeed of any kind written by him – no diaries, no working notebooks, no manuscripts (with the probable exception of his brief contribution to the collaborative play of *Sir Thomas More*).

The information that has come down to us derives largely from public, especially legal, records. This is what we should expect for a man of his social standing; personal records were more likely to be preserved among aristocratic families who kept muniment rooms. Much research has been carried out into Shakespeare's life; new documentary evidence still occasionally turns up, and new theories are constantly devised in the effort to construct a coherent narrative on the basis of what is known. This is often fascinating in its own right, but little of it has any direct bearing on the way we experience the plays and poems as readers and theatregoers, and for my purposes it seems adequate to summarize the more important facts (omitting some of the more mundane ones such as references to his failure to pay taxes and to his purchases of land and other property) while offering brief discussions of those aspects of his life that may seem of most interest to the modern reader.[3]

Shakespeare's father, John, was a glover, wool-dealer, and money-lender in Stratford-upon-Avon who had married Mary Arden, a prosperous farmer's daughter, in or about 1557. Of their eight children, four sons and one daughter survived childhood. William, their eldest son and third child, was baptized in the magnificent Holy Trinity Church on 26 April 1564, and may have been born three days earlier, on 23 April, which happens to be St George's Day. At this time John Shakespeare's fortunes were rising: four years later he became bailiff (or mayor) and justice of the peace; but in later years his prosperity declined, possibly as a result of Catholic sympathies. His youngest son, Edmund, born sixteen years after William, was to follow his brother into the theatre: he became an actor, but died when he was only twenty-seven and was buried on the morning of the last day of 1607 in St Saviour's, Southwark, close to the Globe, to the sound of the tolling of the church's 'great bell', a ceremony for which someone had to pay a pound. We do not know to what company he belonged, or whether he acted in any of his brother's plays.

No lists survive of the pupils at the Stratford grammar school – the King's New School, as it was known – in Shakespeare's time, but his father's position would have qualified him to attend, and we have every reason short of absolute documentary evidence to suppose that he did. If so, he would have left when he was about fifteen. We should be more likely to know if he went to a university, but there is nothing to suggest that this is so. He must have found some kind of work, and whether or not this was in Stratford, he kept up his links with his home town: a bond permitting him to marry Anne Hathaway, of nearby Shottery, was issued on 28 November 1582, when he was eighteen; she was twenty-six, and pregnant. Their daughter Susanna was baptized six months later, on 26 May 1583, and twins, Hamnet and Judith, on 2 February 1585. At some unknown date not later than 1592, and probably several years earlier, Shakespeare entered the theatrical profession, with the result that he had to base himself in London – but his family remained in Stratford, and he kept up his links with his place of birth till he died and was buried there. On 11 August 1596 his only son, Hamnet, was buried there at the age of eleven and a half; we can only conjecture how his father felt about this.

In the same year John Shakespeare, who had approached the Heralds' Office in the hope of gaining a coat of arms shortly after becoming Bailiff of Stratford, in 1568, successfully renewed his application, thereby acquiring official status as a gentleman and conferring gentility upon his family. The draft document, prepared by Sir William Dethick, Garter King-of-Arms, shows a shield crossed with a spear and surmounted by a falcon. The spear is an obvious allusion to the family name; more interestingly, the falcon may also have family associations: Shakespeare's writings show expert knowledge of falconry, so it's quite likely that the choice of a crest reflects his own interests.[4]

At this time Shakespeare had a London base in Bishopsgate, but he showed that he looked on Stratford as his real home by buying a large, three-storeyed house there, New Place, within a year of his son's death; it was demolished in 1759 by an irascible owner who got tired of people coming to ask if they could see Shakespeare's mulberry tree, but we have a drawing of the outside done in the eighteenth century which shows that it had five gables and was an establishment of some grandeur.

It's easy to underestimate how early in his life Shakespeare became prosperous. He was only thirty-three when he bought what is often said to have been the second largest house in Stratford, and in the following year his fellow townsman Richard Quiney, whose son was to marry Judith Shakespeare, addressed to him a letter asking for a loan, probably as a business transaction, of £30 – a large sum, sufficient, for instance, to pay the Stratford schoolmaster's salary for eighteen months, and suggesting confidence in his friend's financial resources. Quiney's is the only surviving letter addressed to Shakespeare; as it was found among its writer's papers it appears never to have been delivered, and we don't know if he got the money.[5] Shakespeare's father died in 1601 and was buried in Stratford; his will is lost, so it may be only coincidence that in May of the next year his son had enough spare funds to buy around 107 acres of arable land along with twenty more of pasturage in Old Stratford; he paid £320 for it – we can get some idea of the magnitude of the investment if we reflect that in the late twentieth century such land would be likely to cost something in the region of £150,000. Four years later, in 1605, he had another spare £440 which he invested in the Stratford tithes, producing an annual income of £60.

Also in 1602, a London law student, John Manningham, recorded a piece of gossip that gives us a rare glimpse into what was being said about the private life of Shakespeare and that of the leading tragedian of his company, Richard Burbage:

> Upon a time when Burbage played Richard III there was a citizen grew so far in liking with him that before she went from the play she appointed him to come that night unto her by the name of Richard the Third. Shakespeare, overhearing their conclusion, went before, was entertained, and at his game ere Burbage came. Then, message being brought that Richard the Third was at the door, Shakespeare caused return to be made that William the Conqueror was before Richard the Third.

Shakespeare seems to have lived in various places in London; in 1604 he had lodgings with a Huguenot family called Mountjoy (the title of the French herald in *Henry the Fifth,* but that play had been written several years before). Eight years later he was called to testify in a court case relating to a marriage settlement on the daughter of the house. The records of the case provide, I suppose, our only direct report of words actually spoken by Shakespeare. Verbatim accounts of what was said in Elizabethan lawcourts are often entertaining in the immediacy with which they convey the tones of the human voice, but unfortunately this is not true here: we get little sense of personality from sentences such as 'He knoweth not what implements and necessaries of household stuff the defendant gave the plaintiff in marriage with his daughter Mary.'

Shakespeare's own daughter, Susanna, married a distinguished physician, John Hall, in Stratford in June 1607, and there his only grandchild, their daughter Elizabeth, was baptized the following February. In 1609 his mother died there, and his increasing involvement with Stratford along with his reducing dramatic output suggests that he may have been spending more time at New Place, perhaps devoting himself to his local business interests. But his London commitments continued: he was there for the Mountjoy case in 1612, and in March 1613 he invested more money in a house in the Blackfriars area. Back in Stratford, life had its problems. In 1615 his daughter Susanna sued a young man called John Lane for slanderously alleging that she had 'been naught' with a hatter and haberdasher, Ralph Smith. At the same period Shakespeare was involved in the disputes about the enclosure of land whose tithes he owned that figure prominently in Edward Bond's play *Bingo* (1973).

Probably in January of 1616, whether or not under a presentiment of death, Shakespeare drafted his will, but more family troubles soon caused him to change its provisions. In February his second daughter, Judith, married Thomas Quiney. The bridegroom had previously conceived a child with one Margaret Wheeler, who, along with her baby, died in childbirth a month later. Quiney was brought to court, admitted his crime, and was sentenced to perform public penance, wearing a white sheet in church on three succeeding Sundays. In the event he got off with a fine and a less public confession, but Shakespeare seems to have altered his will to give Judith greater financial protection. He signed it on 25 March, and died, according to his monument, on 23 April. (The thought that he had died on the day he should have celebrated as his birthday once reduced a young friend of mine to tears.)

The will itself is not a personally revealing document, and has been the site of much controversy arising from conflicting interpretations of contemporary legal practice. Notoriously, all his widow got was the second-best bed, but she would have been entitled by law and local custom to part of his estate. He left most of the rest to his elder daughter, Susanna, and her husband. Among bequests to Judith was his 'broad silver-gilt bowl'; this is the kind of thing that might well survive, but it has not been identified. There are numerous bequests to Stratford friends, including his sword to Thomas Combe and 20s in gold to his seven-year-old godson, William Walker. But only three of his theatrical colleagues are named: he left 26s 8d each to John Heminges, Richard Burbage, and Henry Condell to buy mourning rings. He was buried in a prominent position in the chancel of Holy Trinity Church on 25 April. His widow died in 1623, and his last surviving descendant, Elizabeth Hall, who inherited New Place and married first a neighbour, Thomas Nash (not the writer, whose name is usually spelt Nashe), and secondly John Bernard, knighted in 1661, died in 1670. So Shakespeare's direct line died out.

★

During Shakespeare's lifetime, and in the years following, a number of tributes were paid to the excellence of his art, usually implying nothing but respect for the artist, but with few direct allusions to his character. After Robert Greene attacked him in 1592 as 'an upstart crow' (see page 24), Henry Chettle apologized for having allowed the offensive passage to reach print, saying: 'Myself have seen his demeanour no less civil than he excellent in the quality he professes; besides, divers of worship have reported his uprightness of dealing, which argues his honesty, and his facetious grace in writing, that approves his art.' Ben Jonson probably wrote more than anyone else about Shakespeare; his tribute printed in the First Folio is concerned mainly with his art, though he does claim that

> the race
> Of Shakespeare's mind and manners brightly shines
> In his well turnèd and true filèd lines.

Less formally, in *Timber, or Discoveries made upon men and matter*, apparently a selection of Jonson's notebooks partly prepared for publication, he writes: 'I loved the man, and do honour his memory (on this side idolatry) as much as any. He was indeed honest, and of an open and free nature; had an excellent fantasy, brave notions, and gentle expressions, wherein he flowed with that facility that sometime it was necessary he should be stopped . . .' There is also a certain amount of negative evidence: unlike most of his contemporary writers, Shakespeare had no major clashes with the law, was never imprisoned, so far as we know, and incurred no substantial debts.

None of the known tributes to Shakespeare appeared directly after his death, but it was probably in or soon after 1616 that his legatees Heminges and Condell started work on what is clearly conceived as a memorial volume, the great First Folio edition of his collected plays; it did not appear until 1623, but big books take a long time to prepare, and much work went into this one. Its importance cannot be overstated, for without it we should almost certainly not have had the texts of eighteen of Shakespeare's plays, including some of his greatest, such as *As You Like It*, *Twelfth Night*, *Macbeth*, *Antony and Cleopatra*, and *The Tempest*, which appeared there for the first time. But these must have cost Heminges and Condell – who seem to have taken prime responsibility for the volume – the least trouble, because they undertook considerable editorial work on all the other eighteen plays that had already appeared in print. For these the printers had

normally used a manuscript of the play in a late stage of composition
but before it had been put into rehearsal; for the Folio Heminges and
Condell never simply reprinted the existing editions but always
compared them with theatrical manuscripts in the effort, it would
seem, both to purge them of error and to bring them closer to the plays
as acted. They also included a number of verse tributes, among them
the fine poem by Ben Jonson headed 'To the Memory of my beloved
the author Master William Shakespeare and what he hath left us' – the
one that includes the sentence, 'He was not of an age but for all time.'

The title-page of the First Folio bears one of the two images of
Shakespeare with the strongest claims to authenticity, though neither
can be shown certainly to have been done directly from life. The one in
the First Folio is the engraving by Martin Droeshout which his friends
presumably regarded as an adequate likeness. The other is the
monument in Holy Trinity Church, Stratford-upon-Avon
commissioned from Gheerart Janssen, a stonemason whose shop was
not far from the Globe Theatre; it incorporates a half-length effigy in
which Shakespeare looks older than in the engraving, which may
support the view that the engraving, at least, could have been done
from a drawing made in Shakespeare's lifetime. Among oil paintings
the one (with ear-ring) known as the Chandos portrait has its
defenders; many early copies exist, and it became the dominant source
of eighteenth-century images of Shakespeare.

Those who doubt that Shakespeare wrote the works often claim
that there is nothing to connect William Shakespeare of Stratford-
upon-Avon with the writer, but this is not true. Admittedly,
references to him in local records do not identify him as a man of the
theatre, but neither do they ascribe any other trade or profession to
him. And three pieces of contemporary evidence firmly link the
Warwickshire gentleman (as he became) with the London playwright.
One is his will, with its bequests to Heminges, Burbage, and Condell.
Another is his monument, which bears an inscription linking him
with Socrates and Virgil and stating that with him 'quick nature died',
and that 'all that he hath writ | Leaves living art but page to serve his
wit' (a cryptic remark which I take to mean that everything that he has
written leaves an art that lives, if only on the page, to demonstrate his
genius, with perhaps a pun on page as 'side of a sheet of paper' and
'pageboy'). And third is Ben Jonson's linking in his poem of this 'Star
of poets' with his home territory, as the 'Sweet swan of Avon'.

In the century or so following Shakespeare's death many anecdotes
about him were recorded, with varying, often unassessable, claims to

truth. Sir Nicholas L'Estrange (who died in 1655) told a rather unfunny story about his being godfather to 'one of Ben Jonson's children'. Thomas Fuller (who died in 1661 and seems to have started collecting information by 1643) says that 'many were the wit combats between him and Ben Jonson'. He nicely imagines them in terms of encounters between 'a Spanish great galleon and an English man-of-war: Master Jonson, like the former, was built far higher in learning, solid but slow in his performances; Shakespeare, with the English man-of-war, lesser in bulk but lighter in sailing, could turn with all tides, tack about and take advantage of all winds by the quickness of his wit and invention'. Thomas Plume, around 1657, said Shakespeare was a glover's son and that 'Will was a good honest fellow, but he durst have cracked a jest with him at any time'. John Ward, vicar of Stratford from 1662, felt (like many of his successors, I dare say) a duty on taking up office to find out something about Shakespeare; he noted his resolution 'to peruse Shakespeare's plays and be versed in them, that I may not be ignorant in that matter', and recorded that Shakespeare 'spent at the rate of £1000 a year, as I have heard', and that 'Shakespeare, Drayton, and Ben Jonson had a merry meeting, and it seems drank too hard, for Shakespeare died of a fever there contracted'. Around 1672 John Dryden wrote that Shakespeare 'said himself that he was forced to kill [Mercutio] in the third act [of *Romeo and Juliet*] to prevent being killed by him'. John Aubrey, writing his *Brief Lives*, collected material from William Beeston, son of an actor who had joined the Chamberlain's Men by 1598. His notes include the information that Shakespeare was 'the more to be admired' because 'he was not a company keeper . . . wouldn't be debauched, and if invited to writ he was in pain'. This sits a little uneasily with Manningham's much earlier tale about Richard III and William the Conqueror. Aubrey also says that Shakespeare's father was a butcher; that as a boy Shakespeare 'exercised his father's trade, but when he killed a calf he would do it in a high style, and make a speech'; that 'he was wont to go to his native country once a year'; that 'he understood Latin pretty well, for he had been in his younger years a schoolmaster in the country'; and that on his journeys between London and Warwickshire he used to stay at a tavern in Oxford kept by John Davenant, father of the poet and playwright Sir William Davenant – who would let it be understood that he might have been Shakespeare's bastard son. Late in the seventeenth or early in the eighteenth century Richard Davies, a clergyman, recorded the tale that Shakespeare used to poach deer and rabbits at Charlecote from Sir William Lucy, 'who had him often whipped and sometimes imprisoned, and at last made him fly his native country to his great advancement', and also that 'he died a papist'. A Mr Dowdall wrote in 1693 that a clerk aged over eighty who showed him round Stratford church had told him that 'Shakespeare was formerly in this town bound apprentice to a butcher, but that he run from his master to London, and there was received into the playhouse as a servitor, and by this means had an opportunity to be what he afterwards proved'. The tale that *The Merry Wives of Windsor* was written within fourteen days at the command of Queen Elizabeth dates from early in the eighteenth century. In the first systematic attempt at a biography of Shakespeare, the *Life* published in Nicholas Rowe's edited collection of the plays in 1709, some of the anecdotes previously recorded are repeated and others added.

Oral history is not to be despised, but neither is it to be trusted. In any case, even if we knew for certain that in his youth Shakespeare was a poacher, that he made speeches while butchering animals, that his death may have been accelerated by a bout of drinking, that he was once a schoolmaster, I am not sure that this would have much if any effect on our understanding and appreciation of his works. Admittedly, if, for instance, we knew that he had a strong religious commitment – that he was indeed a committed 'papist' – this might affect our reading of the plays; but the evidence is tenuous and therefore useless. Biography is interesting in its own right, and there is always the possibility that following up a clue might lead to discoveries that would genuinely illuminate the works, but literary interpretation should not be based on biographical speculation.

One area of investigation that relates directly to the relationship between life and works is the matter of Shakespeare's education and his reading in general. We should like to know what books he owned, but unfortunately none is mentioned in his will; they may have been listed in an accompanying inventory that has not survived. Certainly his poems and plays draw at least as heavily for their raw material on books as on life. They are the work of a writer with a classical education, not only full of local allusions to gods, goddesses, mythological figures, and the heroes of antiquity, but more deeply permeated with the techniques of the classical rhetoricians and infused with the imaginative spirit of, especially, Ovid and Virgil. Ben Jonson famously jibed at Shakespeare's 'small Latin and less Greek'; but these matters are relative. Shakespeare may not have had as much Latin as university-educated contemporaries such as Christopher Marlowe, who made extensive direct translations from Ovid and Lucan, but he had enough not only to read Latin works but also, it would seem, to coin words on the basis of Latin roots – words such as abruption, circummured, conflux, exsufflicate, and tortive, all found for the first time in his plays.

Of course, some of the classics were available in translation as well as in editions of the original; the years between Shakespeare's birth and his emergence on the London theatrical scene saw the appearance of the first major translations into English of Ovid, Apuleius, Horace, Heliodorus, Plutarch, Homer, Seneca, and Virgil. Shakespeare seems to have known most of these, and there is no doubt that two of his favourite books were Arthur Golding's English version of Ovid's *Metamorphoses*, first published in 1567, and Sir Thomas North's translation (via Jacques Amyot's French version) of Plutarch's *Lives of the Noble Grecians and Romans*, of 1579.

It is not always easy to be sure whether Shakespeare had read the original or a translation of a classical work. To take a particularly difficult instance, *The Comedy of Errors* is unquestionably based on *Menaechmi* by the Roman writer Plautus; Shakespeare's play is believed to have been written by 1594, and the first English translation of *Menaechmi* did not appear until the following year; but manuscripts often circulated privately, so conceivably Shakespeare had access to the translation before it was printed. On the other hand, Plautus was often studied in schools, and it is necessary to emphasize that the extent of the literary education lying behind Shakespeare's plays is not beyond that of a bright pupil at the local grammar school.

There is no wonder he wrote of a boy creeping unwillingly to school, since classes in a typical Elizabethan grammar school started normally at six in the morning; hours were long, holidays infrequent. And education in these schools centred firmly on Latin language and literature: in the upper classes, the speaking of English was forbidden. At the end of his schooldays an Elizabethan boy would have been as well qualified in Latin as a modern classics graduate. One of the scenes in Shakespeare that seem most likely to be closely related to his own experience is the one in *The Merry Wives of Windsor* (4.1) that shows a schoolmaster taking a boy named William through his Latin grammar; it draws on the officially approved textbook, William Lily's *Short Introduction of Grammar*, which was probably Shakespeare's own introduction to the language. It is something of a paradox that during the twentieth century his plays have largely superseded the classics as the basis for a literary education, because a knowledge of the classics is necessary for a full understanding of them.

Having acquired a good grounding in the classics at school, Shakespeare also managed at some point to develop at least a reading knowledge of French and Italian, and throughout his life must have kept up his reading of English and Continental literature. Whether he ever left England we simply do not know, though there are enough anomalies in the plays for us to feel that geography was not his strong point. His childhood and early manhood saw the publication not only of influential translations of the classics but also of many other books that were to be of great use to him, such as William Painter's *Palace of Pleasure*, a popular collection of tales including the one by Boccaccio that was to form the basis of *All's Well that Ends Well*; Holinshed's *Chronicles*, of great importance for the history plays; Lyly's fashionable *Euphues*; Sir Philip Sidney's prose romance *Arcadia* and his sonnet sequence *Astrophil and Stella*; early books of Spenser's *Faerie Queene*; Thomas Lodge's romance *Rosalynde*, the basis for *As You Like It*; prose romances – including *Pandosto*, the source for *The Winter's Tale* – and other pamphlets by Robert Greene; the early writings of Thomas Nashe; and other books which Shakespeare certainly used or must have read and enjoyed. The greatest early English writer known to Shakespeare was Chaucer, and later in life he discovered, I believe, a kindred spirit in Montaigne, whose *Essays* appeared in an English translation by John Florio in 1603. He was also greatly influenced, throughout his career, by contemporary playwrights whose works he must have seen performed, and in some of which he may himself have acted; Marlowe is only the most conspicuous example.

Montaigne, the first great autobiographer of Western civilization, was an essayist, and his main topic was himself. Shakespeare worked mostly in a medium which calls for concealment of the self, for a compassionate identification with all kinds and qualities of men and women, for the ability, as Keats put it, to take 'as much delight in conceiving an Iago as an Imogen'. The dramatist of his time who has left to posterity the strongest impression of himself as a personality is Ben Jonson; rather than hiding behind his works, Jonson acts as an impresario to them, providing them with a panoply of prefaces, dedications, and introductory epistles, annotating some of them with information (not always entirely truthful) about the learning that has gone into their composition, complaining of faults in their performance and misunderstandings in the way they were received, telling us his views of dramatic composition. He writes poems about himself, about his art and about his contemporaries, and he reveals himself less formally, too, in those unbuttoned, probably bibulous, conversations with William Drummond of Hawthornden in which he refers a couple of times to Shakespeare, saying that he 'wanted art', and jeers implicitly at *The Winter's Tale* because in it Shakespeare 'brought in a number of men saying they had suffered shipwreck in Bohemia where there is no sea near by some 100 miles'.

Jonson was a great talker, confident of his own opinions. If there is one thing I feel sure of about Shakespeare, it is that he was a great listener, capable always of seeing both sides of any question, possessing in a way that his nearest and dearest may even have found infinitely irritating the quality that John Keats, writing to his brothers in December 1817, defined as '*Negative Capability*, that is, when a man is capable of being in uncertainties, mysteries, doubts, without any irritable reaching after fact and reason'.

There is one area of his output in which, rather than appearing as the great ventriloquist, Shakespeare seems to speak in his own person, and that is in his sonnets. Even here one has to say 'seems' because these 154 poems, sophisticated literature as they unquestionably are, do not necessarily represent direct autobiographical utterance. As with other sonnet sequences of the period, a narrative can be extrapolated from them. The poet is a married man. He has a male friend considerably younger than himself. The friend is unmarried; the first seventeen of the poems urge him to marry and beget an heir. The friendship appears to grow in intensity. Necessary separation causes the poet great grief. The friend's friendship with another poet arouses the poet's jealousy. The poet has a 'black' – in whatever sense – mistress who seduces the friend. The mistress is 'the bay where all men ride'. Whereas those sonnets that are clearly addressed to or written about the young man idealize the relationship and celebrate lovers' mutuality, exulting in love's illusory triumph over time, those clearly addressed to the woman revile her for cruelty and infidelity, speak ill of her looks, and explore a self-disgusted emotional and bodily entanglement in language of, at times, gross physicality.

Some readers have argued that the sonnets are not necessarily autobiographical, that they may be, as it were, literary exercises, or forerunners of the dramatic soliloquy as it was to be practised by

Robert Browning, poems deriving wholly or in part from
Shakespeare's imagination. They are certainly not just exercises in an
accepted convention, because they depart in conspicuous respects
from the standard conventions of the amatory sonnet sequence – in
portraying the idealized beloved as a male, for instance; in speaking of
the woman as an object of contempt; and in referring to her faults in
language of overt sexuality. But this might simply illustrate
Shakespeare's originality, representing a deliberate inversion of
convention in what is nevertheless an imagined sequence of events.

It is impossible categorically to deny this reading, but there are
powerful arguments against it. One is that the underlying narrative of
the sonnets emerges so fitfully and cryptically that it is far easier to
think of them as having been composed individually, often as
immediate responses to an actual situation, than as a planned sequence
with a narrative thread. Another relates to the time when they were
written. Stylistically many of them seem to belong to the early 1590s,
when the sonnet sequence was most in vogue; this is also the period
when Shakespeare makes most use of the sonnet form, and of literary
conventions associated with it, in his plays. We can be certain that he
had written some sonnets by the end of the decade, as Francis Meres
alludes in his book *Palladis Tamia* of 1598 to Shakespeare's 'sugared
sonnets among his private friends', and versions of two of those later
printed appeared without Shakespeare's permission in a collection
called *The Passionate Pilgrim* in the following year. But the volume
entitled *Shakespeare's Sonnets, never before imprinted* did not appear until
1609, and even then there is nothing to suggest that Shakespeare had
anything to do with its publication – no author's dedication, for
instance, as there is in each of the narrative poems. If Shakespeare had
conceived of the collection as a series of poems written primarily for
public consumption, is it not likely that he would have had it
published closer to the date of composition? And although some of the
poems are not particularly personal in tone, others, especially among
those concerned with the so-called 'dark lady' (a phrase that does not
occur within the collection) read so much like the anguished
exploration of an intensely private state of mind rather than a
projection of this condition in terms that will make it explicable to an
outsider, that I find it hard to escape the conclusion that they spring
from personal experience.

Admittedly, there are signs that Shakespeare, or someone else,
revised poems in the collection and reordered the whole to give it
greater coherence: if the story they hint at is a personal one, and if the

poems were written at the time of the events they reflect, then some of those about the woman would originally have been interspersed among those concerned with the young man; instead they are massed together at the end. If Shakespeare himself put the poems into the order in which they are printed, this might suggest a desire to make them more assimilable by the uninvolved reader, and perhaps even to disguise their autobiographical nature, but it does not preclude the possibility that he initially wrote some, if not all, for his eyes alone. Certainly, if they are autobiographical, it is difficult to imagine that he would have wished many of them to be seen by his wife and family, or by the persons to whom they relate, especially the woman, without giving them at least the air of a fiction.

The sonnets include marvellous poems, some of them wonderfully lyrical evocations of emotional states experienced in friendship and in love. They also include poems which – like speeches from some of Shakespeare's plays – are memorable less as what is usually thought of as 'poetry', and more as extraordinarily complex and interesting explorations of a psychological condition. In the most intense of the dark woman sonnets the poet seems to be wrestling with conflicting elements within his own nature, in an obsessive entanglement with a woman he knows to be unfaithful to him, a woman he despises just as he also despises himself for being unable to resist his self-destroying lust for her. It is a condition that resembles that of Tarquin in *The Rape of Lucrece*, led compulsively to commit a crime that he knows will destroy him, or Angelo in *Measure for Measure*, wrestling with emotions that he cannot control. Well, perhaps after all they are dramatic sketches, fragments of an imagined psycho-drama inhabited only by invented personae, not products of a real-life drama. After all, if, within a dramatic situation, Shakespeare could write verse about amorous situations as intensely personal as he gave to Proteus (in *The Two Gentlemen of Verona*), to Romeo and to Juliet, to Angelo, or to Helen (in *All's Well that Ends Well*), there is no obvious reason why he should not have been able to give a similar sense of immediacy to verse written within a different convention without its actually being a personal outpouring. Possibly the sonnets are no less dramatic in conception than any of his plays, a brilliantly original variation on the convention of the sonnet sequence. If so, they tell us a lot about Shakespeare's imagination, but not about his day-by-day life.

But what if they are indeed autobiographical? If we could identify the young man, and the rival poet, and the mistress, we might well learn much about Shakespeare himself. But I have no confidence in any of the many different attempts that have been made to discover who they were, and unless new documentary evidence turns up I see no hope of doing so. Still, if we believe the sonnet story we must also, even if we cannot put names to the people involved, accept its implications for Shakespeare's biography. On this reading he had an adulterous entanglement with a woman who was herself adulterous. We know that he led a double life between Stratford and London; perhaps he also led one between his wife Anne and another woman. If we believe the sonnets, too, we must believe that there were times when he experienced a kind of sexual nausea, arousing the desire 'To shun the heaven that leads men to this hell' (Sonnet 129).

What about the friend? Is there any sense in which this, too, was a guilty relationship? – for if it was a sexual one then it must, in a society in which sexual relations between men were punishable by death (even though they were rarely so punished), be regarded as a reason for guilt. There is no question that the poet's feelings for his friend are of passionate intensity; but the possibility that the relationship was sexual seems not to have been mooted until 1824[6] and in more recent times has become a hotly contended issue inextricably tangled with the personalities of the debaters themselves.

Those who deny it argue that the expressions of love between the poet and his friend are not essentially different from those expressed by one man for another in many of the plays, and point out that this was an age in which friendship between men was commonly idealized as a relationship that transcended the love of man for woman. It is possible, for example, to point to Montaigne, an energetic lover of women whose essay 'On Friendship' has often been regarded as one of the age's most moving testaments to the love of one man for another. Of his friend Estienne de la Boëtie he writes (in John Florio's translation): 'If a man urge me to tell wherefore I loved him, I feel it cannot be expressed but by answering, "Because it was he, because it was myself." '[7] Upholders of the idealized interpretation can point, too, to the fact that the poet sees his relationship to the woman, not to the man, as the source of guilt, and even that in one of the poems (Sonnet 20) he seems with exceptional frankness to deny the possibility of a sexual relationship:

> . . . for a woman wert thou first created,
> Till nature as she wrought thee fell a-doting,
> And by addition me of thee defeated
> By adding one thing to my purpose nothing.

But since she pricked thee out for women's pleasure,
Mine be thy love and thy love's use their treasure.

Is that not conclusive? Well, perhaps not; so argues, for instance,
Joseph Pequigney.[8] After all, this is the sonnet in which the poet
describes the young man as the 'master-mistress of [his] passion'; in
which he expresses admiration of the young man's 'woman's face', his
'woman's gentle heart', his 'eye more bright than theirs', adding up to
the impression that 'for a woman wert thou first created': he's
thinking of the man's body, not of his mind, and thinking of it in the
way that a man might think of a woman; the pun in 'pricked thee out'
is a wry joke, implying a high degree of intimacy with the person to
whom it is addressed. Moreover, this sonnet comes early in the
sequence: the relationship could have changed later.

Those who uphold the view that the sonnets imply a sexual
relationship between the poet and his friend rely often on a subtext
which is not ultimately demonstrable. Various degrees of self-
consciousness are possible. It could be argued of Shakespeare, as of
Montaigne, that idealization is simply sublimation. Or it could be
claimed that the idealized language is a kind of code, a series of
metaphors in which the writer conveys but also conceals his true
feelings. One of the problems of work on the sonnets at the present
time is that they have come to be used as a weapon in the arena of
sexual politics, with the result that it is now difficult to deny the sexual
interpretation without appearing to be illiberal. The one writer of
Shakespeare's time who is most generally agreed to foreshadow what
has come to be seen as a homosexual sensibility is his exact
contemporary Christopher Marlowe, who displays a conspicuous and
indulgent interest in male-male relationships. Although there are
intense relationships between men in a number of Shakespeare's plays,
notably those of Antonio and Bassanio in *The Merchant of Venice*,
Antonio and Sebastian in *Twelfth Night*, and Achilles and Patroclus in
Troilus and Cressida, none of these seems to me overtly and sensuously
sexual in the manner of those portrayed by Marlowe. In the end I
should have to say that I don't think we can say for certain that the
relationship between the men in the sonnets, whether or not the
poems are autobiographical, is unequivocally physical, while also
saying that the intensity of the love that the poet expresses for the
young man is so great as to permit this interpretation.

★

Studies of the external record of Shakespeare's life, such as they are, give us – or at least give me, because this is ultimately a matter of personal impression – the sense of an educated, well-read man, though not a scholar, ambitious and well organized, a man who knew how to manage his business affairs and could pursue his financial interests with efficiency, who cared for his family and for his roots in Stratford but cared also for his career and was willing to make sacrifices in his domestic life in order to pursue it, a man who valued his reputation for integrity and preferred to keep out of trouble, who took pleasure in his prosperity and the status it gave him, and who hoped to pass on something of what he had earned to his descendants.

If we admit the sonnets as biographical evidence, we see beneath the controlled exterior a turbulent inner life, passions not easily mastered, self-knowledge wrested with difficulty and pain from the crucible of experience, an intense need to love and to be loved, a desire to idealize the beloved and to abase himself in the process, immense suscep- tibility to emotional pain, a demanding sexuality, a volatility of response that can veer rapidly from one extreme of emotion to its opposite, a belief in the power of the imagination along with an awareness of the fragility of illusion. And we see all this because of the shaping, expressive powers of art, because the man who has suffered all this extremity of passion has also summoned up the self-control, the discipline to shape and contain it within the demanding verse structures of the sonnet form.

And even if we discount the sonnets, are not these impressions akin to those we should receive, too, from the plays? The ambition is there in the range and scope of the work, the determination to master all the dramatic kinds, the restless experimentation, the exploitation of the conventions of popular drama in a manner that never quite loses sight of the need to entertain while constantly stretching the imaginative and intellectual responses of its audiences; the emotional turbulence is there in the frequent depiction of extreme states of mind, both comic and tragic; the sexuality is omnipresent and can be both despicable and glorious; so, too, is the idealizing imagination that can transform man from a 'quintessence of dust' to 'the beauty of the world, the paragon of animals'; and all is projected to us by the deployment of a verbal, rhetorical, and structural artistry that reflects the self-control and determination evident in the more practical aspects of his career.

The elusiveness of Shakespeare's personality is a function of his supremacy as a dramatist. In his plays his nature is, as he writes in Sonnet 111, 'subdued | To what it works in, like the dyer's hand'. This itself tells us something about the man: that he had the power to subdue his own identity and imagine himself into the states of mind of the characters he portrays. But he could also stand aside from these characters, seeing them as constituent parts of an overall pattern that is greater than the sum of its parts. In what follows I shall look at his plays and poems in the attempt to identify some of the ways in which they can work upon our minds and imaginations, and to consider some of the meanings that they have had over the years since they were written; but first I want to write in more detail about his professional career as a man of the theatre.

Notes to Chapter One

1 Terence Hawkes, *Meaning by Shakespeare* (1992), p. 3.
2 T.S. Eliot, 'John Ford', in *Selected Essays*, 3rd enlarged edition (1951), p. 203.
3 A convenient list of contemporary allusions is printed on pp. xl–xlii of the Oxford *Complete Works* (1986, etc.). The best and most comprehensive biographical study is S. Schoenbaum's *William Shakespeare: A Documentary Life* (Oxford, 1975), which includes excellent facsimiles of the documentary evidence; it appeared in revised form, but with fewer illustrations, as *William Shakespeare: A Compact Documentary Life* (Oxford, 1977; paperback, 1978). Schoenbaum's *Shakespeare's Lives* (Oxford, 1970; revised 1991) is a fascinating study of the history of attempts to tell the story of Shakespeare's life. Biographies (often combined with critical studies of the works) and biographical studies frequently appear, and are too numerous to list here.
4 See Maurice Pope, 'Shakespeare's Falconry', in *Shakespeare Survey 44* (Cambridge, 1992), pp. 131–43.
5 Shakespeare as a businessman is the subject of E.A.J. Honigmann's paper ' "There is a World Elsewhere": William Shakespeare, Businessman', in *Images of Shakespeare*, ed. W. Habicht, D.J. Palmer, and R. Pringle (Newark, NJ, London, and Toronto, 1988), pp. 40–6.
6 Schoenbaum, *Shakespeare's Lives*, p. 221.
7 *The Essays of Montaigne*, translated by John Florio, Everyman edition, 3 vols (1910), pp. 201, 203.
8 Joseph Pequigney, *Such is my Love: A Study of Shakespeare's Sonnets* (Chicago and London, 1985), pp. 30–41.

TWO

Shakespeare: Man of the Theatre

When Shakespeare started his professional career English theatre and drama were both on the threshold of a sensational period of development which would produce within the next thirty years a high proportion of the acknowledged masterpieces of English, and indeed of world, drama. It was a time of greatness too in the history of English non-dramatic literature. But the most remarkable feature of the period is that much of its greatest poetry – and literary prose – was written for the theatre and is to be found in the plays even of writers who were nothing like so successful when they wrote in other literary forms. Perhaps for this reason, there has been a long, still-continuing tradition of thinking and writing about Shakespeare as a primarily literary artist, a tradition that prevails even among some of the most advanced literary thinkers of the present time. It was particularly dominant in the 1930s during the first great period of professionally institutionalized Shakespeare criticism.

Even when language-based criticism was at its height an alternative movement was making itself felt, emphasizing the importance of studies not only of the Elizabethan and Jacobean stage but also of everything that has happened to Shakespeare's plays between his time and ours, and which inevitably influences our perceptions of them. Scholars and critics have been increasingly ready to acknowledge that Shakespeare was above all a man of the theatre, and that critical techniques appropriate to works intended to be read are not necessarily suited to those intended for performance.

The distinction between the playwright as literary artist and the playwright as man of the theatre can never be absolute. Even the most literary writers in dramatic form – Fulke Greville, John Milton,

William Wordsworth, Thomas Hardy, T.S. Eliot – must make some use of theatrical, or at least dramatic, conventions; even those who are most deeply imbued with theatrical values – Thomas Heywood, Colley Cibber, Dion Boucicault, Noël Coward, Alan Ayckbourn – depend in part on the exercise of literary skills. The critic of drama, then, must also be a critic of literature, but needs, too, to be constantly aware of the ends that the dramatic artist has in mind, to recognize that in the work of the playwright literary values may often need to give way to theatrical values.

The varied critical approaches to Shakespeare reflect the wide range of appeal that his works exert, and it would be arrogant for those of one critical persuasion to dismiss as irrelevant the work of those whose views they do not share. It is possible to say useful and true things about Shakespeare from a wide range of critical perspectives, and in any case most critics are eclectic in their methods, even in the present highly fragmented state of the art. Moreover, the pendulum of critical thought is constantly swinging, resulting in an emphasis sometimes on the literary, sometimes on the theatrical aspects of Shakespeare's artistry. In this chapter I want to look at certain aspects of Shakespeare's career in an attempt to think about the tension that may have existed within his own mind between the professions of literature and the theatre.

Most of the biographical evidence suggests that Shakespeare thought of himself professionally as a man of the theatre, that it was from the theatre that he drew most of his considerable income, and that his professional colleagues came from the world of the theatre. He was a man of the theatre in at least three different senses: as a business man, as an actor, and as a playwright. How he entered the profession we simply do not know. The conjecture that has been most popular in recent years is that he joined the Queen's Men as an actor in 1587. S. Schoenbaum recounts how, in June of that year, when they were visiting the Oxfordshire town of Thame, one of their actors, William Knell,

> drew his weapon and assaulted his colleague John Towne, a
> yeoman of Shoreditch. Cornered on a mound, and fearing for his
> life, Towne plunged his own sword through Knell's neck. The
> latter died within thirty minutes. A coroner's inquest concluded

that Towne had acted in self-defence, and in due course he received a Queen's pardon. Knell's widow remarried in less than a twelvemonth, taking as her husband the actor John Heminges, who would prove so worthy a friend to Shakespeare. Meanwhile the Queen's Men went about their business. We do not know precisely when they played at Stratford in 1587. . . . Before leaving Stratford, had they enlisted Shakespeare, then aged twenty-three, as their latest recruit?[1]

That theory presupposes that Shakespeare had already displayed some taste for the theatre and, one would hope, some talent as an amateur actor; how he might have acquired such talent is not clear; the amateur drama of the Elizabethan age is an under-researched area.

This is guesswork. It is a fact that the first clear allusion to Shakespeare outside the family context of his youth and early manhood, as well as the first reference to him in print, is as a member of the London theatrical scene. This occurs in the somewhat cryptic passage in a pamphlet of 1592, Robert Greene's *Groatsworth of Wit*, in which we hear of 'an upstart crow beautified with our feathers that with his "tiger's heart wrapped in a player's hide" supposes he is as well able to bombast out a blank verse as the best of you; and being an absolute Johannes Factotum is in his own conceit the only Shake-scene in a country'. Greene is attacking Shakespeare here as both player and writer. The crow, with its ability to imitate its betters, was a proverbial image for the actor, and Greene imitates the line 'O tiger's heart wrapped in a woman's hide!' from Shakespeare's play *Richard, Duke of York*, as it seems to have been known when it was first performed, or *The Third Part of Henry the Sixth*, as it is called in the First Folio. By this time, then, it would seem that Shakespeare was already well established as a playwright – so even if he did start as an actor, he must soon have become a writer.

In 1592 Shakespeare was twenty-eight years old; we know that he was an actor and a writer, but have no certain knowledge of his exact professional affiliations; the history of the London theatre companies is particularly confused and confusing at this time. And the following couple of years were to be a bad time for the profession because of the worst and longest epidemic of plague since the beginnings of theatrical life in London. Matters began to improve in the latter part of 1594. In June of that year a newly formed company under the patronage of Queen Elizabeth's Lord Chamberlain, Henry Carey, first Baron Hunsdon, performed under the auspices of the theatre financier Philip Henslowe at Newington Butts, and on 8 October, 'the time being such as, thanks be to God, there is now no danger of the sickness', Hunsdon asked the Lord Mayor of London that his company should be allowed to perform during the coming winter at the Cross Keys Inn in Gracious Street. It seems likely that Shakespeare was a member of this company from its foundation; at any rate on 15 March 1595 he is named in the accounts of the treasurer of the Queen's Chamber as joint payee, along with William Kemp and Richard Burbage, for two performances given before the Queen at Greenwich during the previous Christmas season. So by the time Shakespeare was thirty he was established as a leading member of the company with which he was to be exclusively associated for the rest of his life.

Elizabethan theatre companies were what would nowadays, I suppose, be called co-operatives: managed and run by their own members. Most of their shareholders were active in the companies' artistic affairs; there are several later direct references to Shakespeare in his capacity as administrator. On 21 February 1599 he was named among the syndicate of men responsible for building and running the Globe Theatre; Shakespeare is the only playwright among them. Half of the rights belonged to Cuthbert and Richard Burbage, so Shakespeare initially owned a tenth share in the company – the proportion fluctuated as the number of shareholders went up and down. On the accession of James I the Lord Chamberlain's Men came under the King's protection, and Shakespeare is among the nine members of the company named, along with 'the rest of their associates', in the royal warrants for the letters patent and in the letters themselves; he is similarly named among the members of the company in the document granting each of them four-and-a-half yards of scarlet cloth nominally intended for livery to be worn in the Coronation procession (though possibly the actors did not process). A major event in the company's fortunes was the acquisition of the relatively small, indoor theatre in the Blackfriars; Shakespeare is one of the seven sharers named in the lease of 9 August 1608. We have no record of whether he was actively involved in the business arrangements for the rebuilding of the Globe after the destruction of the original theatre by fire in 1613; perhaps he decided, in Schoenbaum's words, 'that this was a good time to sell his seventh share of the moiety in the company which he had served, to the best of his abilities, for nigh on two decades'.[2]

One of the ways in which Shakespeare served this company was certainly as an actor, though the evidence, sketchy though it is, suggests that this was the least of his professional capacities. His company's principal tragedian was Richard Burbage. According to a list printed in the 1616 Folio edition of Ben Jonson's works, however, Shakespeare was one of the ten 'principal comedians' in Jonson's *Every Man in his Humour* of 1598, and he is similarly listed as one of the eight 'principal tragedians' in Jonson's *Sejanus*, of 1603. An epigram by John Davies of Hereford, printed in his *Scourge of Folly* in 1610, is headed 'To our English Terence, Master Will. Shakespeare', which seems to imply that Davies thinks of him primarily as a comic playwright, but goes on to speak of him in cryptic terms as an actor:

> Some say, good Will, which I in sport do sing,
> Hadst thou not played some kingly parts in sport
> Thou hadst been a companion for a king,
> And been a king among the meaner sort. . . .

That is too vague to be helpful. Shakespeare is listed first among the 'principal actors' named in the First Folio edition of his own plays. Beyond this the evidence is mostly late and anecdotal, such as the comment in *Historia Histrionica*, of 1699, that he 'was a much better poet than player' – which we can well believe – and Nicholas Rowe's rather desperate statement, in the first formal memoir of Shakespeare, published in 1709, that 'though I have enquired, I could never meet with any further account of him this way, than that the top of his performance was the Ghost in his own *Hamlet*'. (Shaw paradoxically interpreted this as a comment on the importance and difficulty of the role rather than as a reflection of its comparative insignificance.)[3]

As I have implied, we simply cannot know whether Shakespeare was an actor before he became a playwright, though this may seem the more natural progression. Both the dating and the sequence of his early plays are extremely uncertain. He may have started off as a freelance playwright rather than as one attached to a specific company but it seems clear that after he joined the Lord Chamberlain's Men he wrote only for them. We know from Henslowe that many dramatists worked freelance, moving from one company to another as the commissions came in, and often collaborating with one or more other writers. But some of the most successful dramatists of the period had agreements to write exclusively over given periods of time for particular companies, and this must have been an arrangement attractive both to the dramatists, because of the stability and stimulus it would provide, and to the companies themselves in assuring the loyalty of playwrights whose work they valued. Regrettably our earliest surviving detailed knowledge about the contractual arrangements between a dramatist and his company – Richard Brome and the proprietors of the Salisbury Court Theatre – relates to a contract made in 1635 and renewed with revisions in 1638, but there is evidence that similar practices prevailed earlier. Brome was supposed to contribute three plays a year for three years, but found difficulty in reaching this target, and optimistically argued in the lawsuit to which we owe our knowledge of these arrangements that this had been rather a wish than an expectation: members of the company had assured him that although

> they had desired to have three plays yearly for three years' continuance together . . . yet upon trust and confidence and by the true and fair intent and plain meaning of all parties, the plaintiffs neither should nor would exact nor expect from this defendant the performance or composition of any more plays than so many only as this defendant could or should be able well and conveniently to do or perform and that their main purpose in expressing such a number of plays was but only to oblige this defendant to dedicate all his labour and plays totally unto their sole profits.[4]

In the revised terms of the contract Brome was to be paid at the rate of £1 per week. In fact he was not able to produce above two plays a year, and this seems to have been a pretty normal rate of production for other house dramatists of the period, including Shakespeare.

It would be interesting to know the terms of Shakespeare's agreement with his company, and especially whether he received regular payments as house dramatist over and above those due to him as a shareholder; he must have been a far more valuable asset than some of the other sharers, and one might expect this to have been reflected in his wage packet.[5] He died a rich man, but this may be because of his business investments rather than his professional earnings.

It seems clear from the records of Shakespeare's professional life, sketchy though they are, that for most of his career he was very much a theatre professional, deeply involved with his colleagues as business man and actor as well as writer; and given the circumstances of the time it seems likely that he would also have fulfilled a function corresponding to that of the modern director. His professionalism is apparent too from the internal evidence of the scripts that he wrote for this company, which are in most respects expertly crafted to the theatre conditions of his time. He knew that audiences liked comedy, even within a tragic framework. He supplied them with songs, battles, and duel scenes; with ghosts, murders, even rapes and mutilations; with lyrical poetry and robust prose; with dances and masques, processions and pageants; with scenes of heroism and of pathos, of love and of hatred, of death and even of resurrection. His sense of practicality is everywhere apparent: in his tailoring of his plot structures so that they would not require more boy actors than his company could easily command, in the allowance he makes for the practice of doubling, in his obvious awareness of the physical features of the theatres of his time – the stage doors, the opportunities for sound effects, the cellarage from which a ghost could speak or music from under the stage be heard, the trap door from which apparitions could appear, the upper level that could serve as the walls of a castle or a balcony, the flying apparatus that could enable Jupiter to descend from the heavens on an eagle or Juno and Ceres to speak or sing in a state of suspended animation.

We can even tell, on the evidence of texts printed from his own manuscripts, that as he wrote he sometimes had particular actors in mind – Will Kemp for Dogberry and Richard Cowley for Verges, in *Much Ado About Nothing*, are the most conspicuous instances. This suggests that at times he relied heavily on his intimate knowledge of the acting styles and stage personalities of individual members of his company in shaping roles for them, and this impression of confidence in his interpreters is reinforced by other features of the early texts such as the fact that at times, in the haste of composition, he did not trouble to sort out the distribution of roles among certain groups of characters such as the members of the Watch in *Much Ado About Nothing*, leaving this task presumably to the rehearsal process – or, if we think of the texts as works to be printed, to the editor.[6]

Even more indicative of Shakespeare's reliance for the full realization of his intentions on the process of rehearsal and performance is the fact that as he wrote he was clearly concerned very largely with dialogue, with providing his actors with the words that they were to speak, rather than with prescribing the gestures, facial expressions, and actions that should accompany the words, even when such gestures, expressions, and actions are of the highest importance in determining meaning. The result, famously, is Shakespeare's openness to flexibility of interpretation, in both criticism and performance. Two different productions of the same, unadapted text of one of his plays can create an effect as different as if the events had been narrated by, say, Dickens on the one hand and D.H. Lawrence on the other hand.

The conclusion we might draw from this is either that Shakespeare did not wish fully to project his imaginative vision, or that he knew he could rely on the collaboration between himself and his theatrical colleagues not merely to convey emotions not fully expressed in the dialogue, but even at points to fill gaps in the narrative itself. The latter conclusion is the one that seems more likely to me. I do not mean by this that Shakespeare necessarily had hard and fast ideas about how his plays should be interpreted – that there was 'an imaginative vision' as clearly defined as a copyist's model. Probably he expected his actors to make a creative contribution and calculated for this as he wrote. But he was writing as one of a team and knew that he would be deeply involved long after his plays had been handed over to the scriveners for the preparation of the scrolls from which the actors would learn their lines; he would be prepared for these lines to be reshaped, with his involvement, during the rehearsal process itself. Again indisputable evidence of such reshaping is provided by discrepancies between surviving early texts, not only in the heavily revised plays such as *Hamlet* and *King Lear*, but in less drastically altered ones such as *A Midsummer Night's Dream*, with its redistribution of an important speech of Theseus's in the last scene, so that in the revised version it is shared between Theseus and Lysander.

To anyone who has had to do with putting on plays for the theatre all this might seem so obvious as to be not worth saying; but failure to acknowledge the full extent to which Shakespeare was a man of the theatre rather than just a writer for the theatre – let alone just a writer – has had long-lasting and far-reaching consequences, including refusal to admit that he sometimes revised his plays, and failure therefore to acknowledge that Quarto and Folio texts of plays such as *Hamlet*, *Othello*, and *King Lear* represent those plays essentially in unrevised and revised form. This is a hypothesis that has been gaining ground in recent years; it was acted on in the editing of the Oxford Shakespeare published in 1986, and is the main reason why that edition differs so substantially from all its predecessors.

But the belief that Shakespeare was essentially a writer rather than a complete man of the theatre dies hard, and continues to find expression in widely disseminated and influential publications such as the New Cambridge edition of *Hamlet*, where the editor expresses his belief that

> there was a point when Shakespeare had made many alterations
> to his play, mostly reflected in cutting rather than adding
> material, some of which he may have made after preliminary
> discussions with his colleagues among the Chamberlain's men.
> The play then became the property of these colleagues who began
> to prepare it for the stage. At this point what one can only call
> degeneration began, and it is at this point that we should arrest
> and freeze the play, for it is sadly true that the nearer we get to
> the stage, the further we are getting from Shakespeare.

This statement, by a learned and distinguished scholar, seems to me entirely unconsonant with the evidence in its implication that Shakespeare would 'hand over' his text to colleagues who would 'prepare it for the stage' – as if it had not been intended for the stage all along; and as for the idea that the process of rehearsal is one of 'degeneration', and worst of all that 'the nearer we get to the stage, the further we are getting from Shakespeare', this seems to me a denial of all that Shakespeare stood for.[7]

Among the strongest indications that Shakespeare thought of himself as above all a theatre man is the fact that he seems to have had remarkably little concern for the appearance of his plays in print. Only about half of them were printed in his lifetime; none of these has an author's dedication, or any of the panoply of preliminary epistles, dedicatory poems, and the like with which Elizabethan authors were accustomed to adorn their publications. He may sometimes have agreed that a play should be printed, but there is nothing to suggest that he did anything either to prepare the plays for reading or to see them through the press. For him, it seems, performance was publication, the theatre was where they belonged. This appears to have been in line with a widespread policy for dramatists attached to particular companies: we know that companies exerted a degree of control over whether plays written for them were to be printed. The sharers in the Whitefriars theatre in 1608, for example, stipulated that 'no man of the said company shall at any time hereafter put into print . . . any manner of play book now in use, or that hereafter shall be sold unto them upon the penalty and forfeiture of £40 sterling or the loss of his place and share of all things amongst them, except the book of *Torrismount*, and that play not to be printed by any before twelve months be fully expired'. Richard Brome, too, contracted not to allow any of the plays that he wrote under commission 'to be printed . . . without the licence from the said company or the major part of them'.[8]

★

I have concentrated so far on Shakespeare's commitment to the theatre, on the extent to which his talents as a literary artist were subjugated to the dramatic medium. Still, he wrote some works for publication in printed form and may well have taken an active interest in the printing of some of these; he did, it would seem, write verse from internal pressures, as a form of self-expression rather than simply for public consumption; and he also wrote at least a small amount of verse in response to commission. A fine but neglected piece is the poem 'The Phoenix and Turtle', published in enigmatic circumstances but which seems, perhaps paradoxically, to be a piece of occasional verse which nevertheless achieves great intensity of expression. (But perhaps after all it is not paradoxical that a dramatist should be able to express deep emotion to order.) He devised an impresa – a paper or pasteboard shield bearing emblems or mottoes – now lost, for the Earl of Rutland; he wrote the sonnets and 'A Lover's Complaint' possibly without thought of publication and certainly (unless he had a collection of rejection slips) not for immediate publication; he may have written, in unknown circumstances, the poem 'Shall I die?', which aroused such controversy when Gary Taylor rediscovered it in the Bodleian Library (and yes, all right, he may not), and he certainly wrote, and achieved pretty well instant publication for, the two narrative poems *Venus and Adonis* and *The Rape of Lucrece*.

It is these two long poems on which his reputation as a man of letters rather than as a man of the theatre depended in his lifetime, and they are the only two of his works for whose publication by printing he appears to have undertaken direct responsibility. They bear his only known dedications, both to the Earl of Southampton, and it is because of the dates appended to these dedications that we can be more confident about when the poems were written than about any of the early plays. *Venus and Adonis* appeared in 1593, *The Rape of Lucrece* in 1594, each with a dedication dated in the same year. Admittedly Shakespeare could have written the poems long before they were published, but the fact that his highest public poetic output coincides with the highest incidence of plague during his career, and therefore with the time at which he might most urgently have felt that the theatre offered no decent living to a family man, makes plausible the theory that he wrote them shortly before they were published, and that they represent his bid for serious attention as a poet pure and simple.

In this they were successful. *Venus and Adonis* went through sixteen editions before 1640, which means that by that date it had been more frequently reprinted than any of the plays and than most other secular writings of its time; *The Rape of Lucrece* was also a lasting success, though on a smaller scale: it went through eight editions up to 1640. A number of allusions to the two poems survive in both manuscript and printed sources, and it is clear that Shakespeare had an independent reputation as a poet, to such an extent that a character – admittedly, a foolish character, as his name, Gullio (deriving from 'gull', a fool), indicates – in a play put on at the turn of the sixteenth century by students of St John's College, Cambridge declared: 'I'll worship sweet Master Shakespeare, and to honour him will lay his *Venus and Adonis* under my pillow, as we read of one – I do not well remember his name, but I am sure he was a king – slept with Homer under his bed's head.'[9] Gullio (who was trying to remember the name of Alexander the Great) even promotes Shakespeare to the status of pin-up boy, declaring: 'I'll have his picture in my study at the court.' It would be nice to know where he expected to get it.

Shakespeare's sonnets were less successful; the title-page of the first edition, in 1609, reads as if it were announcing a newsworthy event – 'Shakespeare's Sonnets, never before imprinted'; it seems to imply confidence that the volume would do well, but it was not reprinted. The bulk of the sonnets did not reappear in print until John Benson's heavily edited collection of 1640, in which they are rearranged, some are run together as longer poems, some are given independent titles, and a few of the pronouns are altered so that some of those clearly addressed to a man appear to be addressed to a woman. The absence of a reprint has spawned a conspiracy theory, suggesting that the volume was suppressed, but it may simply be that the poems did not hit the taste of the time; the vogue for sonnet sequences was past, and many of Shakespeare's sonnets make for hard reading.

In 1593 and 1594, then, Shakespeare displayed himself to public view as a literary artist; he even described *Venus and Adonis* as 'the first heir of my invention' although he had certainly already written several plays by this time. His narrative poems display many of the same kinds of literary skills as are evident in his plays; or, to put it in a different way, Shakespeare's plays, for all their theatrical qualities, are very much the work of a highly trained and sophisticated literary artist, thoroughly versed in rhetorical techniques, many of which derive from classical sources. The plays are recognizably the product of the same sensibility as that which produced the narrative poems;

and – though I should not wish to suggest that the prose in his plays is not often just as evidently the product of literary art as the verse – it is interesting that those of his plays written entirely in the medium of verse, as well as those which make the most self-conscious use of formal verse techniques, belong, like the narrative poems, to the early part of his career.

In writing of Shakespeare's education I have said something of the extent to which his plays draw on literary sources for their content as well as their verbal forms. Of course he draws on theatrical conventions, and some plays, such as *The Comedy of Errors*, probably *King John*, *Hamlet*, and *King Lear*, derive some of their structure and substance from pre-existing plays. But far more often he went for his raw material to literary, sub-literary, or historical sources: to prose romances such as Thomas Lodge's *Rosalynde* (for *As You Like It*) and Robert Greene's *Pandosto* (for *The Winter's Tale*); to narrative poems such as Arthur Brooke's *Romeus and Juliet*, Chaucer's *Canterbury Tales* and *Troilus and Criseyde*, and John Gower's *Confessio Amantis* (for *Pericles*); to novellas by Giraldi Cinthio (for *Othello*) and Boccaccio (for *All's Well that Ends Well*); to chronicle histories by Hall and Holinshed; to works of classical literature such as Plutarch's *Lives* (for the Roman tragedies), Virgil's *Aeneid*, and the pervasively influential *Metamorphoses* of Ovid; to essays by Montaigne; to the Bible; and to accounts of foreign travels. His plays are pervaded too by themes and devices associated with lyric poetry and the sonnet tradition, with elegy and complaint, with pastoral and romance.

If we think of Shakespeare as a man whose home was the theatre it is only fair, too, to think of him as a man of the study, a man who needed books, perhaps even libraries, who worked not mainly by scribbling on the backs of old actors' parts as he travelled the provinces on horse or mule, but more often at a desk or table, surrounded by books – big, heavy books such as Holinshed's *Chronicles* or Plutarch's *Lives*, books that, however capacious a memory he may have had, must sometimes have been open before him as he wrote, often virtually transcribing passages from them, as he does in, for instance, *Henry the Fifth*, *Macbeth*, *Coriolanus*, *Antony and Cleopatra*, and *The Tempest*. (I have a feeling that there is a higher proportion of direct borrowing in plays written late in his career; did he become less sensitive to accusations of borrowing plumes from other writers – even perhaps, not to put too fine a point upon it, lazier?) There was a strong vein of bookishness in Shakespeare; as Bernard Shaw put it, with his tongue tucked in its usual place, Shakespeare, even in portraying fights, has the habit of 'betraying the paper origin of his fancies by dragging in something classical in the style of the Cyclops' hammer falling "on Mars's armor, forged for proof eterne" '.[10] Shakespeare's 'bookishness' may sometimes have created tensions between the desire for immediate theatrical effect and the urge towards literary self-expression. We also have direct evidence, most obviously in *Love's Labour's Lost*, that he sometimes revised as he wrote because he thought he could make literary rather than theatrical improvements.

There is also – and this is something that Bernard Shaw, who wrote contemptuously of Shakespeare's mind, would have denied – a strong vein of intellectuality in Shakespeare's writing. I am not referring here to the underlying structures of the plays, wonderfully expressive though these often are of a highly intellectual grasp of structural principles, and of an extraordinary capacity to create an amazingly complex web of interrelationships, but more straightforwardly of verbal expression within single passages of prose or verse. It is a characteristic with which Shakespeare's neo-classical critics, particularly, often found fault; it drew upon him, for example, Dryden's accusation that he could be carried away 'beyond the bounds of judgement, either in coining of new words and phrases, or racking words which were in use, into the violence of a catachresis',[11] and in its less successful manifestations was responsible for Dr Johnson's view that 'It is incident to him to be now and then entangled with an unwieldy sentiment, which he cannot well express, and will not reject; he struggles with it a while, and if it continues stubborn comprises it in words such as occur, and leaves it to be disentangled and evolved by those who have more leisure to bestow upon it'.[12] But there are also passages in his plays where difficulty of language is the result of complexity of thought, where he makes demands on his listeners that may have taxed audiences in his time no less than they do in ours.

Shakespeare's language, that is to say, can be difficult in ways for which the passage of time alone is not responsible; Chaucer wrote two centuries before Shakespeare, but anyone who has had enough training in the basics of Middle English to read him knows that once the initial difficulties caused by the passage of time are overcome, Chaucer often makes much easier reading than Shakespeare. It may be that at times the difficulties in Shakespeare's style are the result simply of bad writing, as Johnson suggests, and that he may sometimes be justly accused of bombast, but at other times difficulties are surely the result rather of an attempt to express complex ideas even at the expense of the ready comprehension which may seem most to be desired in a play, where the auditor cannot turn back the page and read again a passage whose meaning he has not fully understood. We find this in an early play such as *Love's Labour's Lost*:

> Light, seeking light, doth light of light beguile;
> So ere you find where light in darkness lies
> Your light grows dark by losing of your eyes.
> Study me how to please the eye indeed
>   By fixing it upon a fairer eye,
> Who dazzling so, that eye shall be his heed,
>   And give him light that it was blinded by.
>
> (1.1.77–83)

We find it in a middle play such as *Troilus and Cressida*:

> Nor doth the eye itself,
> That most pure spirit of sense, behold itself,
> Not going from itself; but eye to eye opposed
> Salutes each other with each other's form.
> For speculation turns not to itself
> Till it hath travelled and is mirrored there
> Where it may see itself.
>
> (3.3.100–6)

And we find it most notoriously in the late plays:

> Affection, thy intention stabs the centre.
> Thou dost make possible things not so held,
> Communicat'st with dreams – how can this be? –
> With what's unreal thou co-active art,
> And fellow'st nothing.
>
> (*The Winter's Tale*, 1.2.140–4)

Shakespeare's willingness at times to allow the urge for full expression of his concepts to take precedence over purely theatrical considerations shows itself also in the sheer length of some of his plays. This is a vexed question, but it is undeniable that some of his plays are much longer than others, and, more importantly, that the longest of them would probably have seemed uncomfortably long to their original audiences. We have no right to adopt a condescending attitude to the audiences that made popular successes of such ambitious, complex, and lengthy plays as *Richard the Third*, *Hamlet*, and *Othello*, but there is evidence that Shakespeare himself, or at any rate the company of which I have argued he was so integral a member, sometimes cut passages, though we cannot always say for certain that this was purely on grounds of length. But it is interesting that the Folio texts of plays such as *Richard the Second*, *Hamlet*, and *King Lear*, texts which are generally agreed to be closer to the plays as acted, are usually shorter than the earlier, Quarto texts, which are closer to the point of conception. For example, the Oxford edition of *Richard the Second* prints at the end of the play 'Additional Passages' representing lines apparently present in the play as first written but not as acted, and a glance at these may well suggest that Shakespeare was vulnerable to the accusation of having over-indulged his verbal fluency, and perhaps that he admitted this himself. This is not, of course, to say that omitted passages such as Hamlet's last soliloquy – 'How all occasions do inform against me' – are necessarily any less fine as writing than passages allowed to stand; only that Shakespeare acknowledged sometimes that he had over-indulged his literary talent at the expense of the overall needs of the play.

Shortening of plays that exist in both unrevised and revised form raises interesting speculations about some of those that survive only in what appear to be pre-performance texts. Heretical it may appear to say so, but I strongly suspect that if we had a text of *Antony and Cleopatra* based on the promptbook used by Shakespeare's company it might turn out to have been pruned of as many lines as the Folio texts of *Hamlet* and *King Lear*, and that we might find abbreviations in speeches such as Ventidius's:

> O Silius, Silius,
> I have done enough. A lower place, note well,
> May make too great an act. For learn this, Silius:
> Better to leave undone than by our deed
> Acquire too high a fame when him we serve's away.
> Caesar and Antony have ever won
> More in their officer than person. Sossius,
> One of my place in Syria, his lieutenant,
> For quick accumulation of renown,
> Which he achieved by th' minute, lost his favour.
> Who does i'th' wars more than his captain can
> Becomes his captain's captain; and ambition,
> The soldier's virtue, rather makes choice of loss
> Than gain which darkens him.
> I could do more to do Antonius good,

> But 'twould offend him, and in his offence
> Should my performance perish.
>
> (3.1.11–27)

Four sententious remarks within seventeen lines would have seemed quite a high proportion even for Polonius. Admittedly, passages which on the printed page look difficult can seem translucently clear when mediated to us through the intelligence and sensibility of a skilful actor, but at least I think it is fair to say that Shakespeare makes more demands of this kind on his actors in his later plays, and that these plays have suffered in popularity as a result. It may even be that this is responsible for the decrease in his output in his later years. At the same time we have to admit that there is no evidence that he turned from the dramatic medium to more exclusively literary forms at the end of his career.

As joint General Editor of the Oxford Shakespeare I committed myself to the theatrical Shakespeare; the texts printed in that edition are, when choice exists, those that stand closer to the plays as acted than as conceived. It is a policy that supposes that for Shakespeare the movement from the text of a play as completed in his mind to a performance text is one of fulfilment rather than degeneration. In this chapter I have tried to present both sides of the coin: to suggest that there may well have existed a tension in Shakespeare's mind between theatrical and literary values. It was a fruitful tension: the theatrical Shakespeare was dependent on the literary, and vice versa. Shakespeare was above all a man of the theatre, but theatre has never been as receptive of great literature as it was in his time. He was born at the right moment.

Notes to Chapter Two

1 Schoenbaum, *Compact Documentary Life* (Oxford, 1977), p. 117.
2 ibid., p. 277.
3 In a review of Johnston Forbes-Robertson's *Hamlet*, 2 October 1897; reprinted in *Shaw on Shakespeare*, p. 85.
4 G.E. Bentley, *The Profession of Dramatist in Shakespeare's Time, 1590–1642* (Princeton, NJ, 1971), p. 121.
5 The matter is discussed by E.A.J. Honigmann, ' "There is a World Elsewhere": William Shakespeare, Businessman', in *Images of Shakespeare*, ed. W. Habicht, D.J. Palmer, and R. Pringle (Newark, NJ, London, and Toronto), pp. 43–4.

6 This kind of indeterminacy is interestingly discussed in M.M. Mahood's *Bit Parts in Shakespeare's Plays* (Cambridge, 1993); see, for example, pp. 8–9.

7 *Hamlet*, ed. Philip Edwards, New Cambridge Shakespeare (Cambridge, 1985), pp. 31–2.

8 Bentley, *Profession of Dramatist*, pp. 266–7.

9 From *The First Part of the Return from Parnassus*, anon., cited by Chambers, vol. 2, pp. 199–201.

10 From a review of a dramatization of Bunyan's *Pilgrim's Progress*, 2 January 1897; repr. in *Shaw on Shakespeare*, p. 223.

11 From the 'Preface Containing the Grounds of Criticism in Tragedy' (1679), printed with Dryden's version of *Troilus and Cressida*; repr. in, for example, Vickers, vol. 1, p. 263.

12 From the preface to his edition (1765), repr. in, for example, *Samuel Johnson on Shakespeare*, pp. 131–2.

THREE

Comedies of Verona, Padua, Ephesus, France, and Athens:

The Two Gentlemen of Verona, The Taming of the Shrew,
The Comedy of Errors, Love's Labour's Lost,
and *A Midsummer Night's Dream*

At the start of his playwriting career Shakespeare seems to have moved restlessly, experimentally, and ambitiously from one dramatic kind to another. In writing about his plays it is convenient to group them according to their form or subject-matter – comedies and tragedies, English histories and Roman histories, 'problem' plays and romances (or 'late plays'), and so on – and this is what I shall do here, but it would be wrong to give the impression that he worked systematically at each kind in turn, gradually perfecting his art in a series of plays that get better and better all the time. We should get a true sense of his development as a dramatist only by looking at his writings in the order in which he wrote them, but this would not necessarily give us the sense of an organic sequence, and in any case is impossible because their exact order is unknown. In even his least mature works he shows himself already to be a highly accomplished writer, but so far as we know, nothing that he wrote in his youth or early manhood has survived except that one of his sonnets – Sonnet 145, which seems to pun on the name of Anne Hathaway – may date from the time of his courtship.[1] He must have written academic exercises (in Latin) as a schoolboy, he may have written verse for his own pleasure, he could even have written plays for amateur performance before joining the professional theatre, but if so we have no record of them.

The dates and sequence of his earliest plays are especially uncertain. In this chapter I shall write about his five earliest comedies, all drawing on common conventions of his time, but each having its own distinct identity, as if he had been deeply anxious to avoid any criticism of repeating himself. So, although each is concerned to some degree with

courtship and wooing, one, *The Two Gentlemen of Verona*, concentrates on a conflict between love and friendship; another, *The Taming
of the Shrew*, presents a highly unconventional wooing and places the
marriage of the central characters in the middle, not at the end, of the
action; another, *The Comedy of Errors*, concerns itself with family
relationships in general and gives little prominence to wooing; and the
fourth, *Love's Labour's Lost*, presents an abortive series of courtships.
Only the last, *A Midsummer Night's Dream*, is centrally concerned with
love and marriage.

My opinion, ultimately unprovable, that *The Two Gentlemen of
Verona* is Shakespeare's first surviving play is based mainly on its
slightness and especially on the difficulty that he seems to experience
in orchestrating scenes in which more than three or four characters are
involved. The play is slight in the sense that it is relatively short, that it
has the smallest cast list of any of his plays, that it is structurally simple
– there is no fully developed subplot – and that it plumbs no great
depths of emotion. In the theatre it has often been expanded with
musical additions; in a production by David Thacker at Stratford-
upon-Avon in 1991, for instance, the action was updated to the 1930s,
a dance band was visible at the back of the stage throughout, and
scenes were interspersed with songs by composers such as Cole Porter
and George Gershwin. Although such additions are not strictly
necessary, they are in keeping with the predominant lyricism of the
play's verse. This is – it is hard to avoid the cliché – a young man's play
not only in the limitations of its technique but also in its concern with
youthful emotions and in its tender tolerance of the follies of first love.
    The title sets up the appropriate expectations: this is to be a play
about a relationship between two men, and the action is to take place
in Italy, traditionally a land of romance. The first scene opens up the
conflict between love and friendship that is to dominate the action: one
of the gentlemen, Valentine, is about to leave for the court of the
Emperor, or Duke, of Milan (Shakespeare appears to have been hazy
about aristocratic titles at this stage in his career); the other, his 'loving
Proteus', is restrained from accompanying him by love for Julia.
These young men are at a crucial stage of life, the stage at which the
demands of love are beginning to take precedence over youthful
camaraderie. It is a theme of permanent interest, reinterpretable in
terms of the age in which the play is being performed. Valentine and

Proteus are very fond of one another; there have been modern productions in which their relationship has been portrayed as more or less overtly sexual, and although this is certainly not explicit in the dialogue, it is not unreasonable as a reading between the lines. What is certain is that they must be young enough for us to take a sympathetic if slightly patronizing interest in their affairs, to feel that Valentine is touching as well as asinine when he fails to realize that the love-letter which Silvia, in what should be a transparently obvious attempt to preserve her modesty, pretends to be writing to someone else is in fact intended for him, and even when the Duke tricks him into giving away the plan by which he hopes to elope with Silvia.

No less perennial in its appeal is the plight of the young women who become entangled with these gentlemen. Julia adores Proteus, but by the time she is expressing her faith in his constancy we already know that, having followed Valentine to Milan, Proteus has not merely fallen in love with his friend's newly acquired girlfriend, Silvia, but has determined to betray both his friend and his sweetheart. The development of this situation produces some of the play's most appealing verse, passages of which would be entirely at home in the poetical anthologies of the period. It cries out for performers who can do justice not only to its lyric grace but to the humour and poignancy with which the play's situations invest it. Julia's rhapsodizing over Proteus's love-letter is touching, but it is funny too because she has had to reassemble the letter from the fragments into which she has torn it in the attempt to conceal her love from her maid, Lucetta – who of course already knows all about it. Constantly the play presents us with situations that are funny to the observers – both on and off stage – but serious to those most directly involved.

At times – and these are the passages that present the greatest challenges to performers – the comedy and the pathos are imperfectly fused. Perhaps the most conspicuous example is the scene in which the Duke, primed by Proteus, waylays Valentine on his way to elope with Silvia. The Duke, pretending to seek advice on how he may pursue a love-affair of his own, winkles out of Valentine the details of his plot; relentlessly and inexorably Valentine entangles himself ever more deeply in the snares the Duke has set for him until the Duke fools him into revealing both the rope ladder with which he was to release Silvia from the tower in which she has been immured and the letter in which he declares his intention. Valentine stands revealed as a complete and utter ass, but his response to the Duke's subsequent sentence of banishment is so deeply felt, so touchingly idealistic, and so gracefully

expressed as to require a complete shift in the actor's presentation of
the character and in the audience's attitude to him:

> And why not death, rather than living torment?
> To die is to be banished from myself,
> And Silvia is my self. Banished from her
> Is self from self, a deadly banishment.
> What light is light, if Silvia be not seen?
> What joy is joy, if Silvia be not by –
> Unless it be to think that she is by,
> And feed upon the shadow of perfection.
> Except I be by Silvia in the night
> There is no music in the nightingale.
> Unless I look on Silvia in the day
> There is no day for me to look upon.
> She is my essence, and I leave to be
> If I be not by her fair influence
> Fostered, illumined, cherished, kept alive.
>
> (3.1.170–84)

At other points, though, comedy and pathos come together with
Mozartian felicity, especially in the ironies that play around Julia in the
pageboy disguise in which she follows Proteus. We hear them in her
little dialogue with the Host of an Inn as, unseen by Proteus, she
overhears his offering of the serenade 'Who is Silvia?':

HOST How now, are you sadder than you were before? How do
  you, man? The music likes you not.
JULIA You mistake. The musician likes me not.
HOST Why, my pretty youth?
JULIA He plays false, father.
HOST How, out of tune on the strings?
JULIA Not so, but yet so false that he grieves my very heart-strings.
HOST You have a quick ear.
JULIA Ay, I would I were deaf. It makes me have a slow heart.
HOST I perceive you delight not in music.
JULIA Not a whit when it jars so.
HOST Hark what fine change is in the music.
JULIA Ay, that 'change' is the spite.
HOST You would have them always play but one thing?
JULIA I would always have one play but one thing.

(4.2.53–69)

The Host's emphasis in his first two lines on the word 'man' paradoxically reminds the audience that he is talking to a girl; the way in which Julia applies the Host's talk of the music to her own situation while appearing to the Host still to be talking about the music generates an interplay of meanings that is both witty and touching; and the hint of bawdy in Julia's last remark – 'thing' had a sexual sense – puts us in touch with earthy reality. The climax of the play's comic ironies comes in the meeting between Julia and Silvia when (in Shakespeare's theatre) the boy actor playing Julia disguised as a boy tells Silvia how, in a Whitsun entertainment, 'he' had dressed 'himself' 'in Madam Julia's gown' to play the part of the forsaken Ariadne with such success that 'his' mistress 'Wept bitterly'.

Shakespeare could have told the story of the aristocratic lovers on its own, but to do so would not have offered his audience the range and variety of entertainment that they had already come to expect from the plays of predecessors such as John Lyly and Robert Greene. He offsets the elegant, witty, and delicate comedy of his main plot with a more robust commentary in the figures of Valentine's and Proteus's servants, Speed and Lance. Speed is the more satirical, Lance the more earthy; Speed thin and mercurial, Lance fat and slow in my book, though not always in performance. Speed offers Valentine a cheeky send-up of his behaviour as a lover:

> you have learned, like Sir Proteus, to wreath your arms, like a malcontent; to relish a love-song, like a robin redbreast; to walk alone, like one that had the pestilence; to sigh, like a schoolboy that had lost his ABC
>
> (2.1.17 ff.)

and so on. It's elegant and witty enough, but dated for a modern audience. Even Shakespeare's most wholehearted admirers are apt to find stilted the passages of wordplay indulged in by the lower classes in the early comedies. Max Beerbohm parodied them effectively in a lament for the absence of Shakespearian comic relief in a play about prize-fighting (*The Admirable Bashville*) by Bernard Shaw:

> SECOND POLICEMAN Canst tell me of this prize-fight? Is't within law?
> FIRST POLICEMAN Aye! To't. For what does a man prize highest? A fight. But no man fights what he prizes, else is he no man, being not manly, nor yet unmannerly. Argal, if he fight the prize, then

is not the prize his, save in misprision, and 'tis no prize-fight
within the meaning of the act.
SECOND POLICEMAN Marry, I like thy wit, etc. etc.[2]

Far more timeless in appeal is the character of Lance whose dog,
Crab, is surely the greatest non-speaking role in the canon. With the
possible but not, I think, likely exception of the bear in *The Winter's
Tale* Shakespeare never repeated this early experiment of giving a live
animal a prominent part in a play's action. He was taking a risk:
animals even more than children are notorious scene-stealers, and
their presence on stage introduces an element of unpredictability that
raises an audience's level of attention while increasing both their and
the actor's sense of danger. But Crab's presence is justified by the way
in which Shakespeare integrates him into the language and even the
action of the play, especially in the two solo speeches that form the
heart of Lance's role. Lance's serio-comic account of his tearful parting
from his family, during all which while his dog 'sheds not a tear, nor
speaks a word', follows aptly on Proteus's affectionate parting from
Julia, a parting which, he says, 'strikes poor lovers dumb'. It also helps
to establish Lance as a figure of unsophisticated but basic human
decency in a way that gives authority to his statement, after learning of
his master's treachery: 'I am but a fool, look you, and yet I have the wit
to think my master is a kind of knave.'

The appearance on stage of an animal raises in the audience's minds
the possibility, and perhaps even the anarchic hope, that it will find a
need to relieve itself in public, to the detriment of the stage illusion and
the embarrassment of the actor. There have been productions of *The
Two Gentlemen of Verona* in which Crab has been played by a dog doll
or a puppet, but my conviction that Shakespeare wanted a real dog is
based on the fact that in Act 4, scene 4, he builds into the play an
anecdote which realizes the audience's fantasies for them: sent as a
present from Proteus to Silvia, Crab 'thrusts me into the company of
three or four gentlemanlike dogs under the Duke's table; he had not
been there, bless the mark, a pissing while but all the chamber smelt
him'. The skill with which this anecdote is related should not be
underestimated: it is a little masterpiece of comic prose. And it has its
part to play in the overall pattern of the action: Proteus's disloyalty to
Julia is contrasted with Lance's self-sacrificing fidelity to his dog, and
his forgiveness of Crab's deed:

I, having been acquainted with the smell before, knew it was

Crab, and goes me to the fellow that whips the dogs. 'Friend,' quoth I, 'you mean to whip the dog.' 'Ay, marry, do I,' quoth he. 'You do him the more wrong,' quoth I, ' 'twas I did the thing you wot of.' He makes me no more ado, but whips me out of the chamber. How many masters would do this for his servant?

'Not many', as a member of a Stratford audience audibly remarked, to her subsequent confusion.

The most problematic scene in the play is the last. The action has reached a climax of complication. Proteus has pursued Silvia into the forest where she is seeking Valentine; when she once more rejects his advances he tries to rape her. Happily, Valentine is on hand to rescue her in the nick of time. With implausible speed, Proteus repents and asks Valentine to forgive him; no less speedily and implausibly, Valentine not merely agrees, with resounding sanctimony, but donates Silvia to his friend:

> Who by repentance is not satisfied
> Is nor of heaven nor earth. For these are pleased;
> By penitence th' Eternal's wrath's appeased.
> And that my love may appear plain and free,
> All that was mine in Silvia I give thee.
>
> (5.4.79–83)

Silvia says nothing; Julia faints. On recovering she accidentally gives Proteus the ring he had given her at parting; she reveals her identity, and now it is Proteus's turn to be sanctimonious:

>   O heaven, were man
> But constant, he were perfect. That one error
> Fills him with faults, makes him run through all th' sins.
> Inconstancy falls off ere it begins.
>
> (5.4.109–12)

In espousing constancy he renounces the implications of his name and returns to Julia. The Duke arrives on the scene, a captive of the comic opera outlaws who are the shadowiest characters of the play, just in time to sort out any remaining complications. Silvia still says nothing.

The basic problem of this scene is that Shakespeare is too obviously manipulating his characters, huddling events together in order to bring the action to a conclusion in which the claims of love and friendship will be reconciled, without fully articulating the emotions his characters are required to undergo. From being a play in which states of mind are expressed verbally, it becomes one in which they have to be projected between the lines. It is not unplayable, as David Thacker showed in his 1991 production: Proteus held a long pause indicative of internal struggle before declaring his penitence, and Silvia demonstrated deep though wordless compassion for him; but it requires a sudden change of gear from one theatrical mode to another. This was the most successful handling of the scene in my experience of the play, but it was difficult not to feel that, rather than realizing Shakespeare's theatrical intentions, the actors were bailing him out.

Probably, over the years, *The Two Gentlemen of Verona* has given more pleasure to readers than to theatregoers. The reverse is true of *The Taming of the Shrew*. Yet it includes some fine writing, some of the best of it in the Induction, in which the drunken tinker Christopher Sly is made to think he is a lord. Here, Shakespeare is fully the poet, writing verse whose very subject–matter is the power of language, as well as of visual art, to persuade, to create illusion, even to transform.

LORD
    We'll show thee Io as she was a maid,
    And how she was beguilèd and surprised,
    As lively painted as the deed was done.
THIRD SERVINGMAN
    Or Daphne roaming through a thorny wood,
    Scratching her legs that one shall swear she bleeds,
    And at that sight shall sad Apollo weep,
    So workmanly the blood and tears are drawn.
LORD
    Thou art a lord, and nothing but a lord.
    Thou hast a lady far more beautiful
    Than any woman in this waning age.

                                                    (Ind.2.53–62)

The tinker's language turns from prose to verse as he accepts the greatness that is thrust upon him:

    Am I a lord, and have I such a lady?
    Or do I dream? Or have I dreamed till now?

> I do not sleep. I see, I hear, I speak.
> I smell sweet savours, and I feel soft things.
> Upon my life, I am a lord indeed,
> And not a tinker, nor Christopher Sly.
>
> (Ind.2.67–72)

It is marvellous theatre as well as splendid verse, which makes all the more strange the fact that it has sometimes been omitted in productions of the play, notably those (for both the BBC television series and the Royal Shakespeare Company) by Jonathan Miller. Admittedly the Sly episodes are not essential to the story of the taming of the shrew, which is performed by a troupe of strolling players as an entertainment for the tinker in his new persona. Admittedly too these episodes create a problem for the director in that Sly soon fades out of the action. In the text as it has come down to us by way of the First Folio, the shrew play soon ceases to be a play within the play and becomes the play itself. Nevertheless the Sly episodes are thematically very relevant to this story of a man, Petruccio, who uses imagination, words, and action to transform a woman, Kate, from a shrew to an obedient and loving wife. To omit them is to strip the play of an important, and humanizing, dimension.

Inhumanity is a charge that has often been brought against the shrew plot. Petruccio is a self-confessed fortune-hunter:

> I come to wive it wealthily in Padua;
> If wealthily, then happily in Padua.
>
> (1.2.74–5)

He declares himself indifferent to physical imperfections in a wife:

> Be she as foul as was Florentius' love,
> As old as Sybil, and as curst and shrewd
> As Socrates' Xanthippe or a worse,
> She moves me not – or not removes at least
> Affection's edge in me.
>
> (1.2.68–72)

And his servant, Grumio, threatens that his master will overcome Kate with physical violence:

> an she stand him but a little he will throw a figure in her face and
> so disfigure her with it that she shall have no more eyes to see
> withal than a cat.
>
> (1.2.111–14)

But Petruccio himself, in soliloquy, tells us of his determination to overcome the resistance that he expects from Kate through an exercise not of the body but of the mind:

> Say that she rail, why then I'll tell her plain
> She sings as sweetly as a nightingale.
> Say that she frown, I'll say she looks as clear
> As morning roses newly washed with dew.
> Say she be mute and will not speak a word,
> Then I'll commend her volubility,
> And say she uttereth piercing eloquence.
>
> (2.1.170–6)

This is a key speech, placed immediately before the first of the wooing scenes, and giving the audience insight into the workings of Petruccio's mind. It can be played with a swagger, but in Miller's television production John Cleese, taking advantage of the intimacy offered by the medium, delivered it with sober thoughtfulness, as if he were deeply conscious that much of his future happiness depended on the success of his strategy. The speech provides an important perspective on the action, inclining us to see the taming process primarily from Petruccio's point of view. There is no hint from him that he will work on Kate by physical means. Except for a mild scuffle or two his wooing is carried out by a combat of wits. Kate succumbs to it with unexplained ease – again the dramatic perspective favours Petruccio – and not until he is in church, an episode that is narrated, not seen, does he begin to exercise physical violence, which even then is directed at the clergyman, not Kate, as we hear in Grumio's description of the wedding:

> when the priest
> Should ask if Katherine should be his wife,
> 'Ay, by Gog's woun's,' quoth he, and swore so loud
> That all amazed the priest let fall the book,
> And as he stooped again to take it up
> This mad-brained bridegroom took him such a cuff
> That down fell priest, and book, and book, and priest.
>
> (3.3.31–7)

We are left in no doubt that this is all part of an act that Petruccio is putting on, just as the Lord and his gentlemen had put on an act to transmogrify Christopher Sly, and as the Lord had instructed the performers of the play within the play to behave before Sly. All this may help Petruccio to retain our sympathy. The physically aggressive behaviour stems from mental calculation of a good-humoured and benevolent kind.

The taming process itself, which begins with the marriage, takes place in two major stages, one aimed at subduing Kate's body, the other at taming her mind. In the first, Petruccio carries Kate bodily away from her father's house; he causes her to undergo the physical tribulations, memorably catalogued by Grumio in another of the young Shakespeare's masterly set-pieces of comic prose, of the journey to her new home; and he knocks her servants around in her presence, throwing food and dishes at them – but not at Kate. Again the action is put in a perspective favourable to Petruccio by a soliloquy – or more properly, perhaps, a monologue addressed to the audience – in which he reminds us of the calculatedness of his behaviour ('Thus have I politicly begun my reign'), compares Kate to a falcon that he is taming, outlines the next stage of his campaign, and claims the audience's sympathy by saying

> amid this hurly I intend
> That all is done in reverent care of her

and by asking, disarmingly,

> He that knows better how to tame a shrew,
> Now let him speak. 'Tis charity to show.
> (4.1.189–90, 196–7)

The next stage of the taming story continues the physical process. Kate ruefully sums up the technique before it begins:

> I . . .
> Am starved for meat, giddy for lack of sleep,
> With oaths kept waking and with brawling fed,
> And that which spites me more than all these wants,
> He does it under name of perfect love.
> (4.3.8–12)

After these recapitulatory and anticipatory passages the taming begins again as Kate is deprived first of food, then of new clothes; and this stage in the process comes almost to an end with the long speech of

Petruccio, addressed to Kate, in which he draws a moral in terms that
bring explicitly to the play's surface the ideas I have been tracing:

> Well, come, my Kate. We will unto your father's
> Even in these honest, mean habiliments;
> Our purses shall be proud, our garments poor,
> For 'tis the mind that makes the body rich,
> And as the sun breaks through the darkest clouds,
> So honour peereth in the meanest habit.
>
> (4.3.167–72)

Or, as Shakespeare puts it in Sonnet 146, 'Within be fed, without be
rich no more'.

Petruccio continues in this vein at some length, stressing the
importance of inherent qualities rather than superficial ones. His long
speech marks a turn in both the action and Petruccio's technique. In
the coda of the scene Shakespeare gently prefigures the next stage, as
Kate contradicts Petruccio's statement ' 'tis now some seven o'clock'
and receives her warning from him:

> I will not go today, and ere I do
> It shall be what o'clock I say it is.

Hortensio's closing line – 'Why, so this gallant will command the sun'
– is also deliberately anticipatory. Now Petruccio is to work on Kate's
mind and, even more importantly, on her imagination. He calls the
sun the moon, Kate contradicts him, and he gives orders to turn back;
but Kate is beginning to learn how to deal with him:

> Forward, I pray, since we have come so far,
> And be it moon or sun or what you please,
> And if you please to call it a rush-candle
> Henceforth I vow it shall be so for me.

It is a spirited reply in its acknowledgement of absurdity. Petruccio
puts her through her paces:

PETRUCCIO I say it is the moon.
KATHERINE I know it is the moon.
PETRUCCIO Nay then you lie, it is the blessèd sun.
KATHERINE Then God be blessed, it is the blessèd sun,
  But sun it is not when you say it is not,

And the moon changes even as your mind.
What you will have it named, even that it is,
And so it shall be still for Katherine.

(4.6.16–23)

There is a new-found articulacy in Kate's style here; and is there not
something of a dig, not wholly submissive, at Petruccio in 'the moon
changes even as your mind'? – it was, after all, women's minds that
were proverbially as changeable as the moon.

The next episode reveals Kate not merely concurring with her
husband in patent absurdity but entering with full imaginative
commitment into what now seems more like a game than a display of
the results of a process of brainwashing, as she addresses old Vincentio
as 'Young budding virgin, fair and fresh and sweet . . .' This time she
agrees immediately when Petruccio contradicts her, claiming that she
has been 'bedazzled with the sun', and the episode passes off
harmoniously. (Peggy Ashcroft made a marvellously comic effect
with an interrogative pause before 'sun', as if to indicate that she was
fully aware of the game they were playing together.)[3] It remains
simply for Kate to demonstrate her affection in public, and this she
does, after a momentary flinching, with 'Nay, I will give thee a kiss;
now pray thee love, stay'.

In my view, Kate's journey can be seen as a process that brings her
to a full realization of her potentialities as a woman rather than as a
process of brainwashing, crushing her into cowed submission; and I
should claim support for this point of view in the contrast between the
disjointedness of her utterances early in the play and the confident
control of language that she demonstrates in the long speech in the last
scene in which she rebukes her sister and the Widow who have refused
to come at their husbands' commands, and speaks of the duty that a
wife owes her husband:

> I am ashamed that women are so simple
> To offer war where they should kneel for peace,
> Or seek for rule, supremacy, and sway
> When they are bound to serve, love, and obey.

(5.2.166–9)

Theatrically, the scene is finely crafted, reaching a climax of suspense
as the audience both on and off stage waits to see if Kate will obey her
husband's command. Ideologically, however, Kate's speech has come
to be seen as one of the points where Shakespeare is of his age rather

than for all time. The sentiments expressed in it, however admirable they may have seemed to the men in Shakespeare's audience, have proved increasingly objectionable at least since the women's movement in the late nineteenth century, when Bernard Shaw wrote: 'No man with any decency of feeling can sit it out in the company of a woman without being extremely ashamed of the lord-of-creation moral implied in the wager and the speech put into the woman's own mouth.'[4] For some people Kate's speech is as much of an obstacle to enjoyment of the play as for others are the nationalistic sentiments of the final chorus of Wagner's *Die Meistersinger*. Expedients have been devised for lessening the offence, by having Kate deliver the speech with tongue in cheek or by causing Petruccio to react with evident embarrassment and shame.

It is possible, however, that Shakespeare himself wished to undercut the speech by presenting this climax of the story of the taming of a shrew as romantic wish-fulfilment on the part of Christopher Sly. One of the great unsolved problems of Shakespeare scholarship is the question of the relationship between the play printed in the First Folio and a related play printed in 1594 with the similar but not identical title, *The Taming of A Shrew*. Did Shakespeare adapt this play, or does it derive from his? In it Sly appears at several additional points of the action, and at the close is carried on stage 'in his own apparel again'. Woken by a tapster, and realizing that he is not a lord after all, he declares:

> O Lord, sirrah, I have had
> The bravest dream tonight that ever thou
> Heardest in all thy life.

Some modern directors have successfully grafted this ending on to the text of the play as conventionally printed. At the very least, a reminder that the play we have been watching started as a play within a play is a useful way of rescuing a fine comedy from ideological dismissal; and it is quite possible that to do so correctly represents Shakespeare's intention at one stage, at least, in the evolution of the text.

It is a paradox that the only play of Shakespeare's with the word 'comedy' in its title, *The Comedy of Errors*, is the one that has most often been dismissed as a mechanical farce. Certainly in performance it can and should be one of his most entertaining plays, but it would not have kept its place in the theatrical repertory if its only merits lay in its ingenious plotting. Its brevity – this is the shortest of all Shakespeare's plays – has counted against it, though not probably at its first recorded performance, in 1594, when it formed part of a tumultuous entertainment offered by students of Gray's Inn to guests from the Inner Temple on 28 December, which was traditionally observed as the Feast of Fools. On that evening the revels became so rowdy that the official guests withdrew, after which 'it was thought good not to offer anything of account, saving dancing and revelling with gentlewomen; and after such sports a Comedy of Errors (like to Plautus his *Menechmus*) was played by the players'.[5] In theatres offering their patrons a full evening's entertainment its brevity has often caused it to be either padded out with songs or performed as part of a double bill. It is amenable to this kind of treatment: Frederic Reynolds at Covent Garden in 1819 and Trevor Nunn at Stratford in 1976 are among those who have successfully turned it into a full-scale musical show.

The fact that the cast list includes two pairs of twins has also been a handicap. Ben Jonson told his friend William Drummond of Hawthornden that he had abandoned an intention to write a play with twins in it 'for that he could never find two so like others that he could persuade the spectators they were one',[6] and later directors of Shakespeare's play have betrayed the same anxiety. On film a single actor can play each pair of twins, as in the BBC television version, and even in the theatre this can be done with a bit of textual adaptation or by using doubles, especially in the final scene, the only one where the twins appear together. But to my mind the idea that the audience should be as bemused by the complications of the action as the play's characters is mistaken. On the contrary, much of the play's comedy depends on the audience's knowing which twin they are watching at any given moment. Certainly we need to be able to share momentarily the illusion that the twins may be mistaken for each other; but also, if our laughter rather than bewilderment is to be provoked, we need to be able to stand somewhat aloof from the fictional situation in an attitude of amused superiority over those who fall into error. In my experience audiences have no difficulty in accepting the convention of identity even in productions of the other play in which Shakespeare uses twins, *Twelfth Night*, where the twin brother and sister are now normally played by members of the opposite sex – as of course they were not in Shakespeare's time. Any director able to cast genuinely identical twins in these plays would be well advised to do something to lessen the resemblance between them.

Whatever the genre indicated by its title, there is no denying that this story of a master and his servant seeking their twin brothers from whom they have been separated since infancy has many of the characteristics of farce: absurdities of plot, stylized action, subordination at times of character to plot, and a dissociation of response in which violence – in the play's climactic episodes in which Antipholus and Dromio of Ephesus, believed to be mad, are forcibly bound and sent off to be 'laid in some dark room' – evokes laughter rather than pity and horror. And as well as adopting many of the play's basic situations from Plautus's *Menaechmi*, a Roman farcical comedy which he may have read at school in the original Latin, Shakespeare increases the possibilities of comic confusion: in Plautus only the masters are twins; in Shakespeare so are their servants, which adds greatly to the plot's complexity. Whereas in Plautus there is no-one whom the brother visiting Ephesus is likely to take for anyone else, in Shakespeare he too can be wrong, about the servants, both (confusingly and improbably) named Dromio. In Shakespeare's play, indeed, every character knows, and may easily encounter, either a twin master or a twin servant or both, and so is liable to error, except for the Abbess, who appears only in the last scene. As the character least susceptible to error she is peculiarly suited to her primary function, that of resolving the complexities of the action. The plotting of this play is an intellectual feat of some magnitude; as E.M.W. Tillyard wrote, 'Shakespeare was able to set his prodigious powers of memory and intellect a satisfyingly exacting task'.[7] It demonstrates the kind of intellectual mastery required for the composition of a fugue.

The mechanical complexities of the play's plot have encouraged directors to stylize the action, treating the characters as puppets rather than people and creating a world of pure fantasy. But to do this is to ignore the fact that Shakespeare made other changes to his source which add elements of high seriousness and emotional depth. This is not merely a play of mistaken identity; it is also a story of separation, seeking, and reunion such as Shakespeare was to use many times in his career, most movingly in his late romances such as *The Winter's Tale* and *The Tempest*. The opening scene, in which Egeon, the father of the twin masters, tells of the shipwreck in which his family and the twin servants were separated is entirely serious in tone. (It derives from the same story that Shakespeare was to use in another of his late plays,

Pericles.) Directors resolved to extract every last ounce of comedy from the text have burlesqued it in a manner that is bound to reduce the impact of the final scene, in which Egeon's distress on apparently being rejected by the son he has cared for from infancy is movingly portrayed.

Shakespeare also modified the comic substance of his source play in ways that deepen its moral dimension. He explores, in a seriously comic way, the proper relationship of husband and wife. One of the twin masters (also confusingly and implausibly bearing the same name, Antipholus) is married to Adriana. When her husband does not arrive home in time for dinner she is unreasonably jealous; her sister rebukes her for her suspicions. The tirade she fires off at the man she believes to be her husband when at last he does arrive is serious in content but comic in context, for this is not her husband after all; the blank innocence on his face as she accuses him of being 'an adulterate blot' is all the comment she deserves: this is not her husband she is addressing, and anyway he is innocent. His reaction 'Plead you to me, fair dame' (uttered by Alec McCowen after a quick glance over his shoulder to see if anyone else was there[8]) sets the seal of comedy upon it.

The theme is continued in the more understandable jealousy that Adriana displays on hearing of Antipholus's advances to her sister (though again it is all based on a misunderstanding). Indeed it warps her view of her husband – 'He is deformèd, crookèd, old and sere' – to the point where her sister asks why she bothers to be jealous of such a man; and then Adriana is restored to our sympathy – and makes us laugh – by her admission that she thinks better of him than in her anger she has admitted.

The climax comes in the last scene when the Abbess, with innocent cunning, traps Adriana into confessing that she has bullied her husband, and then tells her that this is why he appears to be mad. This is corrective, moral comedy in that Adriana's husband is not restored to her until her attitude to him has changed for the better.

More broadly, the play concerns itself with family relationships in general. Forcible separation creates a sense of loss of identity, and this is intensified by failures of recognition brought about by mistaken identity. Although the concept of the absolute external identity of one person with another is easily productive of comedy, it is also frightening. It is a concept that Shakespeare himself, as the father of twins, had special reason to ponder (though as his were not of the same sex they could not have been identical). It brings home to us the mysteries of the human personality, the fact that our sense of identity does not only come from within but depends, too, upon a high degree of constancy in the reactions of those around us. If we were to be treated by people we had never seen before as if we were their 'familiar acquaintance' while not being recognized by those whom we believed to be close to us, madness could well result. In *King Lear* Shakespeare profoundly explores the effect on the king of such reversals of expected behaviour from his family and subjects. And in *The Comedy of Errors* he exploits more than simply the comic possibilities of the notion – frequently characters voice the fear that they are dreaming, mad, or the victims of evil practices. The theme of madness reaches its climax in Act 4, Scene 4, when Dr Pinch is brought in to cure Antipholus of Syracuse of his supposed derangement. Pinch – like the Courtesan – is easily burlesqued. Directors often pick up the modern connotations of the term by which Shakespeare describes him – 'conjuror', which in his time meant exorcist – and make his brief appearance, for he speaks only twelve lines, the occasion for elaborate comic business at the risk of holding up the flow of the action. There has even been a Stratford production in which Pinch sawed a woman in two on stage.[9]

It is the suspicion that Antipholus and Dromio of Syracuse (mistaken for their counterparts of Ephesus) are mad that brings about the resolution of the action as they take refuge in the Priory and come under the care of the Abbess, who shows Adriana the errors of her ways (not all the 'errors' of the title are the result of external confusion). The revelation of the Abbess's true identity is one of the rare surprises that Shakespeare plays on his audience. Usually he keeps us ahead of the characters of the play in knowledge of who is who and what is to happen; not until the final scene of *The Winter's Tale* was he to play a comparable card.

The ending of *The Comedy of Errors* is not simply a matter of untying a comic knot. The fundamental human emotions on which this play can base its claim to be comedy rather than farce are the simple and related ones of sorrow at separation and joy in reunion, and they centre on the figure of Egeon. We have not seen him since the opening scene, condemned to die at sunset unless he can find someone to pay his debts. During the body of the play we are frequently made aware of the passage of time, and all the normal relationships of the main characters have been cast into confusion when he enters in solemn procession to 'The place of death and sorry execution'. His emotion on being rejected by the man he believes to be the son he has tended from birth is given full expression, and only if we are made to believe in its reality will the happiness of the resolution be brought home to us.

Although much of it is written in verse of considerable virtuosity *The Comedy of Errors* is one of Shakespeare's least obviously poetical plays. In it his verbal powers are fully at the service of his overall dramatic aims. Often the situations require no more than swift, economical writing, carrying us along briskly from one comic point to the next. But Shakespeare, already a master of dramatic rhythm, knew that the pace would become wearisome if it remained unvaried. From time to time he relaxes the pace of the ongoing action to allow the inclusion of passages of comic writing in which the situation is not advanced but enlarged upon. Such is Dromio of Syracuse's brilliant description of the kitchen wench who, mistaking him for his twin, presses her attentions upon him:

> Marry, sir, she's the kitchen wench, and all grease; and I know
> not what use to put her to but to make a lamp of her, and run
> from her by her own light. I warrant her rags and the tallow in
> them will burn a Poland winter. If she lives till doomsday, she'll
> burn a week longer than the whole world.
>
> (3.2.96–101)

Having declared that 'She is spherical, like a globe', he is egged on by his master to 'find out countries in her' in a comic catechism which preserves the comic tone while giving us a rest from following the complications of the action. Equally brilliant in a different way is Antipholus of Ephesus's description of Dr Pinch and his efforts to cure him of his supposed madness:

> Along with them
> They brought one Pinch, a hungry lean-faced villain,
> A mere anatomy, a mountebank,
> A threadbare juggler, and a fortune-teller,
> A needy, hollow-eyed, sharp-looking wretch,
> A living dead man . . .
>
> (5.1.237 ff.)

In its matching of style to content, its dramatic economy, its tautness of construction, and its bold interfusion of farce with romance, *The Comedy of Errors* has claims to be considered as Shakespeare's first real masterpiece.

★

For a long time the reputation of *Love's Labour's Lost* was bedevilled by
the idea that it is linguistically difficult and so full of unfathomable
topical allusions as to be incomprehensible. Recent thought suggests
that its topicality has been exaggerated,[10] and a series of highly
successful and enjoyable post-war productions, beginning with those
of Peter Brook at Stratford-upon-Avon in 1946 and Hugh Hunt with
the Old Vic company in 1949, has shown that though it may in places
be hard to read, in performance the listener may be carried happily
through its verbal intricacies by the verve of the writing, the impetus
of the action, and the skill of the performers.

Like *The Two Gentlemen of Verona*, this play shows young men – the
King of Navarre and his three attendant lords – at a crucial stage of
adolescence, but whereas at the start of the earlier play one of the men
is committed to love and the other soon falls into it, here all four are
initially preparing to withdraw for three years from the pleasures of
the world, including female society, and to start a 'little academe' in
which 'The mind shall banquet, though the body pine'. One of them,
Biron, is a reluctant fellow-traveller and expresses his scepticism in
lines that prefigure the course of the play's action:

> Study me how to please the eye indeed
>   By fixing it upon a fairer eye,
> Who dazzling so, that eye shall be his heed,
>   And give him light that it was blinded by.
> Study is like the heavens' glorious sun,
>   That will not be deep searched with saucy looks.
> Small have continual plodders ever won
>   Save base authority from others' books.
> These earthly godfathers of heaven's lights,
>   That give a name to every fixèd star,
> Have no more profit of their shining nights
>   Than those that walk and wot not what they are.
> Too much to know is to know naught but fame,
> And every godfather can give a name.
>
>   (1.1.80–93)

Those lines, embedded in the dialogue of the play, take the form of a
Shakespearian sonnet. They exemplify the frequent intellectuality of
the play's style, the brilliance of its versification, and its self-conscious

literariness. The King points out the paradox that lies behind them: 'How well he's read, to reason against reading!'

The action of the play is structured to form an examination of the tension in these people's lives between reason and instinct, art and nature, wit (in its largest sense) and folly. Already in the first scene the pattern that the King of Navarre is attempting to impose is endangered by Biron's scepticism, and the King recognizes the unreality of his plan when Biron draws his attention to the conflict between private desire and public duty: the imminent arrival of the Princess of France on a diplomatic mission means that it is impossible for the King to obey the rule that he 'must not be seen to talk with a woman within the term of three years'.

The Princess, predictably, brings with her three attendant ladies: Rosaline, Katherine, and Maria; each is to undermine the resolution of one of the men. From the start the action is highly patterned, and the patterning extends to the play's less central characters. One of them, Don Armado, takes to an extreme the verbal affectation that forms an element of the lords' conversation: he is

> A man in all the world's new fashion planted,
> That hath a mint of phrases in his brain.
> One who the music of his own vain tongue
> Doth ravish like enchanting harmony.
>
> (1.1.162–5)

Two others, the schoolmaster Holofernes and the curate Nathaniel, exemplify the intellectual sterility that will result if the lords' determination to study is taken to excess. At the other end of the scale, the constable Anthony Dull is so far from verbal affectation as to be almost without words; this phlegmatic character, eloquent in silence, can come to marvellously comic realization on the stage, as, for instance, during a long scene (5.1) in which Armado, Holofernes, and Nathaniel demonstrate that (as the page Mote says) 'They have been at a great feast of languages and stolen the scraps', at the end of which Dull responds to Holofernes' accurate statement: 'Thou hast spoken no word all this while' with 'Nor understood none neither, sir'. And unregenerate nature is represented by the swain Costard and the wench Jaquenetta, the object of sexual rivalry between Armado and Costard.

The play's patterning is responsible for some of its most pleasing theatrical effects, reaching a climax with the scene in which each of the

lords reveals that he has succumbed to love. Biron, who has already
confessed his love for Rosaline and paid Costard for delivering a letter
to her, enters alone and speaks ruefully of his love. He moves aside –
climbing a tree or in some similar way justifying his later statement
'Like a demigod here sit I in the sky' – as the King enters and reads a
love-sonnet addressed to the Princess. Biron watches as the King
watches Longueville read his sonnet addressed to Maria. Then all
three watch as Dumaine reads his sonnet addressed to Katherine. After
doing so he expresses the ironically redundant wish: 'O, would the
King, Biron, and Longueville | Were lovers too!' Longueville reveals
himself and rebukes Dumaine: 'I should blush, I know, | To be
o'erheard and taken napping so.' The King comes forward and mocks
both of them: 'What will Biron say when that he shall hear | Faith so
infringèd, which such zeal did swear?' Biron hypocritically steps
'forth to whip hypocrisy', mocks each of them, and declares himself
betrayed:

> I am betrayed by keeping company
> With men like you, men of inconstancy.
> When shall you see me write a thing in rhyme,
> Or groan for Joan, or spend a minute's time
> In pruning [preening] me?
>
> (4.3.177–81)

Biron seems indeed to be in an impregnably superior moral position
– when Jaquenetta enters with a letter that turns out to be the one he
has written to Rosaline. He tears it to pieces as soon as he has read it.
Realizing that he too is about to be exposed as a lover, he confesses his
guilt. Left alone, the men admit that, as Biron says, 'We cannot cross
the cause why we were born', and Biron speaks a great hymn to love:

> A lover's eyes will gaze an eagle blind.
> A lover's ear will hear the lowest sound
> When the suspicious head of theft is stopped.
> Love's feeling is more soft and sensible
> Than are the tender horns of cockled snails.
> Love's tongue proves dainty Bacchus gross in taste.
> For valour, is not love a Hercules,
> Still climbing trees in the Hesperides?
> Subtle as Sphinx, as sweet and musical
> As bright Apollo's lute strung with his hair;

And when love speaks, the voice of all the gods
Make heaven drowsy with the harmony.

(4.3.310–21)

A summary of the structure of the scene, while it does nothing like justice to the inventiveness, wit, and eloquence with which the situation is developed, may serve to demonstrate the basic simplicity that makes it so effective in the theatre. I remember once seeing a little girl on the edge of her seat with delight as each of the men fulfilled her dearest expectations by falling so neatly into the trap the dramatist had designed for him.

The end of the scene marks the play's main turning-point. 'Lay these glozes by', says Longueville – properly 'glozes' means 'words not to the point', but John Barton achieved a striking theatrical effect by having the men throw off the academic gowns they had been wearing until now; the would-be scholars had turned into self-avowed lovers.[11] After this the men openly go about their wooing. They do not have an easy ride.

Love's Labour's Lost is not only a witty play about sophisticated and highly articulate people; it is also a play that is profoundly concerned with the social function of wit, wit that can harmlessly entertain but that can also be deployed mockingly in a manner likely to disrupt the smooth functioning of society by causing hurt to its victims; in this play, just as pedantry represents the inhumane superfluity of learning, so mockery is seen as the sterile outgrowth of wit. The play is full of entertainments, informal in the first part, formal in the second, and the entertainments are often the occasion of mockery. The lords mock each other in the involuntary entertainments of the overhearing scene, the ladies mock the lords both in their absence and in the masque of Muscovites put on for their pleasure, and the lords mock the lower orders, especially in the pageant of the Nine Worthies presented to the Princess and her ladies.

The mockery, however, does not go unchallenged, nor does moral superiority lie with the mockers. Just as in *The Two Gentlemen of Verona* the clownish Lance is seen to be less of a knave than his master, so here the lowly Costard turns the moral tables on his betters, both by cheerfully accepting correction of error and by the charity of his apology for Sir Nathaniel after the curate has broken down in face of the lords' mockery:

There, an't shall please you, a foolish mild man, an honest man,
look you, and soon dashed. He is a marvellous good neighbour,
faith, and a very good bowler, but for Alisander – alas, you see
how 'tis – a little o'erparted.

                                                      (5.2.575–9)

The effect on the audience is complex. While we may share the
lords' amusement at the discomfiture of the performers, Costard's
comments direct our attention also to the human feelings of those who
are mocked, and unless the performers of the Worthies are grossly
caricatured by their interpreters, the theatre audience's sympathies are
likely to sway increasingly towards them as the pageant becomes
submerged in mockery, leading to the moment when Holofernes
steps out of his role to rebuke his courtly audience: 'This is not
generous, not gentle, not humble' (5.2.622). The criticism may also
help to readjust the theatre audience's sympathies.

The artificiality of the play, and of the behaviour of those portrayed in
it, is shattered in its closing stages by the intrusion of two elemental facts
of life: birth and death. The pageant of the Worthies disintegrates as
Costard reveals that Jaquenetta is two months pregnant by the actor
playing Hector. Mirth and mockery continue as Costard and Armado
prepare to fight, but all is stilled with the entrance of 'a messenger,
Monsieur Mercadé'. This is one of Shakespeare's greatest *coups de théâtre*.
The messenger brings news of death. He must be a sombre figure, and
his unexpected appearance when the mirth is at its height casts a chill over
the scene. One of the most remarkable things about this highly verbal
play is that the most important communication in it is made wordlessly:

MERCADÉ God save you, madam.
PRINCESS   Welcome, Mercadé,
    But that thou interrupt'st our merriment.
MERCADÉ I am sorry, madam, for the news I bring
    Is heavy in my tongue. The King your father –
PRINCESS Dead, for my life.
MERCADÉ   Even so. My tale is told.

                                                      (5.2.709–13)

After this, the mood changes. The characters of the play take on a
new seriousness; they are forced into new relationships with one
another. The Princess – now Queen – gains in dignity as she
apologizes for 'The liberal opposition of our spirits'. Awkwardly the
men try to resume their wooing, but the time is not ripe. They must

undergo tests to show that they are worthy. The King must go for a year 'To some forlorn and naked hermitage | Remote from all the pleasures of the world'. Biron, at the close of his central speech on love, had asked: 'And who can sever love from charity?' Now Rosaline demands that if he is to win her love he must put his wit to charitable ends, turning from mockery to cheering the sick:

> You shall this twelvemonth term from day to day
> Visit the speechless sick and still converse
> With groaning wretches, and your task shall be
> With all the fierce endeavour of your wit
> To enforce the painèd impotent to smile.
>
> (5.2.836–40)

The unsuccessful outcome of the wooing is presented in a moment of alienation that states one of the play's main claims to originality:

> BIRON Our wooing doth not end like an old play.
>   Jack hath not Jill. These ladies' courtesy
>   Might well have made our sport a comedy.
> KING Come, sir, it wants a twelvemonth an' a day,
>   And then 'twill end.
> BIRON   That's too long for a play.
>
> (5.2.860–4)

The shock of Mercadé's news is beginning to subside, and Armado enters to present 'the dialogue that the two learned men have compiled in praise of the owl and the cuckoo'. The two fine songs –'When daisies pied' and 'When icicles hang by the wall' – that end the play are curiously unintegrated into the action, but before they are sung a stage direction calls for the entry of virtually all who have taken part, lords, ladies, and commoners. The songs provide the play's third formal entertainment, and the only one that is not interrupted by its stage audience. The aristocrats have learned at least a temporary courtesy. A director may surely make a point of the fact that now the lords, the ladies, and their dependants join together to form a respectful audience, permitting the play to end with the consolations of music and the formality of art.

Most of Shakespeare's plays are based, more or less closely, on pre-existing narratives. This fact provoked Shaw's tart praise of Shakespeare's 'gift of telling a story (provided someone else told it to him first)'.[12] Both *Love's Labour's Lost* and *A Midsummer Night's Dream*, however, are spun mainly from his own imagination. They are highly personal plays, revealing of his own attitudes to life and art. Imagination is the subject of some of the best-known lines in *A Midsummer Night's Dream* – Theseus's 'The lunatic, the lover, and the poet | Are of imagination all compact . . .' – and there is a sense in which the entire play is about the power of the imagination: it has been called 'Shakespeare's *Ars Poetica*'.[13]

It has also proved an extraordinarily fertile source of inspiration for other imaginative artists: paintings by Fuseli, Richard Dadd, and Arthur Rackham, orchestral music by Mendelssohn, ballets by Balanchine and Frederick Ashton, films by Max Reinhardt and Peter Hall, the opera by Benjamin Britten, are among the witnesses to its hold on the artistic imagination. Drawing on myth, it has itself taken on some of the qualities of myth, so that it is not now easy to free Shakespeare's play from the associations of its own progeny. Famous productions by Harley Granville-Barker at the Savoy Theatre in London in 1914 and by Peter Brook at Stratford in 1970 both consciously tried to free the play in performance from the accretions of tradition; more complexly, John Caird's Stratford production of 1989 constantly alluded, often mockingly, parodistically, and by antithesis to the play's performance history: Mendelssohn's music was played both straight and in a jazzed-up version, the fairies were presented as caricatures of the way they might be seen in a school production, and Robin Goodfellow (or Puck) entered at one point reading his lines in parodic tones from a copy of the play (my own New Penguin edition, as it happened) which he soon threw away in disgust.

Full of quotable passages, *A Midsummer Night's Dream* is one of the most poetic of plays, on a technical level showing Shakespeare as a master of a wide range of verse techniques, and demonstrating also his capacity to body forth in words the creations of his imagination with the most exquisite delicacy. The play is also a triumph of dramatic counterpoint. Its characters fall easily into three groups, and a major source of the play's delight is the interplay that Shakespeare develops within and between them.

Central to the narrative are two stories of love and wooing. The courtship of Theseus, Duke of Athens, and Hippolyta, Queen of the Amazons, is in its final stage; admittedly Hippolyta's silences in the first scene have opened the way to feminist interpretations in which she is inclined to rebel against Theseus in his support of one of his subjects, Egeus, who is opposed to his daughter's marriage, but the play's framework is the preparations for the ducal wedding which must inevitably form its conclusion.

Combined with this more or less stable relationship are the wooing exploits of the young people, Lysander and Hermia, Demetrius and Helena. Egeus's refusal to allow Hermia to marry Lysander provokes them to elope into the 'wood near Athens' where most of the action takes place, and the move is not merely a physical one from the court to the country, it is also a move of the mind, pointed by a pun: the word 'wood' could mean mad, as Demetrius reminds us when he says he is 'wood within this wood', and within the wood prevails the irrationality associated with love: as Bottom is to say, 'reason and love keep little company together nowadays' (3.1.135–6).

Presiding over the woodland, but unseen – with one exception – by the mortals who visit it, are a second set of characters, inhabitants of fairy land, led by their king and queen, Oberon and Titania, a couple whose marriage is in difficulties. The fairies are among Shakespeare's most original creations; his reading contributed to their making, but only his imagination could have bodied them forth entire and complete in themselves. Not only are they products of an exceptional imagination, they also stimulate those who experience them to imaginative effort: no actors could be as small as the dialogue represents them – cowslips are tall compared to Titania, her attendant Fairy can 'hang a pearl in every cowslip's ear', and her elves 'Creep into acorn cups, and hide them there' (2.1). These images of the miniature are productive of charm and prettiness, but there is also a sinister side to the portrayal of the fairies which some directors have exploited; they can release malevolent as well as benevolent forces of nature, and the quarrel between Oberon and Titania has far-reaching consequences:

> The spring, the summer,
> The childing autumn, angry winter change
> Their wonted liveries, and the mazèd world
> By their increase now knows not which is which;
> And this same progeny of evils comes
> From our debate, from our dissension.
>
> (2.1.111–16)

In production Oberon and Titania have normally been played by adults and the lesser fairies by children, often to delightful effect; they have become assimilated to the conventions of romantic ballet. Logically, however, all of them might as well be played by adults, as perhaps they were in Shakespeare's time and as they certainly were in Peter Brook's production. The discrepancy between what we hear of them and what we see sets up a creative interplay between actors and audience: we have our own contribution to make to the play.

The fairy characters present a kind of over-plot to the central action: Oberon's agent in his dealings with both the human world and his estranged wife is the puck, Robin Goodfellow, a figure of folklore, whose mischief objectifies, and apparently causes, the follies of love; by squeezing love-juice on their eyes he causes both Lysander and Demetrius to transfer their affections from Hermia to Helena; the mortal lovers' affairs will not be sorted out until the dissension between Oberon and Titania comes to an end. For all the literary mastery of the play, its principal turning-point is the wordless dance that marks their reconciliation: 'Come, my queen,' says Oberon:

> take hands with me,
> And rock the ground whereon these sleepers be.
> . . . Now thou and I are new in amity,
> And will tomorrow midnight solemnly
> Dance in Duke Theseus' house, triumphantly,
> And bless it to all fair prosperity.

> (4.1.84–9)

The play's third main set of characters are the Athenian labourers, or 'mechanicals', who gather in the wood to rehearse a play that they hope to present before Theseus on his wedding day. Love and the imagination are aligned in this play as challenges to the reason; just as the young lovers have to struggle to cope with the imaginative demands made on them by their first experience of love, so these 'hard-handed men' make valiant efforts to project themselves into the minds, bodies, and even the building materials of the characters of classical legend that they are to represent in the tragedy of Pyramus and Thisbe. Like the lovers under the influence of the love-juice, they cannot distinguish between illusion and reality; and they fear that their intended audience will share their inability. Lion must tell them that he is really Snug the joiner only pretending to be a lion; Bottom must explain that he has not truly been killed as Pyramus. Their concern for their audience's susceptibilities is touching as well as funny; with remarkable economy Shakespeare has provided the raw material out of which generations of actors, from inexperienced schoolchildren to the most talented of professionals, have created warmly credible characters.

Like the lovers, the labourers come under the influence of the fairies: Robin disrupts their rehearsal, transforms their leader, Bottom, into an ass, and causes Titania to fall in love with him. Bottom's slow succumbing to the power of illusion as Titania tells her fairies to wait upon him and finally winds him in her arms has something in common with Christopher Sly's metamorphosis into a lord. And like Sly (at least in the closing episode preserved in *The Taming of a Shrew*) Bottom is transformed by his experience. He enters the world of dreams in which the young lovers, too, have been living, and, for him as for them, when he emerges from it a memory remains, as of a transforming vision. Tricks have been played; though Robin has reversed the effects of the love-juice on Lysander's eyes, and Oberon has liberated Titania from her illusion, Demetrius is permanently under the spell, as he half realizes:

> I wot not by what power –
> But by some power it is – my love to Hermia,
> Melted as the snow, seems to me now
> As the remembrance of an idle gaud
> Which in my childhood I did dote upon,
> And all the faith, the virtue of my heart,
> The object and the pleasure of mine eye
> Is only Helena.
>
> (4.1.163–70)

Waking, the lovers sense that 'yet we dream'; and Bottom too remembers what has happened to him as if it were a dream:

> I have had a most rare vision. I have had a dream past the wit of man to say what dream it was. Man is but an ass if he go about t'expound this dream. Methought I was – there is no man can tell what. Methought I had – but man is but a patched fool if he will offer to say what methought I had. The eye of man hath not heard, the ear of man hath not seen, man's hand is not able to taste, his tongue to conceive, nor his heart to report what my dream was.
>
> (4.1.202–11)

It is Bottom's sense in this speech that he has had an experience greater than he can comprehend that makes this a role not just for a fine comedian but for a great actor.

After Theseus has heard the lovers' story he ascribes it all to mere imagination: not the creative imagination but imagination that plays tricks on us, so that

> in the night, imagining some fear,
> How easy is a bush supposed a bear!

It is the commonsensical realist's attitude. But Hippolyta sees more in it:

> But all the story of the night told over,
> And all their minds transfigured so together,
> More witnesseth than fancy's images,
> And grows to something of great constancy.
>
> (5.1.21–6)

Theseus allows himself to be governed by reason, whereas Hippolyta knows that illusion and the imagination have an even more important part to play in human affairs.

The importance that Shakespeare ascribes to this idea is shown by the last act of the play. The plot is pretty well over by the end of what we know as Act 4 (the play was first printed with no act or scene divisions, which is probably how Shakespeare wrote it). Yet in performance the last act is consistently the most successful stretch of the action. Partly this is because it contains the broadest comedy. The labourers' play of Pyramus and Thisbe is a brilliant piece of deliberately bad writing, and its parodic comedy is enhanced by the absurdities of its presentation. It provides a constant spur to theatrical inventiveness; any group of actors, whether amateur or professional, seizes joyfully on it as a series of opportunities for comic improvisation. It can provide hilarious entertainment even when abstracted from the rest of the play.

More importantly, though, this comedy has its contribution to make to the overall dramatic scheme. The comical tragedy of Pyramus and Thisbe is a testing of the mechanicals' imaginative responses; they fail, of course; but they do so with immense geniality and goodwill that makes us love them even as we laugh at them. Also, like the play within the play in *Love's Labour's Lost*, it is a testing of the responses of its on-stage audience. Before it begins Theseus admirably (if slightly priggishly) defines an ideal of aristocratic courtesy towards the efforts of the common people: 'never anything can be amiss', he says, 'When simpleness and duty tender it . . . Love, therefore, and tongue-tied simplicity | In least speak most, to my capacity.' Yet Theseus is the first to comment critically upon what he sees; it seems that he is no more capable of living up to his ideals than the workmen are of realizing an ideal performance. As in the earlier play, the criticisms of the audience provoke the performers to answer back: Bottom steps through the imaginary frame dividing audience from performers by responding to Theseus's comment 'The wall methinks, being sensible, should curse again', helpfully acting as commentator on the play in which he is taking part: 'No, in truth, sir, he should not. "Deceiving me" is Thisbe's cue. She is to enter now, and I am to spy her through the wall. You shall see, it will fall pat as I told you.' Bottom's good nature parallels that of Costard, helping to lead our sympathies rather to the performers than to the spectators. Even so, the stage audience's patience is sorely strained, leading to an outburst from Hippolyta that seems at odds with her earlier rebuke to Theseus for his lack of imagination. This time he rebukes her: 'The best in this kind are but shadows, and the worst are no worse if imagination amend them.' Even after this the interruptions persist, to the point where Starveling, with forgivable irritation, offers a prose précis of the speech he was to deliver: 'All I have to say is to tell you that the lantern is the moon, I the man i'th' moon, this thorn bush my thorn bush, and this dog my dog.' (A real dog is not called for in this play.)

Even this does not shame the spectators into silence, but some of their comments show them entering into the spirit of the performance, urging the actors on with 'Well roared, Lion' and 'Well run, Thisbe'. Finally Theseus declares the play 'a fine tragedy . . . and very notably discharged' – though there is no sign of the sixpence a day that Bottom's colleagues had foreseen as his reward.

If the last act is in part a testing, it is also a celebration of the successful outcome of love and, more generally, of good fellowship, tolerance, and understanding. Finally the fairies reappear to exorcize evil influences and to bestow their blessing on the palace, and in an epilogue Robin asks us, too, the real audience, to be charitable in our response. The play may be a vision to us just as its happenings were to those portrayed in it:

> If we shadows have offended,
> Think but this and all is mended:

> That you have but slumbered here,
> While these visions did appear . . .

To us, too, it may appear 'something of great constancy'.

Tailpiece: *Love's Labour's Won*

A tantalizing mystery of Shakespearian scholarship is the existence of two references to a play named *Love's Labour's Won*. One is in the list of comedies printed in 1598 in Francis Meres's book *Palladis Tamia*; the other is in a fragment of a bookseller's list discovered in 1953 which appears to record items sold from 9 to 17 August 1603 by a dealer in the south of England. As well as 'loves labor won', the plays listed (all unascribed) are 'marchant of vennis', 'taming of a shrew', and 'loves labor lost'. The natural inference is that a play by Shakespeare called *Love's Labour's Won* was in existence by 1598 and had actually reached print by 1603. Conceivably this was an alternative title for another play, but the only other comedy believed to have been written by 1598 but not included in Meres's list is *The Taming of the Shrew*, which is named (as *The Taming of A Shrew*) in the bookseller's list. Why such a play should not have been included in the First Folio we can only guess, but we know the titles of many plays of the period that have not survived, and no copy of the first edition of *Titus Andronicus* turned up until 1904. So the exciting possibility remains that someone, sometime, somewhere, may come upon a printed copy of a lost play by Shakespeare.

Notes to Chapter Three

1 Andrew Gurr, 'Shakespeare's First Poem: Sonnet 145', *Essays in Criticism* XXI (July 1971), pp. 221–36.
2 Max Beerbohm, *More Theatres, 1898–1903* (1969), p. 582.
3 In the RSC production by John Barton and Peter Hall, 1960.
4 *Shaw on Shakespeare*, p. 180.
5 Quoted in Schoenbaum, *Compact Documentary Life*, p. 185.
6 *Ben Jonson*, ed. C.H. Herford and Percy Simpson, vol. 1 (Oxford, 1925), p. 144.
7 E.M.W. Tillyard, *Shakespeare's Early Comedies* (1965), p. 47.
8 In the RSC production by Clifford Williams, 1962.

9 Directed by Ian Judge, 1990.
10 See, for example, the Introduction to the Oxford edition, ed. G.R. Hibbard (1990), pp. 49–57.
11 In his RSC production, 1965.
12 *Shaw on Shakespeare*, p. 50.
13 David P. Young, *Something of Great Constancy: The Art of 'A Midsummer Night's Dream'* (New Haven, CT and London, 1966), p. 179.

FOUR

Tragedies of Rome and Verona:
Titus Andronicus and *Romeo and Juliet*

Shakespeare's earliest tragedy was a great success in his own time and has been regarded as a terrible mistake almost ever since. We don't know exactly how early *Titus Andronicus* is; it was acted at the Rose in January 1594, but various pieces of evidence suggest that he wrote it several years before then, and it must be among his earliest efforts.

Titus Andronicus has the distinction of being the only Shakespeare play for which an illustration survives from his own time. This is the drawing apparently made by Henry Peacham in 1595, preserved in the library of the Marquess of Bath at Longleat. It is not a straightforward illustration of a stage performance, because it represents action that does not precisely correspond with any single moment in the play; but it seems to be influenced by theatre practice because, while Titus and other figures wear classical costume, the attendant soldiers, with their pikes, are clearly Elizabethan. Aaron is blacked up with notable thoroughness. Below the drawing is transcribed a mixture of lines from the beginning and the end of the play, along with two invented ones. The document is a fascinating puzzle. We also know of a performance given privately during Christmas festivities in the Rutlandshire manor of Sir John Harington of Exton on 1 January 1596.[1]

Titus Andronicus is the work of an author who was obviously ambitious to write an impressive classical tragedy of revenge, possibly spurred on by the success of Thomas Kyd's *The Spanish Tragedy* written during the late 1580s. Although its setting is ancient Rome its action is, happily, unhistorical; as Terence Spencer wrote, Shakespeare seems to have been anxious 'not to get it all right, but to get it all in'.[2] In some ways it seems designed to demonstrate its writer's learning, owing much in spirit and style to one of Shakespeare's favourite books, Ovid's *Metamorphoses*, which indeed makes an appearance on stage (at 4.1.42). It is also liberally besprinkled with Latin tags. But clearly too Shakespeare was aiming at the popular success that he achieved: the double revenge plot manages to incorporate so many physical horrors that this has come to be regarded as the most notoriously sensational play in the English dramatic repertoire. Ben Jonson's comment on its popularity may not be untinged with envy: in the Induction to *Bartholomew Fair* (1614) one of the actors portrayed sneers that 'he that will swear *Jeronimo* [i.e. *The Spanish Tragedy*] or *Andronicus* are the best plays yet, shall pass unexcepted at here as a man whose judgement shows it is constant, and hath stood still these five and twenty, or thirty years'.

There is no denying the play's horrors. In the opening scene, dominated by the family tomb of the Andronici, the veteran warrior Titus makes a ritual sacrifice (off stage) of the eldest son of his captive Tamora, Queen of the Goths, and also kills (on stage) his own youngest son. The first revenge action gets under way as Tamora incites her sons, Chiron and Demetrius, first to stab Titus's son-in-law, Bassianus, to death (on stage) and then to drag off his wife, Lavinia, to 'satisfy their lust' on her. Bassianus's body is chucked into an on-stage pit into which two more of Titus's sons are tricked into falling so that they can be blamed for Bassianus's murder. Chiron and Demetrius bring on Lavinia, '*her hands cut off and her tongue cut out, and ravished*', to be found by her uncle, Marcus, who delivers a 47-line speech, much of it devoted to describing what he sees, while also comparing her fate with that of Philomela, whose rape is narrated in Ovid. The mutilated Lavinia is brought to her father as he pleads for the lives of his condemned sons; Tamora's black lover, Aaron, tricks Titus into cutting off his own hand (on stage) in the belief that this will save his sons' lives, but soon a Messenger returns with their heads and Titus's hand 'in scorn to thee sent back'. This provokes a ritual vow of revenge followed by a grisly procession of departure:

> The vow is made. Come, brother, take a head,
> And in this hand the other will I bear.
> And Lavinia, thou shalt be employed.
> Bear thou my hand, sweet wench, between thine arms.
>
> (3.1.278–81)

The second revenge action opens with an emblematic scene which appears to be a late addition; it was not printed until the Folio of 1623.

In it Marcus kills a fly; at first Titus rebukes him, but on hearing his explanation that 'it was a black ill-favoured fly, | Like to the Empress' Moor' stabs repeatedly at it. Lavinia uses the stumps of her arms to turn the pages of a copy of the *Metamorphoses* to the tale of Philomela, and then to manipulate a staff with which she writes the names of her ravishers in the sand on which she stands. Aaron brutally kills the Nurse who has brought him the baby he has fathered on Tamora, and there is a final sequence of staged horrors in which Titus cuts the throats of Chiron and Demetrius, serves their mother with a pie in which he has baked their heads, kills his own daughter so that she may not 'survive her shame', and within the time that it takes to speak three lines kills Tamora, is himself killed by the Emperor, and is revenged by his son's killing of the Emperor.

As early as 1678 the dramatist Edward Ravenscroft, who adapted the play for the Restoration stage, had attempted to absolve Shakespeare from the responsibility of having written what he described as 'the most incorrect and indigested piece in all his works', one that 'seems rather a heap of rubbish than a structure',[3] and both his doubts and his criticism have gone on being repeated until well into the twentieth century. In 1785 one John Pinkerton wrote: 'Will no editor shew taste enough to deliver us from nonsense that would disgrace a bedlamite to write or to read?'[4]; and although the play went on being included in editions of Shakespeare's works it was rarely performed, and then only in adaptations which reduced its apparent sensationalism. As recently as 1948 J. Dover Wilson – who thought the play 'would long since have been relegated to the limbo of half-forgotten drama' if Shakespeare's name had not been attached to it – was arguing in his New Shakespeare edition that it is Shakespeare's revision of a script by George Peele. We know that Shakespeare worked with John Fletcher late in his career, and it is perfectly possible that some of his early plays, too, were written in collaboration, but distaste for a play's subject-matter is no good basis on which to base such a theory.

More important than arguments about who wrote the play is the question of whether it has anything to offer today, and in fact it has been defended both explicitly, in critical writings, and implicitly, in a small number of productions that have taken it seriously as a study in evil, vulnerability, grief, and despair. Physical horror is no less rife today in both life and art than it was in Shakespeare's time, and we are perhaps more willing to consider it fit subject for the theatre than were some of our forebears. Merely to catalogue the play's horrors is to misrepresent it: they are presented with much conscious artistry and rhetorical power as part of a seriously projected story of personal and national catastrophe.

It is true that certain aspects of the play's technique have proved troublesome. In what may be the first revival to take the original play at all seriously, at the Old Vic in 1923, the theatre critic James Agate found it 'full of anticipations of *Lear* and *Othello*',[5] but the audience 'laughed when the deaths of Tamora, Titus and Saturninus followed each other within about five seconds, as in a burlesque melodrama'.[6] This is certainly a difficult area of the text, comparable in its very different way with the huddled ending of *The Two Gentlemen of Verona*. At the other extreme, certain areas of the play have seemed overwritten: Peter Brook, in his Stratford-upon-Avon production of 1955, omitted over 650 lines, including Marcus's long, Ovidian description of the ravished Lavinia. Brook also evaded some of its horrors: the severed heads of Titus's sons were concealed in ornate caskets, and Chiron and Demetrius died off stage.

Nevertheless this production realized the play's inner intensity as never before, especially in Laurence Olivier's overwhelming performances as Titus, which established this as a great tragic role. Having initially portrayed him as a 'desperately tired', grizzled old warrior, wrote J.C. Trewin, Olivier 'was able to move out into a wider air, to expand him to something far larger than life-size, to fill stage and theatre with a swell of heroic acting'.[7] As so often, Olivier could find greatness in a simple phrase: 'I am the sea' (3.1.224) was a climactic moment. It was not superficial horrors but the production's incantatory ritualism, and the intensity of suffering suggested by Olivier's rhetorical command, that made work for the ambulancemen stationed regularly at the back of the stalls.

Even more remarkable, not least as the first to play the text uncut, was Deborah Warner's harrowing production at the Swan Theatre, Stratford in 1987. The staging was austerely simple; it could have transferred almost unchanged into a reconstruction of the Globe, which also would have offered an upper level, a stage pit, and such basic properties as coffins, ropes, a ladder, and a dinner table. The director trusted her dramatist; rhetoric was plumbed for its deep sources, which were then brought to the surface so that even the most artificial verbal structures became expressive of emotion. Spoken in hushed tones and with the traumatized figure of Lavinia quivering before us, Marcus's description, which Brook evaded and which may read like a heartless verbal exercise by a bright boy from the local grammar school, became a deeply moving attempt to master the facts, and thus to survive the shock, of a previously unimagined horror. Brian Cox searchingly explored the role of Titus in a performance of unremitting concentration and impassioned integrity, finding the shape of the role in a manner that defined the movement of the play, achieving ever-increasing intensity of suffering up to the mirthless laughter with which he preceded the line 'Why, I have not another tear to shed' (3.1.265) and playing the rest of the role on an upward curve as Titus found release in the action needed to effect his revenge. Inappropriate laughter, an obvious danger, was avoided by the exploitation of all the genuine comedy latent in the text – in Tamora's bombastic accusation of Bassianus before his murder, in the squabble between Titus, Lucius, and Marcus over who shall have the honour of losing a hand in the hope of saving Titus's sons, in Titus's reaction to Marcus's identification of the fly with Aaron, and even in the horror of the climactic banquet – with a last touch of macabre humour, Titus included in his words 'Welcome all' the inhabitants of the pie.

I should never have imagined that the stretch of action which made Old Vic audiences giggle could have been so powerful in its effect. A chorus of servants played its part, squatting in ranks to each side of the stage before the pie was served, stretching forward in horror at the death of Lavinia, bending as Titus stabbed Tamora, gasping as Saturninus killed Titus, and finally rushing off through the audience as Lucius killed Saturninus. This was creative directing and acting; the play emerged as a far more deeply serious work than its popular reputation would have suggested, one that is profoundly concerned with both the personal and the social consequences of violence rather than one that cheaply exploits their theatrical effectiveness. Like David Thacker's later handling of *The Two Gentlemen of Verona* in the same theatre, the production left one puzzling over the relative contributions of the dramatist and his interpreters: is the play really as great as it then seemed? The only answer, I suppose, is that any work of art written to be performed is as great as its performers can make it.

Romeo and Juliet stands at the opposite extreme from *Titus Andronicus*. That was a classical, this is a romantic tragedy; that was set in ancient Rome, this takes place in the Italy of the Renaissance; that was political in its implications, this is primarily a private tragedy within a public setting; that was pretty well unremitting in horror, this bears many resemblances to Shakespeare's romantic comedies; that derived largely from works of classical literature, this is based on a long poem written shortly before Shakespeare was born by an otherwise forgotten poet who died young, Arthur Brooke, who himself based *The Tragic History of Romeus and Juliet*, published in 1562, on a French translation of a story that had already been told in Italian by Matteo Bandello.

The plot of *Romeo and Juliet* has affinities with that of *A Midsummer Night's Dream*; indeed one reason for the theory – it is no more – that the comedy was written just after the tragedy is the belief that the tragedy of Pyramus and Thisbe parodies that of Romeo and Juliet. Like *A Midsummer Night's Dream*, the tale of Romeo and Juliet has acquired the status of myth, but credit for this is not due to Shakespeare alone. Before he wrote, there had been numerous versions of the basic story, and although his play has undoubtedly provided the inspiration for many later works such as Berlioz's glowing dramatic symphony *Roméo et Juliette* – the apotheosis of romanticism in music – Tchaikovsky's popular symphonic poem, and Prokofiev's ballet music, other works, including Bellini's opera *I Capuleti ed i Montecchi*, which is often said to derive from Shakespeare's play, in fact have no direct connection with it. Also, although Shakespeare's play has been frequently performed, it has often been in adapted texts, especially David Garrick's version, first acted in 1748.

Garrick made many changes, most famously – picking up on an idea already used by the dramatists Colley Cibber and Thomas Otway – in the final scene. In Shakespeare's play Romeo dies before Juliet awakes. Garrick, perceiving that Shakespeare had missed a trick here, causes Juliet to wake just as Romeo is about to kill himself and gives them a final duologue in which each in turn displays symptoms of mental instability. To a modern reader this episode may well seem comic:

JULIET And did I wake for this!
ROMEO   My powers are blasted,
   'Twixt death and love I'm torn, I am distracted!
   But death's strongest – and must I leave thee, Juliet!
   Oh cruel, cursèd fate! in sight of heaven!
JULIET Thou ravest; lean on my breast.
ROMEO Fathers have flinty hearts, no tears can melt 'em.
   Nature pleads in vain. Children must be wretched.
JULIET O! my breaking heart!
ROMEO She is my wife; our hearts are twined together.

> Capulet forbear! Paris loose your hold!
> Pull not our heart-strings thus; they crack, they break.
> O! Juliet! Juliet! (*Dies.*)[8]

The fact remains that Garrick made a great scene out of it and that his adaptation of the play supplanted Shakespeare's for close on a century; although it is now scorned, his version of the death scene lives on in Berlioz's dramatic symphony and in Gounod's often exquisite though somewhat neglected opera; even in modern productions directors occasionally point the irony of the climax by causing Juliet to show signs of life to the audience, if not to Romeo, before he dies.

M.C. Bradbrook wrote that the 'core and heart' of the play 'is a love-duet',[9] and there is no doubt that the balcony scene, as it is usually known (though the text calls only for a window), in which the young couple declare their love, has come to symbolize the play in the popular imagination. An image of a young man looking yearningly upwards at a beautiful girl is enough to say 'Romeo and Juliet' even to many who have never seen or read the play. It speaks not merely of love but of first love, for both boy and girl. Though Shakespeare often leaves the age of his characters open, here he is exceptionally careful to impress upon the audience as soon as Juliet appears that she is not yet fourteen, still very much in the bosom of her family and even under the care of her childhood Nurse. And though Romeo is initially in love with the shadowy but chaste Rosaline, whom we never see, she is no more than a foil for Juliet, a moon who fades and dies as soon as Juliet appears:

> But soft, what light through yonder window breaks?
> It is the east, and Juliet is the sun.
> Arise, fair sun, and kill the envious moon,
> Who is already sick and pale with grief
> That thou, her maid, art far more fair than she.
>
> (2.1.44–8)

This is the opening of the balcony scene, and though Romeo speaks metaphorically of 'light' he and we should surely already be able to see Juliet as the source of that light. The language in which he speaks of her is unmatched in its lyricism; there is no wonder either that the scene is often spoken of in musical terms ('a love-duet') or that it has proved such an inspiration to musicians. It is full of idealism, of ardent aspiration, of an adoration that is religious in its intensity:

The brightness of her cheek would shame those stars
As daylight doth a lamp; her eye in heaven
Would through the airy region stream so bright
That birds would sing and think it were not night.
See how she leans her cheek upon her hand.
O, that I were a glove upon that hand,
That I might touch that cheek!
. . .
O, speak again, bright angel; for thou art
As glorious to this night, being o'er my head,
As is a wingèd messenger of heaven
Unto the white upturnèd wond'ring eyes
Of mortals that fall back to gaze on him
When he bestrides the lazy-passing clouds
And sails upon the bosom of the air.

(2.1.61–74)

The darkness of the night opens up the beauty of the heavens; the
lovers inhabit a world that is all their own. It is a world too of
boundless generosity: were Juliet 'as far | As that vast shore washed
with the farthest sea', yet Romeo would 'adventure for such
merchandise'; and Juliet's 'bounty is as boundless as the sea', her 'love
as deep'.

For all the scene's rapture, it is conceived in fully dramatic terms. At
its opening, the lovers are apart, and Juliet is unaware of Romeo's
presence. Each has what is in effect a long soliloquy; each in a private
world seeks to reach out to communication with the other. And when
they do address each other directly they are at first restrained by
consciousness of the feud between their families. Steadily they come
towards each other, but the climax of their encounter comes not with
physical contact but with a silence, a sense of equilibrium, of time
suspended in a perfect communion that needs no words:

JULIET I have forgot why I did call thee back.
ROMEO Let me stand here till thou remember it.
JULIET I shall forget, to have thee still stand there,
    Rememb'ring how I love thy company.
ROMEO And I'll still stay, to have thee still forget,
    Forgetting any other home but this.

(2.1.215–20)

The scene permits too a delicate comedy in the lovers' hyperbole and
their self-absorption; after hearing Juliet say no more than 'Ay me',

Romeo may make us smile with the amazed delight with which he utters 'She speaks', as if this were a feat that could scarcely be expected of one so young; and after Juliet has enjoined him not to swear by the moon, he may seem touchingly puzzled in his response 'What shall I swear by?' – the poor boy is doing his best.

Though the heart of the play may indeed be a love-duet, there is far more to its body than this; the novelist George Moore was quite wrong to describe it as 'no more than a love-song in dialogue'. For one thing, idealism is only one aspect of Romeo and Juliet's love. Famously, their first conversation takes the form of a shared sonnet, a sonnet that is witty as well as lyrical, that uses religious imagery but somewhat subverts it by its admission of physicality; it is a sonnet of courtship, and its climax is not a prayer but a kiss:

ROMEO If I profane with my unworthiest hand
    This holy shrine, the gentler sin is this:
  My lips, two blushing pilgrims, ready stand
    To smooth that rough touch with a tender kiss.
JULIET Good pilgrim, you do wrong your hand too much,
    Which mannerly devotion shows in this.
  For saints have hands that pilgrims' hands do touch,
    And palm to palm is holy palmers' kiss.
ROMEO Have not saints lips, and holy palmers, too?
JULIET Ay, pilgrim, lips that they must use in prayer.
ROMEO O then, dear saint, let lips do what hands do:
    They pray; grant thou, lest faith turn to despair.
JULIET Saints do not move, though grant for prayers' sake.
ROMEO Then move not while my prayer's effect I take.
               He kisses her
  Thus from my lips, by thine my sin is purged.
JULIET Then have my lips the sin that they have took.
ROMEO Sin from my lips? O trespass sweetly urged!
  Give me my sin again.
              He kisses her.
JULIET   You kiss by th' book.

                             (1.5.92–109)

This is a love that seeks, and finds, full physical consummation. Juliet looks forward to her wedding night as an occasion of sexual union:

               Come, civil night,
Thou sober-suited matron all in black,

And learn me how to lose a winning match
Played for a pair of stainless maidenhoods.
Hood my unmanned blood, bating in my cheeks,
With thy black mantle till strange love grown bold
Think true love acted simple modesty.

(3.2.10–16)

And the play's final love-duet is the lovers' doom-laden conversation at daybreak after their marriage night, when Romeo is already banished. He seeks to remain, even at the cost of his life; she urges him to go, to save his life.

There are, then, three love-duets, one in the evening, one at night, and the last at dawn; each represents a moment of tremulous, threatened stasis in the lovers' developing relationship, and each is interrupted by Juliet's Nurse. She is a reminder of the world of daylight reality which endangers their love, and she is also a measure of the greatness of that love. If *Romeo and Juliet* is the most romantic of Shakespeare's plays, it is also, from the opening episode with its ribald jesting between Capulet's servants, the bawdiest. In the scene that introduces us to Juliet her Nurse tells a tale that, looking back to Juliet's infancy, also looks forward to the loss of her virginity: 'Thou wilt fall backward when thou hast more wit.' And the idealism of the balcony scene is prefaced by Mercutio's dirty talk of Rosaline:

O Romeo, that she were, O that she were
An open-arse, and thou a popp'rin pear.

Mercutio is Romeo's best friend, the Nurse is closer to Juliet than her parents; they are parallel forces, the two richest and most strongly individual characters in the play, but each is fatally limited in understanding just where it is most needed. Mercutio, for all the delicacy of imagination suggested in his Queen Mab speech – a virtuoso display for actor and author as well as for the character – expresses a satirically reductive view of love between man and woman: 'this drivelling love is like a great natural that runs lolling up and down to hide his bauble in a hole' (2.3.84–5); and for the Nurse, one healthy young man is very much the same as another; she admires Romeo's physical qualities – 'for a hand and a foot and a body, though they be not to be talked on, yet they are past compare' – (2.4.41–2), but after hearing of his banishment immediately transfers her allegiance to Juliet's official suitor, Paris:

I think you are happy in this second match,
For it excels your first; or if it did not,
Your first is dead, or 'twere as good he were
As living hence and you no use of him.

(3.5.222–5)

The technique of juxtaposing romantic and anti-romantic attitudes to
love is the same as Shakespeare uses in his comedies; here as there the
romantic attitude survives criticism, partly because of the sheer poetic
intensity of the lovers' passion, and also because it includes as well as
transcends the physicality to which Mercutio and the Nurse are
limited.

The love of Romeo and Juliet is not simply the coming together of
two individuals, it is also the union of representatives of the younger
generation of two feuding families. This is both their tragedy and their
glory. The public strife within which the private action takes place is
stated by the opening Chorus and portrayed in the opening scene, and
as the action continues, the lovers' private world is more and more
impinged upon by the world of external reality, of uncomprehending
events, the world in which the innocent Paris becomes the victim of
happenings that he cannot control, in which the senseless family feud
destroys the most precious members of the families. The final scene,
which takes place around and in the tomb of the Capulets, is difficult
to stage with any attempt at naturalism, and the lovers are not at their
greatest in death; Juliet's last moments lack the transcendence
displayed by Cleopatra in Shakespeare's other double tragedy of love.
But, as the opening Chorus had promised, we are offered the
consolation of the burial of 'their parents' strife'; those who remain are
made aware of their responsibilities, old Capulet and Montague shake
hands, and at the end of this highly patterned tragedy that had opened
with a Chorus (often spoken by the actor playing the Prince of
Verona) in the form of a sonnet the action recedes into myth with lines
in the form of the last part of a sonnet as the Prince himself declares:

. . . never was a story of more woe
Than this of Juliet and her Romeo.

So it is, at least, on a straightforward reading of the text. Some
interpreters have denied the qualified happiness of the play's ending,
finding a hollow materialism in Montague's promise to raise a statue
of Juliet 'in pure gold', and aligning this with the Friar's accusation of
Juliet's father, after she has been found, apparently dead, 'The most

you sought was her promotion' (4.4.98). It is a legitimate interpretation, but one that takes the risk of turning the play into social satire rather than tragedy.

Notes to Chapter Four

1 These topics are discussed in the Introduction to E.M. Waith's Oxford edition (1984).
2 T.J.B. Spencer, 'Shakespeare and the Elizabethan Romans', *Shakespeare Survey 10* (Cambridge, 1957), pp. 27–38; quoting from p. 32.
3 Vickers, vol. i, p. 239.
4 Vickers, vol. vi, p. 377.
5 James Agate, *Brief Chronicles* (1943), p. 188.
6 Gordon Crosse, *Fifty Years of Shakespearean Playgoing* (1941), pp. 78–9.
7 J.C. Trewin, *Shakespeare on the English Stage 1900–1964* (1964), p. 235.
8 *The Plays of David Garrick*, ed. H.W. Pedicord and F.L. Bergmann, 4 vols (Carbondale, IL, and Edwardsville, IL, 1981), vol. 3, p. 144.
9 M.C. Bradbrook, *Shakespeare and Elizabethan Poetry* (1951; repr. 1964), p. 111.

FIVE

Five Plays of English History:

Henry the Sixth, Part One, The First Part of the Contention (Henry the Sixth, Part Two), Richard, Duke of York (Henry the Sixth, Part Three), Richard the Third, and King John

Comedies, tragedies, histories: the young Shakespeare was ready to turn his hand to them all, and his ambition is most clearly shown in his three long, interlinked plays about the reign of Henry VI and their climactic sequel *Richard the Third*. As with the early comedies, it is difficult to tell just when they were written, though it was probably between about 1590 and early 1593. No known English dramatist had so far worked on such a scale, nor was Shakespeare himself ever to do so again. The plays as a group are sometimes known as the first tetralogy, but this word gives a misleading idea of their interrelatedness. Though they may be seen as a large-scale celebration of England and the English, possibly reflecting a new mood of national unity following on the defeat of the Spanish Armada in 1588, they do not add up to an artistic unity of the order of, say, Wagner's *Ring*, which is comparable in length of performance. There are signs that Shakespeare's sequence grew in ambition as it proceeded: confusingly, the first play in the historical sequence, *Henry the Sixth, Part One*, was probably written after the first two, as if Shakespeare had not originally intended to dramatize the entire reign. *Richard the Third* is resoundingly climactic and heavily retrospective, but the earlier plays do not give the impression that as Shakespeare wrote he was always conscious of the larger design encompassing all the individual units. Separate works in the series use rather different theatrical conventions; their verbal styles vary, and a development in poetic technique is evident from one to another; *Richard the Third* is a more confidently rounded whole than the three earlier plays.

Nevertheless, and although there is no evidence that playgoers of Shakespeare's time were able to see the plays on consecutive afternoons, their narrative links are stronger than those within any other group of his plays; they are more uniform in verbal style than his later composed sequence, also of four plays – *Richard the Second, Henry the Fourth, Part One* and *Part Two*, and *Henry the Fifth* – dramatizing the immediately preceding period of English history, and *Richard the Third*, in particular, gains greatly in resonance when experienced in conjunction with its predecessors. The enormous success of Colley Cibber's adaptation of this play, which first appeared in 1700 and was for two centuries perhaps the most popular play on the English stage, bears witness to this, for Cibber, though he has often been reviled for the ruthlessness of his changes, had the wit to provide some of the background that Shakespeare's play, acted alone, lacks. The theatre's abandonment of this adaptation during the late nineteenth century has not made the original play as successful at the box-office as Cibber's was, and the most popular versions of the twentieth century, staged and filmed by Laurence Olivier in the 1940s and 1950s, adopted some of Cibber's structural changes and even retained a few of his verbal additions. If we are to experience the play adequately we need to see it in its proper context.

It is only since the Second World War that the theatre has set any great value on the *Henry the Sixth* plays, and even in this time they have rarely been presented singly; on the other hand, they have equally rarely been presented as a complete sequence without extensive adaptation or, at least, abbreviation. New Historicist critics have been concerned to demonstrate that in ostensibly writing about the past Shakespeare was covertly, if not necessarily intentionally, interpreting the politics of his own day. Modern directors have seen that the plays can be related, with greater or lesser degrees of subtlety, to political movements of later times, including our own, and that their presentation of a great sweep of history can provide a thrilling theatrical marathon lasting many hours and demonstrating the skills of a major company. There are many powerful acting roles both within individual plays and spanning more than one, especially that of Margaret of Anjou, who is wooed on behalf of Henry VI in the first play and remains as a figure of retributive justice to curse his murderer, Richard III, in the last. As Peggy Ashcroft splendidly demonstrated, when the plays are performed together this can become one of Shakespeare's greatest female roles. It is interesting that what may well be the fullest and purest presentation of the sequence since Shakespeare's time is that directed for the BBC television series by Jane Howell; its success has been related to the director's recognition of 'the affinity of the tetralogy to a TV series'.[1]

When the plays were first performed it is most unlikely that the first three were given under the repellent labels of *Henry the Sixth, Parts One, Two,* and *Three* bestowed upon them, in all probability, by the compilers of the First Folio, anxious to emphasize the historical spread. On its first appearance in print *Part Two* was described on its title-page as *The First Part of the Contention betwixt the Two Famous Houses of York and Lancaster, with the death of the good Duke Humphrey and the banishment and death of the Duke of Suffolk, and the tragical end of the proud Cardinal of Winchester, with the notable rebellion of Jack Cade, and the Duke of York's first claim unto the crown*; and *Part Three* was only slightly more snappily described as *The True Tragedy of Richard Duke of York, and the death of good King Henry the Sixth, with the whole contention between the two houses Lancaster and York.* These are corrupt texts, but that makes it even more likely that their title-pages indicate, if in extended form, the labels given to them in announcing theatrical performances rather than the Folio designations designed purely for print. They also show that these two plays were considered as a pair, independent of '*Part One*'.

New titles have been invented for modern versions. The Royal Shakespeare Company's cycle, directed and adapted by Peter Hall and John Barton in 1963–4, which compressed four plays into three and added some 1400 lines of skilful pastiche composed by John Barton, called them collectively *The Wars of the Roses* and independently *Henry the Sixth, Edward the Fourth,* and *Richard the Third.* Michael Bogdanov directed them in largely twentieth-century costume with a good deal of adaptation and some interpolation for the English Shakespeare Company in 1987–9 under the same general title, and in 1988 Adrian Noble directed a new, condensed version for the Royal Shakespeare Company under the title of *The Plantagenets.* All these versions, different in style as they were, were received with enthusiasm by both critics and audiences; it is clear that the plays can speak strongly to the twentieth century, even if some tailoring is thought to be desirable before they can do so.

The Elizabethan educational system, preoccupied as it was with the classics, did not offer instruction in English history. Knowledge of the nation's past came mainly from the massive volumes of chronicle history compiled by writers such as Edward Hall and Raphael Holinshed. They were cumulative works; Holinshed drew heavily on

Hall, who incorporated writings of the past such as the life of Richard III by Sir Thomas More (later canonized). Shakespeare was among the readers of these works, and he obviously perceived their value as raw material for plays. In an age of limited literacy the writing of plays about England's past would have particular educational value; they could teach as well as please. Also, like any historical writing, they offered the opportunity for propaganda. Like many of Shakespeare's later plays, these histories show a deeply serious concern with political problems: with the responsibilities of a king, his relationship with his people, the need for national unity, the relationship between national welfare and self-interest, the suffering caused by dissension both between nations and between opposing factions within a nation, often mirrored in the image of a family, whether royal or not. But Shakespeare was primarily not a teacher, or a politician, but an artist and an entertainer, and these are the functions that did most to determine the use of his raw material.

He had few if any models to work from; the only significant surviving play based on English history that may have existed before he began to write is Marlowe's *Edward the Second*, and even that may have been written under his influence rather than the other way round. Although the compilers of the First Folio were to group Shakespeare's plays as comedies, histories, and tragedies, 'histories' is an anomalous label because it refers to content, not to genre. Plays about history can be tragedies – like *Edward the Second* – or, like Shakespeare's *Henry the Fifth*, they can draw heavily on the conventions of comedy; they can also be indeterminate of genre, in which case they may be best described as chronicle histories. And they can draw on non-dramatic literary forms, such as the epic and the pastoral, both of which influenced Shakespeare in his experiments with English history as a topic for drama.

It is clear that he wanted to elevate the material of history, not simply to present a series of events in documentary style. In these early plays he (like the writers he draws on) concentrates on royal and noble figures. Not each of the plays can be described as tragedies – that would be difficult since three of them have the same monarch as their central figure; but they include many tragic episodes, and each of the last two plays in the sequence culminates in the violent death of a king. They are written to hold the attention of theatre audiences, and Shakespeare finds room for much comedy of various kinds; but he also seeks dignity of presentation, largely through language. All four of the plays that he wrote entirely (or virtually entirely) in verse are about English history: *Henry the Sixth, Part One* and *Part Three*, along with *King John* and *Richard the Second*; in these early ones especially he makes extensive use of classical comparisons and of epical narrations. Just occasionally he seems dutifully if laboriously to be filling in the historical background, resulting in plodding lists of place-names and genealogical treatises such as have proved irresistible to parodists:

> YORK The third son, Duke of Clarence, from whose line
> I claim the crown, had issue Philippe, a daughter,
> Who married Edmund Mortimer, Earl of March;
> Edmund had issue, Roger, Earl of March;
> Roger had issue, Edmund, Anne and Eleanor.
> (*First Part of the Contention*, 2.2.34–8)

Usually, however, he treats his source material with characteristic freedom, shaping, omitting, altering, and adding.

Part One, at least, seems to have had real success in its own time. It is presumably the play referred to as 'harey the vj' in the record of what seems to be its first performance on 3 March 1592 by Lord Strange's Men at the Rose.[2] The box-office takings – £3 16s 8d – were the highest of the season, and the play had another fifteen performances during the following ten months. Its success is mentioned in Thomas Nashe's satirical pamphlet *Piers Penniless*, published later in 1592. In a passage aimed at defending the drama against the common accusation that it exerted a morally corrupting influence, Nashe claims that, on the contrary, plays based on 'our English chronicles' do good by celebrating 'our forefathers' valiant acts' and setting them up as a 'reproof to these degenerate effeminate days of ours',[3] and he cites a specific example from *Henry the Sixth, Part One*.

Nowadays this play is the least admired of the series, and the one that has been most heavily cut in adaptation, but it opens with masterly thematic appropriateness in its portrayal of the ritual of national and personal mourning over the body of Henry V, nobly expressed, but rapidly degenerating into a family squabble as news arrives that Henry's triumphs in France, which Shakespeare was to portray in a later play, have been dissipated. The rivalry displayed in this scene between Humphrey, Duke of Gloucester – Protector of the infant Henry VI – and Henry Beaufort, Bishop of Winchester, is to play an important part in both this play and the second one in the series, as does the conflict between Richard, Duke of York, and the houses of Somerset and Suffolk. One of the most admired episodes is the emblematic and formalized scene (2.4) in the Temple Garden, invented by Shakespeare, in which the supporters of Richard Plantagenet, of the house of York, and of the Earl of Somerset, of the house of Lancaster, symbolize their loyalties by plucking respectively white and red 'brier' roses. This scene establishes the opposition between the houses of York and Lancaster which runs throughout the plays and will not be resolved until the closing lines of *Richard the Third*. Towards its close the Earl of Warwick ('the Kingmaker') foreshadows what is to come by prophesying that

> this brawl today,
> Grown to this faction in the Temple garden,
> Shall send, between the red rose and the white,
> A thousand souls to death and deadly night.
>
> (2.4.124–7)

The true hero of the play is Lord Talbot, whose valiant though ultimately unsuccessful exploits against the French at the siege of Orléans are the subject of a lengthy Messenger's speech in the opening scene. The French come to dread him so much that his very name becomes a weapon: after a surprise attack in which the French soldiers 'leap o'er the walls in their shirts' and later 'fly, leaving their clothes behind', one of Talbot's men declares:

> The cry of 'Talbot' serves me for a sword,
> For I have loaden me with many spoils,
> Using no other weapon but his name.
>
> (2.1.81–3)

But Talbot and his no less valiant son die, victims of the enmity between York and Somerset, who fail to send troops to their support. Talbot appears to have been a particular favourite with Elizabethan audiences; illustrating how plays can provide examples of valour, Nashe exclaims:

How would it have joyed brave Talbot, the terror of the French, to think that after he had lien two hundred years in his tomb he should triumph again on the stage, and have his bones new-embalmed with the tears of ten thousand spectators at least, at several times, who in the tragedian that represents his person imagine they behold him fresh bleeding![4]

The French forces are led by Joan La Pucelle, known to later ages as Joan of Arc, who presents herself to the Dauphin as a God-sent saviour:

> Lo, whilst I waited on my tender lambs,
> And to sun's parching heat displayed my cheeks,
> God's mother deignèd to appear to me,
> And in a vision, full of majesty,
> Willed me to leave my base vocation
> And free my country from calamity.
>
> (1.3.55–60)

Although much of what Joan does is the same in Shakespeare's play as in Shaw's *Saint Joan*, Shakespeare, following the chronicles, presents her not as a saint but as a fraudulent witch and a whore. In one scene (5.3) she is shown raising spirits and offering to feed them with her own blood if they will continue to help her, and after the English have captured her she tries to save herself from the stake by claiming that she is pregnant and naming several possible fathers for her child.

This portrayal of Joan brought on Shakespeare the disapproval of critics writing at a time when she was being groomed for canonization; Arthur Quiller-Couch hoped that Shakespeare 'had no hand in the slanderous portrait of Joan of Arc sent down to us under his name'.[5] Theatrically, however, she is a vivid character, often undercutting pomposity with language of colloquial directness. Complimenting the turncoat Duke of Burgundy on his change of allegiance from England to France she remarks: 'Done like a Frenchman – (*aside*) turn and turn again'; and after Sir William Lucy, seeking Talbot on the battlefield, has reeled off the full list of his honours, she deflates the messenger with

> Here's a silly, stately style indeed.
> The Turk, that two-and-fifty kingdoms hath,
> Writes not so tedious a style as this.
> Him that thou magnifi'st with these titles
> Stinking and fly-blown lies here at thy feet.
>
> (4.7.72–6)

The chronology of these episodes illustrates Shakespeare's freedom with his sources: historically Joan was burned in 1431, but in the play she takes part in a battle of 1451 in which Talbot's death is advanced by two years.

Henry VI himself is only emergent as a character in this play, in which most of his time on stage is spent in well-meaning but pathetically inadequate attempts to keep the peace among his brawling nobles. In the closing scenes, however, he timorously agrees to marry Margaret of Anjou, whom he has not so far seen, in the hope that this will help to bring England and France together. Some of the liveliest episodes are those in which the Earl of Suffolk acts as proxy wooer, clearly with an eye to making her his own mistress:

SUFFOLK I'll undertake to make thee Henry's queen,
  To put a golden sceptre in thy hand,
  And set a precious crown upon thy head,
  If thou wilt condescend to be my –
MARGARET   What?
SUFFOLK His love.
MARGARET I am unworthy to be Henry's wife.
SUFFOLK No, gentle madam, I unworthy am
  To woo so fair a dame to be his wife
  (*Aside*) And have no portion in the choice myself. –
  How say you, madam; are ye so content?
MARGARET An if my father please, I am content.

                                        (5.5.73–83)

The play ends in a state of uneasy truce, and very much in the manner of one that looks forward to a sequel, as Suffolk in soliloquy declares:

      Margaret shall now be queen and rule the King;
      But I will rule both her, the King, and realm.

In the play that follows, however, Suffolk is not to be as dominant as this might suggest. *Part One* had begun with the English court apparently united in mourning a death; at the opening of *The Contention* the court has come together to celebrate a marriage as Suffolk hands over to Henry the bride whom he has already married by proxy. In the BBC television production the actor playing Henry offered her a kiss, touchingly pleased by his first sight of her; she inclined her head to take it on her lips, but he kissed her hand instead and retreated into contemplation of the divine. Margaret simultaneously demonstrated her doubts about Henry as a man and her delighted anticipation of the power she would achieve by her marriage.

In both plays courtly formality barely conceals the subcurrents of dissension that rapidly rise to the surface in expressions of personal enmity and rivalry, and Henry's saintly ineffectuality as both man and king is seen to be the cause of both personal and national disaster. His acceptance of the terms negotiated by Suffolk for his marriage, by which England loses Anjou and Maine to the French, infuriates his Protector, Humphrey, Duke of Gloucester, and causes a renewal of the 'ancient bickerings' (1.1.141) between him and Cardinal Beaufort, Bishop of Winchester; equally, Henry's elevation of Suffolk to a dukedom and demotion of York from his post of regent of France feed York's ambition, so that the opening scene ends with a declaration from York parallel to that of Suffolk at the end of *Part One*:

> . . . force perforce I'll make him yield the crown,
> Whose bookish rule hath pulled fair England down.

But immediately we are introduced to another aspirant as Eleanor, Duchess of Gloucester incites her unwilling husband to similar thoughts by recounting her dream of glory:

> Methought I sat in seat of majesty
> In the cathedral church of Westminster,
> And in that chair where kings and queens are crowned,
> Where Henry and Dame Margaret kneeled to me,
> And on my head did set the diadem.
>
> (1.2.36–40)

Women play an important part in this play, and the rivalry between the Duchess and Queen Margaret produces comic bickerings as well as serious consequences: Margaret's resentment against Gloucester's power and his Duchess's pretensions encourages Suffolk to lay a plot that will result in both the Duchess's banishment and her husband's disgrace and eventual death. Shakespeare makes the most of the theatrical possibilities afforded by the conjurations carried out on the Duchess's behalf as she seeks to look into the future but is exposed as the result of Suffolk's plot, and her innocent husband's consequent downfall is pathetically portrayed. But ironically the conjurations which enable Suffolk to expose her treacherous desires also produce an accurate if oracular prediction of his own end. The wheel of fortune is to turn for him, too, and his downfall is hastened by a popular uprising protesting against the part he has played in good Duke Humphrey's death.

The common people, who figure hardly at all in *Part One*, are prominent in *The Contention*, and are responsible for some of its most theatrically appealing episodes, all written mostly or entirely in prose. Not all of them present the commons in a favourable light, but neither are they wholly unsympathetic. The King commands that the quarrel between Horner, the Duke of York's armourer, and his apprentice Peter, who has accused him of saying that York has a better right to the throne than Henry, shall be settled by personal combat. Their fight is grimly comic as Horner drinks himself into such a stupor that he is easily killed; but the timorous Peter, who has enough sense to remain sober, achieves comic dignity as he prepares for what he believes to be certain death:

> Drink and pray for me, I pray you, for I think I have taken my last draught in this world. Here, Robin, an if I die, I give thee my apron; and, Will, thou shalt have my hammer; and here, Tom, take all the money that I have. O Lord bless me, I pray God, for I am never able to deal with my master, he hath learned so much fence already.
>
> (2.3.76–83)

Simon Simpcox, who seeks to gain the King's charity by claiming to have been miraculously cured of blindness, is a rogue, but his wife makes a sudden bid for our sympathy with her claim: 'Alas, sir, we did it for pure need' (2.1.159).

These are dramatized anecdotes interpolated into the historical narrative (though still based on the chronicles); more substantial are the episodes in the later part of the play based on the Peasants' Revolt of 1450, led by Jack Cade. Cade is the Duke of York's tool, 'seduced' by him 'To make commotion, as full well he can, | Under the title of John Mortimer' so that York may 'perceive the commons' mind, | How they affect the house and claim of York' (3.1.356–7, 374–5). The scenes in which he appears paint a lamentable picture of the gullibility, folly, brutality and greed of the commons, with their ambition to 'kill all the lawyers' (4.2.78), culminating in the violence of their wanton execution and beheading of Lord Saye and Sir James Cromer, which breeds a vestige of remorse even in Cade: 'I feel remorse in myself with his words, but I'll bridle it. He shall die an it be but for pleading so well for his life' (4.7.102–3). He falls victim to the fickleness of the mob whom he himself has roused, and dies ignominiously at the hands of Alexander Iden, a Kentish squire with pastoral aspirations.

Two extended soliloquies in the earlier part of the play from York, the one at the end of the opening scene which reveals his machiavellian ambition, and that at the end of 3.2 in which he reaffirms his desire to be king and tells us of the Jack Cade plot, prepare us for his emergence in the closing episodes as the main contender for the crown, and at the opening of the last act, though he has declared that his only aim in bringing an army from Ireland is to oppose the Duke of Somerset, he repeats his aim:

> From Ireland thus comes York to claim his right,
> And pluck the crown from feeble Henry's head.

The civil war that has been brewing throughout the long action finally breaks surface, and at the end of the play York has the upper hand. But Henry and Margaret have merely fled to London, and York is still not king.

The fact that *The Contention* has exceeded its companion plays in popularity may be due in part to its wider range of style and emotional effect. Vigorous prose is particularly welcome in a play where the verse, though often powerful and sometimes eloquent, is not varied enough in style to offer vividly individual characterization of each member of the play's long cast list – though this feature of the text can be mitigated in performance when actors help to individualize the language by their own personal characteristics. Comedy runs through the play, not only in the obvious satire of the commons but in the portrayals of the nobles and the King, too: 'So, there goes our Protector in a rage', says Cardinal Beaufort as Gloucester storms off (1.1.145), and the undignified squabbling between Eleanor and Margaret offers characterful comedy:

> *Queen Margaret lets fall her fan*
> (*To the Duchess*)
> Give me my fan – what, minion, can ye not?
> *She gives the Duchess a box on the ear*
> I cry you mercy, madam! Was it you?
> DUCHESS Was't I? Yea, I it was, proud Frenchwoman!
> Could I come near your beauty with my nails,
> I'd set my ten commandments in your face.
> KING HENRY Sweet aunt, be quiet – 'twas against her will.
> DUCHESS Against her will? Good King, look to't in time!
> She'll pamper thee and dandle thee like a baby.

Though in this place most master wear no breeches,
She shall not strike Dame Eleanor unrevenged!

The exact nature of the relationship between Margaret and
Suffolk is left uncertain, but rises in eloquence on their final parting as
Suffolk declares:

> Here could I breathe my soul into the air,
> As mild and gentle as the cradle babe
> Dying with mother's dug between his lips.
>
> (3.3.395–7)

That final image is one of extraordinary tenderness, matched in the
play only by Henry's wish, in speaking of the dead Humphrey, that he
might 'with [his] fingers feel his hand unfeeling' (3.2.145).

If the play has not established an independent place for itself in the
repertory this is no doubt in part because of its position within a larger
sequence, and also perhaps because some of its theatrical conventions
seem dated by comparison with those used in Shakespeare's later
plays. An example is the frequent grisly if slightly offhand use in its
later stages of severed heads – Whitmore brings on Suffolk's 'head and
lifeless body', Margaret spends an entire scene (4.4) cradling, and
sometimes addressing, it, the heads of Lord Saye and Sir James
Cromer are brought on affixed to poles and made to kiss, and Iden
proudly presents Henry with Cade's head, receiving a knighthood in
return. Theatregoers of Shakespeare's time were no doubt inured to
this kind of thing by public executions and the daily sight of traitors'
heads displayed on London Bridge, but the relative infrequency of
such spectacles in Shakespeare's later histories, as well as in plays by
other dramatists after the early 1590s, suggests that they were part of a
theatrical fashion that soon became outmoded.

A severed head is prominent too in the opening scene of the third play,
when 'Crookback Richard', one of York's three young sons who first
appear in *The Contention*, proudly displays the head of the Earl of
Somerset, whom he has killed at the battle of St Albans, and –
prefiguring the play's end – declares: 'Thus do I hope to shake King
Henry's head.' Civil war is in full flood as power sways from one side
to the other.

At first York seems likely to succeed in his claim to the throne as Henry admits, 'My title's weak' (1.1.135) and agrees to cede his right of succession provided he may remain king during his lifetime, but this does not suit Margaret, who leads the royal forces in support of the claim of their son, Prince Edward. At the end of the play's first movement Margaret herself kills York and orders that his head be cut off and 'set . . . on York gates, | So York may overlook the town of York'. The sight does not cheer her husband's heart as much as she wishes (2.2.2–6).

But before long (at least in terms of dramatic time) Edward, the new Duke of York, and his brothers, supported by the Earl of Warwick, are in the ascendant and commanding that the head of Margaret's ally Clifford, who helped to kill their father and who killed their brother, the young Earl of Rutland, shall replace their father's on the gates of York. Henry is captured and sent to the Tower, and Margaret, with their son, flees to France in the hope of enlisting the support of King Louis. It seems at first that she will fail because Warwick has also gone to France to engineer a political alliance between York, now proclaimed King Edward IV, and the French king's sister, the Lady Bona, but the news that in the meantime Edward has married an English widow turns not only Louis but also Warwick against him, and in a surprise attack by night Warwick, accompanied by French forces, captures Edward and removes his crown.

Warwick sets off to free Henry, and succeeds in doing so, but not before Edward, too, has been rescued and fled to Burgundy; as Somerset says, 'we shall have more wars before't be long' (4.7.91). Returned from France Edward (of York) persuades the Mayor of York, a supporter of Henry, to allow him to enter the city, pretending that he comes only to resume his dukedom (as Richard sagely comments, 'when the fox hath once got in his nose, | He'll soon find means to make the body follow' [4.8.25–6]), and is there once again proclaimed king. He and his men recapture the unfortunate Henry and send him back to the Tower, and battle is re-engaged between Warwick and Edward. Warwick, wounded, is captured; dying, he hears too late that 'The Queen from France hath brought a puissant power' (5.2.31).

The play moves to a climactic encounter between Edward and Margaret at Tewkesbury where Margaret and her son are captured; the brothers kill the young prince, and Richard is about to kill Margaret when Edward holds him back, 'for we have done too much', provoking Richard's sardonic question 'Why should she live to fill the world with words?' (5.5.42–3). Richard slips off to the Tower, where he murders Henry. The play ends with Edward believing himself secure in the throne, exulting in the birth of an heir, delighting in his 'country's peace and brothers' loves', and banishing Margaret to France; but the apparent stability of the situation is undermined by asides from Richard – who compares himself to Judas as he kisses the infant prince – indicating the falseness of Edward's sense of security.

The amount of action that Shakespeare crams into this play might suggest that it is merely a chronicle of events, but in fact he has structured and patterned the happenings recorded in the chronicles, projecting the national and personal conflicts through rhetoric as well as deeds, and offering reflective as well as expository and amplificatory speeches, scenes, and episodes which help to give a sense of perspective on the historical action and to relate it to general concerns. Even scenes of violent action are carried forward on long but passionate speeches which pack an immense theatrical punch. On the page long speeches may seem unexciting, but no-one who saw the Peter Hall/John Barton production of 1963 will forget the ferocity with which Peggy Ashcroft's Margaret verbally attacked Donald Sinden's tethered York as she unleashed her fury at him like a dog baiting a bear, taunting him with the napkin stained in his son Rutland's blood and mocking his aspirations by crowning him with a paper crown:

> Look, York, I stained this napkin with the blood
> That valiant Clifford with his rapier's point
> Made issue from the bosom of thy boy.
> And if thine eyes can water for his death,
> I give thee this to dry thy cheeks withal.
> . . .
> A crown for York, and, lords, bow low to him.
> Hold you his hands whilst I do set it on.
>
> (1.4.80–4, 95–6)

After seeing this production it did not seem surprising that York's line 'O tiger's heart wrapped in a woman's hide' (1.4.138) should have stuck in Robert Greene's memory as he wrote the *Groatsworth of Wit*.

Margaret's is an active rhetoric; more contemplative, as we should expect, is that given to her husband, and Henry's most important scene is one that sets the events of the wars at a distance, reflecting on his own condition as an overburdened king, and offering too an emblematic representation of the follies and horrors of civil war. In York's death scene he is made to stand on a molehill (were molehills more substantial in those days? one is idly inclined to ask) as Margaret taunts him; and at the battle of Towton King Henry sits on a molehill as, withdrawn from the fray at the request of Margaret and Clifford, who have told him candidly that they get on better without him, he meditates on how much happier he would be as a peasant than as a king.

> O God! Methinks it were a happy life
> To be no better than a homely swain.
> To sit upon a hill, as I do now;
> To carve out dials quaintly, point by point,
> Thereby to see the minutes how they run:
> How many makes the hour full complete,
> How many hours brings about the day,
> How many days will finish up the year,
> How many years a mortal man may live.
> When this is known, then to divide the times:
> So many hours must I tend my flock,
> So many hours must I take my rest,
> So many hours must I contemplate,
> So many hours must I sport myself,
> So many days my ewes have been with young,
> So many weeks ere the poor fools will ean,
> So many years ere I shall shear the fleece.
> So minutes, hours, days, weeks, months, and years,
> Passed over to the end they were created,
> Would bring white hairs unto a quiet grave.
>
> (2.5.21–40)

The speech as a whole is a full and classic expression of the pastoral ideal which Shakespeare was to examine in more detail in a very different play, *As You Like It*; it is followed by two formal and clearly emblematic episodes, the first showing a soldier discovering that the man he has killed in battle is his own father, and the second showing another soldier finding that he has killed his own son. Henry moralizes these events, longing for the end of civil strife:

> The red rose and the white are on his face,
> The fatal colours of our striving houses;
> The one his purple blood right well resembles,
> The other his pale cheeks, methinks, presenteth.

Wither one rose, and let the other flourish –
If you contend, a thousand lives must wither.

                                        (2.5.97–102)

Here Shakespeare's thematic concerns are most readily apparent; he is
to revert to this same image of the tragic desolation caused by civil war
in the closing speech of *Richard the Third*:

> England hath long been mad, and scarred herself;
> The brother blindly shed the brother's blood,
> The father rashly slaughtered his own son;
> The son, compelled, been butcher to the sire;
> All that divided York and Lancaster,
> United in their dire division.
>
>   (5.8.23–8)

As a later poet was to put it, 'the subject is war, and the pity of war; the
poetry is in the pity'.[6]

In one of the stranger scenes in this play, and the one that follows
immediately after Henry's lament over the evils of civil war, Lord
Clifford enters, wounded, and with an arrow in his neck. He has been
a supporter of King Henry, but now, at the moment of death, states
the case against him:

> . . . Henry, hadst thou swayed as kings should do,
> Or as thy father and his father did,
> Giving no ground unto the house of York,
> They never then had sprung like summer flies;
> I and ten thousand in this luckless realm
> Had left no mourning widows for our death;
> And thou this day had kept thy chair in peace.
> For what doth cherish weeds, but gentle air?
> And what makes robbers bold, but too much lenity?
>
>   (2.6.14–22)

Henry is saintly, but because he lacks the ability to sway 'as kings
should do' is responsible for thousands of 'mourning widows'. His
quietism has consequences as disastrous for his subjects as the rampant
militarism of his opponents, and in these plays the middle way that is
nostalgically recalled in memories of the humane heroism of his father
Henry V is absent. Usurping ambition breaks surface like a life-force,
a sexual impulse that will not be denied, and it has the kind of amoral
attractiveness of animal sexuality that may come to evil or good.

Diametrically opposite to Henry is Richard of Gloucester, who is to
be his killer. Richard's rise to dominance over his brothers culminates
in the soliloquy, the longest uninterrupted speech in the whole canon,
in which, like his father before him, he expresses his determination to
encompass the crown. Here Shakespeare has found for Richard the
voice that will sound throughout *Richard the Third*, with all its
assumption of self-knowledge, of sardonic irony, of ruthless determination and implacable self-will. His acute consciousness of his
bodily deformity offers the possibility of a psychological foundation
for his evil in thwarted sexuality: love, he says, has forsworn him in
his mother's womb, it is no more likely that he will bewitch sweet
ladies with his words and looks 'Than to accomplish twenty golden
crowns', so he will make his heaven to dream upon the crown,

> And whiles I live, t'account this world but hell,
> Until my misshaped trunk that bears this head
> Be round impalèd with a glorious crown.

His power, he claims, lies in his total self-control; he is the master
actor who can

>   smile, and murder whiles I smile,
> And cry 'Content!' to that which grieves my heart,
> And wet my cheeks with artificial tears,
> And frame my face to all occasions.
>   . . .
> I can add colours to the chameleon,
> Change shapes with Proteus for advantages,
> And set the murderous Machiavel to school.
> Can I do this, and cannot get a crown?
> Tut, were it farther off, I'll pluck it down.
>   (3.2.169–71, 182–5, 191–5)

It is obvious that as he wrote this speech Shakespeare knew he would
go on to write a play with Richard at its centre, and unsurprising that
when that play has been performed on its own actors have sometimes
incorporated parts of this speech into it.

Shakespeare's ambition in writing *Richard the Third* parallels that of its
central character, though with happier consequences. This is the

longest play he had so far written, to be paralleled in his career only by *Hamlet*. In it he deploys all the verbal and rhetorical power at his command along with a remarkable mastery of theatrical effect and dramatic structure. Whereas in his earlier history plays we may occasionally feel that he is being led by his material, here he subordinates a complex mass of historical information to a clearly defined artistic purpose, and he does so partly by making of Richard a more dominating central figure than is to be found in any of his earlier plays. Richard's dominance is one reason why this play may be regarded as a historical tragedy rather than a chronicle play, and why it has held the greatest appeal for star actors. It has come to be thought of as a great showpiece, an opportunity for virtuosity; an actor coming to the role can hardly fail to remember, for instance, Hazlitt's description of Edmund Kean in the death scene: 'He fought like one drunk with wounds: and the attitude in which he stands with his hands stretched out, after his sword is taken from him, had a preternatural and terrific grandeur, as if his will could not be disarmed, and the very phantoms of his despair had a withering power.'[7]

Although there are a number of other impressive roles in the play, including Lady Anne, Clarence, King Edward, Lord Hastings, Queen Margaret, the Duchess of York, Queen Elizabeth, and especially Buckingham, Richard's has the reputation of being one in which the actor can achieve almost complete domination, outshining everyone else, exploiting the role's manifold opportunities for the display of sardonic humour, witty malevolence, and savage ferocity, along with moments of gloomy introspection and conscience-ridden hysteria, and culminating in a fight designed to make the drama critics reach for their pens in speedy emulation of Hazlitt.

But the theatrical reputation of this role is founded, not on Shakespeare's play, but on Colley Cibber's radical adaptation, in which he made the role of Richard – played by himself – even more dominant than it is in the original. Cibber omitted whole characters, including Queen Margaret, added others, rewrote Shakespeare's verse, and added much of his own; he retained only about one-sixth of Shakespeare's play in any form at all, and added long chunks from others, not only the death of Henry VI, with which he opens, but also passages from *Henry the Fifth* and *Richard the Second*. Deplorable though many of his changes are, some of them are understandable responses to the problem of presenting the play on its own rather than as the last in a sequence. Parts of the original are simply unintelligible out of context: the women mourn for men who died in the previous play, Margaret for her son Prince Edward and her husband, the Duchess of York for her husband and her son Rutland; in the climactic scene before the battle in which Richard is killed, the ghosts who come to haunt him include those of Prince Edward and his father Henry VI who died before we entered the theatre. Cibber at least had the courage to face these problems, and for long after Sir Henry Irving abandoned Cibber in favour of Shakespeare (heavily cut) actors continued to make changes that resemble Cibber's. In Olivier's film, as in Cibber, there is no Queen Margaret; and Olivier used some non-Shakespearian lines, including Cibber's 'Richard's himself again', often quoted (along with 'Off with his head – so much for Buckingham') as if it were by Shakespeare. The portrayal in this play of the conflict between an evil tyrant and the forces who oppose him is more abstract than in those that preceded it and has resulted in productions drawing an explicit parallel with later regimes as, for instance, Richard Eyre's at the National Theatre in 1990, set mainly in the 1930s, in which Ian McKellen's coldly evil Richard recalled Hitler in appearance.

On its first publication, in 1597, the play was described as *The Tragedy of King Richard III*, but in the collected edition of 1623 it is grouped among the histories and called *The Life and Death of Richard the Third*. The play is both tragedy and history, but it is an ironic rather than a romantic tragedy. As an ambitious usurper who reaches the throne by murder and loses it to a representative of a new and better order, Richard in many ways foreshadows Macbeth, but he lacks that character's introspection. He has already defined himself as a manipulative ironist in the preceding play of the series; in this one he comments ironically on himself rather than examining himself, often standing outside the action and acting as a chorus to his own play. He has no need of a Lady Macbeth to urge him on, but announces his plan from the start:

> I am determinèd to prove a villain . . .
> Plots have I laid, inductions dangerous,
> By drunken prophecies, libels and dreams
> To set my brother Clarence and the King
> In deadly hate the one against the other.

His comments come sometimes in soliloquy, as here or after the wooing of Lady Anne – 'Was ever woman in this humour wooed?' – and sometimes in asides, as when his mother the Duchess of York (new to this play) says: 'God bless thee, and put meekness in thy breast, | Love, charity, obedience, and true duty', to which Richard replies:

> Amen. (*Aside*) 'And make me die a good old man.'
> That is the butt-end of a mother's blessing;
> I marvel that her grace did leave it out.
>
> (2.2.95–9)

The method reaches a climax, and the trick is made explicit, in the dialogue between Richard and Buckingham on their way to fool the Mayor of London into supporting them:

> RICHARD OF GLOUCESTER
> Come, cousin, canst thou quake and change thy colour?
> Murder thy breath in middle of a word?
> And then again begin, and stop again,
> As if thou wert distraught and mad with terror?
> BUCKINGHAM
> Tut, I can counterfeit the deep tragedian,
> Tremble and start at wagging of a straw,
> Speak, and look back again, and pry on every side,
> Intending deep suspicion; ghastly looks
> Are at my service, like enforcèd smiles,
> And both are ready in their offices
> At any time to grace my stratagems.
>
> (3.5.1–11)

Richard's detachment is comic; we are in his confidence, we see the action through his eyes and share his sense of superiority over his victims. And our appreciation of his wit and cunning is enhanced by the vigour of his language; Shakespeare gives him many flashes of colloquial directness contrasting with the formality of other characters.

All this creates a tension between our aesthetic response to his cleverness and our moral response to the uses to which he puts it. His physical deformity, however, serves as an ever-present reminder of his moral corruption, and Shakespeare characterizes his evil through a continuing sequence of repellent animal images: Lady Anne wishes him worse fortune than she can wish 'to wolves, to spiders, toads, or any creeping venomed thing that lives' and later calls him a hedgehog and a toad; Queen Margaret luxuriates in these images, calling him successively within a single scene (1.3) 'dog', 'elvish-marked, abortive, rooting hog', 'bottled spider', and 'poisonous bunch-backed toad'; later she speaks of him as 'A hell-hound that doth hunt us all to death: | That dog that had his teeth before his eyes, | To worry lambs and lap their gentle blood'; and Queen Elizabeth says:

> O thou didst prophesy the time would come
> That I should wish for thee to help me curse
> That bottled spider, that foul bunch-backed toad.
>
> (4.4.79–81)

History may have suggested this image sequence to Shakespeare, because Richard's personal emblem was the boar; Richmond makes good use of this towards the end of the play:

> That wretched, bloody, and usurping boar,
> That spoils your summer fields and fruitful vines,
> Swills your warm blood like wash, and makes his trough
> In your inbowelled bosoms, this foul swine
> Lies now even in the centry of this isle . . .
>
> (5.2.7–11)

On his way to the throne Richard is an immensely active character, bustling (his own word) from one foul deed to the next, but when he gets there both his high spirits and his sense of irony desert him. His first entry as king, 'in pomp' as the stage direction puts it, is a turning-point, often marked in the theatre by an emphasis on spectacle: the RSC production by Bill Alexander of 1984 in which Antony Sher played Richard interpolated a coronation that recalled in its splendour the most extravagant excesses of the Victorian theatre. Richard's confidence is shaken by Buckingham's failure to respond first to his hints then to his plain demand ('I wish the bastards dead') that the young princes, King Edward's sons, be put to death. He shows consciousness of sin: 'I am in | So far in blood that sin will pluck on sin' (4.2.65–6) and is troubled by remembrance of Henry VI's prophecy 'that Richmond should be king'. He begins to lose control on hearing that forces are massing against him, mistrusts his supporters, strikes a messenger who brings what he wrongly expects will be bad news, and on the eve of the battle admits: 'I have not that alacrity of spirit, | Nor cheer of mind, that I was wont to have' (5.5.26–7).

The climax of the role comes with his soliloquy on awaking in his tent before the battle. Somewhat exceptionally, he and Richmond have both dreamt the same dream: that Richard's victims have successively cursed Richard and blessed Richmond. Richard awakes thinking he is already fighting: 'Give me another horse! Bind up my wounds!' Realizing that he has been dreaming, he starts to examine his conscience:

> O coward conscience, how dost thou afflict me?
> The lights burn blue. It is now dead midnight.
> Cold fearful drops stand on my trembling flesh.
> What do I fear? Myself? There's none else by.
> Richard loves Richard; that is, I am I.
> Is there a murderer here? No. Yes, I am.
> Then fly! What, from myself? Great reason. Why?
> Lest I revenge. Myself upon myself?
> Alack, I love myself. Wherefore? For any good
> That I myself have done unto myself?
> O no, alas, I rather hate myself
> For hateful deeds committed by myself.
> I am a villain. Yet I lie: I am not.
> Fool, of thyself speak well. – Fool, do not flatter.
> My conscience hath a thousand several tongues,
> And every tongue brings in a several tale,
> And every tale condemns me for a villain.
> Perjury, perjury, in the high'st degree!
> Murder, stern murder, in the dir'st degree!
> All several sins, all used in each degree,
> Throng to the bar, crying all, 'Guilty, guilty!'
> I shall despair. There is no creature loves me,
> And if I die no soul will pity me.
> Nay, wherefore should they? – Since that I myself
> Find in myself no pity to myself.
>
> (5.5.133–57)

I quote from this speech at such length because there is ambiguity in its tone: or perhaps it would be more accurate to say a discrepancy between the style in which it is written and the emotions that may be supposed to lie behind it. An actor seeking a grand tragic climax to the role may try to evoke a sympathetic response, treating it as a forerunner of Macbeth's 'Tomorrow, and tomorrow, and tomorrow', but to me it seems rather a cerebral self-examination than an emotional revelation, and this is how Antony Sher treated it. What shook Sher's Richard was his subsequent discovery that he was capable of fear: 'Ratcliffe, I fear, I fear' (5.5.168).

It is understandable that *Richard the Third* should nowadays be treated rather as a tragedy than as a history play, particularly when it is performed out of sequence, because its historical resonances must have meant far more to its original audiences (with whom it seems to have been very popular – the first edition went through five reprints before the play appeared in the First Folio) than they can to us. The man who speaks its last words, Richmond, was Elizabeth I's grandfather; the play celebrates the final establishment of the Tudor dynasty to which the Queen herself belonged. Her subjects had a deadly fear of civil war such as is portrayed in the *Henry the Sixth* plays; the earlier part of her reign had seen serious threats to national unity in, for instance, the religious strife, Mary Queen of Scots's claim to the English throne, and the Spanish menace.

There was constant fear lest what had been gained should be lost; and, with so much power resting in the sovereign, the sudden death of the Queen, especially if she had not appointed a suitable heir, could have swiftly plunged the country into disaster. This fear of anarchy is reflected in *Richard the Third* in the scene (2.3) in which three anonymous citizens discuss Edward's death and its possible conse-quences; they fear to see 'a troublous world', 'the hearts of men are full of fear', there is nothing they can do but 'leave it all to God'. Sins might have to be expiated even to the third and fourth generation, and *Richard the Third* shows the gradual expiation of the sins of the house of York, partly by the functioning of the principle of the self-destructiveness of evil, and partly through the will of God in the figure of the Lancastrian Earl of Richmond.

It is ironic that Richard's personal evil should be destructive of his family's greatness. Shakespeare strongly emphasizes the expiation of guilt in his manner of portraying the deaths of Richard's brothers, Clarence and Edward, showing that he conceives of them not just as individuals but as symbols of national guilt. Clarence had been a traitor; he had married the daughter of Warwick the King-maker who was then in revolt against Edward IV, but later deserted Warwick and was reconciled with his brother. Even the men hired to murder him urge his guilt upon him:

SECOND MURDERER Thou didst receive the sacrament to fight
  In quarrel of the house of Lancaster.
FIRST MURDERER And, like a traitor to the name of God,
  Didst break that vow, and with thy treacherous blade
  Unripped'st the bowels of thy sov'reign's son.

                                                        (1.4.198–202)

Clarence dies penitent and full of holy thoughts. His brother, Edward IV, is equally penitent in death, especially for his failure to prevent his brother's murder; he says to his assembled family:

> O God, I fear thy justice will take hold
> On me – and you, and mine, and yours, for this.
>
> (2.1.132–3)

The final, almost sacrificial act in the self-destruction of the family is the death of the Princes in the Tower, an act which Sir James Tyrell, who has given instructions for their murder, ascribes not to an individual but to the nation, describing it as

> The most arch deed of piteous massacre
> That ever yet this land was guilty of.
>
> (4.3.2–3)

Straight after this comes the great scene of mourning in which the Lancastrian Queen Margaret joins with the Yorkist Duchess of York and Queen Elizabeth to bemoan the fate of their families and pray for vengeance on their enemies.

The strong religious colouring of these scenes increases the sense that the play's happenings represent a working-out of God's purpose to a particular end – that of the establishment of the Tudor dynasty in the person of the Earl of Richmond. We had been introduced to him as a boy in the preceding play, when for once the possibility that someone might come to the throne was stated for him in terms of 'peaceful' majesty rather than by him as an aspiration to power. Richmond is one of the most obviously symbolic figures in the whole of Shakespeare's plays, constantly invoking God, whose minister he claims to be:

> O God, whose captain I account myself,
> Look on my forces with a gracious eye.
> Put in their hands thy bruising irons of wrath,
> That they may crush down with a heavy fall
> Th'usurping helmets of our adversaries.
> Make us thy ministers of chastisement,
> That we may praise thee in the victory.
>
> (5.5.61–7)

This speech is immediately followed by the appearances of the dream-spectres to both Richmond and Richard, a highly stylized scene which not only brings to a climax the formality and patterning of this play but also ties it in with the earlier plays of the series: even the Yorkists confer their blessings on Richmond and curse Richard. The leaders' orations to their forces reflect their differing ideals: Richmond stresses Richard's guilt in the sight of God – 'one that hath ever been God's enemy' – whereas Richard specifically denies conscience, 'a word that cowards use' (and something of a key word in this play).

It has to be admitted, of course, that Richmond's God is no pacifist: Richard's death is bloody, and a modern audience may view with some scepticism Richmond's claim to be God's minister as he delivers the *coup de grâce*. The irony was pointed in Bill Alexander's production where Richmond, glittering in golden armour and holding a sword in the form of a cross, advanced from behind a dying Richard to stab him through the neck of his corslet. Richmond's bloody triumph was signalled by the singing of a *Gloria*.

The last speech of the play, spoken by the new King, Henry VII, ties everything up so comprehensively that it is worth quoting in full:

> Inter their bodies as becomes their births.
> Proclaim a pardon to the soldiers fled
> That in submission will return to us,
> And then – as we have ta'en the sacrament –
> We will unite the white rose and the red.
> Smile, heaven, upon this fair conjunction,
> That long have frowned upon their enmity.
> What traitor hears me and says not 'Amen'?
> England hath long been mad, and scarred herself;
> The brother blindly shed the brother's blood;
> The father rashly slaughtered his own son;
> The son, compelled, been butcher to the sire;
> All that divided York and Lancaster,
> United in their dire division.
> O now let Richmond and Elizabeth,
> The true succeeders of each royal house,
> By God's fair ordinance conjoin together,
> And let their heirs – God, if his will be so –
> Enrich the time to come with smooth-faced peace,
> With smiling plenty, and fair prosperous days.
> Abate the edge of traitors, gracious Lord,
> That would reduce these bloody days again
> And make poor England weep forth streams of blood.
> Let them not live to taste this land's increase,

> That would with treason wound this fair land's peace.
> Now civil wounds are stopped; peace lives again.
> That she may long live here, God say 'Amen.'

The significance of this speech to an Elizabethan audience was so well expounded by E. M. W. Tillyard that it seems best to let him have the last word:

Every sentence of Richmond's last speech, today regarded as a competent piece of formality, would have raised the Elizabethans to an ecstasy of feeling. Richmond gets everything right and refers to all the things they minded about. He is conventionally pious, his first words after the victory being, 'God and your arms be prais'd, victorious friends'. . . . Then he thinks of the immediate problems and asks about the dead. Hearing of them, he begins his last speech,

> Inter their bodies as becomes their birth,

and thereby implies: after thanks to God, the keeping of due degree on earth . . . Then, after degree, mercy:

> Proclaim a pardon to the soldiers fled
> That in submission will return to us.

And lastly an oath, taken with full religious solemnity and duly observed, and the healing of the wounds of civil war, with an insensible and indeed very subtle transfer of reference from the epoch of Bosworth to the very hour of the play's performance, from the supposed feelings of Richmond's supporters to what Shakespeare's own audience felt so ardently about the health of their country. The reference to father killing son and son killing father served at a single stroke both to recall the battle of Towton and to take the audience out of the Wars of the Roses to the wider context of civil wars in general: to Israel, France, and Germany; to the writers of chronicles and the Homilies; to what they had heard endlessly repeated on the subject by fireside or in tavern.[8]

If all Shakespeare's history plays were named after their most vigorous, interesting, and theatrically attractive characters (and those that have the longest role in the play), *King John* would be called *The*

Bastard. It is he – Philip Falconbridge, illegitimate son of Richard Coeur de Lion – who speaks the play's best-known lines:

> This England never did, nor never shall,
> Lie at the proud foot of a conqueror
> But when it first did help to wound itself.
> Now these her princes are come home again,
> Come the three corners of the world in arms
> And we shall shock them. Naught shall make us rue
> If England to itself do rest but true.

They are the last lines of yet another play concerned with conflict between England and France, and they help to explain the fact that some of its most successful theatrical revivals have been at times, such as those of the Napoleonic Wars, when these conflicts have been replayed.[9] Yet it is hard to see *King John* overall as a celebration of England, or even as a play that associates the English cause with heroic values. It is the most satirical of Shakespeare's histories in its treatment of political issues, and John, dominated by his mother, Queen Eleanor, and unredeemed by Henry VI's saintliness, is the most wimpish of its kings, the smallest-minded in his pursuit of selfish aims.

In spite of its scepticism about war, *King John* has not been a popular play in the twentieth century. In part this may simply reflect a judgement on the unevenness of its writing, but I suspect it is also because directors, as well as readers, have difficulty in identifying an appropriate tone for its varying episodes. In the opening scene John's expression of defiance to the French ambassador can be read entirely seriously; only if he is characterized in terms of his later behaviour does it take on a comic tinge. Thus, for instance, Deborah Warner, in her RSC studio theatre production of 1988, reduced John's heroic pretensions to absurdity from the start by having him played by an unusually short actor wearing a baggy greatcoat and often carrying a sword of state that he found grotesquely unwieldy; he became a character desperately, humiliatingly, in search of a dignity denied him by nature.

Perhaps the Warner production cast the character into too restrictive a mould, but Shakespeare's dialogue is often reductive in its presentation of the King's handling of political issues, particularly in the scene where the Kings of France and England wrangle over the respective claims to the English throne of John and his nephew Arthur, orphan son of Richard I's brother Geoffrey, who has the support of the French. Both sides claim Angers; the Citizens are willing to yield to the King of England provided they know who that is; the height of absurdity is reached when John proposes to the King of France that they 'lay this Angers even with the ground, | Then after fight who shall be king of it'. France's ally Austria proposes to fire artillery from the north while France fires from the south; the Bastard is delighted to encourage them in this: '. . . prudent discipline! From north to south | Austria and France shoot in each other's mouth.' Carnage is averted only by a Citizen's proposal for a political marriage between the Dauphin of France and Princess Blanche of Spain, John's niece.

Direct satire emanates mainly from the Bastard, sometimes in sardonic asides – 'Zounds', he says, after hearing the Citizen of Angers' long tirade, 'I was never so bethumped with words | Since I first called my brother's father Dad' – but also in his direct taunting of the Duke of Austria with his repeated 'and hang a calf's skin on those recreant limbs' and above all in his soliloquy after Angers when Shakespeare has him step outside the framework of the play in his speech beginning 'Mad world, mad kings, mad composition!' with his analysis of how the King of France, 'whose armour conscience buckled on', has nevertheless abandoned his support of Prince Arthur's claim to the throne under the influence of 'commodity' – self-interest:

> this commodity,
> This bawd, this broker, this all-changing word,
> Clapped on the outward eye of fickle France,
> Hath drawn him from his own determined aid,
> From a resolved and honourable war,
> To a most base and vile-concluded peace.
>
> (2.1.582–7)

His cynical conclusion, 'Gain, be my lord, for I will worship thee', is to be belied by his later behaviour.

In the earlier scenes of the play Prince Arthur is a political pawn in the conflict between England and France; later, after he has been captured by the English, he becomes its touchstone of humanity – 'The life, the right, and truth of all this realm', as the Bastard is to describe him after his death. One of the play's most dramatic stretches of dialogue is that in which John seduces Hubert de Burgh into promising to dispose of the young prince:

Good Hubert, Hubert, Hubert, throw thine eye
On yon young boy. I'll tell thee what, my friend,
He is a very serpent in my way,
And wheresoe'er this foot of mine doth tread,
He lies before me. Dost thou understand me?
Thou art his keeper.
HUBERT   And I'll keep him so
That he shall not offend your majesty.
KING JOHN
Death.
HUBERT My lord.
KING JOHN   A grave.
HUBERT   He shall not live.
KING JOHN   Enough.

                                            (3.3.59–66)

The understatement of writing like that is more to the taste of modern
audiences than the rhetoric, eloquent though it may be, of Constance
as she mourns her son's loss. Her speech beginning 'Grief fills the
room up of my absent child, | Lies in his bed, walks up and down with
me' (3.4.93 ff) has been seen as a reflection of Shakespeare's own grief
at the death of his son Hamnet in August 1596, and thus as evidence
that the play had not been written by then. The fact that Arthur is not
dead at this point may be irrelevant, but children had died, and
mothers grieved for them, in plays written by Shakespeare before this
date. We do not know exactly when Shakespeare wrote *King John*,
though it obviously belongs in style, and partly in content, with the
early histories. In all of them, and in later plays too, notably *Macbeth*,
the wanton killing of children becomes a symbol of ultimate evil.
Prince Arthur is the most eloquent of Shakespeare's wronged
children; this is a theatrical handicap in the absence of boy actors
trained in the delivery of rhetorical verse. In the past he was often
played by a young woman; this seems no longer to be acceptable, and
the difficulty of finding a boy who can do justice to the verse is a major
obstacle to modern performance. It is a pity, because the scene in
which Arthur persuades Hubert not to put out his eyes (the text,
incidentally, never explains why he is planning to do so) is a powerful
one. His death scene is clumsy, and awkward to stage, but important
not least because it transforms the Bastard from cynical commentator
to involved participant: 'Beyond the infinite and boundless reach | Of
mercy, if thou didst this deed of death, | Art thou damned, Hubert'
(4.3.117–19).

King John's end, poisoned by a monk, is grotesque and ignominious, but productive of more than one kind of eloquence. Hearing
that he has burst into song in spite of his suffering, his young son
Prince Henry speaks elegiacally:

> 'Tis strange that death should sing.
> I am the cygnet to this pale faint swan,
> Who chants a doleful hymn to his own death,
> And from the organ-pipe of frailty sings
> His soul and body to their lasting rest.
>
> (5.7.21–4)

And John's account of his own suffering has a strange beauty that
suspends moral judgement:

> Ay marry, now my soul hath elbow-room;
> It would not out at windows nor at doors.
> There is so hot a summer in my bosom
> That all my bowels crumble up to dust;
> I am a scribbled form, drawn with a pen
> Upon a parchment, and against this fire
> Do I shrink up.
>
> (5.7.28–34)

In the end, then, as the Bastard asserts his undying loyalty to the
memory of his unworthy king, as news comes that an honourable
peace has been made with France, and as all the new King's subjects
swear allegiance to him, we may respond without total disbelief to the
Bastard's final assertion of the power of a united England.

Notes to Chapter Five

1 Lois Potter, 'Recycling the Early Histories: "The Wars of the Roses"
  and "The Plantagenets" ', *Shakespeare Survey 43* (1991), pp. 171–81;
  quoting from p. 171.
2 *Henslowe's Diary*, ed. R.A. Foakes and R.T. Rickert (Cambridge, 1961),
  p. 16.
3 Thomas Nashe, *Selected Writings*, ed. Stanley Wells (1964), pp. 64–5.
4 ibid.
5 A.T. Quiller-Couch, *Historical Tales from Shakespeare* (1899; repr.
  [1910]) p.v.
6 Wilfred Owen, Preface to his *Poems* (1920).

7 *Hazlitt on Theatre*, p. 6.
8 E.M.W. Tillyard, *Shakespeare's History Plays* (1944), pp. 201–2.
9 See, for example, Arthur Colby Sprague, *Shakespeare's Histories: Plays for
  the Stage* (London, the Society for Theatre Research, 1964), p. 15.

SIX

A Poetic Interlude:

Venus and Adonis, *The Rape of Lucrece*, Shorter Poems, the Sonnets, and 'A Lover's Complaint'

It was probably during the months following July 1592, when London theatres had to close because of plague, that Shakespeare sat down for the only time in his life to extended bursts of writing not intended for the stage. The publication in the following year of his narrative poem *Venus and Adonis* is one of the few points where his Stratford and London connections interlock: the poem was entered on the Stationers' Register on 18 April to Richard Field, a Stratfordian three years older than Shakespeare who had served his apprenticeship to a London printer. Field also published Shakespeare's other narrative poem, *The Rape of Lucrece*, in the following year, and, metamorphosed into a Frenchman, he hovers curiously behind the text of *Cymbeline*, written many years later, when the disguised Innogen pretends that the body of Cloten which she believes to be that of Posthumus is actually that of her 'master' Richard du Champ (4.2.379).

Shakespeare's classical education shows itself most directly in these two Ovidian narrative poems. Fashionable and popular in his own time and until twenty or thirty years after he died, they were almost completely neglected from the Restoration until early in the nineteenth century, when Coleridge wrote perceptively and appreciatively about them. Since then they have taken second place to all but a handful of the plays in general esteem, and remain among the least-read of Shakespeare's writings. I suppose this is partly because performed works are more easily accessible than chunks of print, and also because the conventions in which these poems are written are unfamiliar to the general reader; but it is a pity, because they have much to offer both in themselves and in relation to the plays. (Incidentally, both of them read aloud very well.)

Shakespeare was writing in a genre that had only recently become fashionable, with the publication in 1589 of *Scilla's Metamorphosis* by Thomas Lodge, best known now as the author of *Rosalynde*. The English poems written in imitation of Ovid all use their original story (taken usually but not always from the *Metamorphoses*) as a framework or basis for a greatly extended narrative. These are not poems for the reader who is in a hurry to know how it all turns out: the elaboration is at least as important as the story, and is what gives each of the poems its individuality. Along with Marlowe's great comic poem *Hero and Leander*, *Venus and Adonis* and *The Rape of Lucrece* are the best, and best-known, works in this kind, and although *Hero and Leander* did not appear until 1598 Shakespeare may have been able to read it in manuscript before embarking on *Venus and Adonis*. Marlowe's poem is the more sensuous and humorous, Shakespeare's the more intellectually witty.

Venus and Adonis brought Shakespeare much praise in his own time, when it seems to have appealed particularly to young men and women on account of its sophisticated eroticism. Around 1600, for instance, Gabriel Harvey wrote that 'the younger sort takes much delight' in this poem whereas *Lucrece* and *Hamlet* had it in them 'to please the wiser sort'. There are many contemporary allusions and imitations, and in a number of plays lovers quote extracts from the poem to assist them in their wooing, perhaps encouraged by the fact that moralists deplored its supposed tendency to arouse lascivious thoughts.

Whereas Marlowe worked mainly from a late, Greek imitation of Ovid, Shakespeare went directly to the *Metamorphoses*, probably using both the original and Golding's translation. But like Marlowe he creates a long poem on the basis of a short tale. Ovid tells it in only about 75 lines, along with an interpolated tale about twice as long. Shakespeare, in nearly 1200 lines, modifies both the characterization and the events. Most importantly, whereas in Ovid the youthful Adonis returns Venus's love, Shakespeare turns him into a bashful adolescent who shies away from the goddess's embraces: the first part of the poem tells of her wooing of, and sexual assault on, the unresponsive Adonis. This change, characteristic of Shakespeare's attitude to his source material, is responsible for much of the poem's psychological interest as well as for its piquant eroticism. Adonis's innocence and idealism contrast with Venus's experience and (para-

doxically) physical, materialist outlook. It is the goddess who represents lust, the human boy who stands up for love. The tension between his youthful withdrawal from sexual experience and her over-mature anxiety to rush into it provides the dramatic impetus of the poem. Venus admits that Adonis is 'unripe' (l. 128), and he pleads for her understanding in words that suggest greater intellectual than emotional maturity:

> 'Fair queen,' quoth he, 'if any love you owe me,
> Measure my strangeness with my unripe years.
> Before I know myself, seek not to know me.'
>
> (523–5)

That last line encapsulates a persistent theme of Shakespeare's comedies. Adonis's bashfulness is funny, but touching too. It is appropriate to the essentially non-tragic nature of a story with a quasi-tragic ending.

For the rest, the story is easily told. When Venus has exhausted her efforts Adonis declares that he is off 'To hunt the boar with certain of his friends', and resists her efforts to stop him. Waiting fearfully to learn the outcome of the chase, she hears the yelping of his hounds, sees the blood-stained boar, comes upon the defeated dogs, and at last finds Adonis dead. Grieving over his body she prophesies that 'Sorrow on love hereafter shall attend'. Adonis's body melts away, and a purple and white flower springs up in its place. Venus plucks the flower, places it in her bosom, and flies off in her dove-drawn chariot to seek solitude in Cyprus.

Shakespeare's main addition to Ovid's narrative is an episode (259–324) in which Adonis's stallion lusts successfully after a mare and gallops off to the forest with her, thus frustrating Adonis's attempts to escape from Venus's wooing. The contrast between the stallion's uninhibited sexuality and Adonis's bashfulness makes this episode resemble the kind of subplot that Shakespeare introduces into his comedies. Otherwise his amplifications consist mainly of rhetorical elaborations. Among the more conspicuous are Venus's verbal assault on Adonis's chastity (95–174), in which she uses arguments resembling those in the first seventeen of Shakespeare's sonnets; her speech (613–714) on the dangers of boar-hunting, followed by her elaborate explanation of why the night is dark (721–68); Adonis's reply (769–810), culminating in his eloquent contrast between lust and love; the amplifications of Venus's reactions to the sight of the dead Adonis (1033–56); and her lament over his body (1069–1164).

Clearly this is a long poem in that it treats a relatively small amount of narrative material with an expansive, amplificatory leisureliness. Yet it opens with admirable rapidity in a highly concentrated stanza:

> Even as the sun with purple-coloured face
> Had ta'en his last leave of the weeping morn,
> Rose-cheeked Adonis hied him to the chase.
> Hunting he loved, but love he laughed to scorn.
> > Sick-thoughted Venus makes amain unto him,
> > And like a bold-faced suitor 'gins to woo him.

After this there are digressions and, more importantly, many passages in which the narrative halts while emotions are described or expressed. Yet the poem is not slow-moving. The characters' feelings are an important part of the story, and the expression of them is developed with such order, clarity, and ease of versification that the general impression is one of speed.

The quality of *Venus and Adonis* that is most in danger of being underrated is its elegant high comedy. Among the plays it is closest to *Love's Labour's Lost*; like that play it delights in its virtuosity, drawing attention to its own craftsmanship with self-conscious wit. But also like the play, it encompasses a range of styles. The narrator stands at some distance from the events, allowing himself ironic comment, both explicit and implicit, upon them. There is irony in Venus's extended comparison of her own wooing of Adonis with Mars's wooing of her (97–112). There is comedy in the description of the coming together of Venus and Adonis after his horse has escaped:

> He sees her coming, and begins to glow,
> Even as a dying coal revives with wind,
> And with his bonnet hides his angry brow,
> Looks on the dull earth with disturbèd mind,
> > Taking no notice that she is so nigh,
> > For all askance he holds her in his eye.
>
> > > > > > > (337–42)

And there is positive burlesque in the description of Adonis, irritated, opening his mouth to speak:

> Once more the ruby-coloured portal opened
> Which to his speech did honey passage yield,
> Like a red morn that ever yet betokened

> Wrack to the seaman, tempest to the field,
>   Sorrow to shepherds, woe unto the birds,
>   Gusts and foul flaws to herdmen and to herds.
>
> (451–6)

The poem's intellectualism results sometimes in a complication of 'conceited', metaphysical writing that has its counterpart in the elaborate wordplay of the early comedies, but Shakespeare is capable too of the splendidly assured firmness and clarity of Venus's prophecy following Adonis's death and, perhaps most impressive of all, of the pared simplicity of her sight of the dead Adonis:

> She looks upon his lips, and they are pale.
> She takes him by the hand, and that is cold.
> She whispers in his ears a heavy tale,
> As if they heard the woeful words she told.
>
> (1123–6)

Those last lines echo (or anticipate) both the tone and the very words of the messenger of death in *Love's Labour's Lost*: 'the news I bring | Is *heavy* in my tongue . . . My *tale* is *told*' (5.2.711–13).

Readers expecting a romantic approach have been repelled by the intellectualism of *Venus and Adonis* (Hazlitt described the two narrative poems as 'a couple of ice-houses'). Others have taken pleasure in finding in the poem 'touches of nature' reflecting Shakespeare's upbringing in the Warwickshire countryside, but it needs to be recognized that the nature imagery has its function in the poem's overall economy: there is a dive-dapper in the poem, and there were (and are) dive-dappers in the Warwickshire Avon, but the one in the poem belongs there and nowhere else:

> Upon this promise did he raise his chin,
> Like a dive-dapper peering through a wave
> Who, being looked on, ducks as quickly in –
> So offers he to give what she did crave.
>   But when her lips were ready for his pay,
>   He winks, and turns his lips another way.
>
> (85–90)

That stanza exemplifies in little a characteristic technique of the poem. The story is mythological; the events take place in a remote period before the organization of the world has been determined. Its landscape is inhabited by none but the goddess Venus and the mortal Adonis – and by members of the animal kingdom, in which their passions are reflected: the dive-dapper, the lustful stallion, the timorous hare, Wat (679–708), the sensitive snail (1033–5), and the savage boar. In her lament for Adonis, Venus stresses the harmony that existed between him and the animals:

> To see his face the lion walked along
> Behind some hedge, because he would not fear him.
> To recreate himself when he hath sung,
> The tiger would be tame, and gently hear him.
>   If he had spoke, the wolf would leave his prey,
>   And never fright the silly lamb that day.
>
>   (1093–8)

The boar has disrupted this harmony, and the result will be eternal discord: 'Sorrow on love hereafter shall attend.'

In the dedication to *Venus and Adonis* Shakespeare had promised, if the Earl of Southampton should 'seem but pleased' with that poem, to 'take advantage of all idle hours' to honour the Earl 'with some graver labour', and Richard Field's entry for publication of *The Rape of Lucrece* followed that of *Venus and Adonis* by little more than a year. The exceptional warmth of the dedication to the later poem suggests friendship as well as patronage and has supported the conjecture that Southampton, who was twenty years old when *Lucrece* appeared, is the young man addressed in Shakespeare's sonnets. Whether or not this is so, Southampton is the member of the aristocracy with whom we can most confidently say that Shakespeare had a relationship of some kind. If a new cache of Southampton papers were to turn up, biographers of Shakespeare would be pleased to hear of it.

This poem, too, was to be popular. It was respected as a work of more serious moral purpose than its predecessor: in an epigram published in 1614 Thomas Freeman wrote:

> Who loves chaste life, there's *Lucrece* for a teacher;
> Who list read lust, there's *Venus and Adonis*,
> True model of a most lascivious lecher.

But it is also a companion piece to *Venus and Adonis*. Both are Ovidian, both use a stanza form – *Venus and Adonis* the six-line stanza resembling the sestet of a Shakespearian sonnet, *The Rape of Lucrece* the seven-line 'rhyme royal'. One shows rape attempted unsuccessfully by a female, the other shows rape achieved by a male; one treats its topic comically, the other tragically; both are set in pre-Christian times, though one is mythological, the other historical.

For this poem Shakespeare turned not to the *Metamorphoses* but to Ovid's *Fasti* (chronicles). The story had often been told elsewhere, and Shakespeare seems to have known other versions too. He was also influenced, particularly in the later parts of the poem, by the tradition of the 'complaint'; the *Mirror for Magistrates*, which he drew on in his history plays, was well known as a collection of such poems in which the ghosts of historical figures bemoan their fate. As in *Venus and Adonis*, Shakespeare makes a little go a long way: his telling of the tale is about twelve times as long as Ovid's.

The historical story of Lucrece resembles those that Shakespeare uses in his tragedies in its interfusion of personal and political events: Lucrece's ravisher, Tarquin, belonged to the tyrannical ruling family of Rome. During the siege of Ardea a group of noblemen boasted of their wives' virtue and rode back home to see what they were up to. Only Collatine's wife, Lucretia, was virtuously occupied at home in Collatium. The King's son, Sextus Tarquinius, found her attractive. Failing to seduce her, he raped her and went back to Rome. Lucretia committed suicide and her husband's friend, Lucius Junius Brutus, whose father and brother the King had murdered, used the occasion as an opportunity to rouse the Roman people to rebel against Tarquinius's rule and to constitute themselves a republic.

Shakespeare concerns himself mainly with the private events of the story – Tarquin's desire for Lucrece, the rape, and Lucrece's suicide – and compresses the action into a period of no more than forty-eight hours, centring on the events of one night. His opening scarcely looks back to what has gone before; his ending devotes only a few lines to the consequences of Lucrece's suicide. Tarquin is already 'Lust-breathèd' and on his way to violate Lucrece in the opening lines.

> From the besieged Ardea all in post,
> Borne by the trustless wings of false desire,
> Lust-breathèd Tarquin leaves the Roman host
> And to Collatium bears the lightless fire
> Which, in pale embers hid, lurks to aspire

> And girdle with embracing flames the waist
> Of Collatine's fair love, Lucrece the chaste.

As in *Venus and Adonis* the splendid swiftness of the opening stanza plunges us straight into *medias res*, with no immediate explanation of how Tarquin came to act like this – that will come later. And the opening is not merely swift, it is also packed with energy in its suggestion of the destructive power of Tarquin's lust imaged as a fire lurking unseen among embers which will soon burst into flame.

No-one could sustain a long poem at this pitch, nor would the basic narrative material support it. Whereas in *Venus and Adonis* Venus is dominant throughout, in *The Rape of Lucrece* the focus switches from Tarquin in the first part to Lucrece in the second, and this is one of the factors that reduce the impression of unity in the poem. Another is the feeling that the amplificatory technique, which tends to keep us at a distance from the events, is less suited to the personal tragedy of Lucrece (and, in its way, of Tarquin) than it had been to the high comedy of Venus and Adonis. As in the earlier poem, Shakespeare ekes out his material with long, meditative soliloquies, digressive episodes, and (to an even greater extent) moralizing passages. For example, lines 764 to 1036 – more than one-seventh of the whole – consist of an apostrophe by Lucrece to, successively, Night, Opportunity, and Time, and later in the poem almost 200 lines are devoted to Lucrece's description of a painting of Troy, with comparisons of features in it to her own plight. While we may admire the poet's skill in such passages, we may also regret the dilution of the tragic effect.

And the tragic effect can be great. For us who know the later work it is difficult not to hear Macbeth's efforts to screw himself up to the murder of Duncan as we read the account of Tarquin, fully conscious of his wickedness, going to rape Lucrece at dead of night:

> Now stole upon the time the dead of night
> When heavy sleep had closed up mortal eyes.
> No comfortable star did lend his light,
> No noise but owls' and wolves' death-boding cries
> Now serves the season, that they may surprise
>   The silly lambs. Pure thoughts are dead and still,
>   While lust and murder wakes to stain and kill.

> (2. 162–8)

But even if Shakespeare had not written *Macbeth* that stanza would still have been a masterly piece of scene-painting, and it is followed by an admirably direct depiction of both Tarquin's actions and (briefly) his emotions:

> And now this lustful lord leapt from his bed,
> Throwing his mantle rudely o'er his arm,
> Is madly tossed between desire and dread.
> Th'one sweetly flatters, th'other feareth harm.
> But honest fear, bewitched with lust's foul charm,
>   Doth too-too oft betake him to retire,
>   Beaten away by brain-sick rude desire.

The brutality and coldness of Tarquin's next action, reflected in the sound-patterns of the verse, are suggestive of his state of mind:

> His falchion on a flint he softly smiteth,
> That from the cold stone sparks of fire do fly.
> Whereat a waxen torch forthwith he lighteth,
> Which must be lodestar to his lustful eye,
> And to the flame thus speaks advisedly:
>   'As from this cold flint I enforced this fire,
>   So Lucrece must I force to my desire.'

The torch in the night has symbolic force, recalling the imagery of lust in the poem's opening lines, linking especially with the phrase 'lightless fire'. The temperature goes down for a while as Shakespeare starts to amplify the situation, allowing Tarquin a long 'disputation | 'Tween frozen conscience and hot-burning will'. Though excellent in its own terms, the soliloquy lacks the suggestive compression of the descriptive passages that precede it. It may seem odd that Shakespeare, the dramatist, should be more successful in descriptive and narrative passages than in direct speech; perhaps this is because, lacking the need for constant movement that he acknowledges in drama, he permits his characters here to embroider at great length upon an essentially static situation.

Excitement grows again as Tarquin begins his journey to Lucrece's chamber:

> The locks between her chamber and his will,
> Each one by him enforced, retires his ward;
> But as they open they all rate his ill,
> Which drives the creeping thief to some regard.

The threshold grates the door to have him heard,
  Night-wand'ring weasels shriek to see him there.
  They fright him, yet he still pursues his fear.

(302–8)

The participation of inanimate objects in his guilt anticipates Macbeth's

Thou sure and firm-set earth,
  Hear not my steps which way they walk, for fear
  Thy very stones prate of my whereabout . . .

(2.1.56–8)

The next stanza is even more forceful in its combination of simple, direct statement with the image of the torch, now of high associative power, making its way in spite of the effort of the better things of nature to impede its progress:

As each unwilling portal yields him way,
  Through little vents and crannies of the place
  The wind wars with his torch to make him stay,
  And blows the smoke of it into his face,
  Extinguishing his conduct in this case.
    But his hot heart, which fond desire doth scorch,
    Puffs forth another wind that fires the torch.

One could point to many fine passages in the ensuing stanzas: the way that the various obstacles in Tarquin's path are brought together in his mind only to be dismissed as 'accidental things of trial'; his hesitation on the very threshold of Lucrece's room; the nice detail that he uses his knee to push the door open; and the splendid description of the sleeping Lucrece. The lengthy account of his physical assault on Lucrece provides a sustained example of the full strength of Shakespeare's narrative power: it is 'artificial', 'conceited', daring to be a good deal larger than life:

This said, he shakes aloft his Roman blade,
  Which like a falcon tow'ring in the skies
  Coucheth the fowl below with his wings' shade
  Whose crooked beak threats, if he mount he dies.
  So under his insulting falchion lies
    Harmless Lucretia, marking what he tells
    With trembling fear, as fowl hear falcons' bells.

(505–11)

Granted the method, it is also vivid, suggestive, and exciting.

At other points the poem seems to me less effective, yet even the least relevant passages are often fine in themselves. The description (indebted to both Virgil and Ovid) of the painting of Troy on which Lucrece embarks is a brilliant piece of writing, even if we are conscious of the strain by which it is linked to the narrative; and Lucrece's apostrophe to Night, Opportunity, and Time is a distinguished poem in its own right.

Lucrece is caught in a 'double bind': if she kills herself she will (anachronistically, because according to Christian, not Roman thought) sin against her soul; if she does not, she will live a shamed life. She determines on death, but not till she has told her husband all:

> That he may vow in that sad hour of mine
> Revenge on him that made me stop my breath.
>
> (1178–80)

She hopes through death at least to save her reputation. After she has killed herself Brutus pulls the knife from her body and, in lines that have some of the mythic resonance of those in *Venus and Adonis* telling how it came about that love is always attended by sorrow, we are told that

> . . . ever since, as pitying Lucrece' woes,
>   Corrupted blood some watery token shows;
>   And blood untainted still doth red abide,
>   Blushing at that which is so putrefied.
>
> (1747–50)

The composition of *The Rape of Lucrece* seems to have been a formative experience for Shakespeare. In it (along with *Titus Andronicus*) he laid the bases for his later plays on Roman history. He explored many themes that were to figure prominently in his later work: the discrepancy between virtuous appearance and 'inward ill' (91); the conflict of conscience and desire; the folly of ill-directed ambition, which leads men to 'neglect | The thing we have, and all for want of wit | Make something nothing by augmenting it' (152–4); the power of 'soft fancy' to subjugate 'A martial man' (200); the responsibilities of 'princely office' (628); the destructive and the healing powers of time; the relationship between 'private pleasure' and 'public plague' (1478–9); man's desire for honour after death; and the legendary, symbolic quality of historical figures and their deeds.

And just as a basic theme of Shakespearian comedy, the search for, and final achievement of, self-knowledge, is adumbrated in *Venus and Adonis*, so a basic motif of his tragedies, the problem caused by an absence of self-knowledge so disastrous that it is finally destructive of self, emerges in *The Rape of Lucrece*: most movingly, the poem presents the horror of a man who 'still pursues his fear' (308), the relentless powers of self-destructive evil.

Later in his career, Shakespeare was to portray a usurper – like the older Tarquin – who – like the younger Tarquin – is carried helplessly along on the tide of his own evil ambition. Moments before he murders Duncan, in lines in which Shakespeare seems to be acknowledging his debt to his younger self, Macbeth draws the parallel between his crime and Tarquin's:

> Now o'er the one half-world
> Nature seems dead, and wicked dreams abuse
> The curtained sleep. Witchcraft celebrates
> Pale Hecate's offerings, and withered murder,
> Alarumed by his sentinel the wolf,
> Whose howl's his watch, thus with his stealthy pace,
> With Tarquin's ravishing strides, towards his design
> Moves like a ghost.
>
> (2.1.49–56)

In 1594 the theatres reopened, and Shakespeare became a member of the newly formed Lord Chamberlain's Men. Thereafter, with the important exception of the sonnets – the private counterpart to the public narrative poems – and their accompanying poem 'A Lover's Complaint', Shakespeare seems to have devoted his energies to the theatre, with only a few pauses for writing non-dramatic verse. A 90- line poem beginning 'Shall I die?' is firmly ascribed to 'William Shakespeare' in a manuscript collection of poems probably put together in the late 1630s which is now in the Bodleian Library, Oxford. Its existence was no secret, but when Gary Taylor, working on the poems for the Oxford edition of the *Complete Works*, drew attention to it in 1985 it suddenly became the centre of an enormous amount of attention. The stanza form in which it is written has not been found elsewhere in the period, but resembles the lines spoken by Robin Goodfellow over the sleeping Lysander in *A Midsummer Night's*

Dream (3.3.36–46), and there are parallels with plays and poems that Shakespeare wrote around 1593–5. It has a demanding rhyme scheme which creates the impression of a virtuoso exercise, skilful but insubstantial, and if it adds nothing to Shakespeare's reputation, it appealed enough to at least two early readers for them to wish to have copies of it (there is a second, unattributed version in a Yale manuscript). Some scholars, for reasons best known to themselves, have devoted an inordinate amount of effort to trying to prove that Shakespeare did not write it, but as the only piece of external evidence favours his authorship it must remain at least among the Shakespeare apocrypha unless new information comes to light.

Far finer is 'The Phoenix and Turtle', ascribed to Shakespeare in 1601 when it appeared, without title, as one of the 'Poetical Essays' appended to Robert Chester's *Love's Martyr: or Rosalind's Complaint*, described as 'allegorically showing the truth of love in the constant fate of the phoenix and turtle'. Chester's poem seems to have been composed as a compliment to Sir John and Lady Salusbury, his patrons, but we know of no link between this family and Shakespeare.

The poem mounts in intensity through three parts. First it summons a convocation of benevolent birds, with a swan as priest, to celebrate the obsequies of the phoenix and the turtle dove, who have 'fled | In a mutual flame from hence'. The birds sing an anthem in which the death of the lovers is seen as marking the death of all 'love and constancy':

> So they loved as love in twain
> Had the essence but in one,
> Two distincts, division none.
> Number there in love was slain.

Their mutuality was such that 'Either was the other's mine'. In the third part of the poem Love makes a funeral song

> To the phoenix and the dove,
> Co-supremes and stars of love,
> As chorus to their tragic scene.

This funeral song, or threnos, is set off by being written in an even more incantatory style than what has gone before – each of the five stanzas has three rhyming lines, and the tone is one of grave simplicity:

Beauty, truth, and rarity,
Grace in all simplicity,
Here enclosed in cinders lie.

Death is now the phoenix' nest,
And the turtle's loyal breast
To eternity doth rest.

Leaving no posterity
'Twas not their infirmity,
It was married chastity.

Truth may seem but cannot be,
Beauty brag, but 'tis not she.
Truth and beauty buried be.

To this urn let those repair
That are either true or fair.
For these dead birds sigh a prayer.

The poem may have irrecoverable allegorical significance; in the absence of any clue as to what this might have been it is best read as an example of 'pure poetry',[1] a mysterious and mystical elegy that creates and inhabits its own closed world. Though it must have been composed by 1601 its affinities seem to me to lie with the late plays, with, for example, the lyrical strangeness of some of the passages that I quote in my discussion of *Pericles*.

In Chapter One I wrote about the sonnets mainly in relation to Shakespeare's life, but the reason that the collection is nowadays so often reprinted as a gift book has less to do with its biographical significance than with the popularity of individual sonnets as utterances of love that help us to define our own experience. Liberty of interpretation exists in verse as well as in drama: the gender of the person the poet addresses becomes irrelevant, and the jubilant celebration of love in such a poem as 'Shall I compare thee to a summer's day' (Sonnet 18) may speak for any lover of his or her beloved.

The poems are full of contradictions, forming together a kind of anatomy of the shifting moods of love. Some speak with wonderful confidence, often using natural imagery, of the beauty of the loved one, of the power of love to transcend time – 'Love's not time's fool' (116) – of faith in the beloved; others with elegiac lyricism of the pain of

absence and the fact 'That time will come and take my love away' (64).
Some express confidence that time may be conquered by the begetting
of children, or still more by the power of poetry:

> Not marble nor the gilded monuments
> Of princes shall outlive this powerful rhyme,
> But you shall shine more bright in these contents
> Than unswept stone besmeared with sluttish time.
>
> (Sonnet 55)

Some express faith in the beloved's constancy – 'you like none, none
you, for constant heart' (53); others deplore 'Those pretty wrongs that
liberty commits | When I am sometime absent from thy heart' (41).

The lover is remarkably forgiving, even at times to the point of
self-abasement – 'Being your slave, what should I do but tend | Upon
the hours and times of your desire?' (57). In the sonnets concerned
with the woman he is especially aware of love's irrationality, and of
the 'expense of spirit' that 'is lust in action' (129 – a sonnet that might
have come from the lips of Tarquin):

> till action, lust
> Is perjured, murd'rous, bloody, full of blame,
> Savage, extreme, rude, cruel, not to trust,
> Enjoyed no sooner but despisèd straight,
> Past reason hunted, and no sooner had
> Past reason hated as a swallowed bait
> On purpose laid to make the taker mad.

Love is seen as a sickness, a breeder of paradox, a state of mind that
overturns truth:

> My love is as a fever, longing still
> For that which longer nurseth the disease,
> Feeding on that which doth preserve the ill,
> Th'uncertain sickly appetite to please.
>
> (Sonnet 147)

And the couplet of *this* sonnet might have been spoken by Othello:

> For I have sworn thee fair, and thought thee bright,
> Who art as black as hell, as dark as night.

Not all the poems are closely tied in with the sequence; the eloquent and deeply felt Sonnet 146, for instance, beginning 'Poor soul, the centre of my sinful earth', is a general meditation on the relationship between soul and body which would be at home in a religious sequence; indeed its conclusion – 'So shalt thou feed on death, that feeds on men, | And death once dead, there's no more dying then' – resembles the last words of John Donne's Holy Sonnet No. 10: 'death, thou shalt die'.

Just as the sonnets vary in subject-matter, so they also range through a wide variety of poetic styles; some are well-ordered meditations on eternal poetic themes of time, the transience of beauty, and of love, on the power of art and the inevitability of death; others are more narrowly, even enigmatically, related to a particular situation; some are intellectual, witty workings-out of poetic conceits; some, no less intellectual, are tortured, introspective self-communings. Though some seem to belong to the world of *The Two Gentlemen of Verona*, others are closer in tone to *Measure for Measure* or *Troilus and Cressida*.

All this makes the sonnets difficult to read consecutively, as a sequence – a difficulty that is compounded by the fact that the Shakespearian sonnet, ending in a couplet, is a closed form, not naturally leading the reader on to what is to follow. Many attempts have been made to reorder the sonnets into a tidier, more logical sequence, but none has been convincing, and anyhow the endeavour is misguided. The illogicality, the disorder, the violent juxtapositions of mood are themselves part of the sequence's content, making of it not just a collection of assorted poems about love but an exploration of love's 'violent'st contrariety' (*Coriolanus*, 4.6.76).

In the 1609 volume the sonnets are followed by a poem with a separate heading, 'A Lover's Complaint, by William Shakespeare'. Its inclusion may be part of Shakespeare's design: this narrative poem belongs to a well-defined genre, and it was not uncommon for a sonnet sequence to be followed by the complaint, or lament, of a forsaken lover. Here a woman abandoned by her lover tells her woes. As in the sonnets, the young man is irresistibly attractive, but in his treachery he more closely resembles the dark woman. In Shakespeare's plays he comes closest to Bertram in *All's Well that Ends Well*, and the poem may have been written around the same time.

In many ways 'A Lover's Complaint' contrasts with the sonnets: its style is archaic and conscious of artifice, its structure oblique, at an extreme from the directness and personal tone of the more intimate of the sonnets. It employs a series of distancing perspectives: the narrator is a mere scene-setter; having described seeing a love-lorn lass 'Tearing of papers, breaking rings a-twain, | Storming her world with sorrow's wind and rain', he retires to let her tell her tale to 'A reverend man that grazed his cattle nigh'. But this man, too, fades out of sight as she tells her story of seduction and abandonment.

The lass's complaint contains within itself a second, long complaint – her lover's, ultimately successful, speech of seduction, ending with the tears that brought about her downfall:

> O father, what a hell of witchcraft lies
> In the small orb of one particular tear!

She fell, she says, and would fall again if subjected to such persuasion:

> O that infected moisture of his eye,
> O that false fire which in his cheek so glowed,
> O that forced thunder from his heart did fly,
> O that sad breath his spongy lungs bestowed,
> O all that borrowed motion seeming owed
> Would yet again betray the fore-betrayed,
> And new pervert a reconcilèd maid.

And here the poem ends; neither the listener nor the narrator returns. It is a mannered poem that requires the reader to accept its own conventions; although it may seem to stand at a far extreme from the sonnets it accompanies, this may be the point: that it is a kind of obverse companion piece, another, different account of love's torments, and one with its own distinctive voice.[2]

Notes to Chapter Six

1 F.T. Prince discusses it in these terms in his Arden edition (1960, etc.).
2 Other, minor poems, mostly epitaphs, that may be ascribed to Shakespeare are printed in the Oxford *Complete Works* and discussed in the *Textual Companion*, pp. 449–60.

SEVEN

Four More Plays of English History:

King Richard the Second, King Henry the Fourth, Part One, King Henry the Fourth, Part Two, and *King Henry the Fifth*

After dramatizing English history – or certain aspects of it – from the birth of Henry VI to the accession of Queen Elizabeth's grandfather, Henry VII, Shakespeare turned back in the *Chronicles* to the reign of Richard II. Again he was to write an interlinked series of four plays, and in this series it seems to have been even more his concern to make a success of each individual play rather than to create a single overarching structure. This impression derives partly from the fact that his style as both poet and dramatist developed greatly while he was writing the four plays. I don't mean by this that the plays get progressively better, only that Shakespeare could not stand still long enough to write four plays all in the same mode. Also, in practical terms, it may be that his company could not encourage him to write four closely related plays one after another; diversity of repertoire was important to them. The first, *Richard the Second*, is close in both time of writing and in style to *King John*, which it may even have preceded; the other three, *Henry the Fourth, Part One* and *Part Two* and *Henry the Fifth*, though not all that much later in date – *Henry the Fourth, Part One* was probably first acted in 1596, its companion piece within a year or so, and *Henry the Fifth* during 1599 – are far more like one another than they are like any of the earlier histories.

It is only during the twentieth century that the theatre has treated these plays as an interlinked sequence – a tetralogy – and then only sporadically. The Henry VI plays, comparatively rare in performance, have almost always been performed together, though usually, as I have said, in adaptation. But with the understandable exception of *Henry the Fourth, Part Two*, which has suffered in popularity from its status as a sequel, the later written plays (like the earlier *Richard the*

Third) have been regarded as more free-standing, while sometimes being brought together either in themselves or with their predecessors to form an epic sequence. Again, the links already existing in the original texts have usually been reinforced in order to increase the sense of continuity.

To modern audiences *Richard the Second* is the lyrical tragedy of a young, beautiful, and supremely eloquent king betrayed by his supporters, compelled to resign the crown, humiliated, imprisoned, and ultimately murdered in degrading circumstances. It is a play in which remarkably little happens; there are no battle scenes, no severed heads, only one scene of violence. The tournament for which preparations are made early in the play is called off as it is about to begin; we cannot even pinpoint the moment at which Richard yields the crown to Bolingbroke. *Richard the Second* is one of Shakespeare's most obviously literary plays; sensing this I once did a statistical exercise, dividing the number of lines spoken in each of the plays by the number of speeches to see which play has the highest average length of speech; as I suspected, *Richard the Second* came top. It demands a leading actor who can do justice to its long verse paragraphs and to the subtleties of its versification; the supremely lyrical John Gielgud has been the role's greatest exponent. We can enjoy it as an aesthetic experience, a dramatized poem on the age-old themes of the transience of earthly glory and the conflict between worldly and spiritual values.

In its own time, however, it struck home with a topicality that may – or may not – have surprised its author. Ostensibly he was simply dramatizing chronicle history, selecting and arranging from (in this play) a surprisingly wide range of historical sources with his usual freedom, telling the story of the reign of Richard II in a manner that brings it in touch with general ideas and suggests matters of fundamental human concern beyond the particularities of history. Like the plays about Henry VI, but with more emphasis on the central character, *Richard the Second* is much concerned with kingship: with what it means to be a king, with the problems that face a man who has to bear the burden of kingship, to try to live up to its responsibilities and make proper use of its privileges. It is concerned too with the relationship between a king and his country, with the plight of a country that is weakly governed.

Although these are topics of general interest, they had particular significance at the time Shakespeare was writing. Queen Elizabeth was unmarried. In 1595 she was sixty-five years old. She had reigned indomitably for thirty-seven years, but there was no obvious heir; much anxiety was felt about who should succeed her. Voices were even raised proposing that the next ruler should be chosen for merit rather than on hereditary principles. Elizabeth was sometimes accused of being over-influenced by favourites, and for this reason was compared to Richard II. There was a fear that, like him, she might be deposed; and we know that this fear was specifically seen in relation to Shakespeare's play. It was first printed in 1597, not long after its composition, which in itself may suggest that it was regarded as topical; and in this edition the episode of Richard's abdication does not appear. The text appears to have been slightly adjusted so that the break was not too noticeable. There were two reprints in the following year, both lacking the abdication scene. Of course, it is still obvious that Richard gives up the throne, but some form of censorship, whether from outside or on the part of the actors themselves, seems to be responsible. And we know for certain that the play was used as a weapon in the political campaign because in 1601, on the eve of the Earl of Essex's unsuccessful rebellion against the Queen (for which he was to be executed), his supporters hired Shakespeare's company of actors to put on a special performance of *Richard the Second* at the Globe as a gesture of encouragement and defiance.

Obviously, then, the play was felt to be concerned with live political issues. Yet apparently, too, this concern was not felt to be specifically topical, for Shakespeare and his fellows were not punished for their share in the performance. Perhaps this is because Shakespeare was thought to transcend topicality and to write of historical events in a manner that is philosophical and poetical rather than political and topical. Or perhaps he was just lucky. The epilogue to this story is that when the fourth edition of the play appeared in 1608, after the problem of the succession had been resolved and King James was safely on the throne, the abdication episode appeared in print for the first time.

Richard the Second (along with *King John*) is the last of Shakespeare's plays to be written entirely in verse. This is one of the ways in which it looks backward to the earlier histories rather than forward to the later ones. It may help, too, to explain why, at a time of rapid development in dramatic conventions, Essex's supporters had to pay the Lord Chamberlain's Men '£2 more than their ordinary to play it' on 7

February 1601 because the actors regarded it as 'so old and so long out of use that they should have small or no company at it'.[1] Even low-ranking characters who might, in a different context, have been represented in prose are here given the dignity of verse. This confers choric status on them; they seem to be commenting on the action rather than taking part in it. An example is the Welsh Captain who, explaining why he can no longer keep his forces together to await the King's return from Ireland, utters a lament on the state of the country and a prophecy of further disaster:

> The bay trees in our country are all withered,
> And meteors fright the fixèd stars of heaven.
> The pale-faced moon looks bloody on the earth,
> And lean-looked prophets whisper fearful change . . .
>
> (2.4.8–11)

The most obviously choric scene of all (3.4) is that of the gardeners, their occupation part of the metaphor that compares England to a garden. Shakespeare uses their language to reinforce the metaphor, already employed several times in the play, and now fully extended and developed:

> our sea-wallèd garden, the whole land,
> Is full of weeds, her fairest flowers choked up,
> Her fruit trees all unpruned, her hedges ruined,
> Her knots disordered, and her wholesome herbs
> Swarming with caterpillars.
>
> (3.4.44–8)

As a literary expression of the state of the kingdom these lines of beautifully controlled, measured blank verse are fine; as drama they pose problems. Actors playing the gardeners frequently characterize them as comic rustics, dressing and speaking like the gravediggers in *Hamlet* (who of course speak characterful prose), thus drawing attention to themselves, or to the characters they are playing, and away from the meaning of the scene. This is undesirable; but the alternative, to play them as exceptionally well-bred and literate gentlemen who just happen to have taken up gardening as a living, sacrifices any sense of reality of the speakers as people. When I was editing the play I did a little research on the gardeners of great Elizabethan estates, thinking they might perhaps have been the equivalent of modern professors of botany, but was not too convinced by what I found. So I thought John Barton hit upon an ingenious solution in his 1973 production in making them monks: intelligent and literate people who might (as Browning shows in his 'Soliloquy of the Spanish Cloister') also be full-time gardeners.

This scene represents at an extreme level a procedure that can be observed throughout the play, and which is very much bound up with Shakespeare's decision to write it entirely in verse, and in verse of a plangently lyrical, elegiac kind that seems almost to have been created for this play. Action as well as language is stylized. Shakespeare seems to be taking the representation of people and events, as of speech, as far away from a naturalistic mode as he dares, rigorously subordinating credibility of immediate effect to the patterns of imagery and thought that carry the play's deeper meanings. When Mowbray is banished, for instance, he reacts not with an idiosyncratic expression of his capacity to make the best of a bad job (like Kent in *King Lear*), or with a vivid expression of personal hatred and defiance (like Coriolanus), but with a meditation on the idea that in a foreign country his language will be of no use to him: not an entirely implausible reaction, but more important as one in a series of passages concerning the function and power of words, especially a sovereign's words, than as a personal reaction from Mowbray himself. Similarly only a little later, when Bolingbroke and his father, John of Gaunt, discuss the sentence that has been passed, their conversation soon becomes a philosophical discussion on the power of the imagination which is deeply relevant to one of the play's overriding concerns – for the King rules largely by his power over people's imaginations – but far from a naturalistic representation of a conversation between an old father and his newly banished son.[2]

Stress in the play's language on the symbolic aspects of the situations portrayed is paralleled by similarly calculated stylization of action. The scene showing Richard's return from Ireland, for instance, is based on a conventional design, that in which a sequence of messengers bring increasingly bad news. Richard speaks his most confident affirmation of the power of kingship:

> Not all the water in the rough rude sea
> Can wash the balm from an anointed king.
> The breath of worldly men cannot depose
> The deputy elected by the Lord.
> For every man that Bolingbroke hath pressed
> To lift shrewd steel against our golden crown,

God for his Richard hath in heavenly pay
A glorious angel. Then if angels fight,
Weak men must fall; for heaven still guards the right.
(3.2.50–8)

Immediately Salisbury enters to tell him that the Welsh army has defected to Bolingbroke. Richard consoles himself with the thought 'Is not the King's name forty thousand names?'; Scrope enters to report Bolingbroke's success in raising troops in England. Richard calls for his friends Bushy, Bagot, and Green, and learns that they are dead. And he speaks his great meditation on the mortality of kings, 'Of comfort no man speak . . .' (3.2.140 ff.). The action is un-historical; Shakespeare has compressed events that happened over a period of time at two different places, creating a structure that permits a poetic exploration of the polarities of Richard's confidence and despair.

Characters, too, are stylized: Richard's Queen is rather a foil for her husband than a person in her own right; Northumberland is primarily an embodiment of menace; John of Gaunt makes an impact because of his best-known speech, 'This royal throne of kings . . .' (2.1.31–68) – one of those speeches where the actor's main problem is in preventing the audience from singing along with him – but is pre-eminently a mouthpiece for certain ideals of kingship and national pride. There is, however, one supremely important figure and another who is little less so.

As well as being possibly the last of Shakespeare's all-verse plays, *Richard the Second* is also the last of his history plays to be cast in tragic form. Richard II is a kind of passive counterpart to the bustling Richard III. Richard III makes his way to the throne by way of a series of assassinations; Richard II cedes his throne while seeming to make hardly any effort to hang on to it. He and Bolingbroke are like the figures on a weather clock: as one goes in, the other comes out; and, it would seem, with as little exercise of will-power.

Richard fluctuates in his demands on the audience's sympathy. At the start, where he is much seen but little heard, this is left partly to the actor's discretion. The opening quarrel between Bolingbroke and Mowbray is about the murder of Richard's uncle, Thomas of Woodstock, Duke of Gloucester. Historically Richard was deeply implicated in this murder, but Shakespeare leaves the matter vague: F.R. Benson, a famous Richard in the early years of the century, had Richard caress and feed hounds here in bored indifference; later in the play one of the hounds was seen to have transferred allegiance to Bolingbroke. But it would be equally valid to show Richard's silence as the reverse of indifference – rather a careful reticence in case anything he said might be used in evidence against him. In the second scene John of Gaunt declares that he believes Richard guilty, though he holds the kingly office in such respect that he will do nothing to bring the King's guilt to light. This helps to build up sympathy with Bolingbroke, because of the apparent justice of his accusations against Mowbray; and the audience's respect for Richard is undermined in the first scene in which we see him in his private capacity (1.4), in which he admits he has been extravagant and speaks with callous indifference about his uncle's illness; Gaunt's subsequent evocation of what England should be serves as a measure of Richard's disqualifications for the kingly office.

Here we see Richard at his worst. By the time he returns from his Irish campaign the tide of fortune has begun to turn against him, and Shakespeare slowly reinstates him in our favour, encouraged perhaps by Holinshed, who observed in his chronicle how remarkable it was that Bolingbroke should have been advanced to the throne, 'and that King Richard should thus be left desolate, void, and in despair of all hope and comfort, in whom if there were any offence it ought rather to be imputed to the frailty of wanton youth than to the malice of his heart'.[3] Next time the matter of Gloucester's murder is raised it is in the gages scene (4.1) where, though it is taken for granted that Richard instigated the murder, the focus is on the question of whether Mowbray or Aumerle was responsible for executing his orders. Aumerle's vehement denials may be designed to help Richard's cause in the audience's eyes just before he makes great demands on our sympathy in the deposition scene. Shakespeare seems to be manipulating our awareness of historical events, pushing one interpretation forward at one point in the play and a different one at another point according to the needs of the dramatic situation.

It is characteristic of this play of non-events that Richard finally capitulates not to actions but to threats and words. Deprived of kingship, the man who held the office loses also his sense of identity. Although Richard has many solo speeches, so long as he is king they are public speeches. Not until after he has been deposed do we see him speaking not for effect but to himself alone, in prison where he meditates on his solitude. Lacking a public role he has to try to define his true self. He thinks of religious salvation, but realizes the difficulty of attaining it. He thinks of escape, but knows it is impossible. He considers resignation to his fate, and in this thought finds 'a kind of ease'. But none of the roles in which he casts himself satisfies him, because each recalls its opposite:

> Sometimes am I king;
> Then treason makes me wish myself a beggar,
> And so I am. Then crushing penury
> Persuades me I was better when a king.
> Then am I kinged again, and by and by
> Think that I am unkinged by Bolingbroke,
> And straight am nothing.

Contentment, it seems, can come only with oblivion:

> But whate'er I be,
> Nor I, nor any man that but man is,
> With nothing shall be pleased till he be eased
> With being nothing.
>
> (5.5.32–41)

In these lines Richard matures into the status of a tragic hero. He is using his imagination now not to escape from reality but in the effort to accept and so to master it. There is a new toughness about his language in his last scene; he speaks like a man who has come through suffering rather than being vanquished by it. He has developed, we might say, from a lyrical to a metaphysical poet.

The final twist of pathos comes with the entry of the Groom, who has with difficulty got permission to visit his old master, but saddens him with the story of how Richard's horse carried the usurper Bolingbroke to his coronation. The common people have few representatives in the play; the Groom is one of them, and his final allegiance to his master helps to bind us to Richard in his last moments.

In the late stages of *Richard the Second* Shakespeare introduces an episode that looks forward to what is to come. Bolingbroke, the newly crowned Henry IV, asks for news of his 'unthrifty son' Prince Hal and, in words that briefly prefigure the rest of the tetralogy, learning that he is 'As dissolute as desperate', manages nevertheless to 'see some sparks of better hope, which elder days | May happily bring forth' (5.3.1–22). The new king bears his responsibilities heavily; claiming that he had not sought Richard's death he banishes his murderer as Richard had banished him, and ends the play a penitent man, determined to 'make a voyage to the Holy Land'.

Shakespeare seems to have had more direct trouble with the censors over *Henry the Fourth, Part One*. First acted, probably, in 1596, it reached print two years later, but the first edition survives only in a single fragment of eight pages. It was reprinted in the same year, and five more editions appeared before the 1623 Folio. The printing of two editions within a few months, and the fact that one of them was read almost out of existence, reflect the great interest in the play both in itself and as a topic of scandal centring on its main comic character.

The earliest title-page advertises the play's portrayal of 'the humorous conceits of Sir John Falstaff', but we know from various pieces of evidence that when it was first acted this character bore the name of his historical counterpart, the Protestant martyr Sir John Oldcastle; a pun on his name survives in his opening scene, when the Prince calls him 'my old lad of the castle' (1.2.41–2). Shakespeare changed his surname as the result of protests from his descendants, the influential Cobham family, one of whom – William Brooke, seventh Lord Cobham – was Elizabeth's Lord Chamberlain, and thus involved with theatrical matters, from August 1596 until he died on 5 March 1597. Oldcastle had already been portrayed as a reprobate in a play called *The Famous Victories of Henry V* which Shakespeare must have known, although it was not printed until 1598, and then in a debased and shortened text; but this did not exempt him from criticism. Awareness of the character's origins adds to the play's historical resonances. The name Oldcastle was restored in the Oxford edition of 1986 because we felt that among all the hundreds of editions of the play there should be one, at least, in which the character had his original name, but I shall use Falstaff here because Shakespeare continued to use this name in *Henry the Fourth, Part Two* as well as in *The Merry Wives of Windsor*.

At the opening of *Henry the Fourth, Part One* the new king declares it is a year since he resolved to make a crusade to the Holy Land; he is still as melancholy as he was at the end of *Richard the Second*, but this play is to be very different from its predecessor. During the later part of the 1590s, after writing *Richard the Second* and *King John*, Shakespeare turned away from tragedies and tragical histories; the three English history plays that he wrote during the same period as his romantic comedies are imbued with the comic spirit. In them his imagination seems to play even more creatively over the matter of history, with less didacticism and greater artistic freedom. If in *Richard the Second* he seems deliberately to have been limiting his stylistic range, in *Henry the Fourth, Part One* and its successors he revels in his command of a wide range of styles in both verse and prose and of the opportunities it affords him for suggesting idiosyncrasy of character through language. The difference in dramatic mode is striking, as if he suddenly felt a sense of release, of joy in the power of words to project his pleasure in human diversity. As a result the plays are full of rich character parts, large and small, from Falstaff to Francis the Drawer.

The plays are strongly influenced, too, by comic form. Thus, for instance, in *Henry the Fourth, Part One* the King is anguished by both filial and national rebellion; just as in *A Midsummer Night's Dream* Oberon and Titania must be reconciled before the mortals' course of love can run smooth, so the dissolute Prince Harry (or Hal) must reform and be reconciled with his father before rebellion can be put down. In the opening scene the King, after learning of civil troubles both in Wales and in the North which make him realize that he will have to postpone his plans for a crusade, reiterates the complaints about his son that we heard in *Richard the Second*, and contrasts him with Henry Percy, known as Hotspur, who had made a brief appearance in the earlier play. The parallel that Shakespeare draws between these young men is unhistorical, as in fact Hotspur was 'two years older than the King and twenty-three years older than Hal',[4] but it provides him with one of the play's structural foundations.

Before we see either of them the King, wishing 'that it could be proved | That some night-tripping fairy had exchanged | In cradle-clothes our children where they lay', has complained that 'riot and dishonour stain the brow' of his son whereas Hotspur is 'the theme of honour's tongue' (1.1.80–7). 'Honour' is to be very much a key word of this play, a concept we are invited to think about in a variety of contexts. Harry is, in the King's eyes, demeaning himself by associating with Falstaff and his tavern-mates, and the second scene shows them in action, with the Prince agreeing for once to 'be a madcap' by joining Falstaff in a robbery by ambush while concocting with his friends Poins a counterplot to rob the robbers: as Poins says, 'The virtue of this jest will be the incomprehensible lies that this same fat rogue will tell us when we meet at supper: how thirty at least he fought with, what wards, what blows, what extremities he endured; and in the reproof of this lives the jest' (1.2.183–7). Left alone, Harry delivers a soliloquy in which he reveals a different side of himself: although for the present he will 'uphold the unyoked humour' of his companions' 'idleness', he intends later to 'throw off' his 'loose behaviour', believing that the more dramatic his reformation appears, the greater the impression it will create:

> I'll so offend to make offence a skill,
> Redeeming time when men least think I will.
>
> (1.2.213–14)

This speech has been variously interpreted. It may be thought to portray the Prince as a coldly calculating young man, willing to have fun with his friends as long as it suits his purposes while being ready to cast them off at the moment that suits him best: he is 'the sun', they 'the foul and ugly mists | Of vapours that did seem to strangle him'. More charitably, the speech has been seen less as an expression of the Prince's personal feelings than as a conventionalized means by which the dramatist can speak through his character, 'assuring his English audience that this wayward young Prince will emerge untarnished as the splendid King Harry of fame and at the same time . . . inviting them to detect certain ironies in later scenes which might otherwise pass unperceived'.[5] In any case it relates to a problem of which we will often be conscious during this and the two succeeding plays, and which is of permanent interest: the extent to which, in educating himself to be effective in a position of power, a man may have to deny certain aspects of his own humanity. To interpret the plays allegorically is to oversimplify them, but there are elements of the morality pattern in them, and, as the Prince himself indicates, there is a sense in which the red-blooded, amoral behaviour of his companions represents that side of himself which has to be subordinated if he is to achieve the self-control required of a king. 'Ordinary' people play a much greater part in these plays than in the earlier histories, and although this is in part a result of the decision to adopt the plot/subplot conventions of comic form, in part it is also surely a reason for doing so.

Learning of the Prince's part in the Gadshill robbery, the King confronts him with his follies and claims that he, on his way to the throne, had been 'seldom seen' until the right moment, when he 'stole all courtesy from heaven, | And dressed myself in such humility | That I did pluck allegiance from men's hearts' (3.2.50–2); but it is typical of Shakespeare's moral complexity that what the King sees as a virtue in himself has already been scorned by Hotspur in his criticism of what he regards as the hypocritical wiles of 'this king of smiles', 'This fawning greyhound' (1.3.244, 247). Yet Henry uses the successes in war of 'this Hotspur, Mars in swaddling-clothes' (3.2.112) as a rod for Harry's back, accusing his son of being his 'near'st and dearest enemy' (3.2.123). The meeting between King and Prince who are also father and son provokes from Harry an eloquent self-defence with the promise to redeem his reputation in combat against Hotspur, a promise which he excitingly fulfils at the battle of Shrewsbury.

Hotspur is immensely attractive, and rather funny, in his impulsive impetuosity, and even the Prince's parody of him is not intolerant: 'I am not yet of Percy's mind, the Hotspur of the North – he that kills me some six or seven dozen of Scots at a breakfast, washes his hands, and says to his wife, "Fie upon this quiet life! I want work" ' (2.5.102–6). But his commitment to 'bright honour' is presented as an obsession that is in danger of preoccupying him to the exclusion of all else: 'He apprehends a world of figures here, | But not the form of what he should attend' (1.3.206–7). Shakespeare seems to be creating a pattern with Hotspur at one extreme, Harry somewhere around the middle, and at the other extreme, of course, Falstaff.

At least since Maurice Morgann wrote his fine *Essay on the Dramatic Character of Falstaff*, published in 1777, Falstaff has led a life independent of the plays for which he was created. He has appeared in adaptations centred on him, such as Orson Welles's play *Chimes at Midnight* (1960; filmed in 1966) and in independent plays such as *Falstaff's Wedding* (by William Kenrick, 1760); he has been celebrated in essays by writers such as William Hazlitt, A.C. Bradley, and J.B. Priestley, in a gargantuan novel by Robert Nye, and in Elgar's eloquent symphonic study of 1913; he has been the central figure in operas by composers as diverse as Antonio Salieri, Otto Nicolai, Ralph Vaughan Williams, and, supremely, Giuseppe Verdi, in the masterpiece of his old age, *Falstaff* (1893). His visual image, red-cheeked, white-bearded, fat-bellied, and big-booted, has been the subject of many paintings and of pieces of sculpture, has been propagated in porcelain, and has adorned inn signs and beer mats. The finer artists who have depicted him in different media have caught some of the complexity that belongs to a figure extrapolated in varying proportions from three different plays; but the stereotype has been of a rumbustious, fun-loving, womanizing, beer-swilling old rogue.

All these derivatives pay just tribute to the vitality of Shakespeare's imagination and verbal skill in 'creating' (as we say, using an image which is itself a tribute to the power of words) a figure which has had such an impact on other creative artists; but Shakespeare's greatness is no less evident in the fact that Falstaff is fully integral to the play in which he first appears. This is most subtly apparent in the first tavern scene (2.5), written almost entirely in prose, and one of the longest and most richly complex sustained stretches of dramatic action in all his works. The earlier part of the scene is pure comedy as the Prince and Poins bring to fruition their plot to expose Sir John's cowardice at Gadshill. The opportunism which, for better and for worse, is one of the fat knight's most salient characteristics is deployed in masterly fashion in his recovery, with his claim that he was a coward 'on instinct' (l. 276), but the tone darkens on his proposal to have 'a play extempore'.

In their scenes together Falstaff has repeatedly shown his awareness of his young friend's status as the future king, and has expressed his own hopes of benefiting from the succession. With characteristic enjoyment of paradox he, who may more easily be seen as a 'villainous, abominable misleader of youth' (467–8), claims that, on the contrary, it is he who has been misled by the Prince: 'I have forsworn his company hourly any time this two-and-twenty years, and yet I am bewitched with the rogue's company. If the rascal have not given me medicines to make me love him, I'll be hanged.' The relationship is not altogether easy; actors can suggest complex subcurrents of affection, exploitation, even sexuality, on both sides. The Prince and Falstaff are boon companions, yet Falstaff is an old man; he may be giving the Prince some of the intimacy that the King cannot provide, but though they may mock the King in his absence he is a figure of authority to be feared, too. The Prince allows Falstaff to dispatch the King's messenger without seeing him himself, and they jest about the 'villainous news' he brings of the massing of the rebel forces whose leaders include Hotspur, but Falstaff realizes that the Prince may be 'horribly afraid' and that 'thou wilt be horribly chid tomorrow when thou comest to thy father'. Their enactment of this interview in advance of its happening is, as the Hostess says, 'excellent sport, i'faith', but behind the role-playing is a reality that rises slowly to the surface until, with Sir John's climactic 'banish plump Jack, and banish all the world' the Prince acknowledges the truth of the situation with 'I do; I will'. Actors vary in the weight they give to these words, but inevitably the line, and the knocking at the door that follows, cloud the mirthful scene no less fatefully than the entrance of Mercadé at the climax of a similarly long stretch of comic action in *Love's Labour's Lost.*

The tone of hilarity briefly returns, but there is a new sobriety in the Prince as, rising to the dignity of verse for the first time since his early soliloquy, he deals diplomatically with the Sheriff's charges, finally promising that 'The money shall be paid back again, with advantage'. The sun is beginning to emerge from the mists. In the mean time, Falstaff snores behind the arras.

In peace Falstaff is an immensely beguiling figure, but war reveals a darker side to his opportunism, as if Shakespeare were helping us to sympathize with the Prince's inevitable rejection of his values. The strong element of caricature in Falstaff's account of his ragged regiment, 'the cankers of a calm world and a long peace', may mitigate the callousness and selfishness that lie behind his recruiting methods, and we may laugh at the pragmatism of his soliloquy on honour: 'Can honour set-to a leg? No. Or an arm? No. Or take away the grief of a wound? No. Honour hath no skill in surgery, then? No. What is honour? A word. What is in that word "honour"? What is that "honour"? Air' (5.1.131–5). We can hardly fail to enjoy his genius for self-preservation as he plays dead in order to save his life in combat with the Douglas and 'riseth up' in horror at the thought that he may be 'disembowelled' after hearing Harry speak his own epitaph; this is a marvellous moment for the actor. But it is not easy to admire him as, immediately afterwards, he stabs the dead body of Hotspur in the thigh and then claims that he, not the Prince, has killed him. Shakespeare's patterning of his material is clear as we simultaneously see Falstaff at his worst and the Prince at his best.

When we first hear of the play that we know as *Henry the Fourth, Part One*, which is the title it bears in the Folio, it is as *The History of Henry the Fourth*. There is nothing to indicate that Shakespeare originally thought of it as the first part of a two–part play, though it does not bring the story of the King to a conclusion. *Part Two*, on the other hand, was printed in 1600 as *The Second Part of Henry the Fourth*, and bears all the marks of a sequel. This must be partly why it is less often performed than the earlier play. In imaginative range it is in no way inferior, in moral complexity and linguistic subtlety it may even be regarded as superior, but it is less obviously a self-contained unit than *Part One,* which can therefore more easily be played on its own.

The action of the opening scenes, dealing with the aftermath of the battle of Shrewsbury, is far more obviously continuous of the play that has preceded it than the opening scenes of *Henry the Fourth, Part One* are of *Richard the Second*. But there are elements of repetition from the earlier play. The King has even more causes of anxiety, and is still planning his pilgrimage to the Holy Land. He is again the victim of rebellion, led this time by the Earl of Northumberland, the Archbishop of York, and the Lords Hastings and Mowbray (son of the Mowbray of *Richard the Second*), and again his public responsibilities are exacerbated by his eldest son's behaviour.

The Prince seems to have regressed from the reformed state in which we saw him at the end of the previous play. Early on we see the Lord Chief Justice 'that committed the Prince [to prison] for striking him about Bardolph' in censorious conversation with Falstaff, accusing him of having 'misled the youthful Prince' – to which Falstaff again replies with the accusation that 'The young Prince hath misled me' – and informing us by the way that 'the King hath severed you and Prince Harry'. We do indeed see them together less in this play, and the Prince is more clearly troubled in conscience about his relationship with his father. Again the Prince has to work through a reconciliation with his father, this time on his death-bed.

The King of this play is not merely melancholy but ill, and this colours the tone of the whole play. We see him first (3.1) in his nightgown meditating on the burdens of kingship, contrasting his insomnia with the peaceful sleep of his 'poorest subjects', even the ship-boy who can go to sleep in the crow's-nest during a violent storm – it is yet another variation on the pastoral ideal enunciated by Henry VI. 'Uneasy lies the head that wears a crown', he concludes. He appears in only one other scene (4.3), in which he is already on his death-bed. There his attitude to his eldest son is ambivalent; he pays generous tribute to his virtues while reiterating his regret at the bad company he keeps. This draws from the Earl of Warwick an explicit statement of the claim that

> The Prince but studies his companions,
> Like a strange tongue, wherein, to gain the language,
> 'Tis needful that the most immodest word
> Be looked upon and learnt . . .
>
> (4.3.68–71)

So, says Warwick, voicing in commendation what some have seen as the unfavourable interpretation of the Prince's 'I know you all' soliloquy in *Part One*, 'The Prince will in the perfectness of time | Cast off his followers'. When at last the sick King sleeps the Prince enters and, supposing him dead, takes away the crown he believes he has already inherited. The subsequent episode of bitter rebuke, explanation, regret, and reconciliation culminates in the dying King's expression of anxiety about the 'bypaths and indirect crook'd ways' by which he came to the throne and in his advice to Harry 'to busy giddy minds with foreign quarrels', thus looking both back to *Richard the Second* and forward to *Henry the Fifth*. Although the Prince expresses confidence in the rightness of his claim to the throne, doubts will remain. The King's ambition to go to the Holy Land is ironically recalled as he is carried off to die in the Jerusalem Chamber of Westminster Abbey.

The relationship between the King and the Prince provides an emotional centre which gives the play some of the tone of a tragicomedy, and though it has much comedy centring on Falstaff and his tavern-companions, its distinctive quality derives above all from an emphasis on illness and on regret for the past that permeates serious and comic scenes alike. In the opening scene Hotspur's father, the Earl of Northumberland, is 'crafty-sick'; when Falstaff first appears, at the opening of the next scene, he is asking his page what opinion the doctor has expressed of his urine; and throughout the play we hear more of his age, infirmities, illnesses, and need to 'begin to patch up [his] old body for heaven' (2.4.234–5) than we had in *Part One*; his 'immortal part', too, 'needs a physician' (2.2.97). It is clearer, too, than in the earlier play that the tavern he frequents is also a brothel, and a place where disease may be caught (2.4.43–4). His relationship with his whore (as Poins calls her), Doll Tearsheet, is grotesquely poignant; the Prince and Poins look upon it with detached distaste: 'Look whe'er the withered elder hath not his poll clawed like a parrot. . . . Is it not strange that desire should so many years outlive performance?' – but Shakespeare also makes us see it from the old lovers' point of view:

SIR JOHN Thou dost give me flattering busses.
DOLL By my troth, I kiss thee with a most constant heart.
SIR JOHN I am old, I am old.
DOLL I love thee better than I love e'er a scurvy young boy of them all.

And at the end of the scene Shakespeare asks for a rare degree of wordless expressiveness from his performers as, in response to the news that Falstaff has called for Doll, Mistress Quickly urges her: 'O run, Doll; run, run, good Doll!'

Sickness afflicts the nation as well as individuals: 'The commonwealth is sick', and 'we are all diseased', says the Archbishop (1.3.87, 4.1.54), and the King observes 'what rank diseases grow' in 'the body of our kingdom' (3.1.37–8). The past is often nostalgically recalled: Lady Percy movingly recalls that 'miracle of men' her husband, Hotspur (2.3.18–45); the King regretfully remembers the time when his present enemy 'Percy was the man nearest my soul' and, quoting from *Richard the Second*, recalls Richard's prophecy in self-exculpating terms:

> 'Northumberland, thou ladder by the which
> My cousin Bolingbroke ascends my throne' –
> Though then, God knows, I had no such intent,
> But that necessity so bowed the state
> That I and greatness were compelled to kiss –
> 'The time shall come' – thus did he follow it –
> 'The time will come that foul sin, gathering head,
> Shall break into corruption'; so went on,
> Foretelling this same time's condition,
> And the division of our amity.
>
> (3.1.65–74)

And Mowbray recalls and describes the abortive tournament in *Richard the Second,* in which his father and Bolingbroke had prepared to fight (4.1.111–27).

Nostalgic recollection is in part a method of self-examination, an exercise of conscience in the effort to apportion responsibility and, if possible, to exorcize guilt. It is more poetically also an exploration of the effects of the passage of time on people, and it is typical of Shakespeare's technique at this stage in his career that the most emotionally subtle and complex passages concerned with this theme are written in prose which is simultaneously funny and touching in a way that, outside Shakespeare, we are most likely to associate with Chekhov. Our sense of the reality of the present is enhanced by recollections of the past, especially in the scenes set in Justice Shallow's Gloucestershire orchard where Shallow's romanticized memories of his youth – 'Jesu, Jesu, the mad days that I have spent!' – are counterpointed with Falstaff's exploitative reductionism which yet also rebounds back upon himself: 'Lord, Lord, how subject we old men are to this vice of lying! This same starved justice hath done nothing but prate to me of the wildness of his youth and the feats he hath done about Turnbull Street; and every third word a lie . . .' (3.2.298 ff.). A sense of the imminence of death permeates these scenes, but the present continues to make its demands, too: 'And to see how many of my old acquaintance are dead. . . . We shall all follow, cousin. . . . Certain, 'tis certain; very sure, very sure. Death, as the Psalmist saith, is certain to all; all shall die. How a good yoke of bullocks at Stamford fair?' (3.2.32–7).

Henry the Fourth, Part Two is to end not with the death of an old king but with the coronation of a new one. The matter of the education of a prince, the subjugation of natural humanity in the interests of decisive leadership, remains important. The most decisive and successful leader in this play, Prince John, is also its least attractive character. He achieves victory over the rebel forces by a coldly calculated trick, deceiving their leaders into dismissing their armies in the belief that a peace has been concluded and then arresting them on a charge of high treason. It is easy to warm to Falstaff's complaint: 'this same young sober-blooded boy doth not love me, nor a man cannot make him laugh. But that's no marvel; he drinks no wine.' He takes a contrasting view of Prince Harry – 'the cold blood he did naturally inherit of his father he hath, like lean, sterile, and bare land, manured, husbanded, and tilled, with excellent endeavour of drinking good, and good store, of fertile sherry' – but he is mistaken; as the Prince of Wales comes closer to the throne, so he comes more closely to resemble his younger brother.

The Lord Chief Justice, whom we have not seen since early in the play, becomes a touchstone for the new king's qualities in its closing stages. The Prince had boxed his ears and been sent to prison for it; his brother the Duke of Clarence warns the Justice that now he will have to 'speak Sir John Falstaff fair', but the new king, after hearing the Justice's dignified self-defence, confirms him in office with the promise: 'You shall be as a father to my youth.' Acknowledging that 'The tide of blood in me | Hath proudly flowed in vanity till now', he declares his intention to 'mock the expectation of the world, | To frustrate prophecies, and to raze out | Rotten opinion, who hath writ me down | After my seeming' (5.2.117, 125–8). Among those whose expectations will be mocked are Falstaff and his friends. In Gloucestershire, time seems to stand still as songs are sung after supper 'in the sweet o'th' night'; but again the outside world breaks in with a knocking at the door, and an incoherently elated Pistol announces to Falstaff: '. . . thou art now one of the greatest men in this realm.' 'Blessed are they that have been my friends, and woe to my Lord Chief Justice', he says; but we already know better.

It is typical of the constantly, and disturbingly, shifting moral focus of this play that in its closing stages, just as in *Part One* we had seen Falstaff at his worst at the same time as the Prince at his most heroic, so here the spectacle of the new king's coronation, when we see him at his most dignified, is preceded by a sordid little episode in which beadles drag his former companions Mistress Quickly and Doll Tearsheet to prison. 'There hath been a man or two killed about' Doll, alleges the beadle; she is apparently feigning pregnancy with a cushion up her skirt to evade punishment. In performance this episode has been often omitted, perhaps because of its uncomfortable nature, but it makes a calculated contribution to the play's moral pattern. It is as if Shakespeare were warning us of the consequences of excessive tolerance: 'the man is dead that you and Pistol beat amongst you.' The end of the play counterpoints major and minor keys. Sir John and his friends have rushed up from the country to acclaim the King in his coronation procession, but as Falstaff cries, 'God save thee, my sweet boy', the King commands his old enemy the Lord Chief Justice to 'speak to that vain man'. Then, addressing him directly, he declares: 'I know thee not, old man', and speaks of their long friendship as a dream. He has turned away his former self and will similarly turn away those that kept him company. And the one who expresses approval of his banishment of his followers is his sober brother Prince John.

Henry the Fourth, Part Two ends with an epilogue presumably written by Shakespeare himself which speaks with exceptional directness of his and his company's intentions. 'If you be not too much cloyed with fat meat, our humble author will continue the story with Sir John in it, and make you merry with fair Catherine of France; where, for anything I know, Falstaff shall die of a sweat – unless already a be not killed with your hard opinions. For Oldcastle died a martyr, and this is not the man.' One reason for this may be the wish, or obligation, to insist that Falstaff, even under a changed name, does not represent the historical Oldcastle.

The epilogue must have been written when *Henry the Fifth* was still only in the planning stage; Sir John is to appear only as a memory in that play, though whether this was because audience appetite was cloyed we cannot tell. The play itself contains an unusually explicit allusion to current events which enables us to be pretty sure when it was written: the Chorus to Act 5 says:

> Were now the General of our gracious Empress –
> As in good time he may – from Ireland coming,
> Bringing rebellion broachèd on his sword,
> How many would the peaceful city quit
> To welcome him!

The 'General' must be the Earl of Essex, whose 'Empress', Elizabeth, had sent him on an Irish campaign on 27 March 1599; he returned, disgraced, on 28 September, so probably Shakespeare wrote his play in the spring of 1599. It was printed in a corrupt text in 1600.

Like *Richard the Third, Henry the Fifth* is very much the culmination of a series; like that play, it gains in resonance if we are aware of what has gone before. But, also like *Richard the Third*, it can (with perhaps a few textual adjustments) stand on its own, as the success not only of numerous productions independent of the rest of the sequence but also of two major feature films, by Laurence Olivier and Kenneth Branagh, demonstrates. It contains more obvious ingredients for popular success than its predecessors. Though it is a sequel to them in that it continues the story of the Prince of Wales, he is now king, and we are to witness his apotheosis. Here at last is a play with a real hero: not the saintly but ineffectual Henry VI, the lively but villainous Richard III, the devious John, the passive Richard II, the melancholy, conscience-ridden Henry IV, but a young, active, strong, inspiring but thoughtful warrior king who, instead of having to concern himself with 'civil broils', is to lead a victorious campaign overseas. There are fewer indistinguishable nobles in this play, and a wide range of colourful character parts (including a Scotsman, an Irishman, and a Welshman); there is also a love-story, and a resoundingly happy ending.

Henry V was a great national hero to Shakespeare's contemporaries, especially because of his successes against the traditional enemy, France. Referring presumably to an earlier play, Thomas Nashe had written in 1592 of 'what a glorious thing it is to have Henry the Fifth represented on the stage leading the French King prisoner and forcing both him and the Dauphin to swear fealty'[6]; and the play of *Henry the Sixth, Part One*, written round about the same time, opens with an impressive sequence of funeral tributes to this 'king blest of the King of Kings'. The main exponent of this point of view within the play of *Henry the Fifth* is the Chorus, who never speaks less than adoringly of 'the mirror of all Christian kings', 'this grace of kings', 'This star of England'.

The Chorus's well-known apologies for the inability of the Elizabethan theatre to represent 'The vasty fields of France' need not be taken too seriously; after all, its inadequacies were no more evident in *Henry the Fifth* than in many other plays. The effect is rather to glorify the subject-matter of this particular play, to confer epic grandeur on the familiar story, partly perhaps through the classical associations of the device itself; it draws attention to a neo-classical employment of five-act structure in the layout of the narrative. Often in other plays Shakespeare makes us conscious of the artifices of presentation, but only in *Pericles* elsewhere is a chorus figure so prominent throughout the action, and there the presenter is the characterized figure of 'ancient Gower', the poet. Here, the Chorus is anonymous, and is usually played so in the theatre. Whereas the Chorus speeches in *Romeo and Juliet* are often given to the Prince, and the Prologue to *Troilus and Cressida* is usually spoken by one or other of the play's characters, the Chorus here is always thought of as an anonymous presenter, or perhaps as Shakespeare himself. From 1859, when Charles Kean cast his wife as the Chorus (in the figure of 'Clio, a Muse'), until at least 1928, when Sybil Thorndike took the part, these speeches were regularly spoken by a woman, and this is a practice that could usefully be resumed. What is certain is that whoever takes the part must be an accomplished verse speaker, for the choruses are among the chief literary as well as dramatic glories of the play, and one of their main functions is to express the popular perception of Henry as a national hero.

Nevertheless, the action presents a Henry who does not conform simply and easily to the Chorus's view of him. In spite of having written of his youthful indiscretions in the two preceding plays, Shakespeare does not allow us to forget them in this one; rather is it seen as a virtue in him that he has passed beyond them. In the opening scene the Archbishop of Canterbury, no less, declares that at the very moment of his father's death

> Consideration like an angel came
> And whipped th'offending Adam out of him,
> Leaving his body as a paradise
> T'envelop and contain celestial spirits.

More surprisingly still, it turned him into a 'sudden scholar'. In preparation no doubt for the oratory to come, the Archbishop makes much of Henry's new-found rhetorical skill, which is such

> that when he speaks
> The air, a chartered libertine, is still,
> And the mute wonder lurketh in men's ears
> To steal his sweet and honeyed sentences,

all the more remarkably considering his previous 'addiction to courses vain'. Henry's new seriousness of mind is amply demonstrated by the fact that he allows the Archbishop to complete his long and tedious discourse on the Salic laws, paraphrased from Holinshed with little effort of the imagination.

Henry's kingliness is put to the test by the arrival of the French Ambassador with a scornful message and a mocking gift of tennis balls from the Dauphin, to which he responds with his first great display of oratory:

> many a thousand widows
> Shall this his mock mock out of their dear husbands,
> Mock mothers from their sons, mock castles down;
> Ay, some are yet ungotten and unborn
> That shall have cause to curse the Dauphin's scorn.
> But this lies all within the will of God . . .
>
> (1.2.284 ff.)

Although the Dauphin continues to believe that England is 'idly kinged . . . By a vain, giddy, shallow, humorous youth' (2.4.26–8), the Ambassadors are convinced that he is 'too much mistaken in this king'. Henry's appeal to God is significant; throughout the play Shakespeare is careful to temper Henry's warriorliness with claims that he is God's agent. 'O God, thy arm was here' is his reaction to the news of the miraculously light casualties at Agincourt, and in many productions the departure at the end of the scene of the King and his war-stained soldiers singing together *'Non nobis'* and *'Te Deum'*, not required (though permitted) by the text, has been deeply moving.

Although the new King's former tavern-companions take part in the action, they are a dwindling band, and we are often made poignantly conscious of their redundancy to the King's present purposes. 'Now all the youth of England are on fire', says the Chorus to Act 2, and even Bardolph, Pistol, and Nim (who 'dare not fight, but . . . will wink and hold out mine iron' – in other words, keep his eyes shut and brandish his sword in front of him) are off to the wars. But Falstaff 'is very sick, and would to bed', and his old mates know who is to blame: 'The King has killed his heart', says Hostess Quickly. The comic tenderness of her account of his death immortalizes her as well as Falstaff. But Bardolph dies, not in battle but for stealing a 'pax of little price' (3.6.43), and Nim too is hanged, presumably also for stealing. Only Pistol, the born survivor, lives on, and he, says the boy who provides so touchingly shrewd a commentary on the rogues, would have gone the same way as the rest 'if he durst steal anything adventurously' (4.4.69–70).

Fluellen tells the King of Bardolph's crime before he is put to death in terms that might have induced clemency in a less resolute man:

> . . . the Duke hath lost never a man, but one that is like to be executed for robbing a church, one Bardolph, if your majesty know the man. His face is all bubuncles and whelks and knobs and flames o' fire, and his lips blows at his nose, and it is like a coal of fire, sometimes plue and sometimes red. But his nose is executed, and his fire's out.
>
> (3.6.100–7)

Actors have done much with the silence before the King speaks, but when he does his words are plain: 'We would have all such offenders so cut off'; he justifies his severity on the grounds that humane treatment of the French civilians will result in a speedier victory. The only one of his old companions whom he encounters personally is Pistol, and that is when the King is disguised; he offers no sign of recognition, even when Pistol speaks admiringly of him: 'The King's a bawcock and a heart-of-gold . . . I love the lovely bully' (4.1.45–9). The last mention of Falstaff comes from Fluellen in response to Captain Gower's claim that Henry, unlike Alexander the Great, 'never killed any of his friends'. No, says Fluellen, but there are grounds for comparison: 'As Alexander killed his friend Cleitus, being in his ales and his cups, so also Harry Monmouth, being in his right wits and his good judgements, turned away the fat knight with the great-belly doublet' (4.7.38–46) whose name Fluellen cannot remember. Fluellen's intention to point a contrast within the comparison backfires in the light of the Hostess's earlier statement that the King had killed Falstaff's heart.

The King's new-found eloquence which the Archbishop marvels at in the opening scene is shown to contribute largely to his successes in war. His speeches before Harfleur and at Agincourt have become the most admired pieces of war rhetoric in the language. Of course, not everybody likes them, any more than everybody likes 'Land of Hope and Glory' or 'Colonel Bogey'. It is difficult to admire either Henry V the man or *Henry the Fifth* the play without endorsing militaristic values, or at least responding to the theatrical portrayal of a man who embodies these values. In a century during which war has become increasingly abhorrent to civilized people, *Henry the Fifth* has often been either condemned for its ideology or defended with the claim that its portrayal of Henry is fundamentally ironic, that Shakespeare did not really believe what he seems to be saying. This has resulted in some interesting readings of a play which, like many others, carries within itself the possibility of conflicting interpretations.

Henry is stern with the noblemen who betray him as well as with Bardolph; he utters fearful threats to the Governor of Harfleur; at the extreme of provocation, he gives the order for every English soldier to kill his prisoners. Shakespeare might have made it easier for us to endorse Henry's attitude if he had given us more cause to condemn the French; perhaps he could too easily expect his original audiences to do this for him. But if Henry's attitude to war owes more to the Old Testament than to the New, it is shared by many people even at the present day, including some who might deplore it in theory while accepting it in practice; and even those who would dissociate themselves from the words of 'Land of Hope and Glory' may be carried away by its music. What is more, even the speech in which Henry threatens Harfleur shows him to be fully conscious of the horrors of 'impious war'.

Though he has cast off gross company, the King fights alongside his soldiers and, on the night before Agincourt, talks to them (admittedly in disguise) with an honesty unimaginable in Richard II and quite different from his father's 'courtship to the common people' (*Richard the Second*, 1.4.23). His conversation enhances his awareness of the kingly burden, and in a soliloquy which recalls a similar plaint by his father (*Henry the Fourth, Part Two*, 3.1.1–31) and anticipates (historically) one by his son (*Henry the Sixth, Part Three*, 2.4.1–54), he expresses it:

> I know
> 'Tis not the balm, the sceptre, and the ball,
> The sword, the mace, the crown imperial,
> The intertissued robe of gold and pearl,

The farcèd title running fore the king,
The throne he sits on, nor the tide of pomp
That beats upon the high shore of this world –
No, not all these, thrice-gorgeous ceremony,
Not all these, laid in bed majestical,
Can sleep so soundly as the wretched slave
Who with a body filled and vacant mind
Gets him to rest, crammed with distressful bread.

(4.1.256–67)

For all the extroversion of his public utterances, in private he too is a troubled ruler, anxious to expiate 'the fault | My father made in compassing the crown' (4.1.290–1).

Shakespeare's increasing use of comic form in his history plays reaches its climax in *Henry the Fifth*. It includes episodes of courtship and culminates, as comedies conventionally do, with a marriage, one that will unite realms as well as hearts. Shakespeare's confidence that his audience would understand enough French to enjoy the delightful scene in which Catherine is shown learning English (as well as Pistol's scene with the French Soldier, 4.4) should be enough to warn us against patronizing the 'groundlings'; there are few parallels for it in the rest of English drama.

This play too ends with an epilogue, written in the form of a sonnet. Having exhorted us throughout the play to piece out the actors' imperfections with our thoughts, the Chorus apologizes again for the 'rough and all-unable pen' with which his 'bending author hath pursued the story'. His attitude to Henry is still adulatory; he lived only a 'Small time, but in that small most greatly lived | This star of England'. And now, completing the circle, he looks poignantly forward to the dissipation of Henry's achievements in events that he and his fellows have already portrayed:

Henry the Sixth, in infant bands crowned king
　Of France and England, did this king succeed,
Whose state so many had the managing
　That they lost France and made his England bleed,
Which oft our stage hath shown – and, for their sake,
In your fair minds let this acceptance take.

Notes to Chapter Seven

1 The information comes from a deposition of one of the company's leading actors, Augustine Phillips, quoted by E.K. Chambers, *The Elizabethan Stage*, 4 vols (Oxford, 1923), vol. 2, p. 205. Though Phillips does not actually state that 'the play of the deposing and killing of King Richard the Second' played on this occasion was by Shakespeare, the circumstantial evidence is virtually conclusive.

2 The fact that the conversation between Bolingbroke and Gaunt is abbreviated in the Folio text suggests that Shakespeare and/or his colleagues came to feel that it was over-literary as originally written.

3 Modernized from Geoffrey Bullough's *Narrative and Dramatic Sources of Shakespeare*, vol. 3, pp. 401–2.

4 ibid., vol. 4, p. 156.

5 A.C. Sprague, *Shakespeare's Histories* (1964), pp. 55–6.

6 From *Pierce Penniless his Supplication to the Devil*, in *Thomas Nashe, Selected Writings*, ed. Stanley Wells (1964), p. 65.

EIGHT

Comedies of Venice, Messina, France, Illyria, and Windsor:

The Merchant of Venice, Much Ado About Nothing, As You Like It, Twelfth Night, and The Merry Wives of Windsor

Although the attempt to arrange Shakespeare's plays in groups often seems an artificial exercise, there is a conspicuous difference between his comedies up to *A Midsummer Night's Dream* and those written later, in that only the later ones include villainous characters among their cast lists.[1] In these plays the happiness of the comic ending is harder won; to this extent they are 'darker', more intensely romantic, and richer in poetic texture. Yet in them Shakespeare also uses a higher proportion of prose to verse. He is experimenting with conventions of language as well as of plot; it is not too paradoxical to say that some of the most poetical passages in these plays are written in prose; we have only to think, in *Much Ado About Nothing*, of Beatrice's response to Don Pedro's 'out o' question, you were born in a merry hour': 'No, sure, my lord,' she replies, 'my mother cried. But then there was a star danced, and under that was I born', or of speech after speech of Rosalind in *As You Like It*. By the time we reach *Twelfth Night*, however, the most lyrical writing is again in verse.

The first known reference to *The Merchant of Venice*, in 1598 – a year or two after it was written – tells us that it was 'otherwise called *The Jew of Venice*', suggesting that from the start Shylock was regarded as the play's central character. The alternative became the main title in the adaptation of the play of 1701 by George Granville, later Lord Lansdowne, in which it first reappeared after the closing of the theatres, and when Shakespeare's play returned to the London stage, in 1741, it was the triumph of Charles Macklin, playing, as Pope is said to have declared, 'the Jew that Shakespeare drew', that ensured its success. Since then it has never been out of the repertory for long, and has provided a star vehicle for many of the greatest actors not only in Britain but also on the Continent, in the United States, and still further afield; it has often been acted in translation, and there is even recorded a London production of 1919 in which Shylock was played – with resounding success – by a 74-year-old Dutch actor, in Dutch, while the rest of the cast spoke English, receiving their cues from the waving of a handkerchief in the wings by the leading actor's son.[2] Shylock has also taken on a life outside the play in which he appears; in popular parlance his name is synonymous with grasping miserliness.

Shylock's dominance is the more surprising in that the role is comparatively short; he appears in only five scenes. Although he figures in a comedy, most of the leading actors who have impersonated him have been associated especially with tragedy, and undoubtedly one of the reasons that the role has appealed to such actors is its capacity to generate intense emotion. Shylock is in many ways a repellent figure. As soon as the merchant, Antonio, appears, Shylock declares his implacable hatred of him behind his back while speaking ingratiatingly to his face. His servant, Lancelot Gobbo – a more entertaining character, we must hope, for Elizabethan audiences than actors usually succeed in making him today – regards him as 'the very devil incarnation'; his daughter Jessica is so unhappy that she runs away from home; as soon as he hears that Antonio has had losses he determines to insist on what he has previously called the 'merry bond' by which he will be permitted to take a pound of Antonio's flesh when his debts become due; learning of Jessica's flight with her lover Lorenzo he seems to grieve for the loss rather of his possessions than of his daughter and wishes she were dead; and when his suit against Antonio comes to trial he continues to insist on his right to his pound of flesh in face of all attempts at persuasion, and has his knife at the ready even as Portia comes out with the legal quibble that stays his arm.

All this makes for exciting theatre; the trial scene especially is a masterpiece of dramatic pacing. If this were all, Shylock might be no more than the villain of a melodrama, a Mr Punch who can make the audience laugh but whose downfall will only be applauded. But there is another side to Shylock: Antonio does not deny his accusations of racist brutality – 'You call me misbeliever, cut-

throat, dog, | And spit upon my Jewish gaberdine' – and Shylock
makes an eloquent speech of self-defence:

> He hath disgraced me, and hindered me half a million; laughed at
> my losses, mocked at my gains, scorned my nation, thwarted my
> bargains, cooled my friends, heated mine enemies, and what's his
> reason? – I am a Jew. Hath not a Jew eyes? Hath not a Jew hands,
> organs, dimensions, senses, affections, passions; fed with the
> same food, hurt with the same weapons, subject to the same
> diseases, healed by the same means, warmed and cooled by the
> same winter and summer as a Christian is? If you prick us do we
> not bleed? If you tickle us do we not laugh? If you poison us do
> we not die? And if you wrong us shall we not revenge?
>
> (3.1.50–62)

The logic of his conclusion is not impeccable, but this is a piece of
rhetoric, not a legal argument, and an audience may respond rather to
its eloquence than to its reasoning. The moral values of the role are
nicely balanced; directors may sway the audience's responses one way
or the other by production devices or even by making quite small cuts;
actors may emphasize either the comic or the sympathetic aspects of
Shylock.

A few actors have played the role for comedy; Dustin Hoffman, in a
production by Peter Hall (1989), emphasized its irony rather than its
passion; but most have preferred a more sympathetic interpretation,
even seeking tragic effect. Critics, too, have given Shylock their pity;
William Hazlitt – influenced perhaps by Edmund Kean's performance
– wrote:

> we can hardly help sympathizing with the proud spirit, hid
> beneath his 'Jewish gaberdine', stung to madness by repeated
> undeserved provocations, and labouring to throw off the load of
> obloquy and oppression heaped upon him and all his tribe by one
> desperate act of 'lawful' revenge, till the ferociousness of the
> means by which he is to execute his purpose, and the pertinacity
> with which he adheres to it, turn us against him; but even at last
> . . . we pity him, and think him hardly dealt with by his judges.[3]

A crucial point in the theatrical interpretation of the role is
Shylock's final exit. There is nothing obviously climactic about the
last words he speaks:

> I pray you give me leave to go from hence.
> I am not well. Send the deed after me,
> And I will sign it.

Then the Duke says: 'Get thee gone, but do it', and Graziano:

> In christ'ning shalt thou have two godfathers.
> Had I been judge thou shouldst have had ten more,
> To bring thee to the gallows, not the font.
>
> (4.1.392–7)

The text gives us no clue as to how Shylock might leave, and the scene continues equably after he has gone with no suggestion that those remaining have seen anything that might upset them. Yet many actors have chosen to give him a histrionic exit expressive of accumulated emotion. This was one of the most famous moments in Sir Henry Irving's enormously popular performance. A critic wrote:

> The quiet shrug, the glance of ineffable, unfathomable contempt
> at the exultant booby, Gratiano . . . the expression of defeat in
> every limb and feature, the deep, gasping sigh, as he passes
> slowly out, and the crowd rush from the Court to hoot and howl
> at him outside, make up an effect which must be seen to be
> comprehended.[4]

This was an ending that sought a tragic effect, not just by the way Irving spoke the words, by the body language with which he accompanied them, by the whole of his interpretation up to this moment, but also by action invented by the director (in this case no doubt Irving himself) – the action of the crowd's rushing from the court and hooting and howling at Shylock outside. In some performances Irving still further increased the tragic effect of his interpretation by omitting the whole of the last act of the play – in which of course Shylock does not appear. On the other hand Patrick Stewart, in a production by John Barton, portrayed not tragic suffering but a cringing self-abasement, whereas David Suchet, in a revival of the same production, 'chose a non-reacting end'. 'All he has is two lines. Shakespeare deliberately gives him nothing. So I decided not to react at all. I just stay kneeling. . . . The simplicity of the lines is what I play.'[5]

Since Shakespeare's time, and particularly during the past half-century, responses to both the role and the play as a whole have become complicated by racial issues. Shylock has been seen as a symbol of the Jewish race; the play has been regarded as anti-Semitic, or as being dangerously liable to arouse racial prejudice; some communities have banned it; sometimes Shylock's malevolence has been softened in the attempt to save Shakespeare's reputation.

Another way of doing this is to minimize the contrast between Christians and Jews. Although there is a temptation to play Shylock as a realistic character, the play is built on the implausibilities of folk-tale and legend; the story of the pound of flesh had often been told before Shakespeare wrote, and so had that of the beautiful maiden whose father's will dictates that she can be won only by a suitor who makes the right choice among three caskets. It is easy to see the play in terms of contrasts: between the scheming, miserly, legalistic Shylock and the beautiful, generous, merciful Portia; between their religions, Judaism and Christianity; between the money markets of Venice and the idealized landscape of Belmont; between the heights of lyrical poetry associated with the love-plot and the harshness of Shylock's prose. There are other tensions, too: the familiar conflict, in Bassanio, between love and friendship; the opposition, in the story of the caskets, between attractive but hollow superficiality and the rewards given to those 'that choose not by the view'.

But the play's oppositions, though strong, are not simple. The generous Bassanio has been extravagant. Is he also a fortune-hunter, as interested in Portia's money as in her character? Some interpreters have thought so. And what about his friend, Antonio? He is generous to Bassanio, but admits to having treated Shylock with a contempt that might be considered less than worthy of a Christian. And is his generosity to Bassanio entirely disinterested? Recent interpreters, on both page and stage, have read homosexuality into their relationship. Antonio is inexplicably melancholy in the play's opening; is this because he knows he is losing Bassanio to a woman? And if so, does this reduce his moral stature? And could there be any hint that Bassanio is exploiting their relationship in asking Antonio for money in order to further his suit of Portia? In Bill Alexander's 1987 Stratford production, there was no doubt that Antonio's melancholy stemmed from frustrated desire for Bassanio: he reeled as Bassanio spoke in praise of Portia, and kissed him with despairing passion but little response as they parted. In this production, indeed, even Salanio and Salerio (those unmemorable characters known in the theatre as the Salads) were given to kissing each other, presumably to suggest decadence in Venice.

Even Portia is not immune to criticism. She has often been praised as the first of Shakespeare's great romantic heroines. Certainly she provides a worthy antagonist to Shylock, and offers a role that has been as attractive to actresses as Shylock has to actors. It is a richly varied role, ingeniously contrived in its pertness and wit for the boy who must first have played it, but offering also opportunities for sensuous elegance to the actresses who have succeeded him. And in her plea to Shylock to show mercy Portia speaks lines that have caused her to be exalted almost as a saint; Dover Wilson called her 'quality of mercy' speech 'one of the greatest sermons in all literature, an expression of religious thought worthy to set beside St. Paul's hymn in praise of Love'.[6] But perhaps she is not quite such a paragon of virtue as this might suggest. We may forgive her gentle mockery of her first unsuccessful suitor, the affected Prince of Aragon, but in our time, at least, her remark on the discomfited departure of the black candidate for her hand, the Prince of Morocco – 'A gentle riddance . . . Let all of his complexion choose me so' (2.7.78–9) – may raise eyebrows (and is often omitted), and at the trial she has to adopt Shylock's legalism to achieve her ends, good though these are.

The play's openness to interpretation has been theatrically fruitful; we can expect a different experience each time we see it. We may go partly in the hope of experiencing a great Shylock, but a disadvantage of the tradition of treating this as a star role, and especially of building up his final exit as a grand climax, is that it spoils Shakespeare's delicate transition from Venice to Belmont and reduces the impact of the last act, giving rise to accusations that the play is broken-backed. This is a pity because the moonlit love-duet between Christian Lorenzo and Jewish Jessica with which the act begins is as exquisite in its phrasing as the vocal and orchestral harmonies which Vaughan Williams created for his setting of part of it in his 'Serenade to Music', and also because the comedy resulting from the revelation that Portia and her maid Nerissa had been disguised as the lawyer Balthasar and his clerk is integral to a play that is much concerned with the values by which men live. From Shylock's false evaluation of the power of money has come something not far off tragedy; from Aragon's and Morocco's over-evaluation, the one of fine appearances, the other of his own merits, has come comic discomfiture; now from the value that Portia and Nerissa insist that their lovers should place upon their love-tokens comes a delicate and touching game of high comedy. The ring, protests Graziano, was of no value; yet, says Nerissa, it meant much to her:

> What talk you of the posy or the value?
> You swore to me when I did give it you
> That you would wear it till your hour of death,
> And that it should lie with you in your grave.
>
> (5.1.151–4)

And Portia teases her husband in the same way. The comic game uses as its counters the fragility of human happiness, the relativity of values; for a while Portia and Nerissa pretend to be insisting, as Shylock had done, on the letter of the law, but then they relent, as Portia had begged him to do, and the play comes to an elegant if mildly bawdy end with Graziano's ribaldry:

> while I live I'll fear no other thing
> So sore as keeping safe Nerissa's ring.

But a final question remains. What happens to Antonio? His worldly fortunes are mended with all the implausibility characteristic of a comic ending, but how does he stand in relation to the lovers? Do they include him in their happiness as they go off the stage? Does he go off by a different exit? Does he stay alone on stage until the lights have gone down? Or until one of the lovers – which one? – returns to persuade him to join them? And in any case, how does he feel?

We can only find out by going to see the next production.

As if in acknowledgement of the dangers inherent in Shylock's three-dimensionality, Don John, the self-confessed villain ('it must not be denied but I am a plain-dealing villain' [1.3.29–30]) of *Much Ado About Nothing*, is more obviously a mere cog in the plot-mechanism. But whereas Shylock's plot against Antonio is, however narrowly, averted, Don John succeeds in causing 'the most exquisite Claudio' to repudiate his bride at the altar and thus brings about her apparent death. With this play we move towards tragicomedy, yet it is also one of the most delightfully entertaining that Shakespeare wrote. Like *The Taming of the Shrew*, it presents contrasting attitudes to love, and as in that play it is those who sceptically question romantic attitudes who convince us that they have achieved the more enduring relationship.

Although technically the love-affair between Claudio and Hero forms the main plot, it is presented somewhat sketchily and distinctly implausibly. Claudio is young. As usual we don't know just how young; in the theatre it is difficult to sympathize with him unless we can condescend to him, blaming his faults on the callowness of youth. In the opening scene he speaks attractively of his love for Hero to his older friends Don Pedro and Benedick, and is soon to be mocked for displaying the standard symptoms of the lovesick wooer, but we never see him alone with Hero, and she says very little at any point.

Claudio's wooing is done on his behalf by Don Pedro, and he is easily tricked into believing that Pedro 'woos for himself' (2.1.164). Although he is soon disabused of this, it prepares us for the ease with which he falls for the plot by which Don John and his henchmen cause him to believe that Hero has been unfaithful before marriage. Repudiating her in church he bursts into a sententiously ironical diatribe against 'seeming' which contrasts with the revelation, after his departure and Hero's supposed death, that it is precisely Hero's seeming that has convinced the Friar who was to have married them of her innocence, not her guilt. The Friar's conviction that the belief that she is dead indeed will rekindle Claudio's love for her is beautifully expressed:

> When he shall hear she died upon his words,
> Th'idea of her life shall sweetly creep
> Into his study of imagination,
> And every lovely organ of her life
> Shall come apparelled in more precious habit,
> More moving-delicate, and full of life,
> Into the eye and prospect of his soul
> Than when she lived indeed.
>
> (4.1.225–32)

But Claudio's attitude to Hero's grieving father and uncle the next time we see him, and more particularly the way he speaks of them to Don Pedro – 'We had liked to have had our two noses snapped off with two old men without teeth' (5.1.116–17) – is objectionable, and in spite of his expressions of penitence, first on learning of Don John's plot and then more formally at Hero's supposed tomb, it is not easy in the final scene to feel that he deserves the revelation not merely that she is still alive but that she is willing to marry him. Claudio stands in need of forgiveness; the warmth with which Kenneth Branagh's Benedick, in the closing speeches, spoke 'Come, we are friends' (5.4.116) did more to reconcile us to Claudio than anything in the character himself.[7]

Although Claudio and Hero are the central characters in the play's main action, Beatrice and Benedick have been its main theatrical attraction at least since Shakespeare's contemporary Leonard Digges wrote, in lines first printed in 1640, 'let but Beatrice | And Benedick be seen, lo, in a trice | The Cockpit galleries, boxes, all are full . . .' They offer comedy of both character and situation. The 'merry war' between them is established in the opening scene: Beatrice piles comic insults on Benedick both before she sees him and to his face, yet there is no mistaking her interest in him, however it may be expressed; and although Benedick declares himself 'a professed tyrant to their sex' (1.1.161) and an opponent to marriage, he tells Claudio that Beatrice, 'an she were not possessed with a fury, exceeds' Hero 'as much in beauty as the first of May doth the last of December' (1.1.180–2). Beatrice, too, though she says she prays morn and night that God will send her no husband, admits that there is something to be said for Benedick, were it not for his perpetual tattling (2.1.6–26).

Clearly they are fascinated by each other, and Shakespeare gives us a tantalizing hint of an earlier relationship between them that may offer a psychological explanation for this; responding to Don Pedro's 'Come, lady, come, you have lost the heart of Signor Benedick', Beatrice says, 'Indeed, my lord, he lent it me a while, and I gave him use [interest] for it, a double heart for his single one. Marry, once before he won it of me, with false dice. Therefore your grace may well say I have lost it' (2.1.258–63). This window into the past is no sooner opened than it is closed again; the actress may pass lightly by it, it has even been cut, but it became the keystone to Judi Dench's interpretation of the role (RSC, 1976), with its suggestion of an unhealed wound, something still to be worked out. It also raises again the question of age; Beatrice and Benedick do not need to be much older than Claudio and Hero, but modern interpreters have often made them more nearly middle-aged, casting the shadow of the passage of time over their reluctant courtship.

The title *Much Ado About Nothing*, with its openness to wordplay on 'noting', foreshadows a central device in the play's technique, its constant use of overhearings. Don John contrives an overhearing that will trick Claudio into believing ill of Hero; his brother Don Pedro instigates the overhearings that will 'bring Signor Benedick and the Lady Beatrice into a mountain of affection th'one with th'other' (2.1.342–4). Before they begin, however, we have seen enough to suggest that the tricks played on Benedick and Beatrice will lead them on a journey of self-discovery rather than deceive them into believing what is not true. Benedick is funny because we are a step ahead of him on this journey; we can see how his mind is working when, after hearing his complacent expressions of superiority over the lovesick Claudio, his confident assertion that 'till all graces be in one woman, one woman shall not come in my grace', he goes on to speculate what she would be like if she did.

There is at least a touch of vanity in this, and it is on Benedick's vanity that his friends play, making him believe that Beatrice is almost suicidal with love for him, though too proud to reveal it: 'she will die if he love her not, and she will die ere she make her love known, and she will die if he woo her, rather than she will bate one breath of her accustomed crossness' (2.3.167–71). Complacency remains in the assurance with which Benedick, left alone, exclaims: 'This can be no trick' and in the sententiousness of his 'Happy are they that hear their detractions and put them to mending'; it is up to the actor to decide whether to suggest any emerging self-knowledge in Benedick's resounding declaration to the audience, 'The world must be peopled. When I said I would die a bachelor, I did not think I should live till I were married.'

The need for the same trick to be played on Beatrice creates a risk of monotony by repetition, but Shakespeare varies the situation, partly by writing Beatrice's deception in verse, whereas Benedick's had been in prose, and also by causing Beatrice's friends to voice more fundamentally serious criticism of her character:

> HERO . . . nature never framed a woman's heart
>   Of prouder stuff than that of Beatrice.
>   Disdain and scorn ride sparkling in her eyes,
>   Misprising what they look on, and her wit
>   Values itself so highly that to her
>   All matter else seems weak. She cannot love,
>   Nor take no shape nor project of affection,
>   She is so self-endearèd.
>
> (3.1.49–56)

In *A Midsummer Night's Dream* Theseus had said that 'never anything can be amiss | When simpleness and duty tender it' (5.1.83–4); Hero alleges that Beatrice 'never gives to truth and virtue that | Which simpleness and merit purchaseth'. And Beatrice, emerging from hiding, accepts the justice of their criticisms in a shaken reaction that expresses a serious gain in self-knowledge:

> What fire is in mine ears? Can this be true?
>   Stand I condemned for pride and scorn so much?
> Contempt, farewell; and maiden pride, adieu.
>   No glory lives behind the back of such.
>
> (3.1.107–10)

Only insensitive actresses play this speech mainly for laughs; the subdued tenderness of her promise to tame her 'wild heart' to Benedick's 'loving hand' is a necessary prelude to the more mature Beatrice that we see in the later part of the play.

By the end of the second overhearing scene we are ready to believe that Benedick and Beatrice are in love; Shakespeare exploits the comedy inherent in their situation by episodes in which each behaves in the ridiculous ways of the conventional lover, but we do not see them together again until the climactic scene in church at which they become more closely involved with the Claudio/Hero plot. Their presence during Claudio's accusation of Hero and its aftermath offers some reassurance; like the Friar, Beatrice has an instinctive trust in Hero – 'O, on my soul, my cousin is belied' (4.1.147) – and Benedick is worldly-wise enough to suspect Don John of having engineered the situation.

At the end of the scene Benedick, left alone with Beatrice, sees her for the first time with her defences down:

> BENEDICK Lady Beatrice, have you wept all this while?
> BEATRICE Yea, and I will weep a while longer.
>
> (4.1.258–9)

The emotional pressures of what has gone before add psychological plausibility to their subsequent declaration of love, but it is one that remains wholly consistent with all we know of them:

> BENEDICK I do love nothing in the world so well as you. Is not
>   that strange?
> BEATRICE As strange as the thing I know not. It were as possible
>   for me to say I loved nothing so well as you, but believe me
>   not, and yet I lie not. I confess nothing nor I deny nothing. I
>   am sorry for my cousin.
>
> (4.1.269–74)

It is completely unsentimental and totally believable. And it leads into one of the most famous surprise reactions in drama as Benedick asks, 'Come, bid me do anything for thee', and receives the reply 'Kill Claudio'. The severity of Beatrice's demand takes Benedick aback: 'Ha! Not for the wide world', and can disconcert audiences. Only theatre critics ostentatiously in avoidance of the obvious omit comment on how this line is received. Does the audience think Beatrice is joking? Do they laugh? If so, is their laughter amused or defensive? A proper balance between the serious and the comic is not easy to achieve, but the words launch us into the last movement of the play, in which Benedick is to challenge Claudio; Shakespeare re-establishes a comic tone with Benedick's increasing speechlessness in the face of Beatrice's warm-hearted vehemence on behalf of Hero:

> BEATRICE O that I were a man! What, bear her in hand until they
>   came to take hands, and then with public accusation,
>   uncovered slander, unmitigated rancour, – O God that I were a
>   man! I would eat his heart in the market-place.
> BENEDICK Hear me, Beatrice.
> BEATRICE Talk with a man out at a window – a proper saying!
> BENEDICK Nay, but Beatrice.
> BEATRICE Sweet Hero, she is wronged, she is slandered, she is
>   undone.
> BENEDICK Beat—
>
>   (4.1.304–15)

The body of the church scene provides the longest serious stretch of action in the play; although Hero's plight is movingly presented, it remains in the realm of comedy because we know not just that she is innocent but that Constable Dogberry and his men of the Watch, in yet another overhearing, have discovered the plot against her and plan to reveal it.

With this group of characters we are in company similar to that of Bottom and his friends. Foolish, uneducated, incapable of understanding their duties or of carrying them out efficiently, yet they have good intentions, are, to quote Dogberry's first speech, 'good men and true'. They may be foolish, but so are other, apparently wiser inhabitants of Messina; in their inarticulate, fumbling way Dogberry and his men see the truth, they recognize villainy when it lies before them, even though their inarticulacy inhibits them from communicating their discovery.

The device of making Dogberry say exactly the opposite of what he means is not particularly funny once we have got the idea; it amuses us only if the actor projects the impression of a personality that will account for and give rise to the verbal errors on which the comedy depends. In a 1988 Stratford production David Waller achieved a triumph of character-acting by playing Dogberry entirely from his own point of view. He beamed with self-satisfaction as he promised to bestow all his tediousness on Leonato; he made a marvellous prose aria of self-righteousness out of 'Dost thou not suspect my place? . . .', and smirked with pleasure as Don Pedro declared, 'This learned constable is too cunning to be understood', nudging his sidekick Verges into recognition of the compliment. In a performance like this the comic device becomes a comment on the use of language; in spite of all his errors Dogberry's meaning is clear to those who have the patience to try to understand him and the sympathy to mend his errors with their imaginations. Dogberry's words, like Hero's blushes, can be misinterpreted, but truth is in them, waiting to be perceived by those capable of doing so.

The play's ending lies with Beatrice and Benedick; he loves her 'no more than reason', she loves him 'but in friendly recompense'; he takes her only 'for pity', she yields to him 'on great persuasion, and partly to save your life, for I was told you were in a consumption'. As pipers strike up the music for a final dance we can only agree that they were 'too wise to woo peaceably' (5.2.65).

Not much happens in *As You Like It*. Its story, such as it is, is slight and can be followed without difficulty. It is written in a limpid and uncomplicated style with a high proportion of prose; I remember hearing a child in the Stratford theatre say with relief that it 'didn't sound like Shakespeare'. Emotionally it is untaxing; it offers elementary theatrical pleasures such as a sylvan setting, a wrestling match, a cast full of beautiful young people including Shakespeare's most enchanting heroine, set-pieces both serious and comic giving the actors ample opportunity to display their talents, a number of excellent songs, and a fable in which the wicked become good and the good are bountifully rewarded. On the most straightforward level, this is 'As You Like It'.

But there is more to it than this. Even Bernard Shaw, who wrote disparagingly of what he regarded as its 'sham moralizing and stage "philosophy" ', admitted that its 'fascination' 'is still very great'. Finding its production during a Christmas season 'very timely', he suggested that 'The children will find the virtue of Adam and the philosophy of Jaques just the thing for them; whilst their elders will be delighted by the pageantry and the wrestling'.[8] More recently, criticism has helped to show that its easy grace and charm represent a triumph of the art that conceals art; that in fact this is a play of original technique and subtle construction, a highly sophisticated product of Shakespeare's reactions to a variety of theatrical and literary modes that were fashionable around the turn of the sixteenth century, when he wrote it.

As You Like It is a pastoral play; like other exponents of the form, Shakespeare uses it as a basis for an entertainment in which discussion of ideas plays an important though unobtrusive part. His direct source is a non-dramatic pastoral, Thomas Lodge's prose romance *Rosalynde*, which, first published in 1590, had already been three times reprinted by the time he came to write his play. Except for Sir Philip Sidney's *Arcadia* it is the best work of Elizabethan prose fiction, but the play is far from being a straightforward dramatization of the novel. Shakespeare seems to have found it useful rather for its conventionality than for its originality; indeed the very obviousness of the exposition in the opening speeches of his play, sometimes seen as an artless clumsiness, is rather a sophisticated way of putting us in the right frame of mind for a play which will never for long allow us to forget that we are watching a fiction.

As You Like It is full of unrealities, of deliberate and obvious artifice. Though its characters are subtilized and made vivid by the things Shakespeare gives them to say – or even, in the case of the sublimely inarticulate William (is his name Shakespeare's little joke against himself?), by their inability to say virtually anything at all – they are exceptionally stereotyped and literary in origin, and exist on simplified planes of morality. Though this play has two villains –Rosalind's uncle, Duke Frederick, and Orlando's brother, Oliver – the former is little more than a device to set the story in motion by banishing Rosalind, and both of them undergo spectacularly sudden conversions, the Duke at the end of the play, after a fortunate encounter with 'an old religious man' (5.4.158), Oliver in time to woo and win Rosalind's best friend, Celia. The plot's improbabilities were, we may be sure, as evident to Shakespeare as they are to us; it is naïve to take them as mere naïveties.

The most fundamental element of the pastoral tradition is the opposition between court and country and all that is associated with each of them – power and humility, wealth and poverty, industry and leisure, and so on. The speech of Henry VI quoted on page 98 demonstrates the convention in action. In *As You Like It* the opening

scene shows us disorder and discord: the brothers Orlando and Oliver
are violently opposed to each other in character and action; Oliver
persuades Duke Frederick's wrestler, Charles, to treat Orlando
roughly when he takes up the challenge. And there is discord in higher
places: Duke Frederick, before whom the wrestling will take place,
has usurped power from his elder brother, Duke Senior. This is the
world of the court – and not too far from that of *Cinderella* – where we
see 'unregarded age in corners thrown', where the good younger
brother is kept in servitude by the bad older one, and from which a
usurping duke has banished his brother.

But we hear also of a 'better world' to which the elder Duke has
gone:

> he is already in the forest of Ardenne, and a many merry men
> with him; and there they live like the old Robin Hood of
> England. They say many young gentlemen flock to him every
> day, and fleet the time carelessly, as they did in the golden world.
>
> (1.1.109–13)

In these words, with their explicit references to the English
legends of Robin Hood and the classical myth of the Golden World,
Shakespeare again draws attention to the conventions of pastoralism,
with their assumption that in the country – as in the past – is to be
found an ideal way of life where all is simplicity and innocence, where
shepherds live and love in honest contentment and good fellowship,
and where time never presses.

But although Shakespeare uses the convention, he also gently
satirizes it. As often, he manages to juxtapose the expression of an
attitude along with a criticism of that attitude without destroying its
validity. Even a single character can simultaneously hold diametrically opposed opinions: Touchstone, asked how *he* likes it – 'And how
like you this shepherd's life, Master Touchstone?' asks Corin – replies,
in a passage that encapsulates Shakespeare's capacity for evenhanded-
ness:

> Truly, shepherd, in respect of itself, it is a good life; but in
> respect that it is a shepherd's life, it is naught. In respect that it is
> solitary, I like it very well; but in respect that it is private, it is a
> very vile life. Now in respect it is in the fields, it pleaseth me
> well; but in respect it is not in the court, it is tedious. As it is a
> spare life, look you, it fits my humour well; but as there is no
> more plenty in it, it goes much against my stomach.

And then, as if surprised by his own capacity for disputation, 'Hast any philosophy in *thee*, shepherd?' (3.2.11–22).

Touchstone, the jester who accompanies Rosalind and Celia into the forest, is one of the two main characters that Shakespeare adds to Lodge's story, both essentially commentators, little involved in the action: the other is Jaques, a melancholy courtier of Duke Senior. Jaques makes fun of Touchstone in lines that are not far from being a parody of Henry VI's meditations on time:

> 'Good morrow, fool,' quoth I. 'No, sir,' quoth he,
> 'Call me not fool till heaven hath sent me fortune.'
> And then he drew a dial from his poke,
> And looking on it with lack-lustre eye
> Says very wisely 'It is ten o'clock.'
> 'Thus we may see', quoth he, 'how the world wags.
> 'Tis but an hour ago since it was nine,
> And after one hour more 'twill be eleven.
> And so from hour to hour we ripe and ripe,
> And then from hour to hour we rot and rot;
> And thereby hangs a tale.'
>
>   (2.7.18–28)

The idealizations of the pastoral world, with its emphasis on the natural cycle, are mocked here, but its better aspects come up smiling at the end. Juxtaposition of opposites is a common feature of the play's technique. Though the first act shows us mainly the court, with its strife and dissensions, it also shows us old Adam's devotion to his master, and the friendship of Celia and Rosalind.

With the second act we are in the forest, but it is not an escapist's paradise; adversity is experienced in exile as well as being a cause of exile. Rosalind feels a need to disguise herself as protection against danger; when she and Celia arrive in the forest she calls it a 'desert place'; similarly, when Orlando and his servant Adam get there, with Adam fainting and near to death, Orlando says, 'If this uncouth forest yield anything savage, I will either be food for it, or bring it for food for thee . . . Yet thou liest in the bleak air.' And even Amiens's song 'Under the Greenwood Tree' points out that there are enemies in the forest: 'winter and rough weather'. Nevertheless the forest is welcome because the 'winter wind' is not so unkind as 'man's ingratitude', the 'bitter' sky's sting 'not so sharp | As friend remembered not'. A happy life is possible there, but only to those who can make good use of adversity. 'Happy is your grace', says Amiens to the Duke, 'That can translate the stubbornness of fortune into so quiet and so sweet a style.'

This is a pervasive idea in *As You Like It*, projected chiefly in the picture of Orlando imagining that the disguised Rosalind is the true Rosalind. He plays a game, but it is an educative game, one that leads him to a state of heightened self-awareness: the bitterness he experiences in looking 'into happiness through another man's eyes' turns finally to sweetness when he needs no longer to 'live by thinking'. The play's title is not, perhaps, the throw-away phrase it may seem: during its course we see that the quality of human experience is influenced by the attitude that people bring to it, that while the melancholy Jaques will always be melancholy, others will succeed in transmuting 'the stubbornness of fortune' into quietness and sweetness. And the audience has its part to play, and also its reward to reap. As Orlando has to use his imagination in the game of pretending that 'Ganymede' is Rosalind, so we have to use ours in remembering that Ganymede is actually Rosalind; Shakespeare's audience would have had to make the additional imaginative leap required by the fact that a boy was representing Rosalind in the first place, and this element of imaginative game-playing helps to explain why the play has succeeded in the modern theatre with grown men as Rosalind.[9]

As Shakespeare's story passes from court to country, it passes also to one of the commonest topics of pastoral literature: love. The forest is inhabited by a number of lovers, actual and potential; and one pair is straight out of the Renaissance pastoral convention. Hundreds of Elizabethan lyrics present the situation of the faithful, abject lover whose beloved is fair of face but hard of heart; Shakespeare reproduces this situation with Silvius, sighing 'upon a midnight pillow' for Phoebe, who scorns him. In calculated opposition to this is the love-affair of Touchstone and Audrey. There is no languishing here. Touchstone has hardly met Audrey before he is looking for a parson, but he is without any romantic illusions: 'As the ox hath his bow, sir, the horse his curb, and the falcon her bells, so man hath his desires; and as pigeons bill, so wedlock would be nibbling' (3.3.72–4). His attitude is to some extent a criticism of Silvius's, but is itself criticized. Being purely physical it is, as he realizes, temporary; and in the end Jaques will consign him to 'wrangling', for his 'loving voyage is but for two months victualled'. Between these attitudes, and containing both, are those of Rosalind and Orlando.

Like Silvius, Orlando has many of the attributes of the conventional lover: he goes around hanging verses on trees, sighing out his soul in praise of his beloved. But he has enough imagination to enter fully and joyfully into the game that Rosalind proposes to him; and he also has a remarkable capacity to silence criticism, as we see in his encounter with Jaques:

JAQUES The worst fault you have is to be in love.
ORLANDO 'Tis a fault I will not change for your best virtue. I am weary of you.
JAQUES By my troth, I was seeking for a fool when I found you.
ORLANDO He is drowned in the brook. Look but in, and you shall see him.

(3.2.276–82)

The fullest character in the play, the one who embraces most attitudes within herself and resolves them into a rich synthesis of personality, is Rosalind. As she plays her verbal games with Orlando Shakespeare's prose takes wing as never before. She laughs at Orlando's romantic attitudes, at his abusing of 'young plants with carving Rosalind on their barks'; she declares love 'merely a madness', denies the possibility of dying for love, is tremulously aware of love's transience. Yet her love seems as deep and genuine, and in its way as romantic, as any Orlando could wish. Aware of the humorous aspects of love, of the exaggerations of lovers, she is aware too of love's potency. She seems sometimes to laugh lest she cry; her awareness of the possibility of folly becomes a kind of self-awareness born of experience, her boyish disguise a means of revealing while at the same time controlling her emotion. She also is too wise to woo peaceably, but her feelings spill over when she is alone with Celia: 'O coz, coz, coz, my pretty little coz, that thou didst know how many fathom deep I am in love. But it cannot be sounded. My affection hath an unknown bottom, like the Bay of Portugal.' And in this mood even she is not immune from deflating comment: 'I'll tell thee, Aliena, I cannot be out of the sight of Orlando. I'll go find a shadow and sigh till he come.' To which Celia replies, 'And I'll sleep' (4.1.195–8, 205–8).

It is Rosalind, too, who reproves Phoebe for her obstinate refusal of Silvius's love:

> But, mistress, know yourself; down on your knees
> And thank heaven, fasting, for a good man's love;
> For I must tell you friendly in your ear,
> Sell when you can. You are not for all markets.

(3.5.58–61)

This is not moon-sickness, but it shows a healthy appreciation of the value of love. And though she keeps up her disguise as Ganymede effectively for most of the time, it slips when she sees a handkerchief stained with Orlando's blood.

The comprehensiveness of Rosalind's vision makes it fitting that she should be the one who effects the resolution. The converted Oliver is to marry Celia. An outlet for our incredulity is artfully built into the dialogue:

> ORLANDO Is't possible that on so little acquaintance you should like her? That but seeing, you should love her? And loving, woo? And wooing, she should grant? And will you persevere to enjoy her?
>
> (5.2.1–4)

But Shakespeare would not wish us to regard Oliver's conversion, or the wicked Duke's, as psychologically plausible. He is as aware as we are of his own artifice; the improbabilities at the end of the play are as blatant as those at the beginning. Rosalind has only to reveal her femininity to solve all the problems. Shakespeare builds up to her revelation in the patterned dialogue of that quartet of lovers which for me has the contrapuntal harmony, the motion within stillness, of the first-act quartet in Beethoven's *Fidelio*. I look on this as a touchstone of the play in performance. (Another is the wrestling, which too easily gets out of hand.) Its formality as well as its subject-matter lifts the play on to a new level of seriousness as each character declares 'what 'tis to love'; and the enigmatic position of Rosalind, the carrier of the all-important secret, gives to her final speech in the scene something of a consciously oracular quality:

> Tomorrow meet me all together. (*To Phoebe*) I will marry you if ever I marry woman, and I'll be married tomorrow. (*To Orlando*) I will satisfy you if ever I satisfy man, and you shall be married tomorrow. (*To Silvius*) I will content you if what pleases you contents you, and you shall be married tomorrow. (*To Orlando*) As you love Rosalind, meet. (*To Silvius*) As you love Phoebe, meet. And as I love no woman, I'll meet.
>
> (5.2.218–30)

This sets the scene for the climax of concord, heralded by the purely joyful song of love and spring-time, 'It was a lover and his lass'. The solemnity is lightened by Touchstone's final comic set-piece on the lie, and immediately Rosalind and Celia enter 'as themselves', along with Hymen, the Greek god of marriage.

This is one of those moments when the absence of detailed stage directions leaves a lot to the interpreter. Though Hymen may be presented as the god himself (in which case this is the first theophany in Shakespeare's plays, anticipating those of the final romances), directors sometimes feel a need to explain his presence by making him someone, perhaps a forester, whom Rosalind has conscripted into taking on the role. The direction for 'still music' (which I take to mean music that will still the audience into silence) is a clue; though there is no transition from the preceding prose dialogue to Hymen's first speech (or song), the music, the words, and the patterning of the dialogue can all help to give this episode the quality of a vision. The action moves from the world of temporal events to become a symbol of earthly concord won through love:

> HYMEN
>   Then is there mirth in heaven
>   When earthly things made even
>   Atone together.

An ideal state has been won through the destruction of false ideas about love and life, through a facing-up to reality that includes the recognition of the powers of the imagination and art, and a reliance upon the basic humanity of good people.

But of course it is all a fiction. We knew it from the start, and at the end Shakespeare gives the boy who has played Rosalind an epilogue spoken in his own person – 'If I were a woman . . .' – to ease the transition back to real life. The vision fades; but perhaps, like Orlando's game, it has done its work.

Twelfth Night, or What You Will: Pepys found it 'but a silly play, and not at all related to the name or day' (Diary, 6 January 1663), but the title of Shakespeare's last romantic comedy probably alludes to the topsy-turvydom traditionally associated with the last day of the Christmas revels. It has much in common with his earlier comedies: a foreign setting; a pair (but only one pair) of shipwrecked twins whose identical appearance creates both comic and serious complications; a practical joke designed to make one character believe that another loves him; a jester who acts as a commentator on the action; a heroine who disguises herself as a boy; another heroine who is wooed by a man in whom she can take no interest and who falls in love with a woman believing him to be a man; and a hero who transfers his affections from one woman to another. But as always Shakespeare creates something new out of the familiar material; we have no sense that he is writing to a formula. His play follows comic tradition in its concern with wooing and its culmination in marriage; but it is concerned with more than one kind of love, and does not always adopt conventional attitudes to it.

At its opening, love is seen, conventionally enough, as a kind of sickness, at least if taken to excess:

> If music be the food of love, play on,
> Give me excess of it that, surfeiting,
> The appetite may sicken and so die.

But if Orsino begins the scene by trying to cure himself of love, he ends it by seeking to indulge himself still further:

> Away before me to sweet beds of flowers;
> Love-thoughts lie rich when canopied with bowers.

There is clearly something immature in his desire for music and solitude, his emotional volatility, his apparent incapacity to do anything for himself, but any hint of criticism comes only from his own manner of speaking about his love; he induces in audiences a sort of indulgent avuncularity; we may shake our heads over his self-absorption while echoing Polonius's words over Hamlet: 'A is far gone, far gone, and truly, in my youth I suffered much extremity for love, very near this' (*Hamlet*, 2.2.191–3).

The woman he loves, too, is presented somewhat critically. Orsino's servant Valentine tells him that Olivia has vowed to stay indoors for seven years mourning the death of her brother, but when we first see her she allows her jester, Feste, to prove her a fool with a toleration that suggests there is hope for her yet:

FESTE Good madonna, why mournest thou?
OLIVIA Good fool, for my brother's death.
FESTE I think his soul is in hell, madonna.
OLIVIA I know his soul is in heaven, fool.
FESTE The more fool, madonna, to mourn for your brother's soul,
  being in heaven.

(1.5.62–7)[10]

Into this atmosphere of introversion comes a more balanced character, Viola, one of a pair of twins. She also believes her brother, Sebastian, to be dead, but takes a more positive attitude – and, to be fair, she has some faint encouragement to hope that he may have survived the shipwreck that parted them (1.2.3–16). Viola is the active agent in this play, and her separation from her brother provides its structural foundation, creating a tension upon whose resolution the entire outcome of the events depends, and which will not be resolved until the final scene. We soon know that Sebastian is alive and not far away; the complications that arise because of their identical appearance (biologically impossible, since only same-sex twins can be identical) can be resolved only when they come together. The love between them is real; when she is mistaken for him she (unlike her counterparts in *The Comedy of Errors*) is bright enough to realize what this may mean, and she expresses her renewal of hope movingly:

> He named Sebastian. I my brother know
> Yet living in my glass. Even such and so
> In favour was my brother, and he went
> Still in this fashion, colour, ornament,
> For him I imitate. O, if it prove,
> Tempests are kind, and salt waves fresh in love!
>
> (3.4.371–6)

The relationship between Viola and Sebastian adds a non-sexual, familial love-interest to the play.

A different kind of love is that which Antonio conceives for Sebastian after rescuing him from the shipwreck. Antonio feels so tenderly towards the boy that he is willing to risk his life to help him: '. . . come what may, I do adore thee so | That danger shall seem sport, and I will go' (2.1.42–3). His expressions of love are both intense and idealized:

> This youth that you see here
> I snatched one half out of the jaws of death,
> Relieved him with such sanctity of love,
> And to his image, which methought did promise
> Most venerable worth, did I devotion.
>
> (3.4.351–5)

Again, as with the Antonio of *The Merchant of Venice*, modern interpreters have discerned a sexual element in his love (he does use the word 'desire' [3.3.4]); although his role is not large, it is important to the plot; when the disguised Viola, whom he has mistaken for Sebastian, is bewildered by his requests for the return of money he had lent Sebastian, his naming of her brother renews her hope that he may have survived: 'Prove true, imagination, O prove true, | That I, dear brother, be now ta'en for you!' (3.4.367–8), and Antonio's expressions of disillusionment in the last scene with 'that most ingrateful boy' whom he sees by Orsino's side provide an emotional ground-bass against which the joy of the untangling of the complications seems all the more intense. Like Egeon in *The Comedy of Errors* he is an entirely serious character whose capacity for suffering defines the play's emotional range.

Olivia has two other wooers besides Orsino; she forms a kind of passive centre to the action, the means by which its various plots are related. This is a reason why *Twelfth Night* creates so strong an impression of unity; there is less sense of plot and subplot than in some of the other comedies, more of an integrated community. One of Olivia's wooers is the pathetically inadequate Sir Andrew Aguecheek whose friendship with her uncle Sir Toby Belch provides a debased parallel to that between Antonio and Sebastian. They are boon companions, they drink, sing, have fun and play practical jokes together, but there is an uncomfortably economic basis to their relationship. Whereas Antonio bestows his purse upon Sebastian, Sir Toby values Sir Andrew because he is wealthy – 'he has three thousand ducats a year' (1.3.20) – and admits, 'I have been dear to him . . . some two thousand strong or so' (3.2.52–3). The last words they speak in the play, after Sebastian has beaten both of them up, cast an unpleasant retrospective light on their friendship:

> SIR ANDREW I'll help you, Sir Toby, because we'll be dressed together.
> SIR TOBY Will *you* help – an ass-head, and a coxcomb, and a knave; a thin-faced knave, a gull?
>
> (5.1.201–4)

Olivia's other wooer is Malvolio. The name, signifying one who wishes ill, is significant; if *Twelfth Night* has a villain, it is Malvolio, though he may seem more fool than knave. In their opening exchange Olivia accuses him of being 'sick of self-love' (1.5.86); the same charge may be brought against both Olivia and Orsino, but the action is to show that while their sickness is curable, Malvolio's is not. Moral values are delicately balanced. Sir Toby may be drunken and parasitical, but he is attractive as an upholder of merriment and good fellowship; Malvolio, outwardly well regulated and eminently respectable, is self-obsessed and oppressive; the clash between them generates great comic energy as Malvolio, roused from sleep, interrupts the midnight revels of Sir Toby and his companions with his self-righteous pomposity, stimulating Sir Toby's rebuke 'Art any more than a steward? Dost thou think because thou art virtuous there shall be no more cakes and ale?' (2.3.109–11).

Malvolio's self-importance provokes in Sir Toby and his companions the desire for revenge, and his self-love – what Maria, Olivia's waiting-gentlewoman, calls his 'faith that all that look on him love him' – is the 'vice' on which she will work in tricking him into the belief that Olivia is in love with him. The trick resembles the one played on Benedick, but even before Malvolio picks up the love-letter supposedly from his mistress that Maria puts in his way, he is full of fantasies about Olivia – or, more correctly, about the power he hopes to acquire through marriage to his mistress, and about the humiliations that he would be able to impose upon Sir Toby.

During the action of *Twelfth Night* several of the characters change. Olivia comes out of mourning, falls in love with Viola dressed as Sebastian, and marries Sebastian. Olivia's relationship with Sebastian lies on the margins of the action; we are required to accept the speed with which he agrees to marry her as the 'accident and flood of fortune' (4.3.11) that he calls it.

More central, and far more plausible psychologically, is Orsino's shift of affection from Olivia to Viola. The crucial scene in this relationship is that (2.4) in which Feste eases Orsino's love-melancholy with the sad strains of 'Come away, come away, death'. Cesario's eloquent praise of the tune – 'It gives a very echo to the seat | Where love is throned' – stirs Orsino's interest in this strange boy whose 'small pipe is as the maiden's organ', and this, along with the frequent reminders of the possibility, not to say the likelihood, of a shift in his affections, prepares us for his total change of heart when finally Cesario is revealed as a maid indeed.

Orsino's conversation with Viola is the romantic heart of the play, not least in its presentation of Viola. Comedy arises from our knowledge that the supposed boy is a girl, but the poignancy of her situation is made all the keener by the ripples of irony that spread over the scene as the young Duke gives to his younger pageboy the benefit of his experience in matters of the heart. When he is diverted from his own passion to a curiosity about Cesario's love-life the audience is allowed to catch hints that Orsino cannot hear. His advice culminates in a memorable expression of one of the play's most romantically lyrical themes, the traditional one of the transitoriness of beauty:

> For women are as roses, whose fair flower
> Being once displayed, doth fall that very hour.

And there is especial poignancy in Viola's reply, coming as it does from one who is having to hide her love while her beauty is in danger of fading:

> And so they are. Alas that they are so:
> To die even when they to perfection grow.
>
> (2.4.37–40)

Viola's parable of her imaginary sister who 'never told her love' creates a temporary suspension of the flow of time in the play as she looks backward to an imagined past which is at the same time an image of the future that she fears for herself, for she cannot tell whether her imaginary sister died of her grief; but she jolts herself out of her reverie with an acknowledgement of that commitment to action and service – to the present – that helps to make her so attractive a character.

The frustrations of Orsino's love for Olivia combined with his growing interest in, as it seems, a boy create a complex situation, and the intensity of his passion reaches frightening proportions in the last scene in his outbursts of jealousy and anger against Cesario. In the story on which Shakespeare based his play, Barnaby Riche's tale of Apollonius and Silla, the Duke's anger with his servant is more rationally motivated: there, the equivalent of Olivia is actually with child by the Sebastian figure, and is not married to him; on learning this the Duke draws his rapier on the girl who is masquerading as a boy, and she is able to save herself only by 'loosing his garments down to his stomach' and showing 'his breasts and pretty teats, surmounting far the whiteness of snow itself'.[11] This option was not available to Shakespeare.

The character who is least susceptible to change is the one who is least open to love, Malvolio. The limitations of his unyielding sanity are defined largely by the opposition with the play's wise fool, Feste, which is set up in his first scene. Feste points for us the paradox that the conscious fool, or entertainer, requires great intelligence to do his job: 'Wit, an't be thy will,' he prays, 'put me into good fooling!' (1.5.29–30). And as he speaks there enters his opponent, Malvolio, who thinks he has wit, who regards himself as the epitome of sanity and Feste as a 'barren rascal'. The opposition between them reaches a climax in the scene in which Malvolio, imprisoned as a madman, is reduced to the humiliation of pleading his sanity to the Fool whose jesting he had earlier so sternly rebuked. 'I am as well in my wits, fool, as thou art', he claims, and Feste answers: 'But as well? Then you are mad indeed if you be no better in your wits than a fool' (4.2.90–2). It is a scene in which he might have acknowledged his folly, but he is incapable of doing so. Some actors seek sympathy for Malvolio, but Shakespeare makes clear that he ends no wiser and no better than he had begun; Viola tells us that he has had the captain who rescued her cast into prison; Feste, spanning the play's time-scheme, points out that Malvolio is only suffering the revenges inevitably brought about by 'the whirligig of time'; and Malvolio exiles himself from the happy ending with his vindictive cry of 'I'll be revenged on the whole pack of you'.

The resolution of the action comes at the extreme point of the complications caused by Viola's disguise. Antonio suffers because he thinks himself denied by Sebastian, Olivia because she thinks her new husband has rejected her, Orsino because he thinks he has been betrayed by his page. Theatrically the most powerful moment is the silent one when the twins confront each other, the pause before they speak. Virginia Woolf made the point in a review of an Old Vic performance:

> Perhaps the most impressive effect in the play is achieved by the long pause which Sebastian and Viola make as they stand looking at each other in a silent ecstasy of recognition.[12]

But Shakespeare gives them a rapt duologue of slow recognition that strikes with all the wonder and rapture of an achieved impossibility. The love of brother and sister creates a radiance in which other people's problems are solved; as they discover their true identities by each acknowledging the identity of the other, so Sebastian, Orsino, and Olivia achieve a sense of integrity, of achieved self. But the journey towards it has not been easy, and there is gravity at the conclusion of the comedy, and bitterness, too, in Sir Toby's harsh rejection of Sir Andrew and in Malvolio's unregenerate hatred. It was a bad stage tradition that made Viola at the end of the play change rapidly into woman's clothes in a brief show of glamorous femininity. The action ends with Orsino's subdued expectation of happiness expressed in almost spiritual terms:

> Pursue him, and entreat him to a peace.
> He hath not told us of the captain yet.
> When that is known, and golden time convents,
> A solemn combination shall be made
> Of our dear souls.

But the character whose words linger as we leave the theatre is not Orsino but Feste, the jester who has acted throughout almost as the presenter of the action.

Feste has the sadness that comes, we are told, of perfect knowledge. The jokes he makes are sad jokes, the songs he sings are sad songs. He is the artist at the heart of the play, the creator and entertainer who has constantly to strive to make contact with his audience, and who relies on his ability to do so for his very living. He can express his knowledge most easily through the artist's devices of the parable, the enigmatic utterance, the paradox, the ironical playing with words which are his stock-in-trade. He knows that he can learn more from his foes than from his friends because his foes tell him plainly he is an ass, 'so that by my foes, sir, I profit in the knowledge of myself, and by my friends I am abused' (5.1.15–18). But he cannot impose this lesson on others; Malvolio remains himself even though the fool has put the means of self-knowledge within his grasp.

The fool is the wise man of the play, and it is fitting that at the end he remains on stage to sing his song of the wind and the rain which manages at once to mean so little and so much as he looks backward to a time when he 'was and a little tiny boy' and forward to the actors' future efforts to please their audiences. He reminds us that his practice is, as Viola had said, 'As full of labour as a wise man's art' (3.1.65), and of the forces that are inimical to man's happiness – the wind and the rain, knavery and swaggering. In his suggestions of the repeated frustrations and failures consequent upon mortal folly he may remind us too of the intelligence and understanding – such as those of Viola – that are needed rightly to use and control the less rational elements of our natures, that we cannot hope to be fully in control of our destiny but must see ourselves against the backdrop of that great expanse of time that has passed since 'the world begun'. So he may suggest too, as the play has suggested, that by submitting ourselves to chance, by opening our imaginations to experience even if it does seem partly foolish, we may receive the blessings of fortune. Whatever Pepys may have thought, this play is surely one of them.

The Merry Wives of Windsor is exceptional among Shakespeare's comedies. It is the only one to be set in England. Except for one or two passing references to the reign of Henry IV, there is nothing to suggest that the action takes place before Shakespeare's own time. It is a small-town comedy rather than a romantic one, peopled by members of the middle and lower classes, with no aristocrats in the cast list; it is full of details of ordinary life that would have been familiar to Elizabethan Londoners; it includes a substantial passage that seems to link it to a particular occasion; its language is colloquial and up-to-date, with a higher proportion of prose to verse than in any other of his plays. And some of its characters are related in name and personal characteristics to ones who figure also in Shakespeare's plays about the reigns of Henry IV and Henry V. But its exact relationship to these plays is unclear, partly because we cannot be sure of its date. I have put it at the end of this chapter because of its singularities, but it may have been written before any of the plays discussed here except *The Merchant of Venice*. At one point Master Page says that young Fenton 'kept company with the wild Prince and Poins' (3.2.66–7), which takes for granted the audience's familiarity with the events of *Henry the Fourth, Part One*, and it is difficult to believe that Shakespeare had not already written at least one play about Sir John Falstaff before putting him into this comedy, but characters do not simply run over from the history play to the comedy in the way that they do, for instance, in Trollope's novels about Barsetshire or the Pallisers. In the history play Mistress Quickly is the hostess of a disreputable tavern and Sir John is already on intimate terms with her, whereas in the comedy she is a respectable servant to the French Dr Caius, and Falstaff at first does not know her. The comedy also includes characters with the same names and at least some of the same characteristics as ones who crop up in *Henry the Fourth, Part Two* (Justice Shallow and Pistol) and *Henry the Fifth* (Nim); we can't be sure which came first.

It's surprising in a way that we can't put a date to the play which contains what is probably Shakespeare's most extended topical reference, the lines in the last act which compliment the Queen and

link the play with ceremonies held in connection with the Order of the
Garter. Hobgoblin, addressing children dressed as fairies, says:

> Cricket, to Windsor chimneys shalt thou leap.
> Where fires thou find'st unraked and hearths unswept,
> There pinch the maids as blue as bilberry.
> Our radiant Queen hates sluts and sluttery.
>
> (5.5.42–5)

Shortly afterwards Mistress Quickly refers explicitly to the Order of
the Garter – the highest order of knighthood, and one which was (and
still is) in the sovereign's personal gift – and to its connection with
Windsor Castle, where the ceremony of installation has always been
held, in lines that have nothing to do with the dramatic situation (and
that are usually omitted in performance), instructing the fairies to
'Strew good luck . . . on every sacred room' of Windsor Castle, and
especially to clean and perfume those choir stalls in the chapel that are
reserved for Knights of the Garter. They are to create a fairy ring (the
shape of the garter) and to inscribe the motto of the order – '*Honi soit
qui mal y pense*' – in flowers within it. These lines would have been
most topical around the time of a ceremony of installation of Knights
of the Garter, such as the one held in May 1597 when Lord Hunsdon,
patron of Shakespeare's company, received the honour. He was
attended by a 'brave company of men and gentlemen, his servants and
retainers', splendidly costumed and reported as numbering 300,
presumably including Shakespeare and his colleagues. The Queen was
not present at the installation but had attended the feast at the Palace of
Westminster on St George's Day, 23 April. This may have been the
occasion of the compliments, but the first certain references to the play
are in 1602 when it was both entered for publication and printed in a
corrupt text, so it may have been written after 1597 – and, indeed, the
Garter passage may not have been written at the same time as the rest
of the play. The question remains open.

All I have said so far may suggest that this is a more naturalistic play
than Shakespeare's other comedies, one more firmly rooted in
Elizabethan society, but its plot is made up of conventional situations
of literary ancestry. Its central story, of Sir John's unsuccessful
attempts to seduce Mistress Page and Mistress Ford, and of Master
Ford's unfounded jealousy, is in the tradition of the Italian novellas,
short, often racy stories such as Chaucer drew on for some of the
Canterbury Tales, and may derive directly from one in a collection of

1588 called *Il Pecorone* by Ser Giovanni Fiorentino, which seems also to have influenced *The Merchant of Venice*. One traditional aspect of the Falstaff story in the play is the fact that he undergoes a sequence of three humiliations: being dumped into the Thames among a mass of dirty linen from the laundry-basket in which the wives have tricked him into taking refuge; being beaten in his disguise as an 'old woman of Brentford'; and finally, when dressed as Herne the Hunter for a midnight assignation in Windsor Forest, being tormented into a confession by children and others dressed as fairies.

Alongside these episodes Shakespeare runs another traditionally structured tale of the wooing of 'sweet Anne Page' by three suitors: the rich, foolish Abraham Slender (preferred by her father), Dr Caius, a French doctor (preferred by her mother), and the romantic young Fenton (preferred by the girl herself). As the play moves into the verse of the final episodes it draws more strongly on the conventions of romantic comedy: the manically jealous Ford is cured of his obsession, begs forgiveness of his wronged wife, and joins in the plot to trick Falstaff. Anne Page elopes with her favoured suitor, and her new husband, unabashed by the dismay of his rivals, preaches a brief but pithy sermon on the miseries of enforced marriage and is forthwith welcomed into the family circle. Falstaff himself is led to see the error of his ways and is invited to join the celebratory feast. The play ends, not in the disintegration of farce but in a comic harmony in which the outsider joins the society whose moral values he has been trying to subvert.

A legend that surfaces a century after the play had first appeared in print claims that it was written at Queen Elizabeth's 'Command, and by her direction, and she was so eager to see it Acted, that she commanded it to be finished in fourteen days'.[13] Seven years later Nicholas Rowe varied the tale: 'She was so well pleas'd with that admirable Character of *Falstaff*, in the two parts of *Henry the Fourth*, that she commanded him to continue it for one play more, and to shew him in love.'[14] Whether or not there is any truth in these legends, they have not done Shakespeare's reputation any good; the play has been too easily dismissed as a hasty piece of hack work. Arguably, too, Shakespeare himself was unwise to give its central character the name of Falstaff; from early in the nineteenth century the idea of a single Falstaff character drawn, sometimes romanticized, from the history plays has been used as a yardstick with which to beat the Falstaff of *The Merry Wives of Windsor*. 'Falstaff in *The Merry Wives of Windsor*', wrote William Hazlitt in 1817, 'is not the man he was in the two parts of

Henry IV. His wit and eloquence have left him. Instead of making a butt of others, he is made a butt of by them.'[15] And in 1909 A.C. Bradley, while calling the play a 'very entertaining piece', complained that in this 'comedy or farce' which is 'prosaic almost to the end' Shakespeare shows Falstaff 'baffled, duped, treated like dirty linen, beaten, burnt, pricked, mocked, insulted, and, worst of all, repentant and didactic. It is horrible.'[16]

Yet playgoers, less likely to make odious comparisons, have continued to enjoy Falstaff in his Windsor setting, which twentieth-century directors, drawing on the many local allusions in the text, have often depicted with a high degree of naturalism. His language may not be quite as pungent as in the histories, yet the effectiveness of the role lies not simply in the absurdity of comic situations but also in the relish with which he recounts his misfortunes:

> Have I lived to be carried in a basket like a barrow of butcher's offal, and to be thrown in the Thames? Well, if I be served such another trick, I'll have my brains ta'en out and buttered, and give them to a dog for a New Year's gift. 'Sblood, the rogues slighted me into the river with as little remorse as they would have drowned a blind bitch's puppies, fifteen i'th' litter! And you may know by my size that I have a kind of alacrity in sinking. If the bottom were as deep as hell, I should down. I had been drowned, but that the shore was shelvy and shallow – a death that I abhor, for the water swells a man, and what a thing should I have been when I had been swelled? By the Lord, a mountain of mummy!
>
> (3.5.4–17)

Later in the same scene, the excellent verbal comedy of his detailed account of how, in order to escape discovery by Ford in his guise of Master Brook, he was rammed into a buck-basket with a mass of dirty linen, carried to the Thames, and thrown in, is enhanced in performance by the fact that the narration is spoken to Ford himself; as John Dennis wrote, the scene 'gives an occasion for a great Actor to shew himself. For all the while *Falstaff* is making this relation *Ford*, at the same time that in dumb acting he shews a concern and a fellow-feeling to the Knight, shews a great deal of Joy and Satisfaction to the Audience.'[17]

The assumption that a 'great Actor' may be playing the role of Ford is another pointer to the reason for the play's theatrical success; as Dr Johnson realized, it is 'remarkable for the variety and number of the personages, who exhibit more characters appropriated and discriminated than perhaps can be found in any other play.'[18] The later scene (4.2) in which Ford searches the basket, thinking that Falstaff must again be concealed in it, followed by the comic bathos of 'Well, he's not here I seek for', by Ford's beating Falstaff in his disguise as the old woman of Brentford, and by Ford's search of the house, expertly provides opportunities for more robustly physical comedy. And though Ford is at the centre of the play's most farcical episodes, the verse lines in which he asks his wife's forgiveness and pays tribute to her virtue steer the play towards a romantic rather than a farcical conclusion. The wives themselves have some excellent scenes, and Mistress Quickly's garrulities encourage a delightful comic rapport with the audience. Shakespeare's prose can be richly rewarding for a performer who (as Herbert Farjeon wrote of Edith Evans, playing Mistress Page) 'quickens every syllable, recognizes in a choice epithet something as three-dimensional as a living being, reveals new wonders unsuspected and never to be forgotten'.[19] Such a response to language assists in the creation of character, and the play is rich in character parts. Imaginative acting, combined with a trust in Shakespeare's words, can create an impression of individuality in even small roles, such as Simple and Anne Page (who declares that, sooner than marry Dr Caius, she 'had rather be set quick i'th'earth | And bowled to death with turnips').

Many artists have illustrated scenes from *The Merry Wives of Windsor* and it forms the basis for operas in English (including Ralph Vaughan Williams's *Sir John in Love*), French, German (including Otto Nicolai's *Die lustigen Weiben von Windsor*, of 1848), and, supremely, Verdi's greatest comic masterpiece, *Falstaff,* in which the librettist skilfully introduces passages from *Henry the Fourth, Part One* and *Part Two*. Like the Falstaff of *Henry the Fourth, Part Two*, the play, witty in itself, has also been the cause that wit is in other men.

Notes to Chapter Eight

1 Proteus in *The Two Gentlemen of Verona* might be regarded as an exception, though he begins with good intentions. In *A Midsummer Night's Dream* Egeus has the function of a comic antagonist, but is a very minor figure, and not villainous in the sense of Don John (in *Much Ado About Nothing*) or even Duke Frederick (in *As You Like It*).

2 O.J. Campbell and E.G. Quinn, *A Shakespeare Encyclopaedia* (1966), p. 526.

3 Hazlitt, *Characters*, p. 213.

4 From *The Spectator*, 8 November 1879, quoted in A.C. Sprague, *Shakespearian Players and Performances* (1954), p. 116.

5 Judith Cook, *Shakespeare's Players* (1983), p. 86.

6 John Dover Wilson, *Shakespeare's Happy Comedies* (1962), p. 114.

7 This was in Judi Dench's production for the Renaissance Theatre Company, 1988.

8 *Shaw on Shakespeare*, pp. 24, 26.

9 As, for example, in the National Theatre production of 1967, by Clifford Williams, and the Cheek by Jowl production of 1991 by Declan Donellan. In both productions I found that, so far from increasing the play's sexuality (let alone suggesting homosexuality), the casting reduced it, throwing more emphasis on game-playing.

10 It is a curious comment on Shakespeare's use of language for characterization that in all his writings only Feste uses the word 'madonna' and he only of Olivia; the Italian word is first recorded in English as a form of address in 1584, and of a representation of the Virgin Mary in 1646.

11 Bullough, vol. 2, p. 361.

12 Virginia Woolf, *The Death of the Moth* (1942; repr. 1961), p. 45.

13 John Dennis, dedication of *The Comical Gallant* (1702); Vickers, vol. 2, p. 161.

14 Nicholas Rowe, Introduction to his edition (1709), vol. 1, pp. viii–ix.

15 Hazlitt, *Characters*, p. 257.

16 A.C. Bradley, 'The Rejection of Falstaff', in *Oxford Lectures on Poetry* (1926), p. 248.

17 Vickers, vol. 2, p. 165.

18 *Samuel Johnson on Shakespeare*, p. 187.

19 *The Shakespearean Scene: Dramatic Criticisms* (n.d.), p. 21.

NINE

Tragedies of Rome and Elsinore:
Julius Caesar and *Hamlet*

From writing *Henry the Fifth*, in which he portrayed the triumphs of the greatest of English hero-kings, Shakespeare seems to have turned directly to write about the decline of the greatest figure of classical antiquity, the man who was so great that he had even conquered England: 'Julius Caesar – whose remembrance yet | Lives in men's eyes, and will to ears and tongues | Be theme and hearing ever' (*Cymbeline*, 3.1.2–4). *Julius Caesar* was one of the first plays to be acted at the newly built Globe Theatre in 1599, and may even have been composed for its opening. After seeing one of its early performances a Swiss doctor, Thomas Platter, wrote: 'On the 21st of September, after dinner, at about two o'clock, I went with my party across the water; in the straw-thatched house we saw the tragedy of the first Emperor Julius Caesar, very pleasingly performed, with approximately fifteen characters.' (In fact the play has around fifty characters, but with doubling can be performed by a company of sixteen.)[1]

Like the plays on English history which had preoccupied Shakespeare during the previous decade, *Julius Caesar* is a political drama, concerned with affairs of state as well as with individuals; like them, it treats of the effects of usurpation; and again Shakespeare is dealing with actual, not invented, happenings. Not surprisingly, productions have often suggested parallels to the action in later totalitarian regimes, such as that of Mussolini; on the other hand this is perhaps the most purely classical of Shakespeare's plays; in its style he seems consciously to have aimed at a Roman simplicity and directness. This, along with the fact that there are only two small parts for women, and no sex, has given it the reputation of an 'easy' play specially suitable for study by young boys; but it is not short of interpretative problems.

★

Turning from English to Roman history, Shakespeare turned, too,
from one massive source book to another, from Holinshed's
Chronicles to Sir Thomas North's great translation of *Lives of the Noble
Grecians and Romans* by the Greek historian Plutarch, based on a
French version by Jacques Amyot and published in 1579. (There is a
touching tribute to the success of this work in Ben Jonson's play *The
Devil is an Ass* (1616), where Tom Gilthead says he named his son
Plutarchus because

> That year, sir,
> That I begot him, I bought Plutarch's lives,
> And fell so in love with the book as I called my son
> By his name, in hope he should be like him.
>
> (3.2.21–4)

Plutarch's splendid book must have appealed to Shakespeare partly
because it is an idiosyncratic history of people as well as of events, rich
in anecdote, and also for the excellence of North's prose, on which he
often draws closely, sometimes incorporating whole phrases word for
word in his dialogue. But although he was to some extent constrained
by history, as usual he also felt free to remould his inherited material
for dramatic purposes; for instance, the Forum Scene (3.2) compresses into a single stretch of action events that historically occurred in
several different places over the space of some six weeks.

Shakespeare could take for granted Caesar's reputation as perhaps
the greatest ruler in the history of the world, but his very greatness
made him particularly suitable for writers moralizing on the theme of
the vanity of human wishes. So for example Thomas Nashe, writing
on ambition, told how

> when he had conquered Gallia, Belgia, this our poor Albion, and
> the better part of Europe, and upon his return to Rome was
> crowned Emperor, in the height of his prosperity he sent men
> skilled in geometry to measure the whole world that, whereas he
> intended to conquer it all, he might know how long he should be
> in overrunning it. Letters had they directed to all Presidents,
> Consuls, Dukes, Palatines, Tetrarchs, and Judges of Provinces to
> assist them and safe-conduct them. Their commission was not
> only to measure the earth, but the waters, the woods, the seas,

the shores, the valleys, the hills, and the mountains. In this discovery thirty years were spent, from his Consulship to the Consulship of Saturninus, when God wot, poor man, twenty years good before they returned he was all-to-bepoinarded in the Senate House and had the dust of his bones in a brazen urn (no bigger than a bowl) barrelled up, whom – if he had lived – all the sea and earth and air would have been too little for.[2]

And Shakespeare was to make Hamlet more lyrically express similar sentiments:

> Imperial Caesar, dead and turned to clay,
> Might stop a hole to keep the wind away.
> O, that that earth which kept the world in awe
> Should patch a wall t'expel the winter's flaw!
>
> (5.1.208–11)

This sense of the vanity of human ambition is present too in the portrayal even of the living Caesar in Shakespeare's play. Not that there is any doubt of his greatness. He is deferentially treated on his first appearance: 'When Caesar says "Do this", it is performed', says Mark Antony (1.2.12); he makes noble statements:

> It seems to me most strange that men should fear,
> Seeing that death, a necessary end,
> Will come when it will come.
>
> (2.2.35–7)

We are reminded of his conquests, and of his influence over the people of Rome.

But we are frequently reminded, too, that this colossus is but a man. Though Shakespeare allows Caesar his full measure of worldly greatness, he lets us see that the world-conqueror will before long – and sooner than he may expect – be 'barrelled up' in a brazen urn no bigger than a bowl. Characteristically, the theme is sounded even in the opening scene: on the one hand, we see citizens who 'make holiday to see Caesar, and to rejoice in his triumph'; on the other hand the Tribunes, Flavius and Murellus, denigrate Caesar, their comments on the last popular hero, Pompey, suggesting both the emptiness of fame and the fickleness of the crowd, to be much exploited later in the play. Caesar's vulnerability is implicit even in what he says about himself:

> I rather tell thee what is to be feared
> Than what I fear, for always I am Caesar.
> Come on my right hand, for this ear is deaf . . .
>
> (1.2.212–14)

(The deafness is Shakespeare's invention.) And Cassius, trying to persuade Brutus to join the conspiracy against Caesar, is at pains to stress his common humanity with vivid anecdotes designed to prove what anyone must know, that Caesar is a man, not a god.

These anecdotes are part of the play's rhetoric of persuasion. And rhetoric is even more important in *Julius Caesar* than in *Henry the Fifth*. Considered rationally, nothing that Cassius says is remotely adequate as a justification of assassination; yet his powers of persuasion are so convincing that they lessen our sense of Brutus's guilt in capitulating to them. Brutus is deceived not only by Cassius but by himself. Much of his reason for joining the conspiracy against Caesar is fear, not of what Caesar has done, but of what he might do. He succeeds in arguing himself into a frame of mind in which he decides to do something that he knows to be wrong:

> It must be by his death. And for my part
> I know no personal cause to spurn at him,
> But for the general. He would be crowned.
> How that might change his nature, there's the question.
>
> (2.1.10–13)

Caesar is to be executed for a crime he has not yet committed.

Not only is Brutus deceived by rhetoric, he also uses it himself in a manner suggestive of self-deception, trying to dress up the inglorious deed in noble words:

> Let's be sacrificers, but not butchers, Caius.
> We all stand up against the spirit of Caesar,
> And in the spirit of men there is no blood.
> O, that we then could come by Caesar's spirit,
> And not dismember Caesar! But, alas,
> Caesar must bleed for it. And, gentle friends,
> Let's kill him boldly, but not wrathfully.
> Let's carve him as a dish fit for the gods,
> Not hew him as a carcass fit for hounds.
>
> (2.1.166–74)

God-meat or dog-meat, we might retort, the effect on Caesar will be just the same.

Still more obviously ironical is Brutus's attempt to glorify the deed when it is done:

> Stoop, Romans, stoop,
> And let us bathe our hands in Caesar's blood
> Up to the elbows, and besmear our swords;
> Then walk we forth even to the market-place,
> And, waving our red weapons o'er our heads,
> Let's all cry 'peace, freedom, and liberty!'
>
> (3.1.106–11)

As the conspirators stoop to smear their hands with Caesar's blood Shakespeare expands the staged representation of an historical action in a way that breaks across the barriers of time to make us see the emblematic significance of what they do:

> CASSIUS   How many ages hence
>   Shall this our lofty scene be acted over,
>   In states unborn and accents yet unknown!
> BRUTUS How many times shall Caesar bleed in sport,
>   That now on Pompey's basis lies along,
>   No worthier than the dust!
> CASSIUS   So oft as that shall be,
>   So often shall the knot of us be called
>   The men that gave their country liberty.
>
> (3.1.112–19)

Before long the 'peace, freedom, and liberty' of Rome will turn to the senseless killing of Cinna, another of Shakespeare's symbolic figures of innocence, like the boy victims in the English histories, but this time a poet who, presumably, uses words in a search for truth rather than to cloak the truth.

The most conspicuously rhetorical scene in the play occurs in the Forum as first Brutus, then Antony speaks to the Roman people about Caesar's murder. In a sense this scene not merely uses rhetoric but is about rhetoric – about the power of emotively structured speech to sway men, to turn a crowd into a mob, to overwhelm reason with passion. Brutus's speech is in prose, excellent and effective in its laconic way: he has the crowd shouting 'Live, Brutus, live, live! – Bring him with triumph home unto his house – Give him a statue with

his ancestors'; but he has made a major error in his calculations, one
that the more worldly-wise Cassius had warned him of: he has
underestimated Mark Antony. When Cassius had counselled that
Antony should be killed along with Caesar, Brutus had argued against
it:

> Our course will seem too bloody, Caius Cassius,
> To cut the head off and then hack the limbs,
> Like wrath in death and envy afterwards –
> For Antony is but a limb of Caesar.
>
> (2.1.162–5)

This is a mistake that the mature Henry V would not have made. And
when Brutus had given Antony permission to speak in the Forum,
Cassius had warned him, 'You know not what you do.' We in the
audience have had a taste of Antony's eloquence before he addresses
the crowd, and it is partly this that makes the Forum scene so intensely
exciting; it becomes a true battle of wits, and we can take pleasure in
the rhetorical skill with which Shakespeare's artistry credits Antony.
He is no more intellectual in his appeal than Brutus had been, but we
admire his keen intelligence as he manipulates the crowd, appealing to
their sentiment, their memories of Caesar's past greatness, their
greed, and their aggression. We do not need to assume that his rhetoric
has no basis in human feeling. In soliloquy he had expressed grief for
Caesar's death:

> O pardon me, thou bleeding piece of earth,
> That I am meek and gentle with these butchers.
> Thou art the ruins of the noblest man
> That ever livèd in the tide of times.
>
> (3.1.257–60)

But he had gone on to express his intention to avenge Caesar and to
prophesy that his death will result in 'domestic fury and fierce civil
strife'. The consequences of usurpation are the same in Rome as in
England.

In his addresses to the crowd Antony's personal emotion is
subjugated to his desire for vengeance. He is in control of himself and
of the mob: as they rush off crying 'Pluck down benches, windows,
anything!' his calm words are as strong in dramatic effect as any in the
play:

> Now let it work. Mischief, thou art afoot.
> Take thou what course thou wilt.

He is the still centre of the storm he has himself created.

Antony's rhetorical victory does not imply that his cause is any more 'right' than that of the conspirators; but his statements about Caesar help to rehabilitate him in the eyes not only of the citizens of Rome but also of the audience. With Caesar's death we grow less conscious of him as a man among men; the legend begins to reimpose itself; this was, says his murderer, 'the foremost man of all the world'. The consequences of the assassination work themselves out in the second part of the play, and it is Caesar's supporters who gain the victory, helped by dissension among the conspirators. The quarrel between Brutus and Cassius was long regarded as one of the play's theatrical highlights; its reputation has dwindled in modern times, perhaps because the play has been treated more as an artistic unity, less as an actors' showcase than it once was; but it clearly goes back to early in the play's career: in the early seventeenth century Leonard Digges, in the lines referred to in the section on *Much Ado About Nothing* (p. 166), wrote:

> So have I seen, when Caesar would appear,
> And on the stage at half-sword parley were
> Brutus and Cassius: O, how the audience
> Were ravished, with what wonder they went thence,
> When some new day they would not brook a line
> Of tedious though well-laboured *Catiline* . . .

In this scene Shakespeare sustains the play's concern with language, commenting obliquely on these men's excessive dependence on words. Cassius had deliberately perverted the truth; Brutus had, perhaps unconsciously, done the same. Now the pair of them indulge in mutual recriminations on a petty level:

CASSIUS I said an elder soldier, not a better.
   Did I say better?
BRUTUS   If you did, I care not.
CASSIUS When Caesar lived he durst not thus have moved me.
BRUTUS Peace, peace; you durst not so have tempted him.
CASSIUS I durst not?
BRUTUS No.
CASSIUS What, durst not tempt him?

BRUTUS For your life you durst not.
CASSIUS Do not presume too much upon my love.
    I may do that I shall be sorry for.

(4.2.110–19)

The episode cannot increase our respect for them; we may wonder
whether Caesar's human weaknesses would have been any more
dangerous to the state than theirs. There may be irony too in the fact
that it is false words that bring about Cassius's death, when he is
wrongly told that Titinius is dead. (Admittedly the episode is based on
Plutarch, but Shakespeare added the incident in which Titinius's
apparent death is *reported* to Cassius.)

In the Folio, where the play first appeared, it is called *The Tragedy of
Julius Caesar*. It is an odd sort of tragedy in which the hero dies half-
way through the play and has one of the smaller roles; but Shakespeare
was never circumscribed by rules of dramatic composition, and
although Brutus may be regarded as the more tragic character, Caesar
is certainly the dominant force even after his death. His spirit appears
and speaks, briefly, to Brutus in an episode that is close to Plutarch;
some directors have even brought him on as a silent figure of
vengeance in the battle scenes: a mistake, I think. The play works itself
out with the triumph of Antony and Octavius, but it is a muted
triumph, a compassionate rather than a condemnatory conclusion, as
Antony speaks his tribute over the dead Brutus:

> This was the noblest Roman of them all.
> All the conspirators save only he
> Did that they did in envy of great Caesar;
> He only, in a general honest thought,
> And common good to all, made one of them.
> His life was gentle, and the elements
> So mixed in him that Nature might stand up
> And say to all the world 'This was a man.'

Fine words. But are they true? Do we know Brutus better than
Antony? Does Shakespeare end the play with a totally affirmative
statement, or with an implied question? – with an acceptance of the
judgement of history, or a suggestion that it is no more the repository
of final truth than any other of the words of man?

★

The anxieties of the conscience-ridden usurper Henry IV and the moral dilemmas relating to Brutus, seduced (as Cassius says (1.2.312)) to murder his friend by specious arguments, betoken Shakespeare's increasing interest in moral problems – or, to put it slightly differently, his increasing appreciation of the dramatic capital to be made out of nicely balanced moral situations. This finds issue in a number of plays where such matters are paramount, plays which have come to be classified by some critics as 'problem plays' both because they portray characters in morally problematic situations and because they also pose particular problems of judgement for the reader or spectator.[3]

Hamlet, a play about a man required by a ghost which claims to be that of his murdered father to take revenge for his father's murder by himself murdering (or, if you prefer, judicially killing) his uncle, who is also his stepfather, is certainly a problem play in this sense. It also poses many problems both scholarly and critical.

The plot originates in an old Scandinavian folk-tale which probably reached England by way of a French version in François Belleforest's *Histoires tragiques* of 1570; it was not translated into English until 1608. Several references from 1589 onwards show that a play about Hamlet already existed, and there have been guesses that it was by Thomas Kyd, or an imitator, or even that it was an earlier version by Shakespeare himself; but it is among the hundreds of plays from this period that have not survived, so we cannot tell what relationship it bore to the play we know. The first clear reference to Shakespeare's play is its registration for publication on 26 July 1602 when it was described not as a tragedy but as *The Revenge of Hamlet Prince [of] Denmark* and was said to have been 'lately acted by the Lord Chamberlain his servants'.

The play itself survives in three different versions; their relationship is a matter of dispute on which views about when Shakespeare wrote his play, and in what form, depend. In 1603 appeared a short version of only about 2200 lines which seems to have been imperfectly put together from actors' memories; this is usually known as the 'bad' Quarto. The title-page describes it as '*The Tragical History of Hamlet Prince of Denmark*, by William Shakespeare', and says that it had been 'divers times acted by his Highness' servants in the City of London as also in the two Universities of Cambridge and Oxford, and elsewhere'. A taste of its quality is provided by its version of the opening lines of the play's most famous speech:

> To be, or not to be; ay, there's the point.
> To die, to sleep – is that all? Ay, all.
> No, to sleep, to dream. Ay, marry, there it goes,
> For in that dream of death, when we awake
> And borne before an everlasting judge,
> From whence no passenger ever returned,
> The undiscovered country at whose sight
> The happy smile, and the accursèd damned.
> But for this, the joyful hope of this,
> Who'ld bear the scorns and flattery of the world,
> Scorned by the right rich, the rich cursèd of the poor?[4]

In the following year, as if to set the record straight, James Roberts, who had signified his intention to publish the play by entering it in the Stationers' Register in 1602, printed the longest of the surviving early versions, extending to about 3800 lines, describing it as 'Newly imprinted and enlarged to almost as much again as it was, according to the true and perfect copy'. This version, known as the 'good' Quarto, is generally agreed to have been printed from Shakespeare's own manuscript.

But when the play came to be printed in the 1623 Folio it was in yet a third version, some 230 lines shorter than the good Quarto (it omits, for example, Hamlet's last soliloquy, 'How all occasions do inform against me'), and with many verbal differences as well as about 70 extra lines. This seems to represent the play in a revised form in which it had been acted by Shakespeare's company. Critics as well as scholars need to be aware of this fluid textual situation; we cannot assume that any single version of the play has ultimate authority; the Folio seems to be the closest we can get to a performance text, though some or all of its omissions may have been unauthorized.[5] Probably Shakespeare wrote his original play around 1600, following on from *Julius Caesar* and *As You Like It* (in which comedy, incidentally, the melancholy Jaques faintly foreshadows the 'gloomy Dane', as Hamlet, not entirely fairly, has been called).

Some of the critical problems that have been encountered with *Hamlet* were neatly expressed in a skit on the play, *Rosencrantz and Guildenstern*, by W.S. Gilbert, which appeared first in 1874. Hearing of the many different forms in which Hamlet appears ('Sometimes he's tall – sometimes he's very short – | Now with black hair – now with a flaxen wig . . .'), Guildenstern exclaims, 'Oh, he is surely mad!' To which Ophelia replies:

> Well, there again
> Opinion is divided. Some men hold
> That he's the sanest, far, of all sane men –
> Some that he's really sane, but shamming mad –
> Some that he's really mad, but shamming sane –
> Some that he will be mad, some that he *was* –
> Some that he couldn't be. But on the whole
> (As far as I can make out what they mean)
> The favourite theory's somewhat like this:
> Hamlet is idiotically sane
> With lucid intervals of lunacy.[6]

In this passage Gilbert satirizes critical disputes about the play, disputes which have diminished neither in quantity nor in intensity since he wrote.

But there can be no dispute about one aspect of the play: ever since it was first performed it has been, not simply one of Shakespeare's most admired plays, and one of his most frequently performed, but also one of the most popular and influential works ever written in any language. It has been imitated, burlesqued, and parodied; operaticized and balletified; filmed and televised. Other plays, novels, and poems have been based upon it; many phrases from it have entered the language; Hamlet himself – depicted as a young man holding and gazing at a skull – has become a type figure with an existence outside the play; its characters and situations have formed the basis of many works of pictorial art; it has been translated into most of the world's languages, and it has been continually performed in many different versions. In recent years, at least, *King Lear* may have overtaken it in critical esteem, but *Hamlet* continues to exert more genuinely popular appeal; more than any other of Shakespeare's plays it exemplifies his capacity – encouraged, no doubt, by the mixed audiences at the Globe – to appeal on many levels at once. It is one of the world's greatest tragedies; it is also, to put it simply, a good night out at the theatre.

Hamlet comes at the end of a period of some five years during which Shakespeare wrote only one play – *Julius Caesar* – with anything approaching a tragic framework. In the comedies of this period he produced some of his wittiest, most humorous, and most lyrical verse and prose; although there are many differences between them and *Hamlet*, there are also many resemblances. As we have seen, this is the period of his career during which he used proportionately most prose and least verse in his plays, and *Hamlet* contains more prose than any other of his tragedies; also, I suppose, it contains more easy, lyrical verse than any except *Romeo and Juliet*. *Hamlet*, it is often said, 'is full of quotations', and some of these are obviously 'poetical' passages –

> But look, the morn in russet mantle clad
> Walks o'er the dew of yon high eastern hill
>
> (1.1.147–8)

or

> There is a willow grows aslant a brook
> That shows her hoar leaves in the glassy stream . . .
>
> (4.7.138–9)

The prose has a similarly lyrical quality. It is as flexible an instrument of expression as the verse, sometimes capturing the terse utterances of day-to-day speech, but at other times written with consummate artistry, reaching, for example, the heights of Hamlet's meditation on man:

> . . . it goes so heavily with my disposition that this goodly
> frame, the earth, seems to me a sterile promontory. This most
> excellent canopy the air, look you, this brave o'erhanging, this
> majestical roof fretted with golden fire – why, it appears no other
> thing to me than a foul and pestilent congregation of vapours.
> What a piece of work is a man! How noble in reason, how
> infinite in faculty, in form and moving how express and
> admirable, in action how like an angel, in apprehension how like
> a god – the beauty of the world, the paragon of animals!
>
> (2.2.299–309)

Part of the play's appeal lies in the sheer sensuous pleasure of the way it is written.

It is not only in the use of prose that *Hamlet*'s comic antecedents have left their mark. English tragedy has a reputation for frivolity that has embarrassed even the English themselves, so that, for example, Coleridge could not believe that Shakespeare was responsible for the bawdy ironies of the Porter in *Macbeth*, *King Lear* was acted for close on two hundred years without the Fool, and David Garrick omitted the comic gravediggers from his acting text of *Hamlet*. The extreme point of view was expressed by a Frenchman, Voltaire, writing at a time when even Shakespeare's own countrymen were unable to respond to what they regarded as the excessively 'romantic' freedom of his drama. *Hamlet*, wrote Voltaire, is a vulgar and barbarous drama, which would not be tolerated by the vilest populace of France or Italy. Hamlet becomes crazy in the second act, and his mistress becomes crazy in the third. The Prince slays his mistress's father under the pretence of killing a rat, and the heroine throws herself into a river. A grave is dug on the stage, and the gravediggers speak characteristically in riddles while holding skulls in their hands. Hamlet responds to their nasty vulgarities in sillinesses no less disgusting. In the meantime another of the actors conquers Poland. Hamlet, his mother and his father-in-law carouse on the stage; songs are sung at table, there is quarrelling, fighting, killing – one would imagine this piece to be the work of a drunken savage. But amidst all those nasty vulgarities, which to this day make the English drama so absurd and barbarous, there are to be found in *Hamlet*, by a bizarrerie still greater, some sublime passages worthy of the greatest genius. It seems as though nature had mingled in Shakespeare's brain the greatest conceivable strength and grandeur with whatsoever witless vulgarity can devise that is lowest and most detestable.[7]

Voltaire's strictures are directed partly against the unconscious comedy that he finds in the improbabilities and violences of the plot. But he disapproves too of the play's intended comedy – the witticisms of the gravediggers and of Hamlet's conversation with one of them. There is indeed a remarkable amount of intentional humour in this play, a fact which links it rather with the earlier *Romeo and Juliet* than with the later tragedies. It includes several characters who are predominantly funny – Polonius, the gravediggers, Osric – as well as variously good-humoured, genial, and witty episodes among the others. And whereas in *Romeo and Juliet* comedy departs as the action advances, *Hamlet* is shot through with it right up to the last scene. Shakespeare's determination to sustain the possibility of a comic perspective on the tragic action is clear in that the most purely comic characters – the gravediggers and Osric – do not emerge until the last act.

But the play's most richly, complexly comic character is Hamlet himself. If Richard II and Brutus are among his antecedents, so too are Biron and Benedick; he is the only one of Shakespeare's tragic heroes whom we can imagine, in happier circumstances, starring in a romantic comedy. When we see him in his more relaxed moments, with Horatio, the players, and even Polonius and Osric, we may respond to his charm and for a while forget the terrible burden he labours under.

Humour in a tragedy suggests variety, and certainly variety of effect is among the play's most valued characteristics. It has great variety of style in both prose and verse: one has only to think of the characteristic language of such diverse characters as Claudius, Polonius, Osric, the speakers of the play within the play, and Hamlet himself. The diversity of style both reflects and creates an equal diversity of characters: Shakespeare is here the supreme ventriloquist. And along with this goes a wide range of theatrical effect. Tragedy though it is, *Hamlet* is one of the most entertaining of plays. As at a performance of an opera one may look forward to favourite arias or ensembles, so in *Hamlet*, however often one has seen it, there is always fresh pleasure to be had from seeing whether the opening scene will be as chilling as it should, how the Ghost will be made to appear ghostly, what will be made of the players' scenes, Ophelia's madness, the churchyard episode, Osric's foppishness, and the final great ensemble centring on the duel of the last scene. It is a long play, but there is always something to look forward to.

More than most plays, *Hamlet* is a series of opportunities for virtuosity. This is true above all of the role of Hamlet himself. 'Hamlet', wrote Max Beerbohm, is 'a hoop through which every very eminent actor must, sooner or later, jump.'[8] There is no wonder that it has been such a favourite part with actors, and even with actresses. The performer has the opportunity to demonstrate a wide range of ability, to be melancholy and gay, charming and cynical, thoughtful and flippant, tender and cruel, calm and impassioned, noble and vindictive, downcast and witty, all within a few hours. He can wear a variety of costumes, he need not disguise good looks, he can demonstrate athletic ability, he has perhaps the longest role in drama – he could scarcely ask for more, except perhaps the opportunity to sing and dance.

And if the role of Hamlet is the greatest reason for the play's popularity with actors, the character of Hamlet is surely the greatest reason for its popularity with audiences. Hamlet is the most sympathetic of tragic heroes. We are drawn to him by his youth, his intelligence, and his vulnerability. As soon as he appears we are conscious of one of the sources of his appeal: his immense capacity for taking life seriously. It may sound like a slightly repellent quality, but I don't mean to imply that he is excessively gloomy or over-earnest. Often he is deeply dejected: but he has good cause. There is nothing exceptional about his emotional reactions except perhaps their intensity. He has a larger-than-life capacity for experience, a fullness of response, a depth of feeling, a vibrancy of living, which mark him out from the ordinary. He is a raw nerve in the court of Denmark, disconcertingly liable to make the instinctive rather than the conditioned response. This cuts him off from those around him, but it puts him into peculiar contact with the audience. And as Hamlet is to the other figures of the play, so his soliloquies are to the role, for in them Shakespeare shows us the raw nerves of Hamlet himself.

The use of soliloquy is one of the most brilliant features of the play, for in these speeches Shakespeare solves a major technical problem in the presentation of his central character. The young man who takes himself seriously, who persists in explaining himself and his problems, is someone we are apt – perhaps too apt – to regard as a bore. We have all had experience of him, and so probably have most of our friends. On the other hand, the desire to know someone to the depths is fundamental to human nature. Here was both a problem and a challenge: how to let Hamlet reveal himself without becoming an almighty bore? Shakespeare found a double solution. First, he caused Hamlet to conduct his deepest self-communings in solitude, so that there is none of the awkwardness associated with the presence of a confidant. And secondly, the soliloquies are written in a style which presents us not with conclusions but with the very processes of Hamlet's mind.

There had been nothing like this in drama before: nothing which, while retaining a verse form, at the same time so vividly revealed what Shakespeare elsewhere calls 'the quick forge and working-house of thought' (*Henry the Fifth* [5.Pro.23]). Vocabulary, syntax, and rhythm all contribute to the effect. Consider the second half of Hamlet's first soliloquy, beginning with his contrast between his uncle and his dead father:

> That it should come to this –
> But two months dead – nay, not so much, not two –
> So excellent a king, that was to this
> Hyperion to a satyr, so loving to my mother
> That he might not beteem the winds of heaven
> Visit her face too roughly! Heaven and earth,
> Must I remember? Why, she would hang on him
> As if increase of appetite had grown
> By what it fed on, and yet within a month –
> Let me not think on't; frailty, thy name is woman –
> A little month, or ere those shoes were old
> With which she followed my poor father's body,

Like Niobe, all tears, why she, even she –
O God, a beast that wants discourse of reason
Would have mourned longer! – married with mine uncle,
My father's brother, but no more like my father
Than I to Hercules; within a month,
Ere yet the salt of most unrighteous tears
Had left the flushing of her gallèd eyes,
She married. O most wicked speed, to post
With such dexterity to incestuous sheets!
It is not, nor it cannot come to good.
But break, my heart, for I must hold my tongue.

                                        (1.2.137–59)

The anguish that it causes Hamlet to think of his mother's over-hasty marriage is conveyed as much by the tortured syntax as by direct statement; we share his difficulty as he tries – and fails – to assimilate these unwelcome facts into his consciousness, seeking to bring under emotional control the discordant elements of his disrupted universe: his love of his dead father, his love of his mother combined with disgust at her marriage to the uncle whom he loathes, and the disillusion with womankind that this has provoked in him. The short exclamations interrupting the sentence structure point his horror: the rhythms of ordinary speech within the verse give immediacy to the contrasts in phrases such as 'Hyperion to a satyr' and 'Than I to Hercules'; and the concreteness of the imagery betrays the effort it costs him to master the unwelcome nature of the facts which it expresses: his mother's haste to marry 'or ere those shoes were old | With which she followed my poor father's body' – it is as if only by concentrating on the matter-of-fact, physical aspects of the scene can he bear to contemplate it, or bring it within his belief. He ends on a note of utter helplessness: he alone sees the truth; he knows that his mother's actions, which both he and she see as evil, must bring forth evil; but he, the only emotionally honest person there, cannot express his emotion – except to us.

One reason for *Hamlet*'s popularity is the stimulus it provides for discussion and argument. As Peter Hall wrote at the time of his 1965 production, 'It turns a new face to each century, even to each decade. It is a mirror which gives back the reflection of the age that is contemplating it.' And the text in itself is so rich that anyone trying to write about it within a comparatively small scope is bound to select. If I had to say in a phrase what I thought was Shakespeare's central concern in writing the play, other than telling a story, I should say

'Reactions to death'. It is a dead man that sets Hamlet the task that preoccupies him throughout the play, and when we first see Hamlet he is wearing mourning – the only one to do so in a court whose other members are fresh from celebrating a coronation and a royal wedding. Hamlet is silent but not inconspicuous as the new king, his uncle-father, deals with business, passing over his nephew's affairs in favour of those of Laertes. When at last Hamlet becomes an object of attention it is to be rebuked by both his uncle and his newly widowed, newly married mother for continuing to grieve for his father.

In *Twelfth Night* – which seems to have been written after *Hamlet* – Shakespeare shows that excessive grief may be regarded as folly, but Hamlet has just suffered a double psychic shock, and the dramatic perspective of the scene, with Hamlet directly seeking the audience's sympathy at the end of it, encourages us to take his point of view. Nevertheless G. Wilson Knight, in a famous essay, declared that Claudius's 'advice to Hamlet about his exaggerated mourning for his father's death is admirable common sense' and that he and his court 'assert the importance of human life'. For Wilson Knight, Claudius is 'a typical kindly uncle' – except of course that he happens to have murdered his brother, etc. . . .[9] For me, it is the reality of Hamlet's grief that 'asserts the importance of human life'. Hamlet makes the point for us when his mother asks why grief seems so particular with him. 'Seems?' he says: 'I know not seems . . . I have that within which passeth show.' In the first soliloquy, one of the troubles that he cannot comprehend is his mother's inability to experience true grief: 'a beast . . . would have mourned longer'.

Shattered in part by a death, Hamlet himself contemplates suicide, asking that

> this too too solid flesh would melt,
> Thaw, and resolve itself into a dew,
> Or that the Everlasting had not fixed
> His canon 'gainst self-slaughter!

(1.2.129–32)

Perhaps there is a hint of immaturity, of a failure to cope with the demands that life (which includes the dead) makes upon him. Such a sense of failure, of extreme frustration and self-dissatisfaction, marks his next soliloquy, 'O what a rogue . . .' (2.2.552 ff.). Again he is preoccupied with the expression of grief – Hamlet has just seen an actor eloquently conveying the grief of a fictional character, but is tongue-tied in the face of reality. And he blames himself for failing to take the expression of grief a step further, to the action of revenge. Part of him feels that this is what he should do, but the springs of action within him fail to respond, because no action can assuage his grief. In this lies the merciless frustration of grief for the dead. He lashes himself with words – 'Bloody, bawdy villain' – but reaches no resolution; nor is any possible. Hamlet cannot both obey the Ghost and remain himself. This is true both psychologically and physically. One way madness lies, the other death. For him to kill the King would – and will – be to bring about his own death. And though he is attracted by death as a relief from suffering, he also fears it as an 'undiscovered country'. We learn this from his central meditation on death, 'To be or not to be . . .', which poses the idea of death as a great question mark, symbolized by the Ghost and all Hamlet's doubts about it.

Soon after this, Hamlet himself inflicts death. It is both ironical and fitting that his killing of Polonius should be unpremeditated, accidental, and that it should seem almost incidental, for when it happens he is lost in his chief obsession, grief at his mother's remarriage, and his efforts to bring her to a state of self-knowledge. His attitudes are in contrast to those of Polonius's children: Ophelia retreats into madness and finally dies a death that is not far from suicide; Laertes blazes into revengeful anger such as Hamlet might have expected himself to feel (but the antithesis is not complete since Hamlet did not know immediately and directly who had killed *his* father, or even that he had been murdered).

During the long period when Hamlet is absent from the stage – in England – the play is much concerned both with the effects of death on Ophelia and Laertes, and also with the plotting of the King and Laertes to bring about Hamlet's death. And when Hamlet returns, it is to a graveyard in a scene (5.1) which mingles the most relaxed comedy in the play with some of its most deeply serious passages.

The design of the scene, though unobtrusive, is carefully calculated. It follows on immediately from Gertrude's account of Ophelia's drowning, so we know who is to be buried as we hear the gravediggers' humorous, slightly grim but entirely phlegmatic discussion of death in its most physical aspects. Death is seen as the great leveller; the gravemaker alone makes houses that last till Doomsday. Hamlet and Horatio come upon the scene, entering at first 'afar off' and overhearing the gravediggers' conversation. Hamlet comments on the discrepancy between the nature of the gravedigger's task and his way of carrying it out: 'Hath this fellow no feeling of his business that a sings at gravemaking?' The scene moves into its second stage as the gravedigger throws up first one skull and then a second, traditional emblems of mortality which provoke Hamlet to gently satirical disquisition on human vanity. There is melancholy in his awareness of the human fate: 'Did these bones cost no more the breeding than to play at loggats with 'em? Mine ache to think on't.' But there is comedy, too, in his characterization of that traditional butt of satire, the lawyer, whose 'fine pate' is at last full of 'fine dirt'.

The secret that is hidden from Hamlet comes just a little nearer to revelation as the Clown tells in his riddling fashion that he is digging the grave for no man, and no woman, but for 'One that was a woman, sir; but, rest her soul, she's dead'. A layer of comic irony is created by his talking of Hamlet who 'was mad and sent into England', where his madness would not be noticed because 'There the men are as mad as he'. Hamlet probes more deeply into the facts of mortality with his question about how long a man will 'lie i'th' earth ere he rot', and the gravedigger produces the skull of someone Hamlet had known, long ago, quite well: Yorick, who was a jester.

Now we see Hamlet in the attitude that is often taken to epitomize the play, the healthy, handsome young man contemplating a skull. The professional provoker of mirth, once 'a fellow of infinite jest', now abhors Hamlet's imagination and can produce no flash of merriment to mock the grinning of his own skull. And Hamlet draws the moral that the greatest of men will descend to this. His imagination plays obsessively on the theme, tracing 'the noble dust of Alexander' till he finds it 'stopping a bung-hole', and the scene moves for the first time into verse as he speaks (or possibly sings) of Caesar, 'dead and turned to clay', whose dust 'might stop a hole to keep the wind away'.

As Hamlet spoke of Yorick he was provoked especially to thoughts of death as the tester of appearances, of that which 'seems':

Now get you to my lady's chamber and tell her, let her paint an inch thick, to this favour she must come. Make her laugh at that.
(5.1.188–90)

His allusion to cosmetics may induce in us at least a subliminal memory of Ophelia, and of what Hamlet had said to her in the 'nunnery' scene:

I have heard of your paintings, too, well enough. God hath given
you one face, and you make yourselves another.

					(3.1.145–7)

In the scene's next stage an actual funeral appears. From the
skull that had lain in the earth many years we move to the body that is
soon to be lain there: but for a while – and obviously quite deliberately
– Shakespeare does not allow Hamlet to know whose it is. But we
know, and the scene gains in tension as first the Priest reveals that this
is the body of a suicide and then Laertes that it is Ophelia. Hamlet
remains to one side as Laertes speaks his great expression of grief
combined with a curse on the very Hamlet who is watching him:

> O, treble woe
> Fall ten times treble on that cursèd head
> Whose wicked deed thy most ingenious sense
> Deprived thee of! – Hold off the earth a while,
> Till I have caught her once more in mine arms.
> *He leaps into the grave*
> Now pile your dust upon the quick and dead
> Till of this flat a mountain you have made
> To o'ertop old Pelion, or the skyish head
> Of blue Olympus.
>
> 					(5.1.242–50)

Laertes is behaving just as Hamlet wished that he himself had been able
to behave on hearing of his father's death.

And now – for the first time in the play, we may feel – Hamlet
achieves full emotional release. He had rejected Ophelia before, but
now, as he sees her dead, his deepest feelings for her give him his cue
for passion, and for once he speaks to 'real' people as previously he has
spoken only to us. With a passionate acceptance of his own humanity
he cries:

> What is he whose grief
> Bears such an emphasis, whose phrase of sorrow
> Conjures the wand'ring stars and makes them stand
> Like wonder-wounded hearers? This is I,
> Hamlet the Dane.
>
> 					(5.1.250–3)

And this is Shakespeare the dramatic poet with all the stops out. At last
Hamlet has been able to break through his inhibition, to unpack his

heart with – marvellously eloquent – words even at the expense of
seeming comically bombastic, in a great affirmation at once of love, of
personal identity, and of kingship. Forgetting himself, he finds
himself; no longer need he hold his tongue, so his heart need not
break. His sense of irony reasserts itself in the wryness with which,
adopting the conventions of the love-test, he challenges Laertes to
outface him in proof of love, and he demonstrates awareness of the
absurdity of his own bombast in

> Nay, an thou'lt mouth,
> I'll rant as well as thou.

The scene had begun with one kind of comedy, and it ends with
another. From the matter-of-fact attitudes to death of those to whom
gravemaking is 'a property of easiness' it has moved through comedy
and satire to a profound and intense expression of the value of a single
human life and of the anguish that a death can cause.

Though Hamlet ends the scene in what may well seem like a state of
exhaustion, within a few lines, in one of those swift reversals of
emotional state that are characteristic of the role, he is back again in
quiet conversation with Horatio, narrating and justifying his dispatch
of Rosencrantz and Guildenstern to their deaths. And he declares in
measured style his conviction that he will be no less justified in killing
the King:

> is't not perfect conscience
> To quit him with this arm? And is't not to be damned
> To let this canker of our nature come
> In further evil?
>
> (5.2.68–71)

For the final sequence Shakespeare brings on yet another comic
character, the affected courtier, Osric, whom Hamlet treats with the
kind of courtly intellectual superiority that he has previously
displayed to both Polonius and Claudius. Although in the graveyard
scene Hamlet has certainly experienced (as he himself put it) 'tow'ring
passion', the effect on him seems to be a kind of emotional purgation
leading to a condition of equilibrium to which he gives eloquent
expression as he discusses with Horatio the likely outcome of the duel
which he is to fight with Laertes:

We defy augury. There's a special providence in the fall of a
sparrow. If it be now, 'tis not to come. If it be not to come, it
will be now. If it be not now, yet it will come. The readiness is
all. Since no man has aught of what he leaves, what is't to leave
betimes?

(5.2.165–70)

This passage offers the opportunity of divergent interpretations of the state of mind that lies behind it, and thus of how Hamlet
ends the play. For some critics and actors he displays fatalism (A.C.
Bradley's word); for others, 'the calm attainment of a higher
benignity' (H.B. Charlton's phrase), a serene emotional as well as
intellectual acceptance of the fact that death is a part of life. The former
interpretation has informed anti-heroic performances particularly in
more recent times; the latter is more consonant with the concept of a
'princely' Hamlet, and is responsible for the play's reputation as the
most consoling and beautiful of the tragedies.

In the final episode, by whatever process, Hamlet has reached a state
in which he can kill the King as by a reflex action; and now he is
avenging not only his father's death but also his mother's and the act
that is to bring about his own. So evil both private and public is
purged, though not before it had spread like the poison that coursed
through the veins of Hamlet's father.

Hamlet's sense of humour, his courtly grace, does not desert him in
the last few minutes of his life. As usual the courtliness is double-
edged, capable of being interpreted as mockery:

HAMLET I'll be your foil, Laertes. In mine ignorance
   Your skill shall, like a star i'th' darkest night,
   Stick fiery off indeed.
LAERTES You mock me, sir.
HAMLET No, by this hand.

(5.2.201–5)

Even after Hamlet knows he is dying he displays a touch of wry
humour in speaking of the 'fell sergeant, Death' who 'Is strict in his
arrest'; and it is not until this wittiest and most elegantly humorous of
tragic heroes is dead that the play subsides into the sobriety that
Voltaire found fitting in tragedy.

Notes to Chapter Nine

1 Platter wrote in German; the translation here is by Ernest Schanzer: 'Thomas Platter's Observations on the Elizabethan Stage', *Notes and Queries* 201 (1956), pp. 465–7. Schanzer suggests that Platter may have seen at the Rose a play about Julius Caesar which was not by Shakespeare, but no such play is known.
2 From *Christ's Tears over Jerusalem*, in *Thomas Nashe: Selected Writings*, ed. S. Wells (1964), p. 177.
3 The term was first used by F.S. Boas in 1896 in relation to *Hamlet, All's Well that Ends Well, Measure for Measure*, and *Troilus and Cressida*. Ernest Schanzer, in *The Problem Plays of Shakespeare* (1963), reapplied it to relate to *Julius Caesar* and *Antony and Cleopatra* along with *Measure for Measure*.
4 In recent years some scholars have argued that this edition represents not a corruption of the play but an early version by Shakespeare himself. How anyone could believe that Shakespeare even as a schoolboy, or indeed any other professional writer, could have intentionally written lines such as these passes my understanding.
5 The scholarly and critical implications of the textual situation are well expounded in G.R. Hibbard's Oxford Shakespeare edition (1987).
6 Quoted from *Shakespeare Burlesques*, with Introductions by Stanley Wells, 5 vols (London, Diploma Press, 1978), vol. 4, p. 249.
7 Adapted from the translation in H.H. Furness's New Variorum edition, 2 vols (Philadelphia, PA, 1877), vol. 2, p. 381.
8 Max Beerbohm, *Around Theatres* (1953), vol. 1, p. 36.
9 G. Wilson Knight, *The Wheel of Fire* (1930; revised edn, 1949), p. 34.

TEN

Plays of Troy, Vienna, and Roussillon:
Troilus and Cressida, Measure for Measure, and All's Well that Ends Well

I once wrote that *Hamlet* and *Twelfth Night* were followed by 'a period of uncertainty and experimentation before the full, confident achievement of the later tragedies',[1] but that is an over-simplification. Certainly the three plays discussed in this chapter seem to have been written between about 1602 and 1604, but the order of composition of the last two, at least, is uncertain, and probably *Othello* punctuates the group. Still, *Troilus and Cressida*, *All's Well that Ends Well*, and *Measure for Measure* certainly show Shakespeare in a more experimental frame of mind than in the earlier comedies, and each of them portrays a young woman experiencing more serious moral and emotional problems than any in those plays. Although each play has undergone a process of both critical and theatrical rehabilitation during the later part of the twentieth century, their relative lack of popularity over the centuries is among the indicators of the challenges they present to both intellect and imagination. They show that at the height of his success Shakespeare was willing to court unpopularity rather than write to a formula.

Troilus and Cressida is Shakespeare's most esoteric play. It is his third longest, next only to *Hamlet* and *Richard the Third*. Its language is exceptionally difficult, abounding in new words and compounds, often of Latin derivation, coined, it would seem, in imitation of the style of classical epic and of its English translators and imitators such as the poet and playwright George Chapman, whose version of *Seven Books* of Homer's *Iliad*, published in 1598, seems to be among

Shakespeare's sources. It includes two long scenes of debate, one in the Greek camp, the other in the Trojan, which themselves include long philosophical speeches that demand the audience's close attention.

The play is difficult to place generically: on its first printing, in 1609, it was prefaced by an epistle by an unidentified writer declaring that among all its author's comedies, so distinguished for 'savoured salt of wit . . . that they seem (for their height of pleasure) to be born in that sea that brought forth Venus', 'there is none more witty than this'; it is indeed full of wit, often very salty, yet it departs in many ways from the conventions of comedy, and in the Folio, where it appears in a substantially different text, is placed among the tragedies; modern commentators have emphasized its satirical elements. These qualities have given rise to the theory that Shakespeare wrote it for a specialized audience, perhaps at one of the Inns of Court, but this is mere guesswork, complicated by the fact that although the original title-page of the first edition followed the Stationers' Register entry in claiming that the play had been acted by the Lord Chamberlain's Men, it was replaced during printing by a substitute title-page withdrawing this claim which is explicitly denied by the description in the epistle (added at the same time as the title-page was changed) of this as 'a new play, never staled with the stage, never clapper-clawed with the palms of the vulgar'.

Whether or not the play was acted in Shakespeare's time (and the differences between the Quarto and Folio editions show at least that he went on working on the text after he had first composed it, which may suggest that it was), it rapidly fell into a theatrical neglect unparalleled by that of any other play in the canon. Dryden drew on it for his *Troilus and Cressida, or The World Well Lost*, first acted in 1679, but that is essentially an independent work using Shakespeare's play as a source; in the late eighteenth century John Philip Kemble began to prepare an acting version but abandoned the project before putting it into production; and the first known performance of anything resembling Shakespeare's play is an all-male version travestying Homer acted at Munich in 1898. *Troilus and Cressida* had to wait for well over three centuries, until after the First World War, before coming into its own as a play that offers a fundamental interrogation of heroic values along with a painfully realistic portrayal of the growth and breakdown of an intense love-relationship that founders under the pressures of war.

The play emerged largely as the result of amateur, and especially university-based, performers – above all those associated with George

Rylands and the Marlowe Society of Cambridge – and since the late 1930s has received a number of deeply serious and powerful professional productions in the subsidized theatre. Many of these have drawn attention to the play's relevance to later ages by updating the action, though perhaps the finest of all, directed by Peter Hall and John Barton at Stratford in 1960, used historical costumes while setting the action in a sandpit that potently imaged Agamemnon's words, 'What's past and what's to come is strewed with husks | And formless ruin of oblivion' (4.7.50–1). At the time, 'Ban the Bomb' was a common slogan; actors are said to have inscribed the words 'Ban the Horse' in the sand.

For the subject-matter of this play Shakespeare chose the first great event in the recorded history of the world, the Trojan War (the Horse does not appear). The distance of time between the play's historical action and its date of composition is important – and is further complicated for us by the additional distance of time of modern performances from both. Important too is the fact that the war was fought over a woman, Helen of Troy (as the Grecian queen is confusingly known). The destructive power of time over human aspirations is one of the play's philosophical concerns, and so is the value that men place on love, and more generally on human emotion. The play's intertwining of the public events of the war with the private love-story of Troilus and Cressida is adumbrated in Troilus's opening speech: 'Why should I war without the walls of Troy | That find such cruel battle here within?' 'Within' punningly means both 'inside the walls' and 'within Troilus himself': he is desperate for the love of Cressida, and his love is distracting him from the business of war.

Troilus is a more physically obsessive lover than Shakespeare has so far portrayed. His heart is an 'open ulcer'; praise of Cressida's beauty, far from giving him pleasure, lays 'in every gash that love hath given me | The knife that made it' (1.1.53, 62–3). Awaiting Cressida's arrival for a private assignation, he expresses his longing for her in terms that complexly envisage the sense of destruction of the self in sexual passion:

> I am giddy. Expectation whirls me round.
> Th'imaginary relish is so sweet
> That it enchants my sense. What will it be
> When that the wat'ry palate tastes indeed
> Love's thrice-repurèd nectar? Death, I fear me,
> Swooning destruction, or some joy too fine,

Too subtle-potent, tuned too sharp in sweetness
For the capacity of my ruder powers.
I fear it much, and I do fear besides
That I shall lose distinction in my joys,
As doth a battle when they charge on heaps
The enemy flying.

(3.2.16–27)

This is the speech of one who is indeed a 'virgin in the night', as he had earlier described himself in lines ostensibly relating to his prowess in battle but actually collapsing the distinction between love and war just as now he compares his expectations of the 'little death' of sex with the destruction of an army on the battlefield. It expresses a realistic rather than a romantic attitude to love, and one that may well seem adolescent in its overheatedness, but it is not necessarily for that reason reprehensible, unless we ascribe to Shakespeare an undervaluation of the place of sex in love that is not supported even by his portrayals of more idealized lovers.

Cressida also is realistic in her attitudes to love, attitudes that have made interpretation of her character a feminist battlefield. Before they come together she meditates on Troilus's love for her in a sequence of maxims, given extra weight by being cast in the form of rhymed couplets and placed at the end of a scene, that suggest calculation rather than commitment, a willingness to manipulate personal relationships rather than to abandon herself to the beloved.

Women are angels, wooing;
Things won are done. Joy's soul lies in the doing.
That she beloved knows naught that knows not this:
Men prize the thing ungained more than it is.
That she was never yet that ever knew
Love got so sweet as when desire did sue.
Therefore this maxim out of love I teach:
Achievement is command; ungained, beseech.

(1.2.282–9)

Whereas Troilus seems naïve, Cressida may seem disillusioned, even cynical. Yet her knowing remarks are preceded by an avowal that she sees 'more in Troilus thousandfold . . . Than in the glass of pandar's praise may be', and she ends by confiding in us that her love is true, however cold she may appear in public:

> Then though my heart's contents firm love doth bear,
> Nothing of that shall from mine eyes appear.

The speech resembles Prince Hal's 'I know you all . . .' in both its declaration of concealed purpose and its placing within the dramatic structure, and it is equally, and equally fruitfully, open to variant interpretation. Does Cressida speak here from previous personal experience, or is she merely a mouthpiece for proverbial wisdom learned at her mother's knee? The personality and even the age of the performer will affect our view of the matter as much as the director's intentions.

The comedy of *Troilus and Cressida* derives largely from two figures who are more important as commentators than for their roles in the plot, Pandarus among the Trojans and Thersites among the Greeks. Pandarus has become the archetypal go-between; when he brings Cressida to Troilus for a meeting which is obviously intended to lead to rapid consummation, she declares her love unequivocally:

> Prince Troilus, I have loved you night and day
> For many weary months
>
> (3.2.111–12)

and the climax of the scene depends on our belief in the truth at least of what Agamemnon later calls 'the extant moment' (4.7.52). Shakespeare capitalizes on his knowledge that his audience would know the end of the story. The love of Troilus and Cressida is a medieval accretion to the legend of Troy, but it was well known through Chaucer's great poem and through Robert Henryson's continuation, *The Testament of Cresseid*, in which Cressida, who deserted Troilus, is now herself deserted by Diomede and dwindles into a leprous beggar. This gives an intensely ironic poignancy to the lovers' plighting of their troth, in which they look forward to the future in which the play was written and to the still more distant time of its present performance, a time, as Cressida says in lines whose heightened tone betrays Shakespeare's purpose,

> When time is old and hath forgot itself,
> When water drops have worn the stones of Troy
> And blind oblivion swallowed cities up,
> And mighty states characterless are grated
> To dusty nothing . . .
>
> (3.2.181–5)

In that time, true lovers will be compared to Troilus, 'false maids in love' will, as Cressida herself incredulously declares, be called 'As false as Cressid', 'and all brokers-between panders'.

And so to bed.

The rest of the play enacts the outcome that has been ironically predicted. As Troilus leaves Cressida in a scene of dawn parting ironically recalling that of Romeo and Juliet, Cressida implores him to stay in words that again raise questions for us about her previous experience as well as expressing her own regret that she has not held to her policy of aloofness:

> Prithee, tarry. You men will never tarry.
> O foolish Cressid! I might have still held off,
> And then you would have tarried.
>
> (4.2.18–20)

The anguish of her plea that she be not returned to the Grecian camp rubs home the ironical point:

> O you gods divine,
> Make Cressid's name the very crown of falsehood
> If ever she leave Troilus.
>
> (4.2.105–7)

But she is returned, and a crucial episode in the interpretation of Cressida is that in which, on her arrival at the Grecian camp, each leader except Ulysses kisses her in turn. At one time the assumption was that she readily acquiesced and that Ulysses's assessment of her as a 'daughter of the game' was accurate; more recently, performances influenced by feminist thought have portrayed the kisses as forced upon her, ascribing Ulysses's views to patriarchal prejudice.

But her eventual yielding to Diomedes is undeniable, and provides the occasion for one of Shakespeare's most complex experiments in dramatic perspective, the love-scene between Cressida and Diomedes in which, not without remorse, she presents him with the sleeve that Troilus had given her as a love-token, a scene which is observed and commented upon by Troilus and Ulysses and, independently, by the scurrilous Thersites. Cressida's last words in the play – again expressed in rhyming couplets – lament what Hamlet had called the frailty of women:

> Ah, poor our sex! This fault in us I find:
> The error of our eye directs our mind.
> What error leads must err. O then conclude:
> Minds swayed by eyes are full of turpitude.
>
> (5.2.111–14)

The outcome in Troilus is an anguished philosophical examination of the instability of the human personality:

> This is and is not Cressid. . . .
> Instance, O instance, strong as Pluto's gates:
> Cressid is mine, tied with the bonds of heaven.
> Instance, O instance, strong as heaven itself:
> The bonds of heaven are slipped, dissolved, and loosed,
> And with another knot, five-finger-tied,
> The fractions of her faith, orts of her love,
> The fragments, scraps, the bits and greasy relics
> Of her o'er-eaten faith, are bound to Diomed.
>
> (5.2.146, 149–63)

The love-story of Troilus and Cressida is integrated with the story of the Trojan War: it is the war that has brought Cressida into the Trojan camp and that, causing her departure, sets temptation in her way. Those who fight the war include some of the greatest heroes of classical antiquity: Priam, Hector, Paris, and Aeneas among the Trojans; Agamemnon, Ulysses, Achilles, and Ajax among the Greeks. But the way in which they are portrayed asks questions about heroic values and subjects personal reputations to searching scrutiny: Thersites, who acts as a domestic fool to Achilles, is the satirist within the play who adopts a consistently reductive attitude to all the Greeks – and indeed to all experience.

The first scene of debate shows the Grecian leaders worrying over why 'after seven years' siege yet Troy walls stand'; Ulysses says it is because 'the specialty of rule hath been neglected', and he expounds the doctrine of degree – 'Take but degree away, untune that string, | And hark what discord follows' – in a speech sometimes taken to demonstrate Shakespeare's own belief in political orthodoxy, a speech which recalls the emphasis in his early history plays on the chaos caused by civil war: a consequence of neglect of degree is that 'the rude son should strike his father dead'. But the remedy that Ulysses propounds, and that sets up the principal framework for the play's heroic action, itself depends on a deliberate violation of the moral order, the rigging of a ballot. Hector has challenged the Greeks to produce a champion for a trial of personal combat; the obvious choice is Achilles, who spends all his time lolling in his tent while his favourite, Patroclus, amuses him by mimicking the Greek leaders; the proverbially wily Ulysses proposes that, in an effort to rouse Achilles from his lethargy, they should set up a lottery and 'by device' arrange for 'blockish Ajax' to be chosen. So, if Ajax wins, they will praise him as their greatest warrior, whereas if he fails they will hold Achilles in reserve. Ajax's response to flattery produces some of the play's best comedy.

In the Trojan camp, the debate centres on Helen. The Greeks are bargaining for her return; Hector's proposal that 'she is not worth what she doth cost | The holding' leads into a discussion of the subjectivity of value. Hector expresses belief in absolute values and says they should 'let Helen go'; Troilus believes in subjectivity – which, as we know, will be his downfall – and argues that the admiration in which Helen has been held justifies any sacrifice for her sake. Though Hector persists with his argument not only against Troilus but also in face of the claim by Helen's lover, Paris, that 'Well may we fight for her whom we know well | The world's large spaces cannot parallel', ultimately, in a surprising volte-face, he agrees 'to keep Helen still' on the grounds that, as Troilus says,

> She is a theme of honour and renown,
> A spur to valiant and magnanimous deeds,
> Whose present courage may beat down our foes,
> And fame in time to come canonize us.
>
> (2.2.198–201)

Again the play's time-barrier is broken with an appeal to the posthumous reputation of the men we are watching which by its very nature questions the validity of that reputation. Hector is willing to act against his own better judgement, to put thousands of lives at risk, for the sake of fame. The only scene (3.1) in which Helen speaks shows her as so irredeemably silly that we cannot feel much confidence in the wisdom of those who regard her as a fit cause for war: Paris's ambiguous closing praise of her as 'Sweet above thought' may give us cause to think that in Troy as in Athens 'reason and love keep little company together', though here the consequence is more serious than in *A Midsummer Night's Dream*.

Shakespeare's concern in this play to relate particular events to general issues is exemplified in the scene (3.3) in which the Grecian lords taunt Achilles. Ulysses sets up the episode like a play within the play: seeing Achilles standing 'i'th' entrance of his tent', Ulysses instructs his companions to 'pass strangely by him', treating him 'As if he were forgot'. Ulysses will come last in the expectation that Achilles will ask the reason for their behaviour, providing an opportunity for Ulysses to dose him with 'derision medicinable'.

The device works, and the brief passage of action is followed by an extended philosophical excursus upon it. First Achilles reflects on the lack of honour given to men who have 'fall'n out with fortune'. But this is not how things stand with him: 'Fortune and I are friends.' He accosts Ulysses, and they embark on an intricate debate on the relationship between inherent virtue and reputation, on the need for self-esteem to be ratified by the approbation of others, on the idea that a man cannot know his own value until others have told him of it; and Ulysses illustrates his point by exclaiming on the unearned acclamation that 'the lubber Ajax' is receiving while (by implication) noble Achilles fails to put his good qualities to use. And in response to Achilles's bitter question 'What, are my deeds forgot?', Ulysses embarks on his great meditation on the effects of time – 'Time hath, my lord, | A wallet at his back . . .' – which is also an exhortation to Achilles not to rely on his past achievements but to 'take the instant way'. Ulysses is preaching at Achilles, but this is more than 'derision medicinable': his tone is deeply, even at times tortuously, serious, and he rises beyond the 'instant moment' to the poetic eloquence of a lament on the destructive power of time that is profoundly expressive of a disturbing truth that underpins the entire play:

>   O let not virtue seek
> Remuneration for the thing it was;
> For beauty, wit,
> High birth, vigour of bone, desert in service,
> Love, friendship, charity, are subjects all
> To envious and calumniating time.
>
>   (3.3.163–8)

It is characteristic of the deflationary mode of this play that the great event to which it long seems to be leading proves inconclusive: Hector abandons his combat with Ajax on the grounds that their kinship 'forbids | A gory emulation 'twixt us twain' (4.7.6–7), and the opposing leaders come together for a party in the Grecian tents; it is this truce that provides the opportunity for Troilus to observe Cressida with Diomedes.

In the battle scenes of the last act Shakespeare projects both the heroic greatness that has created the reputations of his chief characters and the flaws that tarnish it. Bitter in disillusion, Troilus criticizes his brother Hector for the chivalric 'vice of mercy' (5.3.37) that he is accustomed to show to captive Greeks; Cressida makes a last, written appeal to Troilus, but he tears her letter to pieces, dismissing its contents as 'Words, words, mere words, no matter from the heart'. Free now of the 'battle here within', he devotes himself with reckless valour to the 'war without the walls of Troy'. Hector is implored by his wife, Andromache, his father, Priam, and his mad sister, the prophetess Cassandra, not to fight, but in spite of all the omens he insists that honour is 'far more precious-dear than life' and shows himself the greatest of the warriors.

The climax of the action is, as we have been led to expect, the confrontation of Achilles and Hector, but it is not a purely personal combat and it is one that leaves each combatant open to criticism. Achilles, roused at last to active anger by the death of his beloved Patroclus, determines on Hector's death and summons his Myrmidons – his private army – to help him to effect it. Though Hector fights with unexampled heroism, he makes a mistake comparable to his earlier fault of judgement (at least so far as his own interests are concerned) in agreeing to let Helen go. The episode of the anonymous Greek soldier 'in sumptuous armour' has sometimes been cut in performance but is clearly of symbolic significance. Hector chases him for the sake of his armour; having killed him he addresses the body with ill-judged satisfaction:

> Most putrefièd core, so fair without,
> Thy goodly armour thus hath cost his life.
>
> (5.9.1–2)

Exactly the same will shortly be true of him. Believing himself safe he sets aside his arms, and it is at this moment that Achilles and his Myrmidons come upon him. Though he asks Achilles to exercise that chivalric 'vice of mercy' for which Troilus had criticized him – 'I am unarmed. | Forgo this vantage, Greek' – Achilles instructs his followers to strike.

Verbally, at least, Hector's death is not given the dignity of a tragic climax, though there are enough clues in the text to justify the sombre visual impressiveness with which it was portrayed in the Hall/Barton production. Achilles has instructed his Myrmidons to 'Empale him with your weapons round about', and these menacing figures, masked and bearing massive black shields, closed slowly in on their victim before subjecting him to an ignominious death. So far from being accorded the dignity of funeral rites, Hector's body is dragged off to be tied to the tail of Achilles's horse and 'In beastly sort dragged through the shameful field'. At the end of the play, Troilus appears to have taken Hector's place, speaking a lament for him and declaring that 'Hope of revenge shall hide our inward woe'.

Or is it the end of the play? Though there is reason to believe that in some performances it was, in both the early texts Pandarus then appears, only to be repudiated by Troilus with a blow and the curse 'Ignomy and shame | Pursue thy life, and live aye with thy name'. The person Pandarus is in the process of being turned into the type figure of the pander; he addresses the audience in an epilogue-like speech which wrenches the play into the time at which it is being performed. Without this episode the play may be seen as a tragedy; with it, the ending is less positively conclusive yet even more bleak and bitter. Pandarus has been one of the play's main sources of comedy; now, ridden by venereal disease, cursed by Troilus, he speaks across the centuries, still pathetically adopting the pose of entertainer, but finally, addressing his 'Brethren and sisters of the hold-door trade', bequeathing them nothing but his diseases.

In *Measure for Measure* and *All's Well that Ends Well* Shakespeare employs some of the conventions of comedy that he had used earlier in his career, but adopts a more questioning attitude to them. In both plays – as their titles suggest – ideas are close to the surface; in *Measure for Measure*, especially, the element of debate is important. So it had been in *Troilus and Cressida*, but there it is retrospective: the Grecian leaders debate the reasons for the stalemate in their campaign, the Trojans talk about whether to return Helen to her husband in philosophical rather than practical terms, mulling over a question they must have asked themselves thousands of times before. In *Measure for Measure* Shakespeare sets up a situation in which a debate about the relative claims of justice and mercy, so far from being an argument about abstract ideas, is a matter of immediate and passionate concern to those involved and has life-or-death consequences for one of the play's main characters; the argument pervades the play, and is not resolved until the final episode.

The play's title derives from St Matthew's account of Jesus's Sermon on the Mount: 'with what measure ye mete, it shall be measured to you again' (7.2). So far as the play's own morality is concerned the title offers a false lead, but it alerts the spectator in advance to Shakespeare's exploration of moral issues. Both the artifice of the plot and the unreality of its setting also encourage us to see this as a play of ideas rather than a simple narrative. Vienna, which had a reputation as a centre of vice, was appropriate enough for a story about a state where law has grown lax and sexual immorality is rife, and the social background of a city full of brothels is depicted with a richness of detail reminiscent rather of the later history plays than of the preceding comedies; but a 'naughty house' kept by one Mistress Overdone, with a room called the Bunch of Grapes and frequented by a constable called Elbow whose speech habits are similar to those of Dogberry, and by a young gentleman named Froth who has more money than sense, clearly bears a close relationship to the London in which the play was first performed; and it is a curious Vienna that is otherwise peopled almost entirely by characters with Italian names.

The fragile reality of the play's setting is paralleled by the use of conventional elements in its plot. It opens with the old folk-motif of a ruler – here, a duke – disguising himself in order to move more freely among his people (like Henry V). And the story of a woman who, in seeking to save the life of a male relative, arouses the lust of a man in a position of authority had often been told; the version most clearly known by Shakespeare was an unperformed two-part tragicomedy, *Promos and Cassandra*, written by George Whetstone and published in 1578.[2] Shakespeare's handling of the story sharpens its moral implications. His heroine, Isabella, is not merely, as in Whetstone, a virtuous maiden; she is about to enter a nunnery. Her brother, Claudio, has not, as in Whetstone, been accused (however unjustly) of rape; his union with the young woman, Juliet, whom he has made pregnant has been ratified by a formal ceremony of betrothal and lacks only the church's formal blessing. So Angelo, the Duke's deputy, seems peculiarly harsh in attempting to enforce the city's laws against fornication by insisting on Claudio's execution; and Angelo's hypocrisy in demanding Isabella's chastity in return for her brother's life is correspondingly greater. By adding the character of Mariana, to whom Angelo himself had once been betrothed, and by employing the traditional motif of the 'bed–trick' (also used in *All's Well that Ends Well*), by which Mariana substitutes for Isabella in Angelo's bed, Shakespeare permits Isabella both to retain her virtue and to forgive Angelo without marrying him.

The opening scene, in which the Duke transfers the power of life and death, of 'Mortality and mercy in Vienna', from himself to the ostensibly reluctant Angelo, introduces a concept related to one expressed in the debate between Ulysses and Achilles in *Troilus and Cressida*. There, Ulysses reports a 'strange fellow' as saying that even the most gifted man can be conscious of his good qualities only by reflection,

> As when his virtues, shining upon others,
> Heat them, and they retort that heat again
> To the first givers.
>
> (3.3.95–7)

Here, the Duke tells Angelo that his virtues must be set to work:

> Heaven does with us as we with torches do,
> Not light them for themselves; for if our virtues
> Did not go forth of us, 'twere all alike
> As if we had them not.
>
> (1.1.32–5)

It is a thematic statement whose sexual resonances are explored in the first seventeen of Shakespeare's sonnets, and it is particularly relevant in a play in which a central character is about to enter a nunnery where she will be forbidden to 'speak with men | But in the presence of the prioress'. But Claudio, under threat of death because of the zeal of the new broom Angelo, knows that his sister may be able to speak eloquently on his behalf; her virtues will go forth of her both in the silently persuasive power of her youth and in the 'prosperous art' with which she can 'play with reason and discourse'. On the verge of the contemplative life – we see her literally on the threshold of the priory – Isabella is thrust by necessity into a situation in which she is required to plead with a man in the presence not of a prioress but of the incorrigible, and unfailingly entertaining, reprobate Lucio.

Her first interview with Angelo is prefaced by an episode that sets forth the issue. The Provost (or keeper of the prison) is one of a number of relatively small roles in Shakespeare that offer the opportunity for unobtrusively sympathetic performances, partly because they embody a humane point of view with which the audience can easily identify. At the opening of the scene he speaks tolerantly of Claudio:

> Alas,
> He hath but as offended in a dream.
> All sects, all ages, smack of this vice; and he
> To die for't!

He offers Angelo a warning of timeless relevance. The death penalty is irrevocable:

> I have seen
> When after execution judgement hath
> Repented o'er his doom.

And he tells Angelo, and reminds us, that Isabella is

> a very virtuous maid,
> And to be shortly of a sisterhood,
> If not already.
> (2.2.3–6, 10–12, 20–2)

He speaks of the plight of Claudio's betrothed, 'the groaning Juliet', and Angelo's bureaucratic legalism is pinpointed with deadly accuracy in the word by which he refers to her: 'See you the fornicatress be removed.'

Isabella opens tentatively, declaring her abhorrence of the vice for which Claudio is condemned, but pleading that condemnation should be confined to the vice, not inflicted on him who commits it. When Angelo points out the illogic in her plea she acknowledges that the law is 'just but severe' and seems ready to give up. Lucio prompts her, instructing her how to behave as if he were the director of a play: 'Kneel down before him; hang upon his gown.' Thrilling theatrical tension develops as she plumbs deeper and deeper reserves of eloquence in face of the sustained obduracy with which Angelo – whose blood, Lucio has previously told her, 'is very snow-broth' (1.4.57) – insists that her brother must die. She uses Portia's argument that mercy surpasses temporal power; she appeals to Christian doctrine:

> Why, all the souls that were were forfeit once,
> And He that might the vantage best have took
> Found out the remedy.
>
> (2.2.75–7)

She pleads that the offence is universal, but none has died for it;
Angelo retorts: 'The law hath not been dead, though it hath slept', and
argues that insistence on justice is the most merciful course of action.
Slowly Isabella gains the upper hand, silencing Angelo with unforced
eloquence as she rises first to the aphoristic concision of 'O, it is
excellent | To have a giant's strength, but it is tyrannous | To use it like
a giant', and then to lines that have rung down the ages as a
condemnation of what Hamlet calls 'the insolence of office':

> But man, proud man,
> Dressed in a little brief authority,
> Most ignorant of what he's most assured,
> His glassy essence, like an angry ape
> Plays such fantastic tricks before high heaven
> As makes the angels weep . . .
>
> (2.2.120–5)

The culmination of her case is a plea that Angelo look into his own
bosom and ask his heart 'what it doth know | That's like my brother's
fault'; she is all too successful. Performers of the scene must hint
during its course at the psychological subtext that Shakespeare brings
to the surface in Angelo's closing soliloquy of horrified self-discovery:
that it is the very power of Isabella's eloquence, the deep devotion of
her commitment to her cause, that, rather than working on his sense
of logic, has aroused in him the selfsame sexual desires for which
Claudio has been condemned. It is her modesty that has, as he sees it,
corrupted him, her goodness that makes him 'desire her foully', her
saintliness that has shattered his.

Angelo's equation of sexuality with sin may seem surprisingly
un-Shakespearian (though the surprise may be mitigated if, as the text
does something to suggest, he is shown as a formal puritan); it is
justified by the absence of mutuality, the horror with which Isabella
receives his proposal that he will pardon Claudio if she gives up her
body to him. The proposal is not lightly made: Angelo has prayed for
release from his lust, deploring 'the strong and swelling evil' that he
has conceived: again Shakespeare keeps the moral balance delicately
poised. And it forces Isabella into a morally ambiguous situation: she

must choose between the sin of unloving fornication and the cruelty of bringing about her brother's death. For her, the sin that Angelo proposes is a mortal one; she would lose her soul, her brother only his life. The terms in which she states her decision have proved unappealing to twentieth-century audiences:

> Then Isabel live chaste, and brother die:
> More than our brother is our chastity.
>
> (2.4.184–5)

She also is human, and her actions, like her brother's and Angelo's, may call for understanding and forgiveness.

Her decision leads to the resolution to prepare Claudio for death, 'to his soul's rest', but the disguised Duke anticipates her. Few scenes in Shakespeare better demonstrate what Keats called his 'negative capability', his ability to enter into diametrically opposed states of mind, than that in which Isabella tells Claudio of Angelo's proposal and her reaction to it. It opens with the Duke's great *consolatio*, 'Be absolute for death', spoken in his guise as a friar and suggesting that the role sits easily upon him. In response Claudio claims that he is indeed reconciled to death:

> To sue to live, I find I seek to die,
> And seeking death, find life. Let it come on.
>
> (3.1.42–3)

To Isabella too he declares that if he must die he 'will encounter darkness as a bride, | And hug it in mine arms'.

But the news that Isabella could save his life by sacrificing her virginity shakes Claudio's resolve. The way that Shakespeare portrays Claudio's modulation from total rejection of the idea – 'O heavens, it cannot be!' – to a plea for life has the same kind of subtlety with which Mozart can move through hints in an accompanied recitative that an emotion is working its way to the surface to its full flowering in an aria:

CLAUDIO   Sure it is no sin,
  Or of the deadly seven it is the least.
ISABELLA Which is the least?
CLAUDIO If it were damnable, he being so wise,
  Why would he for the momentary trick
  Be perdurably fined? O Isabel!

ISABELLA What says my brother?
CLAUDIO Death is a fearful thing.
ISABELLA And shamèd life a hateful.

And Claudio launches into his devastating vision of death:

> Ay, but to die, and go we know not where;
> To lie in cold obstruction, and to rot;
> This sensible warm motion to become
> A kneaded clod, and the dilated spirit
> To bathe in fiery floods, or to reside
> In thrilling region of thick-ribbèd ice;
> To be imprisoned in the viewless winds,
> And blown with restless violence round about
> The pendent world; or to be worse than worst
> Of those that lawless and incertain thought
> Imagine howling – 'tis too horrible!
>
>   (3.1.109–28)

Isabella rejects his plea for life in terms that may, according to the tone
in which they are delivered, seem anything from the hysterical
outburst of a young girl who is as frightened of the idea of sex as
Claudio is of death, to the callous condemnation of a self-centred prig:

>   O, you beast!
> O faithless coward, O dishonest wretch,
> Wilt thou be made a man out of my vice?
> Is't not a kind of incest to take life
> From thine own sister's shame? What should I think?
> Heaven shield my mother played my father fair,
> For such a warpèd slip of wilderness
> Ne'er issued from his blood. Take my defiance,
> Die, perish! Might but my bending down
> Reprieve me from thy fate, it should proceed.
> I'll pray a thousand prayers for thy death,
> No word to save thee.
>
>   (3.1.137–48)

A director who seeks sympathy for Isabella will choose a performer
who can play her as an early teenager, no older than Romeo's Juliet;
and this would be compatible with the fact that in Shakespeare's
theatre the role would have been taken by a boy.

With these two passionate speeches, one expressive of a fear of death, the other of a fear of sex, the play has risen to an intensity of emotional expressiveness that is unparalleled in the earlier comedies, and its plot has arrived at a point where, it would seem, an outcome that is tragic to either Isabella or Claudio is inevitable. It is now that the Duke steps forward to take control of the action, and that, at the same time, the dominant mode of the play turns from verse to prose.

The Duke is an equivocal figure. At the opening he serves mainly as a plot device to set the action in motion, though an actor can (as Roger Allam did in Nicholas Hytner's 1987 RSC production) seize on his sense of guilt at the slackness of his rule to humanize the character. The ease with which he assumes the role of friar lends colour to presentation of him as a saintly character, even a Christ-figure, and this may be supported by the evident benevolence of his intentions in the later part of the play, where (anticipating Prospero in *The Tempest*) he becomes a surrogate playwright, inventing action and manipulating the characters as he steers the plot to its resolution. Yet his very manipulativeness, his assumption that he knows best what is good for everybody and even has the right to cause them pain as he attempts to bring it about, may repel. Though he justifies himself with 'Craft against vice I must apply' (4.1.533) it may seem both implausible and morally suspect that he should succeed in persuading Isabella to pretend to agree to sleep with Angelo even though the woman in the bed will actually be Mariana, Angelo's former fiancée, whom he has jilted because she had the misfortune to lose her dowry, but who loves him still. The amount of plotting that the Duke has to do to help the dramatist to bring his play to a conclusion tends to detach audiences from an action in which so far they have been deeply absorbed; it also causes the later part of the play to seem more morally didactic than investigative.

Although Mariana and Isabella agree unquestioningly to the friar-Duke's suggestions, not everyone in the play takes him at his own evaluation. He has disconcerting confrontations with other characters, particularly with Lucio, who is representative of the seamier side of life in Vienna that Angelo is trying to reform on the Duke's behalf, and with Barnardine, a drunken, self-confessed murderer long under sentence of death. Though the scenes in which they appear are fully woven into the play's fabric, and highly if wryly comic in the exasperation they cause the Duke, it is not perhaps over-interpretative to see these confrontations as emblematic of the never-ending struggle of church and state with the unregenerate forces of sexuality and violence. Lucio tells the Duke straightforwardly that it is

impossible to quell lechery 'till eating and drinking be put down'
(3.1.366–7); and Barnardine, 'A man that apprehends death no more
dreadfully but as a drunken sleep; careless, reckless, and fearless of
what's past, present, or to come; insensible of mortality, and
desperately mortal' (4.2.144–7), resolutely refuses to be put to death:
'I swear I will not die today, for any man's persuasion. . . . If you have
anything to say to me, come to my ward, for thence will not I today'
(4.2.56–60). The life-force exerts itself, and there is nothing the Duke
can do about it.

In the play's final stretch of action it is Isabella who suffers most.
Though the Duke has foiled Angelo's plan of having Claudio executed
in spite of Isabella's apparent sacrifice of her virginity, sending to
Angelo the head of 'a most notorious pirate' instead of Claudio's (as he
grimly says, 'Death's a great disguiser'), he tells Isabella that her
brother is dead, excusing his action to us with the statement that he

> will keep her ignorant of her good,
> To make her heavenly comforts of despair
> When it is least expected.
>
> (4.3.106–8)

Entering the city gates in his own person, he pretends ignorance,
defending Angelo who stands by as Isabella tells her story, demanding
justice on the man who has wronged her. Angelo maintains his show
of innocence even after Mariana has told her side of the story, and not
until the Duke reveals that he knows everything because of his
disguise as a friar does Angelo admit his guilt, whereupon the Duke
sends him off with orders to marry Mariana instantly.

Now the Duke turns again to Isabella, declaring that though she
might be willing to pardon her wronger 'For Mariana's sake', yet

> The very mercy of the law cries out
> Most audible, even from his proper tongue,
> 'An Angelo for Claudio, death for death'.
> Haste still pays haste, and leisure answers leisure;
> Like doth quit like, and measure still for measure.
>
> (5.1.404–8)

His didactic intent is clear. He is pretending to expect that Isabella will
behave as Angelo had behaved to her, insisting upon justice in the face
of pleas for mercy, and he maintains his pretence even as Mariana
implores Isabella to join her in begging for Angelo's forgiveness:

Against all sense you do importune her.
Should she kneel down in mercy of this fact,
Her brother's ghost his pavèd bed would break,
And take her hence in horror.

(5.1.430–3)

The Duke makes the issue absolutely plain:

He dies for Claudio's death,

and waits for Isabella's response. The wait can be a long one: Peter
Brook, in his 1950 Stratford production, had his Isabella, Barbara
Jefford, sustain as long a pause as she thought the audience could bear
to indicate the mental struggling she had to undergo before kneeling
and allowing the claims of mercy to override those of justice. Still the
Duke maintains his show of unforgiveness, turning from Isabella to
the Provost and calling for Barnardine to be brought before him. With
him comes the muffled figure of Claudio, and only when Claudio is
revealed to be alive does the Duke drop his pretence.

Isabella's reunion with the brother she had believed dead is a
curiously underwritten episode. In *Twelfth Night* a parallel situation,
the reunion of Viola and Sebastian, is the emotional climax of the play,
celebrated in a long and rapturous duologue. Here, neither brother
nor sister speaks either now or for what remains of the play as the
Duke apportions rewards and punishments, pardoning Angelo and
blessing his marriage to Mariana, condemning Lucio to marry his
'punk', and thanking those who have helped him. Isabella's silence is
particularly surprising since the Duke twice proposes marriage to her,
first on the unmuffling of Claudio, which he admits to be an ill-chosen
moment ('But fitter time for that'), then in the play's last lines:

Dear Isabel,
I have a motion much imports your good,
Whereto, if you'll a willing ear incline,
What's mine is yours, and what is yours is mine.
(*To all*) So bring us to our palace, where we'll show
What's yet behind that's meet you all should know.

How does Isabella react? For long it was automatically assumed that
she would inevitably accept the Duke's proposal, but ever since John
Barton's Stratford production of 1970, in which she was left looking
puzzled in the centre of the stage as a melancholy Duke departed

without her, this has been regarded by many as an excessively patriarchal assumption. Although a director may still cause her to accept the Duke (as she rapturously did in a National Theatre production of 1981, probably in reaction to Barton's), he will at least feel the need to argue the case. Will her virtues best 'go forth' of her as a married woman or as a nun – or will she still wish to keep her options open? Shakespeare has given us no final answer; his interpreters can take their choice.

In *Measure for Measure* a young woman seeks successfully to preserve her virginity by means of the bed-trick; in *All's Well that Ends Well* a different young woman seeks successfully to lose hers by the same means. To this extent the plays may be seen as companion pieces; and *All's Well that Ends Well* resembles the other plays discussed in this chapter in its emphasis on ideas, in the way in which people's behaviour is explicitly related to abstract concepts and in which moral conflicts are explored though not necessarily resolved. Rather than including debates within its structure, it is shot through with moral reflectiveness. There is a conscious intellectuality about this play which may help to explain its relative lack of popularity. But to say this is not to imply that it lacks either psychological interest or theatrical effectiveness; on the contrary, Shaw, who called it a 'bitter play with a bitter title', considered that in its psychological realism it 'anticipates Ibsen',[3] and although it is not among the most frequently performed plays, its theatrical qualities have been amply demonstrated in distinguished productions.

As in *As You Like It*, the woman does the wooing. The action is to be seen largely through the eyes of Helen, the 'poor physician's daughter' whose undisclosed love for Bertram, the young Count of Roussillon, is the focus of the opening scene. Her character, behaviour, and position in society are central to the play's exploration of the nature of human virtue, and of the extent to which it is an innate or an acquired quality. She possesses qualities derived from her recently dead father, Gérard de Narbonne, a man of learning 'famous . . . in his profession', and others achieved by education and upbringing. Bertram's father, too, has recently died, and his mother the Countess hopes that he too will 'succeed [his] father in manners as in shape', while admitting that he is 'an unseasoned courtier' who will need the help of the old lord Lafeu who is to accompany him to the court of the sick King of France.

The relationship between innate and acquired virtue parallels another that has some prominence in the play, that between human action and superhuman will, the extent to which human beings are the playthings of fortune or are in command of their fate. Helen feels that the stars are against her. She despairs of winning Bertram's love because of his superior social position:

> 'Twere all one
> That I should love a bright particular star
> And think to wed it, he is so above me.
> In his bright radiance and collateral light
> Must I be comforted, not in his sphere.
>
> (1.1.84–8)

She acknowledges that her 'idolatrous fancy' idealizes Bertram, yet the strongly sexual basis of her love for him is established by the jaunty tone of her conversation with the 'notorious liar' Paroles, who is to be Bertram's companion, on the topic of virginity; 'Away with't', says he, to which she responds, 'How might one do, sir, to lose it to her own liking?'

The imagery of stars that Helen has used to express the hopelessness of her plight turns to a more positive force as she suggests that the stars are not entirely in control of our destinies:

> Our remedies oft in ourselves do lie
> Which we ascribe to heaven. The fated sky
> Gives us free scope, only doth backward pull
> Our slow designs when we ourselves are dull.
>
> (1.1.212–15)

The language in which she expresses the idea that the divine will in combination with human endeavour may bring about events of an almost miraculous nature looks forwards to Prospero's

> I find my zenith doth depend upon
> A most auspicious star, whose influence
> If now I court not, but omit, my fortunes
> Will ever after droop.
>
> (*The Tempest*, 1.2.182–5)

But it looks backwards, too, to the faith of Shakespeare's most romantic heroines – of Viola, cheerfully adopting the guise of a man after a shipwreck in which she believes her brother to have been drowned, and of Rosalind, exiled, feeling that she goes to 'liberty, not to banishment'. So Helen ends the scene with a linking of the illness from which the King of France is suffering to her own plight. Her skills as a physician may help her to bring about the end that she desires:

> Who ever strove
> To show her merit that did miss her love?
> The King's disease – my project may deceive me,
> But my intents are fixed and v. 'll not leave me.

And heaven too may help her: in following Bertram to Paris with the ostensible aim of curing the King she expresses confidence that the knowledge she has derived from her father will be supplemented and 'sanctified | By th' luckiest stars in heaven' (1.3.243–4), and in persuading the sceptical King to let her practise her art upon him she stresses the notion of the human practitioner as an agent of the divine will. She is God's minister, and God will help the King through her. The passage derives a peculiarly impressive quality through the style in which it is written. Helen moves from blank verse into rhyming couplets, and her statements have a generalized quality which causes her to sound almost as if possessed by a power beyond her own:

> What I can do can do no hurt to try,
> Since you set up your rest 'gainst remedy.
> He that of greatest works is finisher
> Oft does them by the weakest minister.
> So holy writ in babes hath judgement shown
> When judges have been babes; great floods have flow'n
> From simple sources, and great seas have dried.
>
> (2.1.133–9)

In overcoming the King's continued resistance, Helen stresses the impersonal aspect of her power:

> most it is presumption in us when
> The help of heaven we count the act of men.
> Dear sir, to my endeavours give consent.
> Of heaven, not me, make an experiment.
>
> (2.1.151–4)

The King begins to give way, and Helen's style grows even more elevated as she promises that

> The great'st grace lending grace,
> Ere twice the horses of the sun shall bring
> Their fiery coacher his diurnal ring,
> Ere twice in murk and occidental damp
> Moist Hesperus hath quenched her sleepy lamp,
> Or four-and-twenty times the pilot's glass
> Hath told the thievish minutes how they pass,
> What is infirm from your sound parts shall fly,
> Health shall live free, and sickness freely die.
>
> (2.1.160–8)

Tyrone Guthrie, in his 1959 production, brought out the incantatory nature of these lines by causing his Helen to intone them like a spell while standing behind the seated King and moving her hands across his head as if she were using hypnosis. And the King, accepting her ministrations, senses that she is the 'organ' of 'some blessèd spirit' that may achieve the apparently impossible. His promised reward for success, a husband of her choosing, brings Helen a step further to fulfilment of her own plan.

But a more difficult step lies ahead. The physical obstacle of the King's illness is to be replaced by the psychological obstacle of Bertram's attitude towards her. The progression has something in common with that in *The Taming of the Shrew*, where Petruccio proceeds first by physical then by psychological methods.

As a prelude to the joyful revelation of the King's restoration to health, Lafeu makes a generalized statement related to the theme of the divine will working through human agency which, though somewhat tortuous in expression, puts into a nutshell an idea that is fundamental not only to this play but to much else in Shakespeare's work: 'They say miracles are past, and we have our philosophical persons to make modern and familiar things [that are] supernatural and causeless. Hence is it that we make trifles of terrors, ensconcing ourselves into seeming knowledge when we should submit ourselves to an unknown fear' (2.3.1–6). Lafeu suggests that 'clever', excessively rational people try to reduce to a commonplace level matters that are beyond human understanding, reducing the mysteries of the universe to a series of scientific formulae, making 'trifles of terrors' instead of opening their imaginations to the fullness of experience – or, as he puts it, submitting themselves 'to an unknown fear'. Hamlet had expressed it more simply: 'There are more things in heaven and earth, Horatio, than are dreamt of in your philosophy'; Lafeu's idea underlies the opposed attitudes to the supernatural of Gloucester and Edmond in *King Lear* and encapsulates the opposing attitudes of Macbeth and Lady Macbeth in the early scenes of their play, he only too conscious of 'an unknown fear', she trying – for a while with success – to make trifles of terrors, though ultimately, in her sleepwalking when the subconscious rises to the surface, showing that the terrors were terrors indeed. As often in Shakespeare, willingness to take an optimistic view of life, to admit the possibility of providential direction of human affairs, is associated with sympathetic characters, while the denial of such possibility is associated with the wicked. The King's cure, says Lafeu, has been brought about by the 'Very hand of heaven', though working through a 'debile minister', and Helen herself stresses that 'Heaven hath through me restored the King to health'.

A greater task lies before her. Shakespeare presents Bertram as a callow young man, easily swayed and in desperate need of moral guidance, a source of worry to his loving mother as well as to Helen. The play's older characters talk of him, as of Helen, in relation to his father; noting a physical resemblance the King adds, 'Thy father's moral parts | Mayst thou inherit, too'; and he expands on his memories of the old Count, significantly stressing the noble way in which he treated his social inferiors:

> Who were below him
> He used as creatures of another place,
> And bowed his eminent top to their low ranks,
> Making them proud of his humility,
> In their poor praise he humbled.
>
> (1.2.41–5)

Bertram's 'unseasoned' quality is indicated by the King's refusal to allow him to go with the other young noblemen to the wars; he is presented as one who is not yet capable of making a decision for himself, and this may go some way to softening the difficult moment when he refuses to accept a decision that the King makes for him: that he should marry Helen.

Helen comes to Bertram last, after turning down the four other young men whom the King parades before her; the natural sequence in a story where all is expected to end well would be for him to accept her. His refusal turns the situation from fairy-tale into reality:

> I shall beseech your highness,
> In such a business give me leave to use
> The help of mine own eyes.
>
> (2.3.107–9)

A modern audience may well feel that he has a perfect right to refuse; that however useful Helen has been to the King, however much everyone else on stage may admire her, and however well his father was accustomed to behave to those 'Who were below him', Bertram may be left to choose his own wife. But the reason he gives for his refusal is unattractive:

> She had her breeding at my father's charge.
> A poor physician's daughter, my wife! Disdain
> Rather corrupt me ever.

And it provokes from the King one of the play's most thematically central speeches, in which he offers an explicit consideration of the relationship between worldly rank and innate virtue. A person may be of great rank yet no virtue:

> Where great additions swell's, and virtue none,
> It is a dropsied honour.

But good carries its own value along with it, even if it lacks recognition:

> Good alone
> Is good without a name.

So Helen is 'young, wise, fair'; she derives her honour from her own acts, not from her forebears; her virtue and her person are the dowry that she brings to the match; the King can add 'honour and wealth'. 'I cannot love her', replies Bertram, 'nor will strive to do't.'

The King's insistence on the marriage is as embarrassing to Helen as to Bertram. *Measure for Measure* shows us two compelled marriages, those of Angelo to Mariana and of Lucio to his 'punk', but they take place at the periphery of the action. Here Shakespeare offers a more psychologically penetrating portrayal, and the episode of parting between the newly married couple is poignant in the tentativeness with which Helen presses her claim:

BERTRAM My haste is very great. Farewell. Hie home.
HELEN Pray sir, your pardon.
BERTRAM   Well, what would you say?
HELEN I am not worthy of the wealth I owe,
    Nor dare I say 'tis mine – and yet it is –
    But like a timorous thief most fain would steal
    What law does vouch mine own.
BERTRAM   What would you have?
HELEN Something, and scarce so much: nothing, indeed.
    I would not tell you what I would, my lord. Faith, yes:
    Strangers and foes do sunder and not kiss.
BERTRAM I pray you, stay not, but in haste to horse.

                                                    (2.5. 77–86)

In soliloquy she accepts the blame for his refusal to return to France, vividly imagines the dangers of warfare to which, she fears, he is subjecting himself in order to avoid her, and declares her refusal to stay where he might wish to be:

> My being here it is that holds thee hence.
> Shall I stay here to do't? No, no, although
> The air of paradise did fan the house
> And angels officed all. I will be gone,
> That pitiful rumour may report my flight
> To consolate thine ear. Come night, end day;
> For with the dark, poor thief, I'll steal away.
>
> (3.2.125–30)

Helen's disguise as a pilgrim journeying to the shrine of St Jaques at Compostella in Spain suggests the penitence she feels for the 'ambitious love' in which she has offended. Unshaken in her devotion she refuses to see anything blameworthy in the man she loves, but his mother is clearer-sighted:

> What angel shall
> Bless this unworthy husband? He cannot thrive
> Unless her prayers, whom heaven delights to hear
> And loves to grant, reprieve him from the wrath
> Of greatest justice.
>
> (3.4.25–9)

The religious imagery is unavoidable: Helen is the necessary instrument of Bertram's moral salvation, just as she had been heaven's instrument in the King's physical salvation. But his folly persists, in his attempted seduction of Diana in Florence, when again he puts too much faith in inherited honour, too little in inherent virtue. Refusing to give her his ring he claims that

> It is an honour 'longing to our house,
> Bequeathèd down from many ancestors,
> Which were the greatest obloquy i'th' world
> In me to lose.
>
> (4.2.43–6)

Diana turns his words back on him, pointing out that her chastity is at least as important to her as Bertram's ring is to him, and his lust is so great that he parts with it. But Diana, as her name implies, is chaste; the bed-trick comes into play again, and the riddling terms in which Diana speaks of it help to emphasize the play's paradoxes:

> He had sworn to marry me
> When his wife's dead; therefore I'll lie with him
> When I am buried . . .
> Only, in this disguise I think't no sin
> To cozen him that would unjustly win.
>
> (4.2.72–4, 76–7)

Shakespeare's interest in his story as a stimulus to moral debate is apparent in a conversation between the French Captains in which they report that Bertram's reading of a letter from his mother has changed him 'almost into another man' (4.3.5). They blame him for his behaviour to his wife, his folly in incurring the King's displeasure, and his scandalous seduction of Diana. They report the supposed death of Helen and their sorrow that Bertram is unlikely to grieve for it. One thing they have to say in his favour: he has behaved with great valour in the wars; but at home his shame will be no less great. And their conversation culminates in what is perhaps the play's central moral observation, stressing the inevitable mixture in the human makeup of good and bad qualities:

The web of our life is of a mingled yarn, good and ill together. Our virtues would be proud if our faults whipped them not, and our crimes would despair if they were not cherished by our virtues.

(4.3.74–7)

It is no accident that this compassionate comment on Bertram is immediately followed by the exposure of that notable misleader of youth, Paroles.

At the opening of the last scene, too, the Countess seeks compassion for Bertram, begging the King to regard his folly as

> Natural rebellion done i'th' blade of youth.

The King assures her that he has forgiven her son, and Lafeu reminds us of Helen's good qualities by suggesting that Bertram did greatest injury to himself:

> He lost a wife
> Whose beauty did astonish the survey
> Of richest eyes, whose words all ears took captive,
> Whose dear perfection hearts that scorned to serve
> Humbly called mistress.
>
> (5.3.15–19)

(Happily for the performer of the role, Helen is not on stage as these compliments are spoken.) Like Claudio in *Much Ado About Nothing*, but more ironically given the circumstances of his previous marriage, Bertram is willing to show his penitence by marrying at command. His claims that he learned to love Helen after losing her, along with the King's forgiveness, may suggest that the play is to end in a purely romantic conversion of Bertram, but before long he is telling a remarkable series of lies to explain how he comes to be wearing Helen's ring, and is placed under guard for suspected murder. Once again his view of honour is challenged, when Diana appears and Bertram claims that it is ridiculous to suppose that he would have had anything to do with her:

> Let your highness
> Lay a more noble thought upon mine honour
> Than for to think that I would sink it here.
>
> (5.3.181–3)

The entanglements of the plot reach their point of highest complication in Diana's oracular utterances as she is called to give evidence and seeks to do so without revealing the bed-trick; they can be resolved only by the appearance of Helen, a moment of wonder to those on stage of the same order of theatricality as the appearance of the supposedly dead Hero in *Much Ado About Nothing*, and much greater in effect, because of the way it is presented, than that of Claudio in *Measure for Measure*. But Bertram has too much to expiate for this to be a high romantic climax. Though Helen declares herself pregnant she is, she says, 'but the shadow of a wife . . . The name and not the thing'. Bertram's response, 'Both, both. O, pardon', leaves much to the actor. He is likely to kneel, like Isabella as she asks pardon for Angelo. Though the moment can be impressive and moving, it is unlikely to make us feel that heaven has effected through Helen a moral cure of Bertram equivalent to her physical cure of the King. The emphasis is on Helen's virtue, not on Bertram's. It is Helen's generosity that we feel, Bertram who should be grateful. Yet his response to her claim to have fulfilled the conditions he laid upon her is itself conditional:

> If she, my liege, can make me know this clearly
> I'll love her dearly, ever ever dearly.

But so is her offer to renounce him:

> If it appear not plain and prove untrue,
> Deadly divorce step between me and you.

The King's invitation to Diana to choose herself a husband is one that she ought to think twice before accepting, and his last words both to those on stage and to the audience belie the assurance of the play's title. To the first he says:

> All yet seems well; and if it end so meet,
> The bitter past, more welcome is the sweet.

And to us:

> All is well ended if this suit be won:
> That you express content . . .

I have concentrated on the relationship between Helen and Bertram in an attempt to demonstrate the play's moral self-consciousness; this is no less apparent in the parallel relationship of Paroles and Bertram, which is also responsible for much of the play's comedy. Paroles, a subtilized brother of Pistol, is a marvellously rewarding role, as in an entirely different way is the Countess ('the most beautiful old woman's part ever written', said Shaw). The play's verbal styles are perfectly attuned to its subject–matter; it could have been written only by a playwright who was as accomplished in verbal artistry as in dramatic craftsmanship. Although it is based on a story by Boccaccio, from the *Decameron*, it strikes me as a deeply personal play, one in which Shakespeare was wrestling with moral concepts that concerned him closely, as he does in many of his sonnets. And for all its interest in ideas, it is often deeply tender in its portrayal of human relationships; there is a Chekhovian quality in the Roussillon scenes, a subtlety of communication between the Countess and Helen, which was pointed with equal success by Tyrone Guthrie in the autumnal beauty of his 1959 production and by Trevor Nunn in his Edwardian version of 1981. As the lights faded at the end of the latter, Helen and Bertram alone remained on stage, tentatively touching hands; there was still no kiss. A precarious rapport had been achieved; the ending, we felt, might also be a beginning.

Notes to Chapter Ten

1 Stanley Wells, *Shakespeare: The Writer and his Work* (1978), p. 51.
2 The play is reprinted, and the sources are discussed, in vol. 2 of Bullough's *Narrative and Dramatic Sources of Shakespeare*.
3 *Shaw on Shakespeare*, p. 243.

ELEVEN

A Venetian Tragedy:
Othello

Shakespeare's audience must have been surprised by his tragedy centring on a black man: issues of race and colour were important to the play in his time and have remained so ever since. Blackness had been associated with sin and death in a tradition extending back to Greek and Roman times, and in medieval and later religious paintings evil men and devils were regularly depicted as black. Blackamoors in plays before *Othello* are generally wicked, and Shakespeare's own Aaron, in *Titus Andronicus*, is a self-delighting villain, more like Iago than Othello, happy to 'have his soul black like his face'. True, the Prince of Morocco in *The Merchant of Venice* is merely bombastic and foolish, but he is distinguished in a stage direction as 'a tawny Moor', not a blackamoor. Iago calls Othello a 'thick-lips', Brabanzio refers to his 'sooty bosom', and Othello himself declares that his name 'is now begrimed and black as mine own face'. There can be no doubt that Shakespeare thought of him as thoroughly black and that his audience might well have been predisposed to credit the contemptuous terms in which the white Iago speaks of Othello in the opening scene: 'an old black ram', 'a Barbary horse', 'a lascivious Moor'. The actuality of the man would have caused a violent and paradoxical reversal of expectation.

For all this, later ages have often tried to lighten Othello's darkness; in the nineteenth century, particularly, both commentators and actors were repelled by the idea that Desdemona could have married what they called a negro. Charles Lamb found that, while Othello's blackness was acceptable on the page, anyone seeing the play acted must 'find something extremely revolting in the courtship and wedded caresses of Othello and Desdemona',[1] Coleridge thought that for Shakespeare's audience as well as for his own contemporaries 'it would be something monstrous to conceive this beautiful Venetian girl falling in love with a veritable negro',[2] and the greatest stage Othello of Coleridge's time, Edmund Kean, regarding it as a 'gross error to make Othello either a negro or a black . . . altered the conventional black to the light brown which distinguishes the Moors'.[3] This started a practice which became common till the time of Henry Irving, late in the century. There was even a lady from the southern states of America who, in a book published in 1869, argued herself into the belief that 'Othello *was* a *white* man!' (her italics).[4]

Shakespeare certainly expected Othello to be played by a white man in makeup, but in our own time the social pressures of an increasingly multiracial society are making it less likely that this will happen. This may be more justifiable on social than on dramatic grounds. Just as the casting of women in roles originally played by boys affects our responses to the plays, so it is arguable that the casting of a real black man as Othello reduces the play's self-conscious awareness of the paradoxes associated with the differences between external ap-pearance and internal reality, between the apparent honesty of the white Iago and the essential goodness of the black Othello who, says the Duke to Brabanzio, 'If virtue no delighted beauty lack, | . . . is far more fair than black' (1.3.289–90). Iago's words 'Men should be what they seem' (3.3.131) – words spoken as he is labouring with all his intelligence to seem honest, as he is not, and to make Cassio seem dishonest, as he is not, words whose immediate repetition by Othello pathetically reinforces our awareness of his failure to see men as they are, not as they seem – underline the ironies which reach their climax in the black Othello's insistence on what he regards as the paradoxical whiteness of Desdemona's skin as he is about to kill her (5.2.4). Knowledge that the actor's blackness, like Desdemona's guilt, is mere seeming may deepen the irony.

Irony is an intellectual quality, and *Othello* is an intellectual play in the sense that Iago's mind and intuition work overtime as he intrigues to bring about Othello's downfall; his insistence on the power of reason over passion, or instinct, is indeed a sign of his villainy: 'we have reason to cool our raging motions, our carnal stings, our unbitted lusts; whereof I take this that you call love to be a sect or scion', he says early in the play to Roderigo in a strategically placed speech in which he declares his contempt for virtue, his belief in man's power to shape his own destiny, his view of love as 'merely a lust of the blood and a permission of the will'. But Iago's cynicism is opposed to Othello's idealism, his intellect to Othello's instinct, his faith in reason to Othello's dependence on trust, his dismissal of love to Othello's commitment to it. In spite of the intelligence that Shakespeare displays in action, the play owes its popularity over the centuries primarily to the emotions generated by these oppositions, the pathetic suffering of Desdemona and the tragic if temporary corruption of Othello. Its capacity to arouse pity as well as terror made it exceptionally successful in Shakespeare's time, when it became a standby of the King's Men; of a performance at Oxford in September 1609 a don called Henry Jackson, in a letter written in Latin, remarked that in tragedies the players 'moved some to tears not only by their words but even by their actions' – a valuable comment on acting styles – and particularly that Desdemona, lying murdered on the bed, 'by her very countenance invoked the tearful pity of those who saw her'[5]; and an elegy on the death in 1619 of Richard Burbage laments that 'the grievèd Moor, and more beside, | That lived in him have now forever died'. The play contains its own epigraph in Othello's 'O, Iago, the pity of it, Iago!' (4.1.192), bitterly ironic in being addressed to the pitiless agent of his tragedy.

Othello is often called a domestic tragedy, accurately in so far as the fate of individuals in this play is not inseparably linked with national (or, as in *Romeo and Juliet*, dynastic) destiny as it is in Shakespeare's other tragedies. Even more than *King Lear*, it is a tragedy of the family: of a father who feels himself betrayed by his daughter; of a husband who feels himself betrayed by his wife; of a wife unjustly murdered by her husband. And it is not a tragedy that invokes supernatural forces: there are no ghosts, no witches, no apparitions. Nor is it set in a mythical past: the military action between Turkey and Venice – infidels and Christians – which gives especial importance to Othello's posting to the Venetian protectorate of Cyprus draws on recent history: the Turks had in fact attacked Cyprus in 1570 and conquered it in the following year. Moreover *Othello* has the smallest cast of any of Shakespeare's tragedies, and its most powerful scenes take place in private, not in public, culminating in a bedroom (*'Enter Othello, and Desdemona in her bed'* is the Folio's direction for the opening of the scene of Desdemona's murder).

Nevertheless, it is wrong to think of *Othello* as a small-scale play, or as one that portrays familiar characters in an everyday setting. Events that had taken place over thirty years ago in the southern Mediterranean probably seemed more remote in an age of severely limited international communication than they would in our century; Venice itself had romantic connotations, and Shakespeare is at pains to portray Othello as an exotic outsider who is also an exceptional man, as great a warrior as, for example, Macbeth. Though his speech to the Senate tells the intimate tale of how he wooed Desdemona by recounting his life-story while she should have been attending to 'the house affairs', it tells too of his romantic, heroic past,

> of most disastrous chances,
> Of moving accidents by flood and field,
> Of hair-breadth scapes i'th' imminent deadly breach,
> Of being taken by the insolent foe
> And sold to slavery, of my redemption thence,
> And portance in my traveller's history,
> Wherein of antres vast and deserts idle,
> Rough quarries, rocks, and hills whose heads touch heaven,
> It was my hint to speak. Such was my process,
> And of the cannibals that each other eat,
> The Anthropophagi, and men whose heads
> Do grow beneath their shoulders.
>
> (1.3.133–44)

Othello's tales of wonder belong to his past and might even be played as playful embroideries of truth – does he really think he has seen these things? Yet they may also give us an early warning of the credulity that is to be his downfall; as the play progresses his subjection to superstition grows, especially in relation to the handkerchief with 'magic in the web of it' that was Desdemona's 'first remembrance from the Moor', and which in its insubstantiality becomes a symbol of the vulnerability of his love to Iago's machinations: 'Trifles light as air | Are to the jealous confirmations strong | As proofs of holy writ' (3.3.326–8).

A crucial way in which *Othello* is exceptional among Shakespeare's tragedies is the presence within the action of a centrally placed intriguer. Iago is one of the very few characters in Shakespeare who seem wholly dedicated to evil, with no redeeming qualities whatever (the others are Aaron in *Titus Andronicus*, Richard III, and, among the comedies, Don John). Among the men of this play, at least, there is no need of a mediating figure, a norm against which the others can be measured; the absoluteness of Iago's evil, and of its corruptive power, takes the play beyond the limits of naturalism into the realms of myth inhabited by the story of the corruption of Eve: Iago is often likened to the devil. He is also – like Oberon and Robin Goodfellow in *A*

Midsummer Night's Dream, the Duke in *Measure for Measure*, and Prospero in *The Tempest* – a surrogate playwright, controlling the plot, making it up as he goes along with improvisatory genius; also like the playwright, he retreats ultimately into a silence that represents Shakespeare's unsentimental acknowledgement of the mysterious and inescapable power of human evil.

Iago's enmity towards Othello is notoriously vague and various in motivation; Coleridge famously referred to his 'motiveless malignity'. He certainly resents Othello's promotion of Cassio to the rank he himself covets; he also claims both to love Desdemona himself (2.1.290) and to suspect Othello of adultery with his own wife (1.3.379–80, 2.1.294–5); Emilia herself refers to this suspicion: 'Some such squire he was | That turned your wit the seamy side without, | And made you to suspect me with the Moor' (4.2.149–51). But there is a purity about Iago's evil which adds to the mystery of his presentation, as if Shakespeare were suggesting that it is futile to look for normal causes of an essentially abnormal state of mind – though this has not stopped actors from reading between the lines in an attempt to find hidden causes for Iago's actions.

Whatever the psychological bases of Iago's actions – if indeed there are any, for he may be regarded simply as a dramatic function – his dependence on reason gives him a terrifying plausibility. Like others of his kind – such as Edmond in *King Lear* – he can use reason, can seem as we say 'reasonable', to deceive people who are in many ways much wiser than he. It is Othello's 'free and open nature' that makes him 'think men honest that but seem to be so'; Iago is 'honest' to all the world. Only when he is alone – with the audience – does he drop his mask.

The concentration of evil in *Othello* within a single character means that this is more of a social, less of a metaphysical play than Shakespeare's other tragedies. For all his deviltry, Iago works within a social context. There is not in this play the sense of a malignant fate that we feel in *Romeo and Juliet*, there is no morally ambiguous figure such as the Ghost in *Hamlet* or the Witches in *Macbeth*, nor is the force of human evil distributed among a number of people as it is in *King Lear*. Iago, the intriguer, works as a man among men. The product of the evil forces within him is the corruption of a good man into an evil-doer; the consequence is the death of the innocent Desdemona, of Iago's own wife, and of Othello himself. The action is tragic, but it is not cosmic, or even national in its implications.

One of the episodes that Shakespeare added to the tale by Giraldi Cinthio on which he based his play is that of the drunkenness of Cassio. Its function is complex; Othello's condemnation of the resulting brawl serves as a symbol of that control over unruly passions which he is proud of exercising but which will soon be eroded, and the terms in which he expresses it paradoxically associate this black man with the forces of Christianity opposed to barbarism:

> Are we turned Turks, and to ourselves do that
> Which heaven hath forbid the Ottomites?
> For Christian shame, put by this barbarous brawl.
>
> (2.3.163–5)

In plot terms, the episode provides a basis for Desdemona's pleas to Othello for Cassio's forgiveness which will be her undoing. And in his penitence Cassio speaks a brief sermon on temperance which provides both a moral gloss on the significance of the episode and an epitomizing image for the course of the spiritual and moral journey that Othello is to undergo:

> O God, that men should put an enemy in their mouths to steal
> away their brains! That we should with joy, pleasance, revel, and
> applause transform ourselves into beasts! . . . To be now a
> sensible man, by and by a fool, and presently a beast! O, strange!
> Every inordinate cup is unblessed, and the ingredient is a devil.
>
> (2.3.283–6, 298–301)

Othello's enemy will enter by the ears, and Othello too will be transformed from a sensible man to a fool, and then to a beast. Whether he finally reverts to being sensible is one of the major critical questions about the play.

'Sensible man' is an understatement for the Othello we see in the opening scenes; Shakespeare is quick to establish his greatness of soul, the magnanimity and ease of command that make him a great general. The calm dignity with which he averts a brawl between his party and Brabanzio's – 'Keep up your bright swords, for the dew will rust them' (1.2.59) – marks him out as a natural commander. Though not all great stage Othellos have had a physique to match – Edmund Kean, for example, was not a big man, nor indeed was Olivier (though he could seem so) – still an actor of heroic build, such as Paul Robeson or Willard White (in Trevor Nunn's 1989 production), will have a head start in the role. There is a rock-like stability about the man and about his love for Desdemona in the early scenes which even Iago acknowledges – 'The Moor . . . Is of a constant, loving, noble nature' – and which reaches its ultimate expression in his greeting to Desdemona on his arrival in Cyprus, when we already know that Iago is plotting to destroy this stability:

> O my soul's joy,
> If after every tempest come such calms,
> May the winds blow till they have wakened death,
> And let the labouring barque climb hills of seas
> Olympus-high, and duck again as low
> As hell's from heaven. If it were now to die
> 'Twere now to be most happy, for I fear
> My soul hath her content so absolute
> That not another comfort like to this
> Succeeds in unknown fate.
>
> (2.1.185–94)

Soon after this, however, in the aftermath of Cassio's drunkenness, Othello shows a glimpse of the tempestuous forces in his nature that can be released if control gives way:

> Now, by heaven,
> My blood begins my safer guides to rule,
> And passion, having my best judgement collied [clouded],
> Essays to lead the way. 'Swounds, if I stir,
> Or do but lift this arm, the best of you
> Shall sink in my rebuke.
>
> (2.3.197–202)

The background to the great temptation scene (3.3) in which Othello is transformed from a sensible man to a beast is completed by Iago's plain statement of intention:

> whiles this honest fool [Cassio]
> Plies Desdemona to repair his fortune,
> And she for him pleads strongly to the Moor,
> I'll pour this pestilence into his ear:
> That she repeals him for her body's lust,
> And by how much she strives to do him good
> She shall undo her credit with the Moor.
>
> (2.3.344–50)

Shakespeare rejects suspense: there is to be no gradual revelation of Iago's moral stance and of his designs; all the emphasis is to be placed on process, on character in action and on method; we are to witness a battle of will and intellect; the main questions in our minds will be 'How will Iago set about his plan?' and 'Will he succeed?'

In a sense the scene is one of seduction; detaching Othello's affections from Desdemona, Iago attaches them to himself, so that even part-way through the process Othello can say, in words that have more than one layer of meaning, 'I am bound to thee for ever' (3.3.217), and the scene ends, after Othello and Iago have knelt together while Othello swears revenge and Iago dedicates himself to his service, with Iago's words 'I am your own for ever'. But the breaking of the bonds of love, a process in which Desdemona herself ironically plays a part, is intensely painful, shaking the very foundations of Othello's being, and eliciting from him speeches of anguished eloquence as he takes his farewell of the life he has known. Like Troilus in another play about jealousy, Othello does not know whether to believe the evidence of his own senses: 'This is and is not Cressid', says Troilus confronted with incontrovertible evidence of Cressida's infidelity; 'I think my wife be honest, and think she is not', says Othello, demanding ocular proof that his wife is 'a whore'.

Although Laurence Olivier, when he came to play Othello in 1964, memorably marked the destruction of Othello's universe by ripping off the crucifix that he had worn round his neck and relapsing into eye-rolling savagery, the complex intensity of Othello's emotionalism as his inhibitions give way, both here and later in the play as he confronts Desdemona with his suspicions and eventually murders her, presents challenges that few modern actors have been able to accept. The greatest performances in the role seem to have come in the nineteenth century, and especially from Italian actors (playing sometimes in English, sometimes in Italian, and most often in Italian while the rest of the cast spoke English), as if the Mediterranean temperament were especially responsive to the role; and it is no accident that of all operas based on Shakespeare plays it is Verdi's *Otello* that generates the greatest tragic intensity. So, for instance, we read that Tommaso Salvini, the greatest Othello of the later part of the nineteenth century, played him as 'a barbarian, whose instincts, savage and passionate, are concealed behind a veneer of civilisation so thick that he is himself scarcely conscious he can be other than he appears'.[6] Believing that Desdemona weeps for Cassio, we are told, 'he drags her to her feet . . . grasps her neck and head with his left hand, knotting his fingers in her loose hair, as if to break her neck'; alternatively, 'he pounced upon her, lifted her into the air', and 'dashed with her . . . across the stage and through the curtains, which fell behind him'.[7] Unsurprisingly, English actresses tended to decline the honour of playing with him.

The withdrawal from Othello of his sense of his own identity is symbolized in his language by his descent from the sublime eloquence of

> Farewell the tranquil mind, farewell content,
> Farewell the plumèd troops and the big wars
> That makes ambition virtue! . . .

to the gibberish of 'Pish! Noses, ears, and lips! Is't possible? Confess? Handkerchief? O devil!', and in his behaviour by the literal descent from the upright posture of the dignified commander to the ignominious falling down in a trance in which Iago can exult over him. Perdition has caught his soul, and chaos come again – and all because he has lost faith in the woman he loves. The fact that Desdemona (like Hero in *Much Ado About Nothing*) is innocent of the crimes imputed to her emphasizes our sense of the extent to which human beings depend for their sense of identity on stability in the reactions of those around them. The effect of behaviour conceived of as uncharacteristic can be comic, tragic, or both. It causes Antipholus of Syracuse (in *The Comedy of Errors*) to suspect that he is dreaming, bewitched, or mad, drives Hamlet into a frenzy of disillusioned despair over his mother, and will reach its most intensely tragic climax in the madness of King Lear. Othello, for all his rock-like invulnerability in war, is portrayed in ways that show him to be particularly susceptible to Iago's erosion of his confidence in Desdemona. He is a social outsider, late to marry, with little previous experience of women, he admits to the Senate that he 'knows little of this great world . . . More than pertains to feats of broils and battle' (1.3.86–7), and, as Iago's poison begins to work, starts to worry about his blackness, his lack of social graces, and his age.

And it must be confessed that Desdemona contributes to her own downfall, above all in the innocent but ill-judged pertinacity with which she nags Othello to forgive Cassio. Like any dramatic character, Desdemona is open to variant interpretation. More even than in most other plays, Shakespeare is concerned in *Othello* with the way in which we construct our sense of other people's, and indeed our own, identities. Iago is a prime example: until the revelations of the final scene he is 'honest Iago' to everyone except the audience. But Desdemona's actions, and her words, too, can be variously construed. It is in the nuances of the conversation about her between Iago and Cassio that Shakespeare seems most deliberately to draw attention to the way in which the construction of human identity depends on the attitude of mind of the beholder. To the reductive Iago she is 'sport for Jove', 'full of game', with an eye that 'sounds a parley to provocation'; to the idealizing Cassio, 'a most exquisite lady', 'a most fresh and delicate creature', and, though she has an 'inviting eye', nevertheless 'right modest'. (It is a passage that will be echoed later in the disparate reactions of Adrian and Sebastian on the one hand, and Gonzalo on the other, to the island in *The Tempest*.)

For the audience, Desdemona is defined largely in relation to the other two women in the play, Bianca and Emilia. The irony in Bianca's name, which means 'white', parallels that in Othello's skin colour. Bianca's precise status is unclear. In the list of characters appended to the play in the Folio (though nowhere in the text itself) she is described as a courtesan, a word which could mean anything from a courtier's mistress to a prostitute; she has a clearly erotic relationship with Cassio (described by Iago early in the play as 'A fellow almost damned in a fair wife' – whatever that may mean – though there is no other indication that he is married), and is despised by Iago as 'A hussy that by selling her desires | Buys herself bread and cloth', and by the respectably married Emilia as a strumpet, while claiming to be 'of life as honest | As you that thus abuse me'. To caricature her in performance, as is often done, as a rampant whore, blatantly incompatible with Iago's praise of her lover Cassio as one who has 'a daily beauty in his life' (unless Bianca *is* the daily beauty), is perhaps too extreme an endorsement of Iago's point of view, but she is certainly the woman in the play who comes closest to whoredom (which explains why for over 150 years she disappeared from acting versions).[8]

Emilia comes further up the scale of womanhood, yet does not reach the highest standards of morality enunciated by Desdemona, who abhors (Shakespeare cannot resist the pun) to speak the word 'whore' (4.2.166). Of course, Shakespeare is able to show the audience aspects of his characters that are not revealed to the others in the play; so, for instance, he gives us the meditative episode between Desdemona and Emilia in which Desdemona sings the 'song of willow' that will not go from her mind as she prepares for bed at her husband's command after the terrible scene in which he has treated her like a whore in a brothel. The 'poor soul' in the song has 'called [her] love false love', to which he retorted: 'If I court more women, you'll couch with more men'. Desdemona is incredulous that women could 'abuse their husbands | In such gross kind'; she herself would not do so 'for all the world', but Emilia takes a more realistic attitude:

> Marry, I would not do such a thing for a joint ring, nor for measures of lawn, nor for gowns, petticoats, nor caps, nor any petty exhibition; but for all the whole world? Ud's pity, who would not make her husband a cuckold to make him a monarch? I should venture purgatory for't.
>
> (4.3.71–6)

And, responding to Desdemona's repeated expression of incredulity, Emilia launches into a vehement claim that women should have equal sexual rights with men, in a speech which seems far ahead of its time and which indeed appears to be one of Shakespeare's afterthoughts since it is present only in the Folio text, a revision of that represented by the 1622 Quarto. It is 'their husbands' faults', she says, 'If wives do fall.'

> Say that they slack their duties,
> And pour our treasures into foreign laps,
> Or else break out in peevish jealousies,
> Throwing restraint upon us; or say they strike us,
> Or scant our former having in despite;
> Why, we have galls; and though we have some grace,
> Yet have we some revenge.
>
> (4.3.86–92)

Women have 'affections, | Desires for sport, and frailty, as men have', and if men are tempted to stray, they can only expect their wives to do so too.

Passionate as it is, Emilia's speech seems not particularly applicable to her personal situation, and this gives it something of the quality of a manifesto, as if Shakespeare were impelled to speak out for women's rights through personal conviction rather than dramatic necessity. But it provokes from Desdemona the declaration of a superior moral stance, a prayer that she may not 'pick bad from bad, but by bad mend'. She may inadvertently have contributed to her own tragedy, but Shakespeare leaves us in no doubt of her moral integrity, of the purity of her motives. And even if Emilia may be less idealistic in her expressions of sexual morality than her mistress, she rises to moral greatness in the final scene with her passionate defence of Desdemona, her vehement denunciation of her husband, and her determination to die by Desdemona's side. It is the opportunity to display naked emotional commitment in this scene that makes Emilia one of the more rewarding women's roles in the canon.

What of Othello in the play's final stages? After he has recovered from the fit induced by Iago's taunting, he sees himself as a man transformed to a beast: 'A hornèd man's a monster and a beast' (4.1.60). Certainly his behaviour under Iago's influence, culminating in his smothering of Desdemona, is monstrous and beastly: G.H. Lewes wrote of Kean's 'lion-like fury', and 'tiger-like' is Henry James's repeated epithet for Salvini's performance in the murder scene.[9] Yet, convinced of the rightness of his cause, Othello recovers his dignity of speech, grieving over the outward beauty of Desdemona's white skin, 'smooth as monumental alabaster', intoxicated by her 'balmy breath, that doth almost persuade | Justice to break her sword', seeing his intention to kill her as 'a sacrifice', not a murder (5.2.70).

The basic question raised by the play's closing episodes is whether Othello remains a beast or recovers his manly stature. Or, to put it in theological terms, whether he is destined for damnation or 'saves himself' by acknowledging his crime, repenting it, and punishing himself for it. Until early in the twentieth century he was generally regarded as an essentially noble and heroic figure who, in A.C. Bradley's words, 'stirs . . . in most readers a passion of mingled love and pity which they feel for no other hero in Shakespeare . . . And pity itself vanishes, and love and admiration alone remain, in the majestic dignity and sovereign ascendancy of the close. Chaos has come and gone; and the Othello of the Council-chamber and the quay of Cyprus has returned, or a greater and nobler Othello still.'[10] This is the attitude that had found expression in the performance of the American actor Edwin Booth, who played the killing of Desdemona as 'a righteous immolation'; after all his suffering, this Othello was finally 'calm, in the concentration of his despair . . . He is not doing a murder: he is doing what he thinks to be an act of sacrifice.'[11]

Although this interpretation, accepting Othello's self-evaluation, can be challenged, it is compatible with at least some aspects of the text. There is surely pathos in the eloquence – though some have called it bombast – with which Othello expresses horror at what he has done even before he knows of Desdemona's innocence:

> O insupportable, O heavy hour!
> Methinks it should be now a huge eclipse
> Of sun and moon, and that th'affrighted globe
> Should yawn at alteration.
>
> (5.2.107–10)

And the intensity of his suffering when he knows the truth is awesome in its vision of purgatorial suffering:

> Whip me, ye devils,
> From the possession of this heavenly sight,
> Blow me about in winds, roast me in sulphur,
> Wash me in steep-down gulfs of liquid fire!
>
> (5.2.284–7)

Perhaps he relapses into inarticulacy in his next line: 'O Desdemon! Dead Desdemon! Dead! O! O!'; but no beast ever made utterance like this. To the onlookers, Othello is the 'man' (5.2.289), Iago the 'viper'. And in his last big speech he recovers the authority with which he had addressed the Senators of Venice. To an extent it is a speech of self-exculpation. He asks to be remembered as

> one that loved not wisely but too well,
> . . . one not easily jealous but, being wrought,
> Perplexed in the extreme.

But it is a speech also of self-condemnation, and it culminates in self-execution.

The alternative to what has come to be regarded as the 'romantic' interpretation of Othello's closing moments is that his self-execution does nothing to exculpate him. Even in the nineteenth century at least one actor – Salvini – had sustained Othello's bestiality to the end, killing Desdemona as one who would 'do a butchery, not perform a sacrifice', and his own death was no less horrific: he 'cuts his throat with a short scimitar, hacking and hewing with savage energy, and imitating the noise that escaping blood and air may together make when the windpipe is severed'.[12]

More recently, the trend among both critics and actors has been to reject the concept of an Othello whose suicide redeems him. T.S. Eliot, in an influential essay published in 1927, remarked that he had 'never read a more terrible exposure of human weakness – of universal human weakness – than the last great speech of Othello. . . . What

Othello seems to me to be doing in making this speech is cheering himself up.' This view of Othello as a self-dramatizing figure who escapes into illusion was developed by F.R. Leavis, who referred to his 'obtuse and brutal egoism'. Other critics have rushed to Othello's defence, but Laurence Olivier admitted to the influence of Leavis in his National Theatre performance of 1964. He made himself up as a full-lipped, sinuous black man, padding on to the stage in sandalled feet, toying with a long-stemmed pink rose. This was an Othello who seemed almost insolently confident of his power to charm as well as command; the performance displayed amazing vocal virtuosity which thrilled some spectators but struck others as self-regarding, as if the actor had the faults that Leavis attributed to Othello. Protesting against this, Dover Wilson (in a letter to *The Times*) wrote that this was an Othello in which he 'could discover no dignity . . . at all, while the end was to me, not terrible, but horrible beyond words'.

The openness to variant interpretation of Othello's end, and indeed of his character as a whole, is yet another instance of the capacity of the Shakespearian text to respond to the imaginative needs of those who read, perform, or watch it. To some extent it is the result of selection. The full scope of Shakespeare's major plays is rarely encompassed by either reader or performer. Actors make textual choices, and shape their interpretations by selecting among the infinite range of possibilities of emphasis that the roles afford. Especially in the past, though often in the present too, the plays have been given in shortened versions which inevitably affect interpretation: so, for example, Salvini, whose greatly altered and abbreviated acting version made Othello even more of a star role than it is in the original text, followed a tradition established by Macready of ringing down the curtain on Othello's death (as does Boito's libretto for Verdi), consequently omitting Cassio's praise of Othello as 'great of heart'. Henry James (who intensely admired Salvini's performance, even though 'he played in Italian while his comrades answered him in a language which was foreign only in that it sometimes failed to be English'[13], wrote of it: 'Of course it simplifies, but any acting of Shakespeare is a simplification. To be played at all, he must be played, as it were, superficially.'[14] Henry James might have added that any critical reading of Shakespeare, too, is a simplification. No less than actors, critics are inevitably selective in their readings, influenced as much in their construction of the play by personal temperament as are Iago and Cassio in their divergent responses to Desdemona. So Othello the character and *Othello* the play fluctuate in the imaginations of successive generations of readers and playgoers, and, though each actor and critic may be temporarily confident of having understood them aright, defy final definition.

Notes to Chapter Eleven

1 From Charles Lamb's essay 'On the Tragedies of Shakespeare, considered with reference to their fitness for stage representation' (1811, much reprinted).
2 S.T. Coleridge, *Shakespearean Criticism*, ed. T.M. Raysor, 2 vols (London, 1960), vol. 1, p. 42.
3 F.H. Hawkins, *Life of Edmund Kean*, 2 vols (London, 1869), vol. 1, p. 221.
4 Cited in the New Variorum edition, ed. H.H. Furness (Philadelphia, PA, 1886), p. 395.
5 Cited and translated by Gino J. Matteo, *Shakespeare's Othello: the Study and the Stage 1604–1904* (Salzburg, 1974), p. 26.
6 Joseph Knight, cited Matteo, ibid., p. 220.
7 E.T. Mason and J.R. Towse, cited by Marvin Rosenberg, *The Masks of Othello* (Berkeley, CA, 1961), p. 113.
8 Matteo, *Shakespeare's Othello*, p. 215.
9 Henry James, *The Scenic Art*, ed. Allan Wade (London, 1949), pp. 174–5.
10 A.C. Bradley, *Shakespearean Tragedy* (1904, etc.; repr. 1957), pp. 155, 161.
11 William Winter, cited Matteo, *Shakespeare's Othello*, p. 227.
12 Knight, cited Matteo, ibid., pp. 219–20. It must be admitted, nevertheless, that for Henry James Salvini retained throughout 'to my sense at least, the tremor of a moral element' (p. 175).
13 James, *Scenic Art*, p. 169.
14 ibid., p. 173.

TWELVE

Tragedies of Ancient Britain and of Athens:

King Lear and *Timon of Athens*

The three uneasy comedies, *Troilus and Cressida*, *Measure for Measure*, and *All's Well that Ends Well*, and the tragedy of *Othello* (probably written after the first but before one or both of the others) all centre not simply on love, courtship, and marriage but on specifically sexual matters. Sex plays a part in *King Lear*, too, but in this play, written probably in the later part of 1605, Shakespeare broadens his canvas to produce his most profound exploration of what it means to be human. For Hazlitt *King Lear* was 'the best of all Shakespeare's plays' because 'it is the one in which he was the most in earnest'.[1] For many theatregoers earnestness is not a particularly appealing quality, and the awesome depths of both mental and physical suffering portrayed in *King Lear* have given it a reputation as the most forbidding of English tragedies, the one that has most affinities with the religious-based ritualism of Greek drama. You don't go to see *King Lear* for a cheerful night out; it induces in those who experience it the same kind of reverential humility as Beethoven's *Missa Solemnis* or the Sistine Chapel.

Although we know both from an entry in the Stationers' Register and from the title-page of the first edition, of 1608, that it had been performed before King James on Boxing Day 1606, it does not seem to have been one of Shakespeare's most popular plays in his own time; and from the appearance of Nahum Tate's radical adaptation in 1681 until well into the nineteenth century, theatregoers were regularly offered a version that reduced its rigours and diminished its emotional impact.

Tate was a minor dramatist who achieved performance mainly by reworking other people's plays, including Webster's *The White Devil*,

Jonson's *The Devil is an Ass*, and Shakespeare's *Richard the Second* and *Coriolanus* as well as *King Lear*. As a poet he was regarded highly enough to be appointed poet laureate in 1692, but he is remembered today mainly as the author of 'While shepherds watched their flocks by night' and of the libretto for Purcell's opera *Dido and Aeneas*. The modern reader is likely to be nauseated by Tate's complacent self-gratulation in the dedication of his version of *King Lear*: 'I found the whole to answer your Account of it, a Heap of Jewels, unstrung and unpolisht; yet so dazling in their disorder, that I soon perceiv'd I had seiz'd a Treasure.' His adaptation has been greatly reviled, yet what Tate does to Shakespeare is not essentially very different from what Shakespeare himself does to the writings on which he draws as sources – such as the old play of *King Leir* whose republication in 1605 may have acted as a stimulus to composition. Tate shortens Shakespeare's play, removing entirely the character of the Fool, whose language must have seemed particularly dated and difficult to Restoration audiences; he modernizes the language at many points; he adds a love-story, removing the King of France and turning Edgar and Cordelia into virtuous lovers who come together at the end; most notoriously, he makes 'the Tale conclude in a Success to the innocent distrest Persons', preserving the lives of Lear, Kent, and Gloucester and sending them off into peaceful retirement. Edgar ends the play optimistically, declaring to Cordelia:

> Thy bright Example shall convince the World
> (Whatever Storms of Fortune are decreed)
> That Truth and Vertue shall at last succeed.

Considered as a Restoration heroic play Tate's *King Lear* must be accounted a success; indeed it was performed for longer than most other plays in the history of the British theatre. It has earned the obloquy of posterity not because of its own demerits but because it kept Shakespeare's play off the stage for a century and a half.

This means that some of the most famous performances of the title role, by actors such as David Garrick, John Philip Kemble, and Edmund Kean, were given in a text that owes as much to Tate as to Shakespeare. Garrick played the role first at the age of twenty-four and continued to do so to the end of his career, when he was close on sixty; his utterance, kneeling, of Lear's curse on Goneril was so impressive, Hazlitt writes, that

The first row in the pit stood up in order to see him better; the second row, not willing to lose the precious moments by remonstrating, stood up too; and so, by a tacit movement, the entire pit rose to hear the withering imprecation, while the whole passed in such cautious silence, that you might have heard a pin drop.

At Garrick's last performance, in 1776, he caused 'Even the unfeeling Regan and Goneril, forgetful of their characteristic cruelty', to play 'through the whole of their parts with aching bosoms and streaming eyes'[2]; but, though he restored some of Shakespeare's lines in place of Tate's paraphrase, he never played the tragic ending.

Edmund Kean was allowed to die as Lear in 1823, and Macready restored the Fool (played by a woman) in 1838, but it was left to Samuel Phelps at Sadler's Wells in 1845 to base a production squarely on Shakespeare's text. Even Henry Irving in 1892, though his acting edition took Shakespeare as its point of departure, cut over 1500 lines – not far off half the play – removing much of the Gloucester plot and running the storm scenes together.

Tate's supplanting of Shakespeare means, too, that all critical estimates up to and beyond the early twentieth century are based on reading, not on performance. Not all these estimates are entirely favourable. Much critical response to the play has been ambivalent, admitting its grandeur while expressing unease with some features of both its substance and its form. Johnson defended Tate's happy ending, remarking that he had been 'so shocked by Cordelia's death that I know not whether I ever endured to read again the last scenes of the play till I undertook to revise them as an editor'. Charles Lamb, who scorned Tate and wrote eloquently of Shakespeare's play, nevertheless regarded it as unactable. To A.C. Bradley it was 'Shakespeare's greatest achievement' but '*not* his best play'; it 'is too huge for the stage', 'imperfectly dramatic', and 'its comparative unpopularity is due, not merely to the extreme painfulness of the catastrophe, but in part to its dramatic defects'. Critics have struggled, not always even to their own satisfaction, to understand its dramatic conventions and its structural principles, so that, for example, Allardyce Nicoll wrote that 'it is not planned with that all-pervading subtlety which characterises' the other 'great' tragedies.[3]

Only in recent years has it come to be recognized that the structure of the play for long known as *King Lear* is to a significant extent the product of eighteenth-century editors. The version printed in 1608 as

The True Chronicle History of the Life and Death of King Lear differs in
many respects from that which appeared in the First Folio of 1623
under the title of *The Tragedy of King Lear*. The Folio lacks about 300
lines present in the Quarto, including the dialogue in which the Fool
implicitly calls his master a fool (Sc. 4.136–51) – possibly the result of
censorship on behalf of King James, known as 'the wisest fool in
Christendom'; Kent's account of the invasion of England (Sc. 8.27–
33); Lear's mock trial, in his madness, of his daughters (Sc. 13.13–52);
Edgar's generalizing couplets at the end of that scene beginning

> When we our betters see bearing our woes,
> We scarcely think our miseries our foes;

the brief, compassionate dialogue of two of Gloucester's servants after
his blinding (Sc. 14.97–106); parts of Albany's protest to Goneril
about the sisters' treatment of Lear (Sc. 16); the entire scene in which a
Gentleman tells Kent of Cordelia's grief on hearing of her father's
condition (Sc. 17); the presence of the Doctor and the musical
accompaniment to the reunion of Lear and Cordelia (Sc. 21); and
Edgar's account of his meeting with Kent in which Kent's 'strings of
life | Began to crack' (Sc. 24.210–18). Moreover the Folio adds about
100 lines not present in the Quarto, mostly in short passages,
including Kent's statement that Albany and Cornwall have servants
who are in the pay of France (3.1.13–20), Merlin's strange prophecy
spoken by the Fool at the end of 3.2, and the last lines of both the Fool
and Lear himself. And several speeches are differently assigned.

For over a hundred years after Shakespeare's death these two
versions of the play were kept apart, available to readers in reprints of
the Quarto and of the Folio; but in the early eighteenth century, when
straightforward reprints of the Folio came to be replaced by edited
collections of the complete works, passages from the Quarto were
incorporated into the Folio, and for close on 300 years this conflated
text – with minor variants from one edition to another – is what was
known as *King Lear*. The theory that evolved to account for this
procedure is that each of the two early versions derived from a single,
lost archetype variously misrepresented by the surviving printed
versions, and that this lost archetype can be hypothetically reconstructed by collapsing the variant versions into one, adding passages
that occur in only one of the two versions, and making a choice
between the local variants in passages that are common to both.
Among those who from time to time questioned this theory was

Harley Granville-Barker, a man of the theatre who was also a scholar, and who, like others before him, was not entirely happy with the play. In his *Preface*, first published in 1927, he wrote critically of the scene found only in the Quarto, regarding it as 'a carpentered scene if ever there was one', and one that he 'could better believe that Shakespeare cut . . . than wrote'. Granville-Barker was sceptical of the wisdom of conflation, writing that

> the producer is confronted by the problem of the three hundred lines, or nearly, that the Quartos give and the Folio omits, and of the hundred given by the Folio and omitted from the Quartos. Editors, considering only, it would seem, that the more Shakespeare we get the better, bring practically the whole lot into the play we read. But a producer must ask himself whether these two versions do not come from different prompt books, and whether the Folio does not, in both cuts and additions, sometimes represent Shakespeare's own second thoughts.[4]

In this passage Granville-Barker was half a century ahead of his time, for in the late 1970s and early 1980s a mass of bibliographical and other evidence was brought forward to support the theory that the Quarto and Folio texts, so far from each misrepresenting a single lost play, are independent witnesses, if not to two 'different prompt books', at least to two distinct Shakespearian versions, one printed from his original manuscript written out before the play had been put into rehearsal, the other from a text that incorporated changes – cuts, additions, and substitutions – made for performance. This belief formed the basis of the decision made by the editors of the Oxford Shakespeare of 1986 to print two independent texts of *King Lear*, one edited from the Quarto, the other from the Folio. The disentangling of the two versions reveals plays that are clearer and simpler to read and to perform than the conflated version. It ought to enhance appreciation of the play; some of the structural defects that have troubled readers of the past can now be seen to be the creation of Shakespeare's editors rather than of the playwright himself; as Granville-Barker wrote, 'Where Quarto and Folio offer alternatives, to adopt both versions may make for redundancy and confusion.' The reader who wishes to come closest to Shakespeare in the heat of original composition will prefer the Quarto-based version; the reader who is more interested in the theatrical realization of the text by the company of players of which Shakespeare was a member will prefer the Folio. And the reader who is interested in the way the process of rehearsal and production may transmute a text will wish to compare the two. The Folio's changes streamline the play's action, removing some reflective passages, particularly at the ends of scenes. They affect the characterization, particularly of Kent, Edgar, and Albany, partly through significant differences in the play's closing passages. Structurally, the main differences lie in the presentation of the military action in the later part of the play: in the Folio Cordelia is more clearly in charge of the forces that come to Lear's assistance, and they are less clearly a French invasion force.

In whatever version the play is performed the role of the King is always seen as one of the most formidable challenges open to an actor, one that can crown a career – or undermine it, for even great actors, Kean, Irving, Charles Laughton, and Olivier among them, have failed to scale the role's heights. Though Lear is unquestionably an old man – 'four-score and upward' – the part is not necessarily best played by an old actor. Burbage was under forty when he created the role; perhaps because of the stamina that it demands, many of the most successful performances have come from men in their middle years. As accounts of past performances make clear, it has many theatrical high points, among them Lear's curse on Goneril; his bewildered 'O, reason not the need . . .' as he tries and fails to understand why his daughters will not yield to his demands; his ragings against the storm to which their cruelty consigns him; his discovery of humility as he kneels to pray for all 'poor, naked wretches'; his mad dialogue with the blinded Gloucester; the infinitely touching episode of his reunion with Cordelia, the daughter whom he had banished; his entry carrying her body in his arms – 'Howl, howl, howl, howl!' – and his dying lamentations over her corpse.

But the role is not merely the succession of actors' points that accounts of earlier performances might suggest. Certainly it demands the capacity to make powerful local effects, but it demands too the ability to weld the points into a whole. The actor must encompass not only Lear's grandeur in decay, his noble fury against his daughters which, coming from one in whom nature 'stands on the very verge | Of her confine' (2.2.320), seems also like the defiant ragings of mortality itself against the inevitability of death, but also the grotesque comedy inherent in the absurdities of Lear's behaviour and in the inconsequentialities of his madness; the sense of a man who, however painfully, learns from his mistakes – of one who, formerly deaf, learns to listen, who passes from the self-willed blindness of the arrogant through the disconnected shafts of insight of the mad to the

impotent wisdom of the humble; who at last, though too late, learns
the value of the love and loyalty that, in his folly, he had rejected. It is a
developing role, and the actor must chart the changes in the King
while convincing us that he is the same man from beginning to end.

I have compared the experience of seeing *King Lear* to taking part in
a religious ritual, and this is not simply because of what Hazlitt called
the play's 'earnestness'. It derives in part from the very style in which
it is written: its frequent invocations – 'Thou, nature, art my goddess',
'Hear, nature; hear, dear goddess, hear', 'You nimble lightnings',
'Blow, winds, and crack your cheeks!', 'World, world, O world!',
'All blest secrets . . .'; its impressive oaths – 'by the sacred radiance of
the sun . . .'; its prayers – Lear's 'Poor, naked wretches . . .',
Gloucester's 'O you mighty gods . . .'; Lear's aborted sermon – 'I will
preach to thee . . . When we are born, we cry that we are come to this
great stage of fools'; and Cordelia's request to Lear, 'hold your hands
in benediction o'er me'. The play's characters, especially Lear himself,
seem constantly to be trying to break through the barriers that divide
the terrestrial from the spiritual, to draw on elemental forces of nature
in the attempt to transcend the limitations of humanity. Time after
time they interrupt what they are saying to each other in order to
appeal to the heavens or, more specifically, to the gods, often
collectively, sometimes individually – to Apollo, to Jupiter, and to
Juno. Shakespeare never lets us forget that we are in a pagan world (a
fact that was responsible for a long tradition, extending at least as far as
the television film in which Olivier plays Lear, of setting the action in a
mock-up of Stonehenge). It is as if he were trying to examine the
values by which we live without the preconceptions of Christianity,
yet at the same time, perhaps inevitably, the play's language is
permeated with terms that must carry Christian associations for
audiences conscious of the Christian tradition. The Fool employs
parable in the effort to divert Lear from his folly, and the overall action
itself, with its basic structure of an arrogant king who learns humility
through suffering, has an element of parable that enables the story to
convey meaning in even the most simplistic retellings.

The play recalls the literature as well as the forms of religion too, in
its obvious concern with moral and ethical issues exemplified in its
frequent use of moralizing remarks, often proverbial in origin, and
structurally in its resemblances to the morality plays popular half a
century before it was written. The moral status of characters in those
plays is always clearly defined, and *King Lear* is unusual among
Shakespeare's plays in the patness with which its characters, too,

divide into good and bad. Lear and Gloucester occupy middle ground, but Lear has two bad daughters, Goneril and Regan, and one good, Cordelia; Goneril's husband, Albany, is good (if weak); Regan's, Cornwall, is bad. Gloucester has one good son, Edgar, and one bad, Edmond.

The stereotyping is reinforced by suggestions of illegitimacy: Edmond is literally as well as figuratively a bastard, and Lear asks Goneril, 'Are you our daughter?' (1.4.201, 232) and calls her 'Degenerate bastard'; to Regan's 'I am glad to see your highness' he responds, 'If thou shouldst not be glad | I would divorce me from thy mother's shrine, | Sepulchring an adultress' (2.2.300–4). However distastefully to modern susceptibility, Shakespeare adopts the convention by which the bastard, who lies outside the ties of family, is seen also as being detached from the human race. The degree to which this is mere convention on the one hand, or suggestive of a psychologically induced condition, on the other, is questionable. It permits an actor playing Edmond to suggest that his evil is the result of his father's preference for the legitimate over the illegitimate offspring; and rather similarly, when Judi Dench played Regan in a Stratford-upon-Avon production, she did so with a stutter and said in discussion that she hoped it helped to suggest how Regan came to be as she was – she stuttered only in Lear's presence, and he showed impatience at it; the implication was that what Lear calls her 'filial ingratitude' was a reaction against parental tyranny. Such a seeking out of rational causes and psychological explanations for the state of soul of Shakespeare's characters is understandable in those who have to portray them as human beings, but it may reduce our sense of the ultimate mystery of human evil. Shakespeare does not suggest that all would be well with the world if only God were a universal psychoanalyst.

Like Iago in *Othello*, the evil characters in *King Lear* are notable for rationality. The attitude of mind displayed by Goneril and Regan after Lear has banished Cordelia and Kent is eminently sensible:

> GONERIL You see how full of changes his age is. The observation we have made of it hath been little. He always loved our sister most, and with what poor judgement he hath now cast her off appears too grossly.
> REGAN 'Tis the infirmity of his age; yet he hath ever but slenderly known himself.
>
> (1.2.288–93)

This reasonableness is so insidiously plausible that directors have sometimes been taken in by it; Peter Brook, in his 1962 production, portrayed Lear partly through the sisters' eyes, an unruly old man offering more encouragement to his followers to be rowdy than the text demands: on his return from hunting his demand for food – 'Let me not stay a jot for dinner' (1.4.8) – was reinforced by his overturning a table. Like Goneril and Regan, Edmond, too, is on the side of common sense; just as Iago regards love as 'merely a lust of the blood and a permission of the will', so Edmond denies that the planets influence men's lives, aligning himself with those 'philosophical persons' who, according to Lafeu in *All's Well that Ends Well*, 'make modern and familiar things supernatural and causeless'. As often in Shakespeare, belief in self-determination is allied to a denial of supernatural influence; rationality in an evil character is opposed to credulity in a more sympathetic one; Gloucester's attributions of the ills of his time to 'These late eclipses in the sun and moon' is to Edmond a mere 'evasion of whoremaster man', yet Gloucester, flawed though he is, has more access to virtue and wisdom than the rationalist Edmond.

The schematic elements in the characterization of *King Lear* are reflected in its structure. This is Shakespeare's only tragedy to have a fully developed subplot parallel to that involving the named central character. Shakespeare has chosen to juxtapose the story of a man who is driven mad with that of one who has his eyes torn out. Both men suffer, but in Lear the centre of suffering is the mind, in Gloucester, the body. Of course the one involves the other. The physical storm into which Lear is banished – or banishes himself – forces him to ever-increasing dependence on his own body, uncushioned by ritual, ceremony, and the comforts of the court. But his reiterated expressions of fear that he will go mad show his concern that the body will continue to be guided by the mind. The process of physical suffering makes him question the need for bodily comforts, 'superfluity' such as the gorgeous clothing of Regan whose need he had questioned in retaliation for her claim that he no longer needs servants (2.2.442). But his mental anguish is greater than his physical pain and, paradoxically, reduces it:

> This tempest in my mind
> Doth from my senses take all feeling else
> Save what beats there: filial ingratitude.
>
> (3.4.12–14)

Yet he turns from self-pity to express kinship with the 'poor, naked wretches' who depend on body alone; his experience teaches him to 'feel what wretches feel' and to recognize the need for a fairer distribution of 'the superflux'. The image of the naked body is brought before us with grotesque pathos when Gloucester's good son Edgar, virtually unclothed in the guise of a bedlam beggar, emerges from a hovel, provoking Lear to reduce himself to the same state of unprotected, elemental humanity:

> Is man no more than this? Consider him well. Thou owest the worm no silk, the beast no hide, the sheep no wool, the cat no perfume. Ha, here's three on 's are sophisticated; thou art the thing itself. Unaccommodated man is no more but such a poor, bare, forked animal as thou art. Off, off, you lendings! Come, unbutton here.
>
> (3.4.96–103)

It is at Lear's moment of decision to depend on nothing but flesh and blood that his mind deserts him.

Gloucester's physicality is emphasized in the chatting about his 'whoreson' Edmond at the opening of the play, and it is obviously by conscious design that the appalling scene of his blinding follows immediately on that in which he shows practical kindness to the demented and exhausted king. Johnson regarded 'the extrusion of Gloucester's eyes' as 'an act too horrid to be endured in dramatic exhibition, and such as must always compel the mind to relieve its distress by incredulity',[5] while excusing it as a concession to the taste of its time. Even in our age its horrors have been evaded: Jonathan Miller, in a 1989 production at the Old Vic, had it played off stage. But though we may flinch from it, it is a necessary challenge to the audience's sensibility, an uncompromising acknowledgement of the power of human evil, and its symbolic force is evident in the fact that as soon as Gloucester loses the ability to see literally he gains the ability to do so metaphorically.

His bastard son Edmond has deceived him into the belief that his legitimate son Edgar is false to him; now, as he calls on Edmond to 'enkindle all the sparks of nature | To quite this horrid act', Regan disabuses him:

> Thou call'st on him that hates thee. It was he
> That made the overture of thy treasons to us . . .

Now, blind, he 'sees' the truth:

> O, my follies! Then Edgar was abused.
> Kind gods, forgive me that, and prosper him!
>
> (3.7.86–7, 89–90)

Like Lear, he is learning through deprivation. Lear had learned to 'feel what wretches feel', and wished to 'shake the superflux to them'. Now Gloucester, stumbling his way to Dover, as he gives a purse to the apparently mad beggar who is in fact his true son Edgar expresses the need in man for a proper balance of physical and mental qualities: the 'superfluous and lust-dieted man' – he who is excessive in both material possessions and sensual gratification – is the man who 'will not see | Because he does not feel'; and there is complex irony in the use of the word 'see' by the newly blinded man who would still have been able to see literally if through proper 'feeling' he had been able to 'see' the truth about his own sons.

Lear, too, in his madness, vividly expresses the idea that physical suffering can bring mental revelation – that people will not begin to see until they learn to feel: 'When the rain came to wet me once, and the wind to make me chatter; when the thunder would not peace at my bidding, there I found 'em, there I smelt 'em out' (4.5.100–3). And Gloucester's paradox is repeated, as if to drive it home:

> LEAR Your eyes are in a heavy case, your purse in a light; yet you
> see how this world goes.
> GLOUCESTER I see it feelingly.
> LEAR What, art mad? A man may see how this world goes with no
> eyes.
>
> (4.5.142–7)

This is in the bizarre episode at Dover Cliff: the dialogue between the mad king and his blind nobleman which brings them together at the nadir of their fortunes yet shows them, in spite of their afflictions, as in some senses wiser and better men than when we first saw them.

A moralistic view of the play's action would see Lear's madness and Gloucester's blinding as punishments appropriate to the faults of those who endure them: Lear has erred in the mind, Gloucester in the body. And indeed Shakespeare not only shows both Lear and Gloucester learning morals about basic human behaviour from their experiences but also allows one of the play's other characters to draw a moral with simplistic harshness when Edgar, speaking to the defeated Edmond, attributes their father's suffering to his sensuality: 'The dark and vicious place where thee he got | Cost him his eyes.' But the final stretches of the action take *King Lear* far beyond the simplicities of the morality play as one hammer-blow of fate succeeds another, driving out of our minds any illusion that the characters may simply be getting what they deserve.

At one point it begins almost to look as if the story might be going to end in what Tate called 'a Success to the innocent distrest Persons'. Rescued by the forces of Cordelia, now Queen of France, Lear is restored at once to sanity and to the love of the daughter whom he had banished. The scene of their recognition and mutual forgiveness links this most tragic of plays to the comic tradition, to the reunion of the living with the supposedly dead – fathers and daughters, fathers and sons, brothers and sisters, husbands and wives – in plays from each stage of Shakespeare's career, ranging from *The Comedy of Errors* to *The Tempest*. In all those plays one of the relatives believes that the other has come back from the grave; the extraordinary thing about *King Lear* is that the King believes this of himself – and regrets it:

> You do me wrong to take me out o'th' grave.
> Thou art a soul in bliss, but I am bound
> Upon a wheel of fire, that mine own tears
> Do scald like molten lead.
>
> (4.6.38–41)

This cosmic image linking hell and heaven, fusing the Christian tradition with classical mythology (in its recollection of Ixion), prefaces an episode whose legendary pathos derives both from the situation portrayed and from the simplicity of the language in which it is written.

Shakespeare's use of language in this play is amazingly subtle, creating an inexhaustible network of resonances; it is possible, for example, to trace intricate patternings of imagery of seeing initiated by Goneril's claim that she loves Lear 'Dearer than eyesight' (1.1.56) and emerging into the action of the play with the blinding of Gloucester when he is not merely deprived of eyesight but has his eyes actually torn out and cast upon the stage; and the play's implicit investigation of what it is to be a man is conducted partly through a multiple series of allusions to animals, from Lear's comparison of himself with a 'dragon' (1.1.122) to his posing of the unanswerable question 'Why should a dog, a horse, a rat have life, | And thou no breath at all?' spoken over the dead body of Cordelia.

But although language is as it were the nervous system of the play, linking all its parts into a single intercommunicating organism, it is always at the service of the dramatic situation and rarely if ever flowers into detachable passages of obvious 'poetry'. (Interestingly enough, one of the most obvious in the Quarto version, the Gentleman's description of Cordelia's grief at hearing of her father's plight – 'You have seen sunshine and rain at once . . .' – was the victim of the blue pencil in the revision represented by the Folio text.) This play's verbal austerity is such that a critic has written: 'Perhaps one reason why *King Lear* has been mistaken for an unactable play is that it is so nearly an unreadable play.'[6] Yet to say this is not to say that the language is invariably 'difficult'; for example, after the mighty image with which Lear greets the sight of his banished daughter their dialogue of forgiveness and reconciliation is carried forward in language of the utmost simplicity, largely using monosyllables and phrases that we ourselves might speak in an entirely everyday domestic context, phrases such as 'I feel this pin prick', 'You must not kneel', 'Do not laugh at me', 'And so I am, I am', 'I know you do not love me', 'No cause, no cause', 'You must bear with me', phrases which in themselves have no poetic charge but which in the context both of the dramatic situation and of all the action and the language, much of it knotty and contorted, that have gone before fall with the benediction of the song-like passages that emerge from the no less complex emotional strivings of some of Beethoven's late piano sonatas.

But the consolations of the reunion scene, though real, are short-lived. The play's closing episodes give great prominence to the sense and sight of the human body as a corpse: their import is foreshadowed by Edgar's words to his despairing father, 'Men must endure | Their going hence even as their coming hither.' Regan sickens and dies, poisoned by her sister; Edgar narrates the story of his father's death; a Gentleman enters carrying the 'bloody knife' with which Goneril has stabbed and killed herself; her body and Regan's are brought on to the stage; Lear, whom we had last seen speaking a vision of an eternity in which he and Cordelia would 'sing like birds i'th' cage', carries in her dead body with the lacerating, animal cry of 'Howl, howl, howl, howl!', seeks in her face for signs of life, boasts 'I killed the slave that was a-hanging thee', and, after we have heard that Edmond too is dead, himself dies gazing at Cordelia.

The ending of *King Lear* has been regarded as too bleak; in particular, from Dr Johnson onwards complaints have been voiced that the death of Cordelia is a gratuitous sensationalism. But like the blinding of Gloucester, which also has offended, it is essential to the play's design. In the opening scene Lear, failing to see the beauty of Cordelia's truth, had banished her. Now, in a total reversal of the crisis of that scene, all his attention and all of his love are focused upon her. Through feeling he has been brought to see, and his last words, bringing to a climax the imagery of sight that has run through the play, are 'Look there, look there'. It is at Cordelia that he, and those on stage, and we, all look: Cordelia dead, but Cordelia who has lived; Cordelia who has loved her father and to whom now, nakedly true to his own emotions, he gives out pure and merited love. And it is love that distinguishes man from the animals, love that enables Lear to transcend his limitations even as he is defeated by them, love that enables him to die unselfishly. Cordelia is dead, she will 'come no more', but she has existed; Goneril and Regan are dead too, and their bodies are there before us – a tableau of the dead that echoes that of the living in the opening scene. Uncompromisingly the play acknowledges the power of evil, the inevitability of death, the frailty of the human body, while also asserting the spiritual values that can give meaning to life. At the end, death comes as a release:

> Vex not his ghost. O, let him pass. He hates him
> That would upon the rack of this tough world
> Stretch him out longer.

Though we can talk of *King Lear* in abstract, universal terms, part of its power comes from its relevance to ordinary life, and modern productions tend to abandon the 'Stonehenge' approach, with its generalizing tendency, in favour of a more socially oriented style, inviting us to make connections between the play and the world around us. Thus Deborah Warner's National Theatre version of 1990 had Lear careering on to the stage in a wheelchair on his first entrance, wearing a clown nose and blowing squeakers, clearly in the middle of his eightieth birthday party; and at the Old Vic the discomforts of the hovel scene uncomfortably reminded members of the audience of the plight of the homeless whose squalid, improvised accommodation under the arches of Waterloo Bridge they had passed on the way to the theatre. The play is more than a social tract, but equally it is more than a philosophical treatise: a work of art that, though it is capable of temporal and local application, also reaches down to the deepest concerns of the subconscious mind.

★

Reviewing one of the rare productions of *Timon of Athens* – a fine one
directed at Stratford-upon-Avon in 1965 by John Schlesinger with
Paul Scofield as a memorable Timon – Bernard Levin summarized the
play's action in a single sentence: 'Timon, generous beyond reckoning
in the days of his wealth, turns to the blackest misanthropy when his
friends prove false in the time of his need.'[7] Even more than *King Lear*
this is a schematic play, a parable in which elements of the design lie
close to the surface, and in which characters are more important for
their contribution to the play's pattern of ideas than as individuals.
Indeed, many of them lack personal names.

The play's prevailing tone is set by the emblematic opening episode
in which, before Timon himself enters, an unnamed Jeweller shows to
a Merchant a jewel that he hopes to sell to Timon, a Painter shows to a
Poet a flattering portrait of Timon, and the Poet summarizes his
allegorical poem in which the personified figure of Fortune is seated
on top of a 'high and pleasant hill'; when she summons to her a man 'of
Lord Timon's frame' many ranks of men climb after him, but

> When Fortune in her shift and change of mood
> Spurns down her late belovèd, all his dependants,
> Which laboured after him to the mountain's top
> Even on their knees and hands, let him fall down,
> Not one accompanying his declining foot.

Nowhere else does Shakespeare so obviously incorporate into a play
lines that could have stood before it as an 'argument', or a summary,
of its action. And in the action that follows, the play's scenario sticks
through its sometimes inadequate flesh and blood like the skeleton of
an emaciated body.

In the first act action and counter-action are interwoven. Consecutive episodes are clearly designed to demonstrate Timon's prodigal
generosity as first he offers to redeem an imprisoned friend from debt
and then bestows money upon one of his own servants so that he may
marry the woman he loves. The Poet, the Painter, and the Jeweller are
all offered rewards for their labours and invited to dinner, and the
scene is rounded off with an episode in which more unnamed lords
praise Timon and look forward to tasting of his bounty. In the
following scene our impression of Timon's magnanimity is reinforced
when he refuses the repayment that Ventidius is unexpectedly able to
offer as the result of his father's conveniently sudden death, and a
formal entertainment at the banquet followed by the distribution of

more lavish gifts provides an opportunity for much obsequious honouring of the host.

Even in this opening act Timon does not go uncriticized, and we hear early warnings of his fall. The cynic philosopher Apemantus rails against Timon's flatterers, claiming that there is no such thing as an honest Athenian and acting as a satirically deflating chorus rather in the manner of Thersites in *Troilus and Cressida*, though with what seems to be more genuine grief at human folly:

> O you gods, what a number of men eats Timon, and he sees 'em not! It grieves me to see so many dip their meat in one man's blood; and all the madness is, he cheers them up, too.
>
> (1.2.38–41)

More urgent if more sympathetic warnings come from Timon's steward, Flavius, who reveals to us, though not yet to his master, that funds are running out.

At the opening of the second act Timon's creditors start to put pressure on him, and the shape of the subsequent stretch of action is set up by his misplaced expressions of confidence that his friends will stand by him. So we have a series of satirically entertaining scenes in which, to the disgust of his faithful servants, Timon's friends show themselves in their true colours, culminating in that in which the enraged Timon, besieged by his creditors' servants, instructs Flavius to invite them all to another banquet at which, he says, 'My cook and I'll provide.' Deluded into supposing that Timon remains his hospitable self the guests apologize sycophantically for their importunities, but the scene, and the first part of the play, come to an ironical climax as '*The dishes are uncovered and seen to be full of steaming water [and stones]*', and Timon beats his guests out of the house. The scene is rounded off by a delightful little coda as the disconcerted lords seek for the belongings that they have lost in the fray, and one of them sums up the situation with 'One day he gives us diamonds, next day stones'.

Timon's last words in this scene mark both the turning-point of the play and a total reversal of his character:

> Burn house! Sink Athens! Henceforth hated be
> Of Timon man and all humanity!

The best-known comment on *Timon of Athens* is John Dover Wilson's description of it as 'the still-born twin of *Lear*',[8] and the second part of the play brings us close to *Lear* in theme as well as in structure. In both men the shock of disillusionment after being betrayed by those they have trusted provokes a rejection of the society in which they have lived and more generally a series of bitter reflections on mankind and especially on human sexuality. Turning his back on Athens Timon curses it and all its inhabitants in a great tirade during which, like Lear in the storm, he exposes his body to the elements, declaring

> Nothing I'll bear from thee
> But nakedness, thou detestable town.
>
> (4.1.32–3)

He 'will to the woods, where he shall find | Th'unkindest beast more kinder than mankind'.

In the play's second part the patterning is even more evident than in the first. The scene following Timon's tirade provides a different perspective on the action as a group of his servants – Athenians themselves – speak with unselfish regret of their noble master's fall and condemn those who have betrayed him. Like both Lear and Gloucester, Timon has faithful followers, even though he finds it difficult to credit their loyalty. Flavius's recapitulatory, moralizing speech at the end of the scene seems designed to restore any sympathy that Timon may have lost by his intemperance; just as servants support and comfort Gloucester after his blinding, and Kent and the Fool follow Lear into the storm, so Flavius declares: 'I'll follow and enquire him out. . . . Whilst I have gold I'll be his steward still.'

After this the play is virtually an interrupted soliloquy in which Timon, now living in a cave, curses mankind, especially that part of it that dwells in Athens, and receives a sequence of visitors whom he treats to diatribes on, especially, the corruptive power of gold. As in *King Lear*, language and symbol are often indistinguishable, here particularly in the opposition between roots – man's basic necessities – and gold, which Timon finds in abundance in the woods where it is of no value to him, and which now he gives away contemptuously as a means of harming men rather than of doing them good. To the warrior Alcibiades, marching against Athens, he offers gold as a help to destroy the city that has rejected them; to the pair of prostitutes who accompany him, as a force for damning themselves and others.

The play's central encounter comes when the natural misanthrope, Apemantus, confronts the man whose 'change of fortune' has thrust misanthropy upon him, pointing out 'Thou'dst courtier be again |

Wert thou not beggar' (4.3.242–3). In defence, Timon says that
Apemantus never knew a better state, memorably comparing himself
to the oak whose leaves

> have with one winter's brush
> Fell from their boughs, and left me open, bare
> For every storm that blows.
>
> (4.3.265–7)

Starting off as 'the worst of men' (276), Apemantus had no distance to
fall. The exhilarating theatricality of this scene derives from the
energy, intelligence, and even glee with which the natural and the
enforced misanthrope delight in insulting each other, and the heart of
the scene is Apemantus's comment: 'The middle of humanity thou
never knewest, but the extremity of both ends. When thou wast in thy
gilt and thy perfume, they mocked thee for too much curiosity; in thy
rags thou know'st none, but art despised for the contrary' (302–6).
Like Lear at his worst, Timon sees mankind as a parade of beastliness,
and the episode ends with the two men chucking stones as well as
insults at each other.

   Reduced to the level of a beast Timon begins to think of death, but
his sufferings are not yet over. The arrival of a group of thieves
provokes another great outburst in which all nature is seen as a prey
upon itself:

> The sun's a thief, and with his great attraction
> Robs the vast sea. The moon's an arrant thief,
> And her pale fire she snatches from the sun.
> The sea's a thief, whose liquid surge resolves
> The moon into salt tears. The earth's a thief,
> That feeds and breeds by a composture stol'n
> From gen'ral excrement. Each thing's a thief.
>
> (4.3.438–44)

King Lear's reconciliation with Cordelia is also a reconciliation with
humanity; the nearest that Timon comes to this is with the re-
appearance of his steward, Flavius, as a reminder that even in Athens
there are men capable of compassion, love, and loyalty, and therefore
that Timon is mistaken in his wholesale denunciations of the human
race. Fleetingly Timon acknowledges this:

>Forgive my general and exceptless rashness,
>You perpetual sober gods! I do proclaim
>One honest man – mistake me not, but one,
>No more, I pray – and he's a steward.
>How fain would I have hated all mankind,
>And thou redeem'st thyself! But all save thee
>I fell with curses.
>
>(4.3.496–502)

And to this 'singly honest man' he gives gold with the injunction that he

>   show charity to none,
>But let the famished flesh slide from the bone
>Ere thou relieve the beggar.

As if to show that Flavius is the exception that proves the rule the Poet and the Painter turn up again, still seeking after their own profit, still showing lack of knowledge both of other men and also of themselves. Finally two Athenian Senators arrive begging Timon to return to lead the city's forces against those of the invading Alcibiades. The idea does not appeal to Timon, and he treats them with bitter but controlled sarcasm.

The logical outcome of Timon's withdrawal from the human race is a further retreat into the refuge of death; only extinction can bring him what he desires. At the end of his flyting with Apemantus he had declared himself 'sick of this false world' and advised himself

>   presently prepare thy grave.
>Lie where the light foam of the sea may beat
>Thy gravestone daily.
>
>(4.3.380–2)

Now he declares:

>   My long sickness
>Of health and living now begins to mend,
>And nothing brings me all things.
>
>(5.2.71–3)

A strange otherworldliness enters his speech as he sends the Senators back to Athens with the message:

Timon hath made his everlasting mansion
Upon the beachèd verge of the salt flood,
Who once a day with his embossèd froth
The turbulent surge shall cover.

(5.2.100–3)

We do not see Timon die, nor do we know who, if anyone, buries him in the grave he has prepared for himself. An illiterate soldier discovers his gravestone, makes an impression in wax of the misanthropic epitaph inscribed upon it, and takes it back to Athens where Alcibiades speaks compassionately of the dead man.

There is something symbolically appropriate in the idea that Timon may have buried himself, but the sketchiness of the plotting here is typical of the text as a whole. Editors tidy up some of its many loose ends, but as first printed, in the 1623 Folio, it clearly derives from a manuscript that still needed a lot of work on it before it could have been put into production. Stage directions give information that is at odds with what happens in the text; characters are inexactly identified – lords are given names at some points but referred to only as lords at others, so that it is not clear who should say what; there is uncertainty about the monetary value of the talent; names occur in variant forms; more subjectively, the style of writing fluctuates, and the verse is often highly irregular.

Perhaps the most conspicuous evidence that the play is unfinished relates to Alcibiades. He figures sketchily in the earlier scenes as a warrior on whom Timon bestows bounty. Then, after Timon has invited his false friends to the mock banquet, we suddenly have a scene with Alcibiades at the centre as he pleads passionately before the Athenian Senate for the life of an unidentified and unseen friend who has apparently killed a man in indeterminate circumstances. His petition is refused, and he himself is banished in spite of his great services to the state. The contribution that this scene was intended to make to the play's structure is easily inferred: it adds to our sense of the corruption in Athens, helps to justify Timon by replicating the private hypocrisy and ingratitude of his supposed friends on the highest and most official level, and provides an opening for a counter-action in which Alcibiades, rather than retreating into bitter misanthropy like Timon, will lead his forces against his own city. Its relation to the main plot seems designed to be the same as that of Gloucester's blinding in *King Lear*, but it is inadequately worked out and imperfectly integrated into the overall dramatic structure.

All the evidence, then, points to the conclusion that *Timon of Athens*, as we have it, is unfinished. There is no evidence that it was acted in Shakespeare's time, though it is conceivable that a more finished version existed and was put into production. But as the compilers of the First Folio usually worked from theatrical manuscripts, and as there is some reason to suppose that they did not originally intend to include this play in their volume, it seems probable that the play was abandoned. We can't tell why this should have happened, but it may be related to the fact that modern scholarship has shown pretty conclusively that Shakespeare worked on this play in collaboration with the young playwright Thomas Middleton, born in 1580, who by 1606, when *Timon of Athens* seems most likely to have been written (soon after *King Lear*), was already the author of several satirical comedies of London life. Some of the textual dislocations are most easily explained as the result of imperfect collaboration, and a number of scenes display a high concentration of linguistic forms characteristic of Middleton as well as other distinctive features of his dramatic style such as the use of unnamed characters and irregular versification.[9]

Though the unfinished state of this play's text causes problems to its theatrical (as well as to its critical) interpreters it also leaves them with exceptional freedoms, and in its comparatively infrequent revivals the text has usually been substantially altered to give it greater coherency and to flesh out passages that seem inadequately realized.[10] The play's satire on the power of money, which attracted Karl Marx, has appealed, too, to modern directors who have used updated costumes and settings to create a heightened sense of social realism, interpreting the play primarily as a satire on the values of a materialistic society. This is true to some of its facets but may undervalue the tragic potential that lies within the character of Timon himself, a role in which the disparate indications of character and personality are difficult to fuse into a consistent whole, but which nevertheless contains within itself seeds that in the performance of a great actor can grow beyond satire to tragedy.

Notes to Chapter Twelve

1 William Hazlitt, *Characters*, p. 119.
2 *London Chronicle*, 21–3 May 1776, cited in Odell, vol. 1, p. 454.
3 These and other criticisms of the play are cited in Stanley Wells, 'The

Once and Future *King Lear*', in *The Division of the Kingdoms*, ed. G. Taylor and M. Warren (Oxford, 1983; repr. 1986).

4 Harley Granville-Barker, *Prefaces to Shakespeare* (1927; two-volume edn, 1958), vol. 1, pp. 332, 328–9.

5 *Samuel Johnson on Shakespeare*, p. 222.

6 Winifred M.T. Nowottny, 'Some Aspects of the Style of *King Lear*', *Shakespeare Survey 13* (Cambridge, 1960), pp. 47–57; quoting from p. 49.

7 *Daily Mail*, 2 July 1965.

8 John Dover Wilson, *The Essential Shakespeare* (1932), p. 131.

9 *Textual Companion*, p. 501.

10 The play's stage history up to Peter Brook's production of 1974–5 is usefully surveyed by Gary Jay Williams in an appendix (pp. 161–85) to Rolf Soellner's book *Timon of Athens: Shakespeare's Pessimistic Tragedy* (Columbus, OH, 1979).

THIRTEEN

A Scottish Tragedy:
Macbeth

Macbeth has a well-deserved reputation as one of Shakespeare's most sheerly exciting plays, a fast-moving murder story laced with witchcraft and offering the theatrical pleasures of a ghost, apparitions, a sleepwalking scene, and climactic battles culminating in a hand-to-hand combat in which the villain-hero is killed by his virtuous adversary. Macbeth himself is more like Richard III than any of the intervening tragic protagonists. Both men are great warriors who come to the throne not by warfare but by murder. Both sink further and further into blood as they struggle to extricate themselves from the consequences of their deeds, and both are tormented by conscience. The fates of both men are inextricably linked with those of their countries, and each of them is finally defeated in personal combat by a representative of the forces of virtue who thereby purges the state of evil and restores the health of the nation. Each play, too, is concerned not with some remote or fictitious country but with a period or setting related closely to the lives of its first audiences. *Richard the Third*, as we have seen, ends with the triumph of the grandfather of Queen Elizabeth, the reigning sovereign at the time it was written. In *Macbeth* Shakespeare portrays a supposed ancestor – Macbeth's comrade, Banquo – of her successor, James I, and draws attention to the continuity of the line in a strange episode which makes the connection explicit.

Macbeth was written probably in 1606; King James VI of Scotland had come to the English throne in 1603, and soon afterwards Shakespeare's company, the Lord Chamberlain's Men, came under royal patronage as the King's Men. While it seems simplistic and reductive to suggest that Shakespeare wrote *Macbeth* to flatter King

James, there are enough points of contact between play and sovereign to make it likely at least that as he wrote he had his royal patron's tastes and interests in mind.

Set in Scotland, the play opens thrillingly with the appearance in thunder and lightning of three witches, who are to figure prominently in the action. Witchcraft was widely practised in Shakespeare's time, and James had a special interest in it – with good reason, since at one time several Scottish women were trying hard to destroy him by methods such as casting into the sea cats bound to the severed joints of dead bodies with the hope of raising storms while James was sailing to Denmark. At their trial in 1591 it was said that they had asked the devil why their spells had failed, to receive the reply 'Il est un homme de dieu' – a phrase echoed in *Macbeth* when Banquo, James's ancestor, claims 'In the great hand of God I stand' (2.3.132).[1] James's own credulous book on the subject, *Demonology*, had appeared in Edinburgh in 1597, and was reprinted in London in the year of his accession. His investigations resulted in the detection of so many frauds that as time passed his credulity waned, but in 1616, years after *Macbeth* was written, he investigated a case at Leicester in which he heard of a boy who suffered from fits. The boy's symptoms were not understood to be the result of natural illness, he made accusations of witchcraft, and as a result nine people had been hanged and another six were in prison awaiting trial. The King managed to get the boy to confess that his accusations were fraudulent and those in prison were released; not much could be done about the others, though James did rebuke the judges for carelessness in having had them put to death.[2]

More direct links with James come in Shakespeare's portrayal of Banquo. In Holinshed's *Chronicles*, where Shakespeare found the story, Banquo is implicated in the murder of King Duncan; in the play, though he is subjected to the same kind of temptation as Macbeth, Shakespeare causes him to withstand it. There is good dramatic reason for this, but it may reasonably be interpreted also as a sensible diplomatic move when one considers the episode, scarcely required by the action (and often cut in more recent performance), in which Banquo's blood-stained spirit appears to Macbeth pointing to a show of eight kings, the last bearing a glass which, says Macbeth,

> shows me many more; and some I see
> That twofold balls and treble sceptres carry.
>
> (4.1.136–7)

This clear allusion to James's unifying of the kingdoms of England and Scotland, symbolized by his investiture with two sceptres and one orb, breaks the play's time-barrier to link the historic action not merely with the time of the play's original performance but beyond that, since then James was the only king to have been so crowned. Whether the description of the English king Edward I touching for the King's Evil (4.3.140–59) would have been pleasing to James is a moot point[3]; its presence in the play can be justified on aesthetic and intellectual grounds, but again it has often proved dispensable, and Malcolm's statement that the King 'To the succeeding royalty . . . leaves | The healing benediction' (4.3.156–7) is easily seen as a strained compliment to that same 'succeeding royalty'.

The matter is complicated by the state of the only surviving text, which shows signs of adaptation. It is Shakespeare's shortest surviving tragedy, and includes episodes (3.5, and parts of 4.1) that there is good reason to believe are not by Shakespeare. These episodes feature Hecate, who does not appear elsewhere; they are composed largely in octosyllabic couplets in a style conspicuously different from the rest of the play; and they call for the performance of two songs, identified in the original version of *Macbeth* only by their opening words, that survive in full in *The Witch*, a play of uncertain date by Thomas Middleton, who appears to have collaborated with Shakespeare on *Timon of Athens*. It seems likely that Middleton, for reasons unknown, adapted Shakespeare's play some years after it first appeared.[4]

The play's framework of national destiny has proved less attractive to later ages than the personal tragedy of Macbeth played within it; many modern productions adjust the text to throw even more emphasis on Macbeth and his Lady, some even suggesting that the action takes place entirely within Macbeth's mind. There are signs that Shakespeare himself found the depiction of national and political issues the less inspiring part of his task, particularly in the long (well, it always seems long) scene in which Malcolm, the rightful heir to the Scottish throne, tests the integrity of Macduff, who is leading the rebellion against the tyrant, by pretending that he would make a far worse ruler even than Macbeth. Intellectually, as critics have laboured to show, the scene is entirely justifiable, and the writing is never less than competent, but the dramatic mode seems artificial and stilted by comparison with that of the bulk of the play, and the emotional temperature is low; it seems significant that here (as in the opening scene of *Henry the Fifth*) Shakespeare's wording is close to that of his historical source, as if he were dutifully versifying history rather than being taken over by it.

Theatrical emphasis upon the figures of Macbeth and his Lady is justified by Shakespeare's technique of character portrayal in this play. In, for example, *Romeo and Juliet* and *Hamlet* he uses his stylistic virtuosity to bestow the impression of individuality on a wide range of characters so that even minor roles – like the servant, Peter, and the Apothecary in *Romeo and Juliet*, and the courtier Osric and the gravediggers in *Hamlet* – have their own distinctive voices. This is not how he works in *Macbeth*. Here, as if to draw attention to the play's moral and ethical structure, even major roles are drained of individuality. In Holinshed, for example, Duncan is a weak king, too 'soft and gentle of nature', 'negligent . . . in punishing offenders', 'slothful' to the point of cowardice. Shakespeare builds him up into a symbol (rather than a portrait) of an ideal king. True, he is not a warrior, but this is not made a ground for criticism, and although there is nothing in the text to show how old he is, it is probably a sound tradition to play him as an old man. Everyone treats him with respect and affection, he is generous in praise and honours where they are due, and in return he receives the love and duty of his subjects. To Macbeth he is 'the gracious Duncan' who

> Hath borne his faculties so meek, hath been
> So clear in his great office, that his virtues
> Will plead like angels, trumpet-tongued against
> The deep damnation of his taking-off.
>
> (1.7.17–20)

Above all, he is a king: Shakespeare stresses throughout the play the holiness of true kingship. Duncan's murder is compared to sacrilege, to the desecration of a temple. When his body is discovered, Macduff cries:

> Most sacrilegious murder hath broke ope
> The Lord's anointed temple and stole thence
> The life o'th' building.
>
> (2.3.66–8)

Duncan is the sort of role – there are many of them in this play – that an actor probably does not get much fun out of playing. He is important not as a personality but for the associations he is made to carry: of generosity, fruitfulness ('I have begun to plant thee,' he says to Macbeth, 'and will labour | To make thee full of growing' [1.4.28–9]), grace and sanctity. With his murder these virtues lose sway in

Scotland; the need for them in a well-run commonwealth is impressed on us again briefly towards the end of the play, in the English scene, when we hear of the King of England to whom sick people are brought for cure: a virtuous king brings practical benefits.

Banquo is similarly treated. In Holinshed we are told of Macbeth that, 'communicating his purposed intent with his trusty friends, amongst whom Banquo was the chiefest, upon confidence of their promised aid he slew the King at Inverness'. In Holinshed Macbeth has Banquo killed not because, as in Shakespeare, he fears his 'royalty of nature', but simply because of the prophecy that Banquo's descendants would inherit the throne. There are good artistic as well as political reasons for this change: to have given Macbeth any accomplice other than his wife would have diminished his stature. And Shakespeare needs a representative, not of the ideal good against which Macbeth sins in murdering Duncan, but rather of a more normal human attitude, though still a virtuous one, that will help to keep Macbeth in perspective. We see Banquo first with Macbeth, but immediately a distinction between them is established. Though both hear the witches' prophecies, their reactions differ. Macbeth seeks a way of bringing them to pass, whereas Banquo treats them simply as unfulfilled prophecies – and ones that may have come from the devil's emissaries. Increasingly Banquo is aligned rather with Duncan than with Macbeth; they two share the passage about the temple-haunting martlet (1.6.1–9) that helps to associate them with the fruitful forces of nature, and although Banquo lacks Duncan's halo of sanctity, he possesses 'royalty of nature', courage, and 'a wisdom that doth guide his valour | To act in safety' (3.1.51,54–5).

The real parting of the ways between him and Macbeth comes just before Macbeth murders Duncan. Banquo has been disturbed by his encounter with the witches: strange thoughts trouble him – whether an awareness of temptation in himself or a suspicion of Macbeth is, perhaps deliberately, left uncertain. Sleepless, he prays that the 'Merciful powers' will restrain in him 'the cursèd thoughts that nature | Gives way to in repose'. He tells Macbeth of his dreams:

> I dreamt last night of the three weird sisters.
> To you they have showed some truth.

Macbeth replies in lines that brilliantly suggest an uncertainty of how far he can go with Banquo:

> I think not of them;
> Yet, when we can entreat an hour to serve,
> We would spend it in some words upon that business
> If you would grant the time.

Banquo agrees:

> At your kind'st leisure.

And Macbeth seems encouraged to go further:

> If you shall cleave to my consent when 'tis,
> It shall make honour for you.

But now Banquo withdraws:

> So I lose none
> In seeking to augment it, but still keep
> My bosom franchised and allegiance clear,
> I shall be counselled.
>
> (2.1.19–28)

It is a measure of Shakespeare's subtlety in composing a dialogue of nuance that Banquo can express both to Macbeth and to us his imperviousness to temptation without actually having been tempted.

From this point on, Macbeth is alone with his wife; he has severed his last link with normal humanity. When Banquo hears of Duncan's murder he makes his position unequivocally clear:

> Fears and scruples shake us.
> In the great hand of God I stand, and thence
> Against the undivulged pretence I fight
> Of treasonous malice.
>
> (2.3.128–31)

Macbeth's awareness of Banquo's suspicions, and his anxiety to ensure that the succession shall fall to his own descendants, are no doubt powerful reasons for the attempted assassination of Banquo and his son, but still more powerful is the awareness that Banquo's presence causes in him of the evil to which he has succumbed. As he thinks of Banquo, he becomes possessed by consciousness of his sin:

> For Banquo's issue have I filed my mind,
> For them the gracious Duncan have I murdered,
> Put rancours in the vessel of my peace
> Only for them, and mine eternal jewel
> Given to the common enemy of man
> To make them kings, the seed of Banquo kings.
>
> (3.1.66–71)

To the audience, Banquo stands as a measure of normality against which the lack of balance in the mind of the tragic hero can be measured. To Macbeth he is as it were an embodied conscience, not to be stilled even by death.

In Duncan and Banquo, then, Shakespeare was less intent on 'creating character' than on fashioning the component parts of a balanced composition. Even greater bareness of characterization is to be seen in many of the other figures of the play. Caithness, Mentieth, Lennox, Ross, Angus – they sound like extracts from a tour guide to the Highlands, and have no more individuality than decreasingly important railway stations along a minor branch line.

Even more obvious stylization is to be found in the play's representatives of evil. The three witches are a theatrical problem: too often far more of a nightmare for the director than for the audience. Members of Shakespeare's original audience would have been closer to the practice of witchcraft than most of us, for whom bearded women savour more of sideshows at a fair than of someone living at the other end of the village whom one believed, and who believed herself, to have supernatural powers of evil action. Shakespeare presents the witches from, so to say, a position of belief: not as women pretending to other people that they have supernatural powers, but as creatures who genuinely believe themselves to have such powers, and who visibly accomplish deeds for which no rational explanation is offered. They can apparently think as one, continuing and completing each other's sentences, they have not only the appurtenances of human witchcraft – a cauldron, horrible things to cast into it which they represent as, for instance,

> Root of hemlock, digged i'th' dark,
> Liver of blaspheming Jew,
> Gall of goat, and slips of yew
> Slivered in the moon's eclipse,
> Nose of Turk, and Tartar's lips,

> Finger of birth-strangled babe
> Ditch-delivered by a drab –

(4.1.25–31)

they can not only vanish in a manner that is convincing at least to
Macbeth and Banquo (though in the theatre we may be conscious of
the trickery by which it is done) but they can also call up apparitions
for which no rational explanation seems possible either to those who
see them in the play or to us. The vagueness that surrounds them – our
uncertainty as to the exact nature of their powers – creates a sense of
disembodiment, so that we feel them as an emotion – three wicked
shudders – rather than see them as people. Theatre directors have to
have them represented by actors, but their horror may be better
conveyed by not taking Shakespeare's implicit stage directions too
literally than by having them chuck into a cauldron plastic spiders and
the like that are no more frightening than the sort of Hallowe'en
horrors that can be bought from a children's joke shop. Adrian Noble
got a much better effect by having them roll round their mouths bits of
bread left over from the Macbeths' feast and then slowly spew them
out.[5]

The witches confound our sense of reality. Their evil counter-
balances the virtues projected in, especially, Banquo and Duncan; they
are anti-natural, and – even more importantly to the effect of this play
– they are equivocal, blurring distinctions between what is and is not.
The equivocal is frightening, and its omnipresence in *Macbeth* is what
makes this such a frightening play. It reminds us that there is indeed
more in heaven and earth than philosophy can account for, reawaken-
ing the subconscious fears that we normally keep suppressed,
frightening us by its sense of dangers lurking behind things familiar,
of what Shakespeare's contemporary Thomas Nashe called 'the
terrors of the night', sudden unidentifiable shrieks, movement where
we had expected stillness, a knocking at the door at dead of night,
motiveless attacks, nightmares that terrify us even though we know
them to be dreams, the possibility that ghosts really do exist. It turns
us all into children, frightened to watch yet too fascinated to stop
watching,

> Like one that on a lonesome road
> Doth walk in fear and dread,
> And having once turned round walks on,
> And turns no more his head

> Because he knows a frightful fiend
> Doth close behind him tread.[6]

The witches are the catalysts to this fear, the equivocal aspects of
their being announced with wonderful compression in the brilliant
little opening scene:

> When shall we three meet again?
> In thunder, lightning, or in rain?
>
> When the hurly-burly's done,
> When the battle's lost and won.
>
> That will be ere the set of sun.
>
> Where the place?
>
> > Upon the heath.
>
> There to meet with Macbeth.
>
> I come, Grimalkin.
>
> Paddock calls.
>
> > Anon.
>
> Fair is foul, and foul is fair,
> Hover through the fog and filthy air.

The disturbance of the weather, the hurly-burly of warfare, the
turmoil in nature when fair is foul and foul is fair, when values are
reversed, all help to create the sense of evil as a denial of nature, a
disturber of the peace, yet at the same time something which is itself,
however mysteriously, in and of nature. The idea recurs throughout
the play, not only in relation to the central characters but in, for
instance, Lennox's description of the storm on the night of the
murder, when 'the earth | Was feverous and did shake' (2.3.59–60), in
the choric episode between an Old Man and Ross recounting the
horrors of the night, 'unnatural, | Even like the deed that's done'
(2.4.10–11), and in the crimes of which Malcolm falsely accuses
himself. But it is not simply that things behave in a manner that is
contrary to nature: at the same time they appear to be what they are
not. Not only does what has been fair become foul; it retains its fair
appearance, so that it is simultaneously fair *and* foul. This idea again is
carried through the play with ever deepening irony: 'There's no art |
To find the mind's construction in the face', says Duncan about the

thane of Cawdor: 'He was a gentleman on whom I built | An absolute trust' (1.4.11–14) – and at that moment enters Macbeth, the new thane of Cawdor whose treachery will exceed that of his predecessor; 'look like the innocent flower, | But be the serpent under't', says Lady Macbeth to her husband (1.5.64–5); 'This castle hath a pleasant seat', says Duncan on entering the building where, we know, he will be murdered (1.6.1); 'False face must hide what the false heart doth know', says Macbeth shortly before he kills Duncan (1.7.82).

Equivocation comes before us almost in person in the grimly comic figure of the Porter who so often tempts directors to rend the play apart by the way he is played, presumably under the illusion that Shakespeare not only expected but desired his clowns to speak more than is set down for them, to break the play's continuity with a display of comic virtuosity, not to say vulgarity. Shakespeare gives his clowns all they need, and all we need from them; the Porter's comedy is of the play, not excrescent to it, he is porter at once of Macbeth's castle and of hell-gate, his drunken fantasies are the counterpart of Macbeth's hallucinations, and, admitting an 'equivocator that could swear in both the scales against either scale, who committed treason enough for God's sake, but could not equivocate to heaven' (2.3.8–9), he reminds us of Macbeth's willingness to 'jump the life to come'. 'I had thought to have let in some of all professions that go the primrose way to th'everlasting bonfire': in that characteristic pun on the word 'professions' we are reminded of those who profess themselves other than they are, the serpent under the flower. Possessed of the throne, Macbeth and his Lady

> Must lave our honours in these flattering streams
> And make our faces vizors to our hearts,
> Disguising what they are.
>
> (3.2.34–6)

Malcolm, who is really virtuous, makes himself appear wicked as a means of testing Macduff's integrity; thus 'fair', by making itself appear 'foul', proves the truth of Macduff's apparent fairness.

Above all, equivocation is expressed through and in the witches and other people's reactions to them. Banquo sees that things may not be as fair as they seem; some doubt seems latent even in his encouraging remark to Macbeth when they two together first hear the prophecies:

Good sir, why do you start and seem to fear
Things that do sound so fair?

(1.3.49–50)

And he asks them 'I'th' name of truth, | Are ye fantastical or that
indeed | Which outwardly ye show?' He remains severely sceptical,
while Macbeth is carried away on a flood of speculation. Banquo's
warning note is clear enough, and important as an anticipation of what
is to come: 'oftentimes', he says, 'to win us to our harm | The
instruments of darkness tell us truths, | Win us with honest trifles to
betray's | In deepest consequence' (1.3.121–4). But Macbeth, while
seeing that the direction his thoughts are taking may be an evil one,
will not face up to the need to make a clear judgement:

This supernatural soliciting
Cannot be ill, cannot be good . . .
                              function
Is smothered in surmise, and nothing is
But what is not.

(1.3.129–41)

This deeply human awareness of the anomalous in his own nature, the
sense of an undertow of evil cutting beneath the bank and shoal of
time, is one of the things that make Macbeth's plight so moving, and
cause us to be more deeply involved with him than with Banquo.
Banquo is in the great hand of God; Macbeth is a cause of greater
concern just because his judgement is less clear.

The overt expression of the witches' equivocal nature comes in the
set of prophecies delivered by the apparitions in the cauldron scene
(4.1). In spite of Banquo's warning, Macbeth continues to place his
trust in the weird sisters; he accepts their oracular statements at face
value; these prophecies do indeed seem fair, it does seem impossible
that Birnam Wood will come to Dunsinane, and there seems no reason
why Macbeth should not feel confident after he is told that 'none of
woman born | Shall harm Macbeth'. But after all, the first apparition
has warned him against Macduff: 'beware Macduff, | Beware the
thane of Fife', and it is at his own risk that he, who has been so apt to
create a false impression, should take their other statements at face
value. It is Macbeth's powers of self-deception that bring about his
final overthrow. The ambiguous nature of the witches symbolizes the
power of choice that he is given, and in the play's last minutes we have
a vivid visual symbol of the destructive force of his self-deception

when the army led by Malcolm and Macduff adopts the device of carrying the branches of trees as camouflage, so that it seems as if Birnam Wood really did move towards Dunsinane. The tables are turned; Macbeth's bloody instructions return to plague the inventor; the fair appearances of evil are foul at heart.

The army that brings the tyrant's reign to an end comes to its victory bearing 'leafy screens'. Besides providing a climactic false appearance, the action also, in its use of the green branches of trees, reminds us of the good things of nature, and of their association during the course of the play with the virtuous characters and with the good way of life in man and in the state. Duncan and Banquo have been associated in our minds with growth and with fruitfulness. On the other side are the weird sisters, inevitably associated with forces opposed to nature: with storm and tempest, savagery and murder. Caught in the middle are the play's central figures, Macbeth and his Lady. In both of them we witness a conflict between natural and unnatural forces.

The evil within Macbeth and his Lady constantly finds expression in a need to suppress natural human feeling. So in a great invocation Lady Macbeth makes a fiercely conscious effort to subdue her womanhood:

> Come, you spirits
> That tend on mortal thoughts, unsex me here,
> And fill me from the crown to the toe top-full
> Of direst cruelty. Make thick my blood,
> Stop up th'access and passage to remorse,
> That no compunctious visitings of nature
> Shake my fell purpose, nor keep peace between
> Th'effect and it. Come to my woman's breasts,
> And take my milk for gall, you murd'ring ministers,
> Wherever in your sightless substances
> You wait on nature's mischief. Come, thick night,
> And pall thee in the dunnest smoke of hell,
> That my keen knife see not the wound it makes
> Nor heaven peep through the blanket of the dark
> To cry 'Hold, hold!'
>
> (1.5.39–53)

The speech, impressive in itself, reverberates through the play. 'Come to my woman's breasts, | And take my milk for gall' is recalled soon afterwards when, inciting her husband to murder Duncan, she declares:

> I have given suck, and know
> How tender 'tis to love the babe that milks me.
> I would, while it was smiling in my face,
> Have plucked my nipple from his boneless gums
> And dashed the brains out, and I so sworn
> As you have done to this.
>
> (1.7.54–9)

'Milk' becomes something of a symbol of merciful nature, prepared for by Lady Macbeth's statement that her husband's nature 'is too full o'th' milk of human kindness' (1.5.16–17) and recalled when Malcolm deceptively declares that he would

> Pour the sweet milk of concord into hell,
> Uproar the universal peace, confound
> All unity on earth.
>
> (4.3.99–101)

Similarly, Lady Macbeth's invocation to night is soon to be paralleled by Macbeth's:

> Come, seeling night,
> Scarf up the tender eye of pitiful day,
> And with thy bloody and invisible hand
> Cancel and tear to pieces that great bond
> Which keeps me pale.
>
> (3.3.47–51)

The play is full of similar links: its poetic texture is dense, creating a claustrophobic, self-contained world: words such as 'blood' and 'night' recur again and again, accumulating fresh and more complex associations all the time.

In the earlier part of the play the subjugation of natural instincts seems easier for Lady Macbeth than for her husband. There is an exultant ring to her declarations of savagery; she cannot understand her husband's mental torment. He has to 'bend up . . . each corporal agent' to what he admits to be a 'terrible feat' (1.7.79–80); contemplating his bloodstained hands, he cries in agony:

> Ha, they pluck out mine eyes.
> Will all great Neptune's ocean wash this blood
> Clean from my hand? No, this my hand will rather

> The multitudinous seas incarnadine,
> Making the green one red.
>
> (2.2.57–61)

But his wife takes a more severely practical point of view:

> A little water clears us of this deed.
> How easy is it then! Your constancy
> Hath left you unattended.
>
> (2.2.65–7)

For her 'The sleeping and the dead | Are but as pictures'; for him the mere thought of the unnaturalness of his contemplated deed conjures up a horrified vision of the universe in mourning:

>   this Duncan
> Hath borne his faculties so meek, hath been
> So clear in his great office, that his virtues
> Will plead like angels, trumpet-tongued against
> The deep damnation of his taking-off,
> And pity, like a naked new-born babe,
> Striding the blast, or heaven's cherubin, horsed
> Upon the sightless couriers of the air,
> Shall blow the horrid deed in every eye
> That tears shall drown the wind.
>
> (1.7.16–25)

At first, then, there is a clear contrast between the two. As the play progresses their roles are reversed. Lady Macbeth's imagination begins to work. Both of them, who had called upon night to cover their deeds, find that Macbeth 'hath murdered sleep' (2.2.40); they are afflicted nightly with terrible dreams; they had turned day into night, and now their own nights are rendered indistinguishable from day. Lady Macbeth had denied imagination. She had committed the mistake of those referred to by Lafeu in *All's Well that Ends Well* who 'make modern and familiar things supernatural and causeless. Hence is it that we make trifles of terrors, ensconcing ourselves into seeming knowledge when we should submit ourselves to an unknown fear' (*All's Well that Ends Well*, 2.3.2–6). The 'unknown fear' – fear of the unknown – is terribly present from the start to Macbeth; he denies it after great struggle. Lady Macbeth seems not to fear it at all; but when her imagination begins to work her 'seeming knowledge' gives way to the horrified questionings of the sleepwalking scene which shows with an extraordinary anticipation of the theories of Freudian psychology the release in sleep of the subconscious fears and other emotions that Lady Macbeth had succeeded in suppressing in her waking life. She had thought that a little water would clear her of her deed; now she finds that 'All the perfumes of Arabia will not sweeten this little hand' (5.1.48–9). She ends in a mental disintegration revealing her 'great perturbation in nature'.

Macbeth's progress is in the opposite direction. In him we see a slow death of the imagination, proceeding from an extreme sensibility through great though self-inflicted suffering to a state of almost complete emotional sterility. He has denied the prompting of nature. By usurping the throne he has plunged his country into unnatural turmoil. He has tried to restore order, but his crime makes this impossible; so the banquet, traditional symbol of social harmony, which begins in order – 'You know your own degrees; sit down' (3.4.1) – is broken by the entry of Banquo's ghost, reminder of the host's crime, and ends in disorder – 'Stand not upon the order of your going, | But go at once.'

Gradually Macbeth finds himself forced by sheer impetus of accumulated evil into a career of escalating crime: 'I am in blood | Stepped in so far that, should I wade no more, | Returning were as tedious as go o'er' (3.4.135–7). He becomes a mass murderer – no wonder the play has continued to seem relevant to the twentieth century – committing his worst crimes with none of the awareness of evil that he had felt in murdering Duncan:

> The castle of Macduff I will surprise,
> Seize upon Fife, give to th'edge o'th' sword
> His wife, his babes, and all unfortunate souls
> That trace him in his line.
>
> (4.1.166–9)

The bonds of nature are seen to be indivisible in the external and the internal world. Macbeth had desired to 'Cancel and tear to pieces that great bond | Which keeps me pale' (3.2.50–1), but his crimes against external nature are against his own nature, too, and this brings retribution, retribution that he had himself foreseen, the retribution of an 'even-handed justice'. He had expressed his willingness to 'jump the life to come' (1.7.7), but the very phrase is ambiguous: he finds that he is plunged into hell not in a life after death but in a death in life.

His expressions of pretended suffering on the discovery of Duncan's body forecast the suffering that he is already beginning to undergo:

> Had I but died an hour before this chance
> I had lived a blessèd time, for from this instant
> There's nothing serious in mortality.
> All is but toys. Renown and grace is dead.
> The wine of life is drawn, and the mere lees
> Is left this vault to brag of.
>
> (2.3.90–5)

At this stage we still hear some of the hyperbole of conscious dissimulation; later comes a piercing, realized vision of despair that comes purely from the private world:

> My way of life
> Is fall'n into the sere, the yellow leaf,
> And that which should accompany old age,
> As honour, love, obedience, troops of friends,
> I must not look to have, but in their stead
> Curses, not loud but deep, mouth-honour, breath
> Which the poor heart would fain deny but dare not.
>
> (5.3.24–30)

Macbeth has, as he says, 'supped full with horrors' (5.5.13); he is scarcely capable of emotional response: 'I have almost forgot the taste of fears' (5.5.9); and so when news arrives of his wife's death his reaction is less a statement of personal grief than a denial of the validity of human emotion. This is Shakespeare's way of showing us the dust and ashes of Macbeth's self-destroyed soul:

> She should have died hereafter.
> There would have been a time for such a word.
> Tomorrow, and tomorrow, and tomorrow
> Creeps in this petty pace from day to day
> To the last syllable of recorded time,
> And all our yesterdays have lighted fools
> The way to dusty death. Out, out, brief candle.
> Life's but a walking shadow, a poor player
> That struts and frets his hour upon the stage,
> And then is heard no more. It is a tale
> Told by an idiot, full of sound and fury,
> Signifying nothing.
>
> (5.5.16–27)

Up to a point, *Macbeth* offers the satisfactions of fiction as defined by
Oscar Wilde's Miss Prism: 'The good ended happily, and the bad
unhappily.' But the play's morality is not as simple as this. Macbeth's
'Tomorrow' speech is a meditative point of repose before the turmoil
of the conclusion. But his despair is not absolute. As the witches'
equivocations are stripped bare, as he hears how Birnam Wood 'began
to move' (5.5.33), he pulls himself together with a last assertion of
physical heroism: 'Blow wind, come wrack, | At least we'll die with
harness on our back' (5.5.49–50); he refuses to 'play the Roman fool'
(5.10.1), and remains courageous to the end. Shakespeare gives him
no dying speech. He defies Macduff even after learning that his enemy
was 'from his mother's womb | Untimely ripped' (5.10.15–16), goes
out fighting, and returns only to be slain.

This did not satisfy later adapters. Sir William Davenant, in his
Restoration version of about 1663, gave Macbeth a moralizing last
speech: 'Farewell, vain world, and what's most vain in it – Ambition.'
And when David Garrick revived the play in 1744 he added a
considerably longer dying speech that seems indebted to Marlowe's
Doctor Faustus:

> 'Tis done! the scene of life will quickly close.
> Ambition's vain, delusive dreams are fled,
> And now I wake to darkness, guilt and horror.
> I cannot bear it! Let me shake it off. –
> 'Twa' not be; my soul is clogged with blood.
> I cannot rise! I dare not ask for mercy.
> It is too late, hell drags me down. I sink,
> I sink – Oh! – my soul is lost forever.
> Oh! (*Dies*)[7]

That is banal because it is too explicitly moral. Both Davenant and
Garrick reduce the play to a demonstration of the folly of ambition,
and Garrick makes the hero condemn himself to a hell which is far less
appalling than the vision of desolation that Shakespeare had already
caused him to express on hearing of his wife's death.

The ending of Shakespeare's play shifts the focus from the personal
to the political; Macduff's entrance with Macbeth's severed head – a
reversion to an earlier dramatic mode that is often softened in modern
productions – signals a happy ending for Scotland if not for the play's
central characters who, in Malcolm's closing speech, are dismissed as
'this dead butcher and his fiend-like queen'. But this is even more of an
over-simplification than Mark Antony's assessment of Brutus, a

reduction to two-dimensionality of characters whom we have experienced with three-dimensional vividness. Though *Macbeth* is a profoundly moral play, it is not, like Malcolm, moralistic.

Notes to Chapter Thirteen

1 D.H. Willson, *King James VI and I* (London, 1956), pp. 104–5.
2 ibid., p. 311.
3 Nicholas Brooke in his Oxford edition (1990, p. 72) points out that though James 'did indeed touch occasionally' he did so 'with great reluctance, and serious theological doubts caused him to modify the ceremony'.
4 *Textual Companion*, pp. 543–4.
5 This was in his RSC production of 1986.
6 S.T. Coleridge, *The Rime of the Ancient Mariner*, Part VI.
7 *The Plays of David Garrick*, ed. H.W. Pedicord and F.L. Bergmann, 4 vols (Carbondale, II and Edwardsville, II, 1981), vol. 3, p. 72.

FOURTEEN

Tragedies of Ancient Egypt and Rome:
Antony and Cleopatra and *Coriolanus*

The tragedies to which I, like most other writers on Shakespeare, have devoted most space – *Hamlet*, *Othello*, *King Lear*, and *Macbeth* – are traditionally regarded as the 'big four'. This is an attitude that solidified in and has continued to be encouraged by A.C. Bradley's still classic study *Shakespearean Tragedy* (1904), and it has perhaps resulted in an unfair undervaluation of Shakespeare's other tragedies. But it has to be admitted that, both before and since Bradley wrote, these four tragedies are the ones that have been both most extensively performed and most highly valued as representative studies of human nature. Coleridge is not the only one to have fancied he had 'a smack of Hamlet' himself[1]; *Othello* is easily seen as a universally applicable parable of good and evil, of the terrible ease with which love may be perverted and innocence destroyed; every old man, said Goethe, is a King Lear[2]; and *Macbeth* speaks to us all of the corruptions inherent in power.

If Shakespeare's last two tragedies, *Antony and Cleopatra* and *Coriolanus*, have exerted a less universal – though still great – appeal it may be because their central characters invite us not so much to identify with them as to wonder at them; an impression that is reinforced by the fact that they are given virtually no soliloquies in which to reveal themselves to the audience. They are exceptional people in both their deeds and their personalities, larger than life, surprising us and even sometimes themselves by the way they behave. So in *Antony and Cleopatra* Enobarbus, responding to Antony's 'Would I had never seen her!' speaks of Cleopatra rather as a travel agent might speak of the Taj Mahal or the Niagara Falls: 'O, sir, you had then left unseen a wonderful piece of work, which not to have been blessed withal would have discredited your travel.'

This attitude to the central characters is related to their origins in both literature and history. In these two plays Shakespeare draws closely again on Sir Thomas North's translation of Plutarch's *Lives*, which had already provided raw material for *Julius Caesar*. But in spite of their common source, the plays are very different. As a story, *Antony and Cleopatra* is as much a sequel to *Julius Caesar* as *Henry the Fifth* to *Henry the Fourth, Part Two*, and there are a few references to the events of the earlier play; but the differences of tone, structure, and ethos make it difficult to think of one as a continuation of the other, and, unlike the English history plays, they are rarely performed together.[3] Plutarch wrote anecdotal rather than chronicle history; he delighted in the vagaries of human behaviour, and Shakespeare clearly shared his enjoyment. No less importantly, North's translation is so vivid, so memorably expressed, that Shakespeare incorporates phrase after phrase from it into these plays.

Even some of Shakespeare's self-consciously poetical passages, such as Enobarbus's famous description of Cleopatra beginning 'The barge she sat in', are moulded out of North's prose. The barge's poop was 'of gold', writes North,

> the sails of purple, and the oars of silver, which kept stroke in rowing after the sound of the music of flutes, citherns, viols, and such other instruments as they played upon in the barge. And now for the person of her self: she was laid under a pavilion of cloth of gold of tissue, apparelled and attired like the goddess Venus commonly drawn in picture, and hard by her, on either hand of her, pretty fair boys apparelled as painters do set forth god Cupid, with little fans in their hands with the which they fanned wind upon her. Her ladies and gentlewomen also, the fairest of them were apparelled like the nymphs Nereides, which are the mermaids of the waters, and like the graces, some steering the helm, others tending the tackle and ropes of the barge, out of the which there came a wonderful passing sweet savour of perfumes that perfumed the wharf's side, pestered with innumerable multitudes of people.

In Plutarch this passage describes Cleopatra's first impact on Antony; Shakespeare places it after we have already experienced her in many moods, and turns Plutarch's picturesque description into an erotic vision:

> The poop was beaten gold;
> Purple the sails, and so perfumèd that
> The winds were love-sick with them. The oars were silver,
> Which to the tune of flutes kept stroke, and made
> The water which they beat to follow faster,
> As amorous of their strokes. For her own person,
> It beggared all description. She did lie
> In her pavilion – cloth of gold, of tissue –
> O'er-picturing that Venus where we see
> The fancy outwork nature. On each side her
> Stood pretty dimpled boys, like smiling Cupids,
> With divers-coloured fans whose wind did seem
> To glow the delicate cheeks which they did cool,
> And what they undid did. . . .
> Her gentlewomen, like the Nereides,
> So many mermaids, tended her i'th' eyes,
> And made their bends adornings. At the helm
> A seeming mermaid steers. The silken tackle
> Swell with the touches of those flower-soft hands
> That yarely frame the office. From the barge
> A strange invisible perfume hits the sense
> Of the adjacent wharfs. The city cast
> Her people out upon her . . .

(2.2.199–221)

One passage is rich prose, the other great poetry; it is extraordinary how Shakespeare succeeds in incorporating so much of North's phraseology into a verse structure – a feat made the easier by the fluidity characteristic of his verse style at this stage in his career. And the passage gains in effect by being placed in the mouth of Enobarbus, the detached observer who has seemed least likely to be seduced by Cleopatra's wiles.

The story that Shakespeare found in Plutarch provided him with the basis for a play that has much in common with his earlier tragedy of *Romeo and Juliet*. In both plays the tragedy is brought about by the clash between the demands of a private love-relationship and those of the outside world. But these are middle-aged lovers with more than their full share of amatory experience; the language of this play, like that of *Romeo and Juliet*, is steeped in sexuality, but the youthful idealism of the earlier play is replaced by a mature, realistic acknowledgement of inextricable sensual entanglement: indeed, Antony's sense of shame at the hold that Cleopatra exerts over him resembles at times the self-disgust of the persona of the sonnets' relationship with his dark lady: 'my five wits nor my five senses can | Dissuade one foolish heart from loving thee', says Shakespeare as sonneteer; 'I must from this enchanting queen break off', says Antony; 'Ten thousand harms more than the ills I know | My idleness doth hatch' (1.2.121–2).

The external forces opposing the lovers are on a different scale in the two plays; whereas the action of *Romeo and Juliet* is confined largely to Verona, *Antony and Cleopatra* takes the whole world as its setting. No other play of Shakespeare's is so vast in scope, or so constantly invokes a sense of what he elsewhere calls 'all the world's vastidity' (*Measure for Measure*, 3.1.67). It is a long play, but not his longest: shorter by over 200 lines than *Coriolanus*, for instance, which nevertheless does not give the same impression of size. This derives rather from the scope of the play's action, the range of its characterization, and above all the prodigality of its language.

Our sense of the broad scope of the play's action is created partly by the ease and fluidity with which the conventions of Shakespeare's theatre permit him to move between the two opposing poles of Egypt and Rome, the one associated with freedom and sensuality – 'I'th' East my pleasure lies', says Antony (2.3.38) – the other with self-discipline and austerity, while also taking in a number of stops on the way. From beginning to end the play is full of to-ings and fro-ings, of messengers and ambassadors, some anonymous, some named characters who may have other functions in the action, carrying news and messages from one location to another: shaming Antony, besotted in Alexandria, as soon as we see him and Cleopatra, with news of what is going on in Rome and in the large theatre of war in which his forces are fighting without him; or telling Caesar in Rome of how Antony 'wastes the night in revel' in Alexandria while Pompey's power increases; or, when Antony has torn himself away from Cleopatra and returned to Rome, carrying messages and gifts from him to her while she simultaneously sends 'twenty several messengers' to him; or, climactically, announcing to her that Antony has married Caesar's sister, Octavia, and, after she has recovered enough from the first shock to summon the terrified messenger back into her presence, describing her rival with anguished circumspection; or, when Antony has returned to Egypt, after his break with Caesar, bringing news that precipitates the sea-battle of Actium; or, after the humiliated Antony has followed Cleopatra's fleet in retreat from the battle, negotiating with Caesar on their behalf and then returning with the information that Caesar will make terms with Cleopatra only if she sends Antony away or has him executed; or securing Cleopatra's agreement 'to lay [her] crown' at Caesar's feet and then being sentenced to a whipping when Antony finds him kissing her hand; or telling Caesar that Antony is ready for the second part of the battle; or telling Enobarbus, who has defected from Antony, that his master has sent his possessions after him 'with his bounty overplus'; or, after the enraged Antony has lost the second stage of the battle as the result (he believes) of Cleopatra's treachery, bringing him, on her instructions, the false news that she has killed herself; or coming, too late, to admit that this was a trick; or bringing news to Caesar of Antony's suicide; or asking the victorious Caesar on Cleopatra's behalf what he intends to do with her; or reassuring her that Caesar will treat her well while deceptively putting her under armed guard; or, finally, telling Cleopatra that Caesar intends to lead her in triumph in Rome. The use of messengers is in part a technical device necessitated by the historical action, but Shakespeare makes artistic capital out of it, creating a sense of continual movement and urgency, giving impetus to an action that might otherwise seem episodic and plotless.

The geographical scope of the action, wide enough in itself, gains in effect from the hyperbolical terms in which the protagonists are portrayed and indeed in which they think of themselves. The tone is established in the opening scene, where Antony is described as 'The triple pillar of the world' and declares that Cleopatra must 'find out new heaven, new earth' if she is to set a limit to his love; rather than attend to the messengers from Rome he would 'Let Rome in Tiber melt, and the wide arch | Of the ranged empire fall', and before long Cleopatra is describing him as 'The demi-Atlas of this earth, the arm | And burgonet of men'.

Tragedy traditionally afflicts persons of high rank, but Antony and Cleopatra are not merely monarchs but monarchs of monarchs who have kings as servants; at a ceremony of enthronement in Alexandria Antony proclaimed even his illegitimate offspring by Cleopatra 'the kings of kings'; jointly they levied 'The kings o'th' earth for war', assembling

> Bocchus, the King of Libya; Archilaus
> Of Cappadocia; Philadelphos, King
> Of Paphlagonia; the Thracian King Adallas;
> King Malchus of Arabia; King of Pont;
> Herod of Jewry; Mithridates, King
> Of Comagene; Polemon and Amyntas,

>   The Kings of Mede and Lycaonia;
>   With a more larger list of sceptres.
>
>   (3.6.69–76)

They are accused of having 'kissed away | Kingdoms and provinces';
after Antony's first defeat in battle he is said to have 'had superfluous
kings for messengers | Not many moons gone by'; and Cleopatra,
glorifying Antony after he has died, describes her dream of him as one
whose

>   legs bestrid the ocean; his reared arm
>   Crested the world. His voice was propertied
>   As all the tunèd spheres, and that to friends;
>   But when he meant to quail and shake the orb,
>   He was as rattling thunder. For his bounty,
>   There was no winter in't; an autumn 'twas,
>   That grew the more by reaping. His delights
>   Were dolphin-like; they showed his back above
>   The element they lived in. In his livery
>   Walked crowns and crownets. Realms and islands were
>   As plates dropped from his pocket.
>
>   (5.2.81–91)

Their state is not merely monarchical but godlike: at the opening of
the play Antony at his greatest is said to have been like the god Mars;
the image recurs, and Cleopatra is his Venus; closer to home, she is
said to have taken upon herself 'th'habiliments of the goddess Isis' and
to have held audiences in this garb. Even Antony's feasts are on the
grandest possible scale – the report that in Egypt he had 'Eight boars
roasted whole at a breakfast and but twelve persons there' is dismissed
by Enobarbus as 'but as a fly by an eagle'. And the grandeur of
impression that Antony makes on those around him, as well as the
play's prodigality of language, is shown by the way in which an
anonymous Ambassador, wishing to express his sense of comparative
insignificance, declares, 'I was of late as petty to his ends | As is the
morn-dew on the myrtle leaf | To his grand sea' (3.12.8–10). In the
face of images such as this it is difficult to uphold the view that
'intoxication with language' is characteristic only of the young
Shakespeare.

But if the play's language were merely hyperbolical in its figuring
forth of the central characters it would suffer from the limitations of
tone that have caused John Dryden's heroic tragedy *All for Love; or,*

The World Well Lost, which is based in part on Shakespeare, to seem
only of its age, finely conceived and written though it often is. It lacks
the counterbalancing subtlety of nuance and portrayal of pettiness as
well as magnanimity, the squalor as well as the grandeur, that
contribute to the extraordinary range of Shakespeare's characterization. We see this even in the minor characters: in, for instance, the
bawdy chatter of Cleopatra's women with the Soothsayer in the play's
second scene by which Shakespeare reinforces our sense of the
hedonism of the Egyptian court:

> SOOTHSAYER Your fortunes are alike.
> IRAS But how, but how? Give me particulars.
> SOOTHSAYER I have said.
> IRAS Am I not an inch of fortune better than she?
> CHARMIAN Well, if you were but an inch of fortune better than I,
>   where would you choose it?
> IRAS Not in my husband's nose.

We see it in the bluntness with which Agrippa speaks of Cleopatra's
relations with her earlier lover, Julius Caesar: 'He ploughed her, and
she cropped' (2.2.235). And we see it wonderfully in the sheer
psychological realism in Cleopatra's interrogation of one of the play's
anonymous messengers about her rival Octavia:

> CLEOPATRA Is she as tall as me?
> MESSENGER   She is not, madam.
> CLEOPATRA Didst hear her speak? Is she shrill-tongued or low?
> MESSENGER Madam, I heard her speak. She is low-voiced.
> CLEOPATRA That's not so good. He cannot like her long.
> CHARMIAN Like her? O Isis, 'tis impossible!
> CLEOPATRA I think so, Charmian. Dull of tongue, and dwarfish.
>   (3.3.11–16)

Such dialogue, with its invitation to acting between lines and pairs of
words as well as on them, suggesting in the Messenger a cautiously
diplomatic choice of epithets, quick shifts of attitude to accommodate
the wishes of his listener, and in Cleopatra a capacity to hear precisely
and only what she wants to hear, is a gift to both performers. It is
brilliantly comic writing which is also part and parcel of the depiction
of Cleopatra as a woman of 'infinite variety', a 'character' in the sense
of someone whom we experience not as a 'representative' woman but
as one who is uniquely, unpredictably, and gloriously herself.

Like *Romeo and Juliet*, *Antony and Cleopatra* is a double tragedy, a tragedy of lovers whose fates are inextricably entangled in death as well as in life. It offers a more rounded, and more frequently critical, perspective on its lovers than the earlier play, while also allowing us a sense of knowing them so intimately in their strengths as well as their weaknesses that criticism is lost in admiration in the etymological sense of that word, a wonder that excludes judgement: *Antony and Cleopatra* is the least moralistic of Shakespeare's plays. And of course the love of Antony and Cleopatra is doomed not just by external circumstances but by the combination of personal character with public responsibility, the fact that for Antony, at least, the pursuance of his love requires the sacrifice of his status as a 'triple pillar of the world'. He is not only, like Romeo, a lover, he is also, like Macbeth, a warrior, but a warrior in decline.

Antony is more often subjected to adverse criticism than Cleopatra, especially in relation to Octavius Caesar, his moral as well as his political adversary. In the play's opening lines he is said to have degenerated from a godlike warrior to no more than a doting sex machine – 'the bellows and the fan | To cool a gipsy's lust' – and he himself soon acknowledges justice in the criticism in declaring 'These strong Egyptian fetters I must break, | Or lose myself in dotage' (1.2.109–10); indeed his awareness of how other people see him, of the bitterly humiliating consequences of his love for Cleopatra, helps both to arouse sympathy with him and to convince us of the power of that love. We see him in a sequence of humiliating situations, his political supremacy threatened in his absence from Rome by Pompey, his independence hampered not simply by his love for Cleopatra but by the wiles she exerts to bend him to her will, his self-respect undermined by a failure in battle such that, says Scarus, 'Experience, manhood, honour, ne'er before | Did violate so itself' (3.10.22–3), compelled to acknowledge Octavius Caesar as 'Lord of his fortunes' and to beg his permission either to live in Egypt or, if that is not granted, to be allowed to 'breathe between the heavens and earth, | A private man in Athens' (3.12.14–15), deserted by his most faithful follower Enobarbus, betrayed a second time in battle by Cleopatra, shamed into trying to kill himself when his servant Eros chooses to commit suicide rather than inflict death upon his master, and then even bungling his own suicide attempt. He is humiliated too by the passage of time, the greying of his hair, his sense that – though 'There's sap in't yet' (3.13.194) – his affair with Cleopatra is the last of many flings.

The play's imagery works constantly to emblematize the meta-
morphic effects of time, the subjection of the physical world to
process, and the consequent vulnerability of all its grandeur, all the
achievements of man, all human emotion and all individual identity.
Rome will indeed 'in Tiber melt', Egypt may 'melt . . . into Nile',
authority 'melts' from Antony, and Shakespeare gathers together
these threads of the play's language and centres them upon Antony as,
betrayed a second time by Cleopatra and recognizing that the hearts of
his followers 'do discandy, melt their sweets | On blossoming Caesar',
he finds in the ever-changing shapes of clouds, the way in which 'That
which is now a horse even with a thought' becomes 'indistinct as
water is in water', an image of his own transience, a realization that he
too 'cannot hold this visible shape', his only consolation the know-
ledge that 'There is left us | Ourselves to end ourselves'.

Although Philo's denigration of Antony, in the play's opening
speech, as a once-great warrior who is now no more than a gigolo
need not be regarded as objective truth, the play gives us no direct
evidence of his prowess in battle; if at times we may even sympathize
with Caesar's description of him as 'the old ruffian', we can admire the
rueful self-knowledge with which he acknowledges his subjection to
Cleopatra, and there is no doubt of his continuing capacity to inspire
devotion and love in men as well as in women.

Rather as with Richard II, Shakespeare gives us a more favourable
perspective on Antony as the play progresses. His largeness of spirit,
characterized as 'bounty', is forcibly demonstrated in his generosity
on hearing that Enobarbus has deserted him, sending after him not
only his 'chests and treasure' but 'gentle adieus and greetings', and
acknowledging 'O, my fortunes have | Corrupted honest men!' As the
Soldier who brings the news to Enobarbus says, 'Your Emperor |
Continues still a Jove', and the depth of Enobarbus's remorse, which
appears to be solely responsible for his death, reflects favourably upon
Antony. He dies nobly, concerned for Cleopatra's safety, and asking
her to remember him at his best. Caesar, learning of his death – 'tidings
| To wash the eyes of kings' – pays him the tribute of tears (5.1.26–8),
and in Cleopatra's dream-vision of Antony recounted to Dolabella her
imagination purges him of all dross, a man metamorphosed into a god
'past the size of dreaming'.

I said that *Antony and Cleopatra* resembles the sonnets in its emphasis
on the destructive power of time, but it resembles them too in its
counterbalancing suggestions that the power of human love, and of
the imagination, can transcend the effects of time. Shakespeare's

earlier double tragedy, *Romeo and Juliet*, ends with an idealized image of its lovers transmuted into golden statues, but Juliet's death follows hard upon Romeo's, and she has nothing to say about him. The long stretch of action that separates Antony's death from Cleopatra's creates theatrical problems in requiring the audience to suffer not just one but two tragic climaxes, but the transcendence of Cleopatra's expressions of love for Antony as and after he dies increases our admiration for her as well as for him, and she even more obviously than he reveals new and greater aspects of herself during the play's closing stretches. But to the very end Cleopatra is a morally ambivalent and enigmatic figure, encompassing within herself the extraordinary range of response for which Antony prepares us in the play's opening scene as he marvels at the way in which all her moods – chiding, laughing, weeping, even perversely nagging at him to hear Caesar's messengers – are becoming to her, and 'how every passion fully strives | To make itself, in thee, fair and admired'.

These qualities are apparent in her throughout the play. There is no wonder that Cleopatra is so coveted a role: this is Shakespeare's greatest comic as well as his greatest tragic woman character. She is a consummate performer, manipulating Antony with as self-conscious an art as Petruccio manipulates Kate:

> See where he is, who's with him, what he does.
> I did not send you. If you find him sad,
> Say I am dancing; if in mirth, report
> That I am sudden sick.
>
> (1.3.2–5)

And when he arrives with his news from Rome, she does indeed – as the knowing Enobarbus has predicted – put on a pretence of sickness, expecting him to say that he wishes to return to his wife, Fulvia, and adopting the ploy of 'You were full of affection when you wanted to stay with me; now I see you in your true colours', but doing so with incomparable eloquence:

> When you sued staying,
> Then was the time for words; no going then.
> Eternity was in our lips and eyes,
> Bliss in our brow's bent; none our parts so poor
> But was a race of heaven.
>
> (1.3.33–7)

And the unexpected news that Fulvia is dead, so far from taking the wind out of her sails, provides more grist to her mill as, rebuking Antony for failing to mourn, she claims, 'Now I see, I see, | In Fulvia's death how mine received shall be': only the first of many tricks she plays on her lover.

The tricks reach a climax when, seeking to draw him back to her after she has betrayed him at Actium, she sends false news of her own death, which Antony receives not with the indifference she had hypocritically predicted but, disastrously for her, with the determination to join her not in oblivion but in Elysium:

> Where souls do couch on flowers we'll hand in hand,
> And with our sprightly port make the ghosts gaze.
> Dido and her Aeneas shall want troops,
> And all the haunt be ours.
>
> (4.15.51–4)

The infinite tenderness of Antony's vision here reasserts his love for her after its most terrible crisis; I shall not forget how Olivier, as long ago as 1951, spoke the lines with extended arms waving gently in the air, as if ready to release his soul on its way to join Cleopatra. But, typically, this expression of love was achieved by means of a trick; Cleopatra is, as Antony has said, 'cunning past man's thought' (1.2.137), and her behaviour is full of paradoxes and inconsistencies, swinging from one extreme to another, at one moment treating Antony's messenger with condescending grace and generosity, the next, on hearing that Antony has married Octavia, haling the innocent bearer of news up and down (as the original stage direction has it) like a fishwife, threatening him with the direst tortures and drawing a knife on him herself. Such fluctuations of mood are productive of comedy, and, as in *Hamlet*, comedy plays constantly over the surface of the play to the end, most obviously in the figure of the Clown who brings Cleopatra her instrument of death.

Certainly, as Antony dies Cleopatra plumbs new emotional depths, lamenting his departure in cosmic terms:

> O see, my women,
> The crown o'th' earth doth melt. My lord!
> O, withered is the garland of the war.
> The soldier's pole is fall'n. Young boys and girls
> Are level now with men. The odds is gone,

> And there is nothing left remarkable
> Beneath the visiting moon.
>
> (4.16.64–70)

Although it might be argued that Cleopatra is acting a part here, just as
it is sometimes argued that Othello does at his end, if so she does it
with striking plausibility, and her grief is reinforced by the reactions of
those around her, even Caesar. She is no less eloquent in contemplating and bringing about her own death. In *Antony and Cleopatra*, as in
his other Roman plays, Shakespeare appears to endorse the choice of
suicide rather than (as in, for instance, *King Lear*) presenting it as an
evasion of responsibility: 'it is great', says Cleopatra,

> To do that thing that ends all other deeds,
> Which shackles accidents and bolts up change,
> Which sleeps and never palates more the dung,
> The beggar's nurse, and Caesar's.
>
> (5.2.5–8)

And when the time comes, urged on by the thought of the indignities
to which she will be subjected if Caesar captures her and leads her in
triumph through Rome, she dies with incomparable dignity, claiming
to be purged of all baser elements:

> I am fire and air; my other elements
> I give to baser life.
>
> (5.2.284–5)

But her sensuality remains – 'The stroke of death is as a lover's pinch, |
Which hurts and is desired'; and so does her sexual jealousy: she fears
that her waiting woman, Iras, having died before her, may seduce
Antony before she herself arrives. Cleopatra sees death not (like
Hamlet) as a sinking into silence, or (like Macbeth) as the end of a
meaningless tale, but as the ultimate consummation of her relationship with Antony – 'Husband, I come' – and dies triumphantly as both
queen and woman. And even in the latest moments of her life, after
she has determined on suicide, she remains the manipulative, cunning
woman we have seen earlier. Directors sometimes omit the episode
with Seleucus in which she tries to cheat Caesar of her 'money, plate,
and jewels', but this risks sentimentalization. Shakespeare portrays
her, not as a woman who steadily develops, maturing finally into a
dignified and immaculate tragedy queen, but as a woman to be

wondered at in her complexity to the end, 'A lass unparalleled', as Charmian calls her, closing her eyes in death.

For the onlookers, *Antony and Cleopatra* ends in a manner typical of Shakespearian tragedy: its closing words, spoken by Caesar, are

> Our army shall
> In solemn show attend this funeral,
> And then to Rome. Come, Dolabella, see
> High order in this great solemnity.

But for the protagonists it ends, like a comedy, with the expectation of marriage.

Like *Antony and Cleopatra*, *Coriolanus* too is based on Plutarch, and incorporates much of the language of North's translation into its dialogue. Nevertheless the tone of the plays is very different. Whereas *Antony and Cleopatra* seems supple, sensuous, and relaxed, that of *Coriolanus*, as if in deliberate contrast, is characteristically austere, knotty, and forbidding, as if in writing it thoughts and words came to Shakespeare in such abundance that desire for clarity was at times outweighed by unwillingness to dilute the complexity of the verbal experience.

Here are none of the pleasures of the East: we are back in Rome, in very ancient Rome at a time when it is striving for survival against the depredations of neighbouring peoples such as the Volscians, and the play tells a story of enmity: enmity between nations, between the classes of a single nation, between members of the same family, and between the opposing elements in a man's own nature. The enmity finds vent in both physical violence and verbal invective: no other play unleashes such energy of abuse. It is scarcely softened by scenes of affection; there are, it's true, a few domestic episodes, but the play's main female character is the hero's mother, not his wife, and she is a formidable matriarch who embodies within herself the values of a martial society.

Comforting her daughter-in-law, Virgilia, for Coriolanus's absence, Volumnia states an ethos precisely opposed to that which Cleopatra encourages in Antony: 'If my son were my husband, I should freelier rejoice in that absence wherein he won honour than in the embracements of his bed where he would show most love'

(1.3.2–5). And she boasts that even when he was a boy she 'was pleased to let him seek danger where he was like to find fame'. Fame and honour won in the service of one's country matter more to her even than life: 'Hear me profess sincerely: had I a dozen sons, each in my love alike, and none less dear than thine and my good Martius, I had rather had eleven die nobly for their country than one voluptuously surfeit out of action.' She delights in the thought of the blood that may have been spilt in the battle, even if it is her son's, and ecstatically imagines the scenes of bloodshed.

A more peaceable frame of mind is only feebly represented by Virgilia: 'His bloody brow? O Jupiter, no blood!' The point is reinforced by the tale Virgilia's friend Valeria tells about Coriolanus's young son, whom she admires not for his sweetness but for his ferocity:

> I'll swear 'tis a very pretty boy. O' my troth, I looked upon him o' Wednesday half an hour together. He's such a confirmed countenance! I saw him run after a gilded butterfly, and when he caught it he let it go again, and after it again, and over and over he comes, and up again, catched it again. Or whether his fall enraged him, or how 'twas, he did so set his teeth and tear it!
>
> (1.3.59–66)

Volumnia makes explicit the connection with his father with her comment: 'One on's father's moods'. Shakespeare is suggesting in Volumnia a set of values that he expects to be foreign to his audience; the story, that is, is not to be told simply from the perspective of his own time but will represent a real attempt to penetrate and understand, though not necessarily to judge, an alien culture. This aspect of the play justifies Terence Spencer's claim that 'to write *Coriolanus* was one of the great feats of the historical imagination in Renaissance Europe'.[4] But if we heard only Volumnia's point of view, there would be no moral perspective; Virgilia's comment – 'O Jupiter, no blood!' – introduces more humane values, and the juxtaposition produces a comic response. Indeed, although Shaw was no doubt indulging his customary love of paradox when he called *Coriolanus* 'the greatest of Shakespeare's comedies' (apparently because the hero is among Shakespeare's most 'admirable descriptions of instinctive temperaments'[5]), still the play does generate far more comedy in performance than is readily apparent from the printed page.

Shakespeare's clear intention in this scene, the first in the play to involve Roman women – a scene that he himself invented – was to portray the values of an alien society, and this is indicative of the interest that Plutarch's life of Coriolanus held for him. What kind of people, he seems to be asking, were they who could behave in this fashion? What were the values by which they lived, and into what dilemmas were they forced by them? What can cause a great warrior and a national hero so to despise his fellow men that he cannot behave with ordinary civility to them? Or, to put it differently, why should a great soldier be such a total failure as a statesman? What could have impelled Coriolanus, after he had been acclaimed by his countrymen, to behave so violently towards them that they banished him? What family background could have produced such a man? Were his bad qualities a necessary corollary of his good ones? How did he come to join forces with the man who had been his greatest enemy? What motives could induce him to go back on this decision at the cost of his own life?

Questions such as these certainly interested Shakespeare (which is not to say that he thought he could answer them). Like *Antony and Cleopatra*, and more than most of Shakespeare's other plays, *Coriolanus* is concerned with human character: with the individualities, the oddities, of those who take part in it, and the way such characteristics can shape national as well as personal destinies. And when we think of the play in these terms we can see how the way in which Shakespeare tells this story of ancient Rome may well have related excitingly for audiences of his time to what was then going on in England, and why for later audiences, too, it has often seemed surprisingly topical, so that, for instance, Nahum Tate, adapting it as *The Ingratitude of a Commonwealth* in 1681, could remark on its 'resemblance with the busy faction of our own time' – an allusion to the Popish Plot. Politically motivated productions have been common; at the Comédie Française in 1932 the play provoked right-wing demonstrations, in Germany during the 1930s school editions drew admiring parallels between Coriolanus and Hitler, yet a Moscow production shortly afterwards is said to have portrayed Coriolanus as 'a superman who had detached himself from the people and betrayed them'. In 1963 the Berliner Ensemble presented a version based on an unfinished adaptation by Bertolt Brecht that reduced Martius's stature as both warrior and statesman; Brecht's play ends with the Tribunes in charge of Rome, and with Brutus refusing to allow Martius to be mourned or commemorated. Günter Grass's play which is known in English as *The Plebeians Rehearse the Uprising* shows Brecht rehearsing his version of *Coriolanus* as news gradually reached the theatre of risings within Berlin against the imposition by the Party on the Government of new labour regulations. Perhaps in reaction, John Osborne in 1973 published a 'reworking' of Shakespeare's play called *A Place Calling Itself Rome* that adopts an emphatically right-wing attitude.

The seeds of Shakespeare's interest in Coriolanus lie in a passage early in Plutarch's *Life* which well expresses both the enigma and the fascination of the hero's character. Plutarch regards Coriolanus as

> a good proof to confirm some men's opinions that a rare and excellent wit, untaught, doth bring forth many good and evil things together. . . . For this Martius' natural wit and great heart did marvellously stir up his courage to do and attempt notable acts. But on the other side, for lack of education, he was so choleric and impatient that he would yield to no living creature; which made him churlish, uncivil, and altogether unfit for any man's conversation. Yet men marvelling much at this constancy – that he was never overcome with pleasure nor money, and how he would endure easily all manner of pains and travails – thereupon they well liked and commended his stoutness and temperancy. But, for all that, they could not be acquainted with him, as one citizen useth to be with another in the city.[6]

These sentences express some of the enigmas about Coriolanus that Shakespeare was to explore in dramatic rather than expository form. Plutarch is interested by the combination in his hero of 'good and evil things together', and in the fact that he was forbidding even to those who greatly admired him. These characteristics of Coriolanus are expounded in the opening scene, even before we see him, as the citizens, incensed to rebellion by famine, determine to proceed especially against 'Caius Martius' in spite of 'services' that, they acknowledge, 'he has done for his country'. And this scene introduces too the four kinds of enmity that I identify in the play.

Enmity between nations – the Romans and the Volsci – forms the play's broad framework from the moment in the opening scene when a messenger brings the news 'the Volsces are in arms' (1.1.224), but the national enmity is rapidly epitomized into a personal one, between Caius Martius – who will be granted the cognomen, or surname, of Coriolanus as a reward for capturing the enemy town of Corioli – and the Volscian leader Tullus Aufidius. The statement of this is suggestive of one of the play's profoundest and most elusive ambiguities, the

relationship of hatred and love. Martius speaks of his enemy in terms
of the highest respect:

> They have a leader,
> Tullus Aufidius, that will put you to't.
> I sin in envying his nobility,
> And were I anything but what I am,
> I would wish me only he.
>
> (1.1.228–32)

When soon afterwards we see into the Volscian camp, we find their
leader less generous in his reference to Martius, whom nevertheless he
obviously respects as an enemy:

> If we and Caius Martius chance to meet,
> 'Tis sworn between us we shall ever strike
> Till one can do no more.
>
> (1.2.34–6)

The meeting comes soon: *Coriolanus* is exceptional among
Shakespeare's plays in that the scenes of battle are concentrated in the
early part of the play, not, as is more common, in the last act. So we
not only hear, we also see that Coriolanus is a warrior at the height of
his powers, possessing the virtue he values above all others, valour. In
this Shakespeare again follows Plutarch, who says: 'Now in those
days valiantness was honoured in Rome above all other virtues'
(words which Shakespeare puts into the mouth of the Roman general
Cominius: 'It is held | That valour is the chiefest virtue'). This is
climactically demonstrated in the scene of personal combat between
the leaders (1.8) which establishes one of the play's chief visual images
– that of two opposed warriors – and which ends in the defeat of
Aufidius, who is spared only because (as the original stage direction
has it) '*certain Volsces come in the aid of Aufidius. Martius fights till they be
driven in breathless.*' This provokes in Aufidius a declaration of enmity
so great that he will stop at nothing; he will forgo the 'honour' that
means so much to his enemy and stoop to any means of conquering
him:

> Where I find him, were it
> At home upon my brother's guard, even there,

> Against the hospitable canon, would I
> Wash my fierce hand in's heart.

> (1.9.24–7)

We shall not see Aufidius again until, much later, Coriolanus, banished from Rome, will seek out his enemy 'at home' and offer to serve him. This remarkable confrontation initiates the revived attention to the enmity between the Roman and Volscian leaders which is to find issue in the closing scenes.

The national enmity is strongly felt, but can only with difficulty be distinguished from the personal. Characteristically, major political issues finally resolve themselves into personal ones. We see this even in the curious little scene – often omitted in performance – between a Roman and a Volscian spy which starts the play's final movement (4.3). So far as the narrative goes, it simply keeps us up to date about the state of the war and shows us that the Volscians are hoping to be able to take advantage of the civil strife in Rome and to 'come upon them in the heat of their division'. More important is the totally calm, matter-of-fact attitude of the soldiers to the events in which they are involved. This Roman is a traitor to his country – but an entirely cheerful one. 'I am a Roman', he says, 'and my services are, as you are, against 'em.' And when he has conveyed his information these members of opposed nations go off for a drink together. Like so much else in the play, the episode jolts us to a consideration of the values that motivate men's actions. That this Roman is a traitor means nothing at all to him. But his exit is immediately followed by the entrance of his great superior, Coriolanus, dressed now 'in mean apparel, disguised and muffled'.

In his only real soliloquy Coriolanus meditates on the change by which he, too, has come to change his allegiance and is now entering the town whose widows he has made, preparing to offer comradeship to his greatest enemy:

> O world, thy slippery turns! Friends now fast sworn,
> Whose double bosoms seem to wear one heart,
> Whose hours, whose bed, whose meal and exercise
> Are still together, who twin as 'twere in love
> Unseparable, shall within this hour,
> On a dissension of a doit, break out
> To bitterest enmity. So fellest foes,
> Whose passions and whose plots have broke their sleep
> To take the one the other, by some chance,

Some trick not worth an egg, shall grow dear friends
And interjoin their issues. So with me.
My birthplace hate I, and my love's upon
This enemy town. I'll enter. If he slay me,
He does fair justice; if he give me way,
I'll do his country service.

(4.4.12–26)

The warriors confront one another again, but this time Coriolanus
bares his throat to Aufidius, inviting him to take revenge if he will.

The remarkable speech in which Aufidius seems to renounce
enmity and accept Coriolanus's offer of service typifies the play's hard
imagery and, in its exploration of the narrow dividing line between
love and hate, provides some justification for readings of the play's
subtext (as in Tyrone Guthrie's Nottingham production of 1963 and
the BBC television version) that find a sexual foundation to the
relationship between the warriors. Aufidius asks to

                           twine
Mine arms about that body whereagainst
My grainèd ash an hundred times hath broke.

Embracing Coriolanus, he claims to

                         contest
As hotly and as nobly with thy love
As ever in ambitious strength I did
Contend against thy valour,

(4.5.107–9, 111–14)

and declares that the sight of Coriolanus gives him more pleasure than
that of his bride as she crossed the threshold of his house. But the
union is an uneasy one, and as they jointly march against Rome our
awareness of Aufidius's mounting though hidden enmity intensifies
the drama of the scenes in which we first hear of Cominius's failure to
shake Coriolanus's purpose against Rome, then witness Menenius's
pathetic failure on a similar errand, and finally watch while the man
who has declared 'Wife, mother, child I know not' hears the
supplications of wife, mother, and child. The almost silent presence of
Aufidius during these scenes is a reminder of the danger that hangs
over Coriolanus; and our knowledge of this danger prevents us from
sympathizing with the Romans' jubilation on hearing of the ladies'

success. When Coriolanus brings to the Volscians the news that he has made a treaty with Rome, the warriors confront each other again, and Aufidius works on his followers' feelings to incense them against Coriolanus by calling on their national pride. Both national and personal vengeance are taken as 'the conspirators draw their swords and kill Martius', and Aufidius humiliates him by standing on his body.

While national enmity provides a broad framework for the play, much of the drama results from the civil strife that prevails within Rome itself. In the city there are two main parties – the patricians and the common people – each represented by a number of individuals. Though Coriolanus is a patrician, he is so right-wing that he virtually forms a party on his own. (It is identification with this attitude that informs fascist interpretations.) So the internal enmity is three-cornered. There is that between the patricians – including Coriolanus – and the common people, and that between Coriolanus and his fellow patricians, including his immediate family, resulting from his refusal to employ the diplomacy they advocate as a means of keeping the peace between the opposed parties. This situation, too, becomes apparent in the opening scene; again the strife is seen to be the result of personal characteristics, and is therefore far from simple. Martius, says one of the citizens, is the worst of the patricians, 'chief enemy to the people' (1.1.7–8), responsible in part for their lack of food, and they want to kill him.

Yet even they, in this extremity, cannot deny his good qualities; and they relax into a discussion of his character, admitting the good services he has done his country, while claiming he did them for the wrong reasons – pride, and the desire to please his mother. One of them states a principle that will be echoed elsewhere in the play, and that epitomizes a universal dilemma: 'What he cannot help in his nature you account a vice in him.' Similarly, later, his enemy, Aufidius, will say of the pride that Coriolanus has shown in his dealing with him,

> Yet his nature
> In that's no changeling, and I must excuse
> What cannot be amended.
>
> (4.7.10–12)

It is a central dilemma in human relations. What allowances should we make for disagreeable characteristics that are nevertheless an in-escapable part of the personality of our fellows, the obverse of their good qualities? Finally the dilemma is insoluble: we can only go on tolerating until we can tolerate no longer; and this is what happens in the play.

The discussion about Martius is followed by the appearance of another of the patricians, Menenius, a father-figure to Martius and one who, we are told, 'hath always loved the people'. Certainly he knows how to handle them, as he shows in his good-humoured fable of the belly. This parable illustrative of relationship, of the mutual dependence necessary among the individual members of a well-organized commonwealth – as of a family – is one of those thematically important speeches that Shakespeare often places early in a play's action; it expounds an ideal against which pragmatic failures may be measured. Menenius's diplomacy contrasts violently with the contempt that Martius pours upon the citizens as soon as he appears upon the stage. His ferocious attack leaves us in no doubt why they should hate him, if not the entire class to which he belongs. He accuses them, above all, of inconstancy:

> With every minute you do change a mind,
> And call him noble that was now your hate,
> Him vile that was your garland.

It is ironical that when eventually they become constant in their hatred of him they force him into the fault of inconstancy himself.

As the conflict between Rome and the Volscians is represented by the personal conflict between Martius and Aufidius, so the conflict between the patricians and the people resolves itself largely into a tussle between Coriolanus and the two Tribunes, Junius Brutus and Sicinius Velutus. These are the people's representatives, but they are also the manipulators of the people, shrewd but sinister figures, always seen together, like Rosencrantz and Guildenstern, and carrying with them an aura of intrigue and self-seeking.

The national enmity draws attention away from the civil strife for a while, though even in the scenes of battle against the Volscians Martius is infinitely contemptuous of the soldiers to whom he owes part of his success. The effect is subtly complex, for the scorn he pours on his men is inseparable from the anger and energy that impel him in his fights against the common enemy, and that indeed inspire his soldiers to do what they can to support him. For a while his success in battle causes the commoners to forget their hatred of him, and he becomes a popular hero, sure to be elected to the consulship, were it not that the Tribunes are determined to sway the voters against him. It is certainly a comment on the fickleness of the mob that after they have given Coriolanus their votes the Tribunes can then persuade them to revoke their decision. Brutus and Sicinius give them detailed instructions how to behave; it's very like the situation in *Julius Caesar* in which Mark Antony stirs up the Roman people against the conspirators who have killed Caesar just after they have approved the deed. Just as Mark Antony, having incited the mob to vengeance, stands back and says:

> Now let it work. Mischief, thou art afoot.
> Take thou what course thou wilt,

so the tribunes, having persuaded the citizens to reverse their decision, watch them go, and Brutus says, 'Let them go on.' Sicinius's rejoinder reveals the element of personal self-seeking in their plot, reminiscent of the worst excesses of the trade union movement:

> To th' Capitol, come.
> We will be there before the stream o'th' people;
> And this shall seem, as partly 'tis, their own,
> Which we have goaded onward.
>
> (2.3.260–3)

Responsibility is neatly divided.

Much of it is shown, too, to belong to Coriolanus, and under the influence of family and friends he tries to repair the damage caused by his arrogant behaviour. Throughout the long stretch of the play in which the conflict between Coriolanus and the common people occupies the centre of attention, sympathies are excitingly manipulated as we watch the persuasion brought to bear on Coriolanus to try to repair the situation, the efforts he makes to control himself, the scheming of the Tribunes to make him lose control, and finally the inevitable explosion as Sicinius makes the accusation:

> you have contrived to take
> From Rome all seasoned office, and to wind
> Yourself into a power tyrannical,
> For which you are a traitor to the people.
>
> (3.3.66–9)

The sentence of banishment is pronounced, provoking the most memorable of Coriolanus's expressions of his hatred of the populace, the speech beginning

> You common cry of curs, whose breath I hate
> As reek o'th' rotten fens, whose loves I prize
> As the dead carcasses of unburied men
> That do corrupt my air: I banish you.
>
> (3.3.124–7)

Coriolanus is no longer the enemy within the state, but has become identified with those outside it.

Coriolanus's attitude to the common people causes much friction between himself and his family, and I suggest that this is the third area of conflict with which the play is centrally concerned. The relationships among members of this family are odd. Volumnia cares more for her son's achievements than for his safety; she glories in the number of wounds he receives; but she won't identify herself entirely with his characteristics:

> Thy valiantness was mine, thou sucked'st it from me,
> But owe thy pride thyself.
>
> (3.2.129–30)

Though she shares his contempt for the common people, she does not scruple to advise him to disguise his true nature in order to have his way with them. To deceive them about his feelings, she says,

> no more
> Dishonours you at all than to take in
> A town with gentle words, which else would put you
> To your fortune and the hazard of much blood.
> I would dissemble with my nature where
> My fortunes and my friends at stake required
> I should do so in honour.
>
> (3.2.58–64)

It is a paradoxical statement. We may ask what sort of honour this is that allows her to dissemble with her nature. Her son, at least, fails to dissemble with his, and as a result of his banishment places himself in a position in which he is required, not to flatter his enemies, but to pretend hatred for those he loves. This leads to the play's most emotionally loaded scene (5.3), in which Coriolanus, in the Volscian camp, listens to the entreaties of his family.

In this scene Coriolanus tries to deny his own nature, to keep the pretence that he has been able to renounce all personal as well as national ties. It is a pretence in which he has so far believed, but the sight of his family forces him to a truer self-recognition:

> I melt, and am not
> Of stronger earth than others.
>
> (5.3.28–9)

In the discussion that follows he tries to distinguish between personal and national interests, hoping he can show his affection for his family without having to renounce his enmity to Rome, but his mother insists, and with great eloquence, that once more he must compromise. If he conquers Rome, he conquers her. If he loses the fight against Rome, she will suffer the humiliation of seeing him 'led | With manacles through our streets'. She succeeds. Coriolanus, as the famous stage direction has it, *'holds her by the hand, silent'* in a moment of submission which is also a moment of self-examination and an acceptance of his fate.

> O mother, mother!
> What have you done? Behold, the heavens do ope,
> The gods look down, and this unnatural scene
> They laugh at. O my mother, mother, O!
> You have won a happy victory to Rome;
> But for your son, believe it, O believe it,
> Most dangerously you have with him prevailed,
> If not most mortal to him. But let it come.
>
> (5.3.183–90)

He knows he has signed his own death warrant. But he knows, too, that he has done the right thing, seeking no longer a godlike aloofness from natural emotion but accepting instead the full burden of his own humanity, the need to acknowledge relationship. At the same time he accepts the inevitability of his own death. 'But let it come' is the parallel in this play to Hamlet's 'The readiness is all', to 'The ripeness is all' in *King Lear*. But it is the final paradox of the mother-son relationship in *Coriolanus* that Volumnia, in calling forth a full expression of her son's love for her, brings about his death. Thus closely are love and hate related.

The fourth conflict within the play is that within the hero himself. Coriolanus is not an obviously introspective character, but he is often torn in different ways as the result of external circumstances. In particular, he is often required to act a part that he feels to be against his own nature. Several times Shakespeare uses the image of the actor. When we first hear that Coriolanus will have to ask the people for their votes if he wishes to be consul, he asks to be excused on the grounds that

> It is a part
> That I shall blush in acting.
>
> (2.2.145–6)

His mother, asking him to do this, requires him to 'perform a part | Thou hast not done before' (3.2.109–10). And his response to this is central to the play's concern with personal integrity, with the extent to which it is possible to dissemble with one's own nature, with the point at which playing a part becomes self-betrayal.

> Well, I must do't.
> Away, my disposition; and possess me
> Some harlot's spirit! My throat of war be turned,
> Which choired with my drum, into a pipe
> Small as an eunuch or the virgin voice
> That babies lulls asleep! The smiles of knaves
> Tent in my cheeks, and schoolboys' tears take up
> The glasses of my sight! A beggar's tongue
> Make motion through my lips, and my armed knees,
> Who bowed but in my stirrup, bend like his
> That hath received an alms! I will not do't,
> Lest I surcease to honour mine own truth,
> And by my body's action teach my mind
> A most inherent baseness.
>
> (3.2.110–23)

There is comedy in the way that Coriolanus works himself up into such a frenzy of determination, so vividly imagining what he will do that he realizes the full baseness of it and so refuses to do it; but the formulation

> I will not do't,
> Lest I surcease to honour mine own truth,
> And by my body's action teach my mind
> A most inherent baseness

is central to the issues of honour and integrity which the play so often puts before us.

The external enmity of the citizens of Rome towards Coriolanus causes him at last to become the enemy of Rome itself – of all that had previously tied him to his birthplace. But he succeeds in acting this role successfully until he hears the pleadings of his family; here the conflict between himself and those he loves becomes inseparable from that between the opposing elements of his nature, and in allowing his natural instincts to prevail and giving up the false role he has been playing he becomes the enemy to himself on a physical level, but saves his soul – or at least his integrity – in the process.

The picture that Shakespeare creates of Coriolanus is essentially a dramatic one. Though certain characteristics – his pride, his desire for fame – are frequently referred to, there is nothing static about him. Other characters of the play are constantly appraising and reappraising him. I suppose he is the only one of Shakespeare's tragic heroes to have an epitaph spoken for him in the first act. Titus Lartius, believing that Martius cannot possibly have survived his entry into the city of Corioles, is in the midst of a valedictory eulogy when he reappears, 'bleeding, assaulted by the enemy'. His valour is celebrated most fully in the speech that Cominius makes on his behalf to the Senate, a speech deliberately intended to praise him; yet one of the most interesting assessments of him comes from his enemy, Aufidius, in a speech which itself might have been an epitaph:

> First he was
> A noble servant to them, but he could not
> Carry his honours even. Whether 'twas pride,
> Which out of daily fortune ever taints
> The happy man; whether defect of judgement,
> To fail in the disposing of those chances
> Which he was lord of; or whether nature,
> Not to be other than one thing, not moving
> From th' casque to th' cushion, but commanding peace
> Even with the same austerity and garb
> As he controlled the war: but one of these –
> As he hath spices of them all – not all,
> For I dare so far free him – made him feared,
> So hated, and so banished.

That is a balanced assessment such as could have come from an objective observer; and Aufidius follows it with words of admiration:

> But he has a merit
> To choke it in the utt'rance.

And he expands into a general remark that is interesting in relation to the play's insistence on fame and on the relativity of judgement:

> So our virtues
> Lie in th' interpretation of the time,
> And power, unto itself most commendable,
> Hath not a tomb so evident as a chair
> T'extol what it hath done.
>
> (4.7.35–53)

Coriolanus's virtues 'Lie in th' interpretation of the time', and Shakespeare does not limit the interpretation we may wish to put upon them. His play is free-standing; we may make our own judgement, we may abstain from judgement. During the course of the play we have seen a man who has commanded admiration and love, hatred and contempt; we have seen the attitudes of those who come into contact with him reverse themselves; we have been shown something of the complexity of those attitudes and of what creates them; we have seen a man transformed from being a national hero to one who seems scarcely to own a name. Just before he dies, one of the more humane among his enemies tries to restrain the mob that has been incensed against him:

> Peace, ho! No outrage, peace.
> The man is noble, and his fame folds in
> This orb o'th' earth.

Yet neither the man's nobility nor his fame protects his body from outrage against the fury of his attackers. He dies ignominiously, and the ignoble hysteria of Aufidius's trampling upon him is excused by a reference to Coriolanus's own instability, as if to remind us that his nobility was qualified:

> His own impatience
> Takes from Aufidius a great part of blame.

But Aufidius has the grace to repent of his rage, and ends the play with the words 'he shall have a noble memory. Assist' – words which link the historical with the actual situation. In stage presentation

Coriolanus has achieved fame such as he sought, and because of the arts of an historian, a playwright, and the actors, his virtues lie in the interpretation of *our* time.

Notes to Chapter Fourteen

1 S.T. Coleridge, *Table Talk*, 24 June 1827.
2 Cited by Kenneth Muir, Arden edition (1952, etc.) p. lii.
3 The principal exception was at Stratford in 1972 when Trevor Nunn directed a season of 'The Romans' yoking together *Titus Andronicus, Julius Caesar, Antony and Cleopatra* , and *Coriolanus.*
4 T.J.B. Spencer, *Shakespeare: The Roman Plays,* Writers and their Work, no. 157 (1963), p. 40.
5 *Shaw on Shakespeare*, p. 215.
6 *Shakespeare's Plutarch*, ed. T.J.B. Spencer (Harmondsworth, Mx, 1964), pp. 296–7.

FIFTEEN

Romantic Plays, Mainly of the Mediterranean:

Pericles, The Winter's Tale, Cymbeline, and
The Tempest

If Shakespeare's career had followed a neat pattern, *Coriolanus* would have come before *Antony and Cleopatra*, whose incandescent poetry foreshadows that of his late comedies, and *Pericles* would have followed both. In fact there is reason to believe that *Pericles* preceded *Coriolanus*; it was entered in the Stationers' Register on 20 May 1608, and appeared in print in the following year. But it is natural to consider it with the plays written after Shakespeare's last tragedies because these plays form – with the exception of the history cycles – the most closely interrelated group among his output. Their relationships lie not, like those of the histories, in common characters and in consecutive narratives, or even in dramatic structure, but in plot motifs, in ideas, and in certain dramatic techniques, especially of characterization. The label 'romances' is convenient as an indicator of the literary and dramatic tradition to which they belong, and on which Shakespeare had already drawn in his earlier comedies, but they are just as properly called tragicomedies, since all of them bring major characters close to death. More neutrally, they are often known as the late (or even last) plays. It is possible to object to this term on the grounds that Shakespeare, who was only in his mid-forties when he wrote them, had – so far as we know – no reason to suppose that he was approaching the end of his career. At the same time it is not unreasonable to see these plays as the work of a man who is conscious of the pressures of time. All of them present a touching contrast between innocence and experience imaged in the relationship between older and younger generations, and in all of them the representatives of the younger generation offer to their elders the hope of renewal and regeneration.

Whatever label we give to these plays, it should not be taken to indicate uniformity: Shakespeare remained a restless experimenter to the end of his career, and his late plays differ from one another in many aspects of content and technique, as well as in ultimate effect; nevertheless, the resemblances are striking and undeniable. All their plots include highly improbable, often even miraculous, happenings, asking us to suspend disbelief and to watch and listen with the wide-eyed wonder of children at a pantomime. Their settings are remote and unrealistic, and their structure tends to the episodic. Chance, fortune, and the gods are frequently invoked as agents of the action; the sea plays a large part: storms and shipwrecks are common. The presentation of characters often avoids psychological realism and tends instead to the general and the ideal. Motivation and causation may be slight, links between sections tenuous. The stories span large areas of space and time, telling of high-born families which are often broken up, perhaps by accident or war; leading characters undergo great suffering, even apparent death; royal children are separated from their parents soon after birth and brought up ignorant of their true identity; lovers too are parted. Though the separation may be purely physical, it may also be, on a deeper level, the result of dissension and strife, so that reunion needs to be accompanied by repentance, forgiveness, and reconciliation, drawing attention to serious moral and ethical issues. Suffering is overcome, obstacles to reunion and reconciliation are removed (sometimes as a result of supernatural intervention), and harmony is restored, though with enough reminders of earlier discord to discourage complacency.

Theatrically, there is a tendency towards greater use of spectacle than in earlier plays, which has given rise to the theory that they were designed especially for the facilities provided for the indoor Blackfriars theatre and to satisfy the expectations of its audiences, which may have been more sophisticated than those normally attending the Globe; but the theory needs to be approached with caution since *Pericles* was performed before the King's Men took over the Blackfriars, and also because the company continued to use both playhouses and to play elsewhere, too.

All the dramatic characteristics of these plays can be found in Shakespeare's earlier work, especially his comedies, but they are present in greater concentration in the late plays; and the resemblances among these plays are more than superficial. All of them have a wide emotional as well as geographical range. Shakespeare was never one-track-minded. Even those of his plays that employ a relatively narrow focus, such as *Richard the Second* and *King Lear,* have a range of emotional impact. *Timon of Athens* shows the extremes of a man's experience, but, as Apemantus says, little between them: 'The middle of humanity thou never knewest, but the extremity of both ends' (4.3.302–3). In the late plays Shakespeare shows a wish to encompass the extremes in a yoking of opposites which will confine a full range of human experience within the local and temporal limitations of a play, and will synthesize the disparate elements in a manner that allows each to exert its energy.

Pericles is in many ways problematical. Like *Titus Andronicus* it was very popular in its own time. The Quarto of 1609, highly defective though it is, was reprinted five times by 1635, and Ben Jonson's envious allusion in 1629 to 'some mouldy tale like *Pericles*', written shortly after his own play, *The New Inn*, had been shelved after a single performance, shows that it continued to draw the theatrical crowds. Also like *Titus Andronicus*, it fell into disfavour after the Restoration and has been little performed since. But whereas *Titus Andronicus*'s fall from favour results from distaste for the text of the play as written, *Pericles*'s relative unpopularity may reasonably be ascribed to the fact that it survives only in a badly damaged text: one of the commonest clichés of Shakespeare scholarship is the statement that 'the authentic Shakespearian voice' is not heard until the beginning of Act 3, Pericles's Lear-like invocation to the elements beginning

> The god of this great vast rebuke these surges
> Which wash both heav'n and hell; and thou that hast
> Upon the winds command, bind them in brass,
> Having called them from the deep.

The play performed before Jacobean and Caroline audiences must have differed considerably from that offered to readers of the time, which is also the only form in which it has come down to us. For many years editors have regularized and patched up this text in the effort to minimize its deficiencies, which are fully apparent only to readers of the Quarto itself, but nothing can be done to bring it back to the condition in which it was first acted. And even when edited by scholars with more than customary boldness, it still calls out for more restoration work before it can be satisfactorily performed.[1]

There are also reasons to believe that in *Pericles*, as in *Timon of Athens*, Shakespeare worked with a collaborator, perhaps George Wilkins, whose play *The Miseries of Enforced Marriage*, published in 1607, gave Shakespeare's company a popular success, and whose book of the play, *The Painful Adventures of Pericles Prince of Tyre*, published in 1608, before the play itself reached print, borrows both from it and from another prose version of the tale, Laurence Twine's *The Pattern of Painful Adventures* (written by 1576), which had also served as a source for the play. It may be because Heminges and Condell knew that *Pericles* had been written in collaboration, or because they could not get hold of a reliable text, or from some combination of these and other factors, that they did not include it in the First Folio.[2]

The basic narrative of *Pericles* is the old and oft-told tale of Apollonius of Tyre on which Shakespeare had drawn early in his career in the framework of *The Comedy of Errors*: here it becomes the story of a young prince who suffers shipwreck, wins a bride in a tournament, loses her when, as he believes, she dies in childbirth during another storm at sea, and leaves his daughter in the care of foster parents; when she has reached maturity she is threatened with murder, abducted by pirates, and sold into a brothel where her invincible virtue has a disastrous effect on trade. Pericles, reduced by grief to a comatose state in which he has spoken to no-one for three months, is restored to normality as the result of a chance meeting with his daughter, and reunited with his wife through the agency of the goddess Diana, who appears to him in a vision.

Reading the play with sympathy – or, still better, seeing it well performed in a sensitively prepared acting version – we may imagine that the authentic text stood high among Shakespeare's achievements. Jonson's description of it as 'mouldy', though jaundiced, is not entirely unfair: this is a deliberately and self-consciously old-fashioned play, retelling an old tale – as its very first line, 'To sing a song that old was sung', declares – and using the old-fashioned device of a presenter, in the person of the late-medieval poet John Gower, to frame and control the far-flung narrative. An archaic style is adopted for Gower's choruses, a naïve tone in order to induce the proper mood for a tale of wonder. Written for the most part in the octosyllabic couplets used by the poet in his long poem *Confessio Amantis*, where Shakespeare read the story, on the page the choruses may appear merely quaint; in the theatre, spoken confidingly, they can be curiously engaging, breaking down any resistance we may feel to the improbabilities of the tale by the frank acknowledgement that this is

what it is, an old tale with no pretensions to reality or even to literary
sophistication:

> If you, born in these latter times
> When wit's more ripe, accept my rhymes,
> And that to hear an old man sing
> May to your wishes pleasure bring,
> I life would wish, and that I might
> Waste it for you like taper-light.
>
> (1.11–16)

'Waste it for you like taper-light': the image suggests the flickering of a
slowly dwindling candle as the story-teller weaves his magic and
holds his listeners from their beds. In *Henry the Fifth* the tone of the
Chorus is bracing, hortatory, stimulating our minds to co-operate
with the performers in re-creating actual events; Gower's is relaxing,
hypnotic, ingratiating, wooing our imaginations and freeing them to
accept the archetypal and symbolic aspects of the story he tells. He has
come from the grave to tell his tale, and the tale itself will tell of
restorations from death to life.

Just as the tale as a whole appeals to the audience's sense of wonder,
so individual episodes represent the effect of wonderful events on
characters within the story. A scene that, in my experience, is
unfailingly effective in the theatre is the one in which, after the chest
holding Pericles's supposedly dead wife, Thaisa, has been washed
ashore in the terrible storm that required it to be cast overboard, it is
brought to the physician Cerimon. Hoping for gold, he and his
companions open it to discover the body of a queen with a paper
identifying her and asking whoever may find her to give her burial.

Wonder follows upon wonder, and Cerimon's companions guide
our reactions with their exclamations of 'Most strange!', 'Is not this
strange?', and 'Most rare' as Cerimon slowly revives the sleeping
queen. The solemnity of his ministrations is enhanced by the 'still and
woeful music' for which he calls; silences are as telling as words as he
watches for signs of life; we hold our breaths along with those on stage
as he demands 'I pray you, give her air', and we share their relief and
joy as at last he announces:

> Gentlemen,
> This queen will live. Nature awakes, a warmth
> Breathes out of her. She hath not been entranced

>   Above five hours. See how she 'gins to blow
>   Into life's flow'r again.
>
>   (12.89–93)

This is truly theatrical writing, but it is poetical too, and the delicate imagery and expressive rhythm of that last sentence are characteristic of a vein of compassionate eloquence pierced with sudden simplicities which is heard at its finest in Pericles's lament over his queen:

>   A terrible childbed hast thou had, my dear,
>   No light, no fire. Th'unfriendly elements
>   Forgot thee utterly, nor have I time
>   To give thee hallowed to thy grave, but straight
>   Must cast thee, scarcely coffined, in the ooze,
>   Where, for a monument upon thy bones
>   And aye-remaining lamps, the belching whale
>   And humming water must o'erwhelm thy corpse,
>   Lying with simple shells.
>
>   (11.55–63)

This is genuinely dramatic poetry both in its form, as an apostrophe to the supposed corpse, and in the way that it creates – partly as a result of the delicate handling of rhythmic and musical effects – an impression of distilling the emotion felt by the character who speaks it; if it tells us more about Pericles than we already know, it does so not by requiring the actor to offer a direct depiction of his psychological state, but by inviting him to project Pericles's complex, almost surreal, vision of the fate of his wife, buried at sea. It calls for exceptionally sensitive verse-speaking, a necessary qualification throughout the play in the actor playing the title role.

Gower weaves the net, but Pericles is the character who holds the play together, a strong role, but one that calls for the ability to convey interior emotion rather than to display more active passions. As in many folk- and fairy-tales, the characters are presented in morally simplified form. Pericles is a wholly virtuous and largely passive figure, patient under the many tribulations he has to undergo, and in his daughter Marina, child of the sea, passivity becomes an active force after she has been captured by pirates and cast into a brothel, opposing itself to the corruption around her and effecting conversions by its own simple, almost mystic power. Diana, goddess of chastity, is the tutelary deity of the play. Thaisa's first words on being restored to life are 'O dear Diana', Pericles, leaving his infant daughter in the custody of Dionyza, swears 'By bright Diana' that his hair will remain 'unscissored' until she is married (13.27–30), Thaisa becomes a handmaid in Diana's temple at Ephesus soon after her rescue, and in the play's concluding stages Diana appears to Pericles and to us in a vision that guides him to reunion with his wife.

Marina's call on Diana to help her to preserve her chastity after she has been sold into the brothel is thus more than a passing allusion: it links her with the mother whom she does not know and with the supernatural forces which she hopes will guard her. But the Bawd turns aside her prayer with a ribald jest – 'What have we to do with Diana?' – and there is comedy too in the reaction of the Gentleman who, finding 'divinity preached' in the brothel, departs declaring, 'I am for no more bawdy houses. Shall's go hear the vestals sing?' (19.4–7). More serious is Marina's encounter (in, regrettably, a badly damaged area of the text) with Lysimachus, the Governor of Mytilene, who comes to the brothel to 'do the deed of darkness' but leaves ashamed of his 'corrupted mind', giving Marina money to relieve her condition and offering more help in the future. Marina's moral steadfastness in the face of danger resembles her father's, and brings similar rewards.

In contrast with the play's portrayals of ideal virtue are a number of villainous characters. The incestuous father and daughter whose guilty secret Pericles fathoms in the opening scene, and Marina's wicked guardian Dionyza who seeks to have her murdered because she outshines her own daughter in beauty and virtue, are little more than cardboard figures, but the Pander and the Bawd who run the brothel, along with their man Boult, are more colourful characters in whom villainy lightly worn achieves a degree of moral complexity. Their realistic, earthy attitude to sex, their total failure to understand Marina's scruples, their horror that 'she has here spoken holy words to the Lord Lysimachus', should amuse; there is brilliant black comedy in these scenes, but in them, even more than in the Eastcheap scenes of *Henry the Fourth, Part Two*, we are left in no doubt that trading in the flesh is a sordid calling:

> BAWD The stuff we have, a strong wind will blow it to pieces, they are so pitifully sodden.
> PANDER Thou sayst true. They're too unwholesome, o' conscience. The poor Transylvanian is dead that lay with the little baggage.
> BOULT Ay, she quickly pooped him, she made him roast meat for worms.

(16.17–23)

On the stage even more than in print Marina is a desperately touching figure as she stands listening to their materialistic assessment of the commercial value of her body, and the instruction to Boult to 'Crack the ice of her virginity, and make the rest malleable', is horrifying, but Boult, like other Shakespearian rogues before and after him, has his moment of self-defence as he responds to Marina's protests:

> What would you have me do? Go to the wars, would you, where
> a man may serve seven years for the loss of a leg, and have not
> money enough in the end to buy him a wooden one?
>
> (19.195–8)

It is the sea, agent of so much that happens in the play, that takes the comatose Pericles to Mytilene, where Lysimachus is able to further his intention of doing Marina good by recommending her, 'with her sweet harmony | And other choice attractions', as one who may be able to draw the King out of his trance-like state. As in all the romances, there is a strong sense in *Pericles* that life is controlled by inscrutable, if ultimately beneficent, powers, symbolized by sea and storm. So Marina, mourning the death of her nurse, Lychorida, laments:

> Ay me, poor maid,
> Born in a tempest when my mother died,
> This world to me is but a ceaseless storm
> Whirring me from my friends.
>
> (15.69–72)

But out of the tempest comes a calm of which music is the apt symbol.

Instrumental music had helped to restore Marina's mother to life, and now she sings in the attempt to drag from the depths of despair the ageing, unkempt man who is a stranger to her. The scene of recognition and reunion of father and daughter has antecedents in many of Shakespeare's plays, most obviously in *King Lear*, but conspicuously also in the coming together of brother and sister in *Twelfth Night*. Like Lear, Pericles has to be coaxed back to consciousness from a state that is close to death. Also like Lear, he is a reluctant Lazarus, seeming at first to prefer to remain on the other side of consciousness. 'You do me wrong to take me out of the grave', says Lear; and Pericles initially repulses Marina's attempts to recover him. Her methods resemble the therapy offered nowadays to patients suffering from coma, and there is a sense that she has to dig deep into the victim's subconscious in order to make any impression on him. Her song – both words and music are lost – makes no immediate impact, though it may be taken to have, perhaps, the same kind of releasing effect on Pericles's imagination that Gower's speeches have on ours; she goes on to speak, not of Pericles's plight, but of the 'wayward fortune' that has 'rooted out [her] parentage', and these are the hooks that reach down into Pericles's subconscious and drag speech out of him.

> My fortunes, parentage, good parentage,
> To equal mine? Was it not thus? What say you?
>
> (21.86–7)

'What parentage?' is a question that Sebastian had asked of his sister Viola 'Whom the blind waves and surges [had] devoured', and Pericles echoes another of Sebastian's questions, 'What countryman?', as he asks Marina, 'what countrywoman? Here of these shores?' Her answer has the enigmatic character that encapsulates the mystery of the concluding complications of some of Shakespeare's comedies:

> No, nor of any shores,
> Yet I was mortally brought forth, and am
> No other than I seem.

She is of no shores because she is a child of the sea; in the enigma lies the answer to Pericles's plight. He is impelled to go on talking by this maiden's resemblance to his wife – 'My dearest wife was like this maid, and such | My daughter might have been' – and his praise of Thaisa as 'another Juno, | Who starves the ears she feeds, and makes them hungry | The more she gives them speech' takes us back strangely to Cleopatra, who 'makes hungry | Where most she satisfies'. Recognition is struggling to the surface, and the power of love is drawing him out of himself: 'Thou show'st | Like one I loved indeed.' He goes on interrogating her, intrigued by her claim that her griefs might equal his, and she – like the chaste Diana, also a repository of secrets, in *All's Well that Ends Well* – remains the centre of our as well as his attention as the possibility that she is his daughter rises slowly to the surface of his mind. Though he cannot believe that she has suffered 'the thousandth part' of his endurance, yet he acknowledges that she looks 'Like patience gazing on kings' graves, and smiling | Extremity out of act'. (Again, Viola in *Twelfth Night*, remembering her imaginary sister's sitting 'like patience on a monument' and 'smiling at grief', seems to have come to Shakespeare's mind.) Questions pile upon one another, and the stark simplicity with which, unaware of its significance, she tells him her name – 'My name, sir, is Marina' – reaches to the roots of his being.

But this is only the turning-point of this extraordinarily protracted episode in which Pericles's patience, the quality he has so notably displayed throughout the action, is put to its final test; his wonder grows as he encourages her to tell her story and she says first that she is a king's daughter, then that she was 'Called Marina | For I was born at sea', then that her 'mother was the daughter of a king', then that the nurse's name was Lychorida, and at last, after she has recounted what happened after her father left her in Tarsus, that she is 'the daughter to King Pericles, | If good King Pericles be'. Still Pericles does not identify himself to her, but the intensity of his emotion finds expression in a call to his counsellor Helicanus expressive of two ideas that recur in these plays: the close relationship between the apparent extremes of pain and joy, and the capacity of the young to renew their parents' lives:

> O Helicanus, strike me, honoured sir,
> Give me a gash, put me to present pain,
> Lest this great sea of joys rushing upon me
> O'erbear the shores of my mortality
> And drown me with their sweetness!

The sea that took wife and daughter away has restored his daughter and is now a 'sea of joys' that threatens to drown him in happiness, and his apostrophe to Marina epitomizes the theme of renewal that lies at the heart of the romance vision:

> O, come hither,
> Thou that begett'st him that did thee beget,
> Thou that wast born at sea, buried at Tarsus,
> And found at sea again!
>
> (21.178–85)

Still he has not identified himself to Marina, but as she names her mother and kneels for his blessing the recognition and reunion are complete.

From the impassivity of coma Pericles has progressed to a state where he is, as he says, 'wild in [his] beholding', and at this point music is heard again – this time, the music of the spheres, audible only to Pericles (and, probably, the audience), music that draws him back into a sleep now of restoration, not withdrawal, in which the goddess Diana herself appears to him and to us, summoning him to her temple at Ephesus. It is, as Gower points out, by the exercise of our imaginations – our 'fancies' thankful doom' – that he can travel there so quickly, and the sacrifice he performs before Diana's altar reaps its reward as one of the vestals – no virgin she – swoons on hearing his story and is identified as Thaisa by the same Cerimon who had restored her to life; Pericles's joy is so extreme that all his past sufferings are redeemed, and again he expresses the idea that joy will overwhelm the sense of personal identity: 'on the touching of her lips' he expects to 'Melt, and no more be seen'. As Marina too identifies herself to her mother the family reunion is complete, and news of Marina's betrothal to Lysimachus extends the hope of renewal of happiness beyond the time-span of the play's action and into a new generation. Gower, in his final chorus, suggests that the audience, like Pericles, will be rewarded for patience by 'New joy'.

Like *Pericles, The Winter's Tale* is based directly on an old tale, and deliberately draws the audience's attention to its fictive origins. Of all these plays, this is the one where Shakespeare was working most closely from an earlier printed book in the way that he worked from Lodge's *Rosalynde* for *As You Like It* or from Plutarch for the Roman plays. For *The Winter's Tale* the book was *Pandosto*, a prose romance written by his old rival Robert Greene and published by 1588, around the time Shakespeare was embarking on his career as a dramatist.

Pandosto is a repository of romance conventions which, in spite of its crude construction and often slack prose, was popular for a phenomenally long time. It had been reprinted four times by the time Shakespeare came to write his play, probably in 1610, and went on being read and printed for at least 150 years. It seems to have appealed especially to a not very highly educated class of reader. In Shakespeare's lifetime it was said that a typical chambermaid 'reads Greene's works over and over',[3] and the same kind of girl is shown reading it in Samuel Richardson's novel *Clarissa*, published in 1747–8. It was about this time that scholars took over from the chambermaids and started reading and reprinting the book as a Shakespearian source – there is a version of it, oddly rewritten into Augustan prose, in Mrs Charlotte Lennox's three-volume anthology *Shakespear Illustrated* of 1753–4. Probably it owed its popularity to its presentation of basic human situations in an undemanding manner, and it may well be this very quality that recommended it to Shakespeare as the basis for a play. Just as composers write some of their best songs to undistinguished lyrics, so Shakespeare may have found *Pandosto* particularly useful because in it Greene had assembled well-worn themes and stock situations of pastoral romance into a pattern on which he could play variations.

Shakespeare makes no attempt to hide the unoriginal nature and improbable aspects of a story that in some respects he left even more improbable than he had found it. His very title prepared his audiences for a tale of romantic implausibility – a mid-sixteenth-century book, *A Short History of Anti-Christ* by J. Olde, classes 'winter's tales' along with 'old wives' tales' – and during the play itself we are reminded of the old-fashioned nature of the story we are watching. This play too has a Chorus, but instead of calling Greene back from the grave to tell his tale, Shakespeare brings on the emblematic figure of Time, complete with hour-glass, not as a narrator throughout the action but only as a commentator who, covering the 'wide gap' of time in the middle of the action, alludes to the old-fashioned nature of the story he is telling; he will, he says,

>   make stale
> The glistering of this present as my tale
> Now seems to it.
>
>   (4.1.13–15)

Within the action too, especially towards the end when marvellous events crowd upon one another, the death of one of the characters is said to be like 'an old tale still', and the possibility that someone believed dead should be still alive would be 'hooted at like an old tale'. At such points Shakespeare shifts the play's focus, inviting the audience momentarily to detach itself from the play and to recall similar fictional situations, perhaps even their memories of *Pandosto* itself, and also the centuries of tradition that lie behind it.

Pandosto provided Shakespeare with a basic structure for his narrative. The novel is made up of two distinct stories, the one inserted into the other. The split story is that of Pandosto himself, the equivalent of Shakespeare's Leontes. The first part of the book tells how, falsely believing his wife to have committed adultery with his best friend and to be bearing his child, he casts off his newborn daughter in the belief that she is his friend's bastard; his wife dies of shame and grief. This could be a self-contained story except for one fact: the baby has been left floating on the ocean. The middle part of the book too is almost self-sufficient: it begins with the discovery of the abandoned infant, and goes on to tell of her childhood, her romance, and her elopement with her lover. Travelling by sea, the lovers are driven on the shore of Pandosto's kingdom, and only now do the two stories begin to merge as Pandosto is reunited with his lost daughter. Shakespeare takes over this story with one important change that provides him with so remarkable a *coup de théâtre* that if you don't know what it is, you should read no further, but see the play first. The introduction of several important new characters is only one of the ways in which Shakespeare strengthens the continuity of the action.

Rather like *King Lear*, the play opens with a conversation in courtly prose setting up the initial situation, establishing the play's geographical bounds of Sicily and Bohemia, the one ruled by Leontes, the other by his boyhood friend Polixenes, and emphasizing the apparently unshakable intensity of a continuing friendship which is such 'that they have seemed to be together, though absent; shook hands as over a vast; and embraced as it were from the ends of opposed winds'. Any experienced playgoer knows that this cannot last, and in the next scene, in which we see Polixenes insisting that his visit to Leontes's court, already nine months long, must come to an end, Leontes's sexual jealousy rapidly becomes apparent. Absence of expressed motivation, so often a feature of romance stories, is acute here.

In Greene, though the onset of jealousy is not portrayed with any great subtlety (it is in fact described in a paragraph that Greene, with characteristic opportunism, took over word for word from an earlier book), it is a gradual process. In Shakespeare, however, it develops with what many actors have felt to be implausible suddenness. Some, such as John Gielgud in Peter Brook's Phoenix Theatre production (1951), have acted between the lines to suggest that Leontes is already jealous when the play begins. Other directors have invented behaviour between Polixenes and Hermione that provides reasonable cause for suspicion. Yet others have devised ways of showing how the behaviour of Hermione and Polixenes, innocent enough in itself, appears to Leontes's diseased imagination – in Trevor Nunn's 1969 production, for instance, a sudden change of lighting halted the action which continued with a mime in which Polixenes and Hermione acted with the lasciviousness that Leontes ascribes to them while reverting to innocuousness when the lighting changed back. Some critics have found an explanation for Leontes's jealousy in his very love for Polixenes, suggesting that he 'projects upon his wife the desires he has had to repudiate in himself'.[4] Though such an explanation may seem acceptable on the printed page, the text offers little if any opportunity to project it in the theatre. Perhaps it is best to apply to Leontes the words that Emilia speaks of 'jealous souls':

> They are not ever jealous for the cause,
> But jealous for they're jealous. It is a monster
> Begot upon itself, born on itself.
>
> (*Othello*, 3.4.157–9)

There is also a strong case for presenting Leontes when we first see him in the state of normality from which he is so unhappily to descend, giving us, however briefly, a standard against which to measure his aberrant behaviour and to which he can be seen to return in the later part of the play. For this reason, although the language of the scene's opening speeches may suggest the formality of the court, directors not uncommonly give it a domestic quality, showing Leontes initially happy in the company of his friend and family: Trevor Nunn set it in a nursery with the King, his Queen, his son and his friend all playing happily together and riding a large wooden horse, and Peter Hall, after initially rehearsing it as a public scene, finally decided to play it in private.[5] It is reasonable too to show Hermione as heavily pregnant here; it is not without point that Polixenes's stay at Leontes's court has been said to have lasted for nine months.

However sketchy the motivation of Leontes's jealousy may be, once it has descended it is projected with vivid immediacy as a self-consuming, almost fanatical state of mind, impervious to suggestion, incapable of admitting the possibility of error. Although the mode of romance often favours the type over the individual, it is important to Shakespeare's purpose here that we see Leontes not as a representative figure but as a man whose state of mind is peculiar to himself. His language as he expresses his vision of Hermione's adultery and of its effect on him is so introverted as to be, at times, almost unintelligible:

> Affection, thy intention stabs the centre.
> Thou dost make possible things not so held,
> Communicat'st with dreams – how can this be? –
> With what's unreal thou coactive art,
> And fellow'st nothing.
>
> (1.2.140–4)

That passage – even after it has been subjected to editorial interpretation – is one of the most notoriously obscure in the canon, and some of the attempts to explain it recorded in the New Variorum edition are even more bewildering than the passage itself, but it is certainly ironical in its emphasis on the liability of the mind to construct something out of nothing, and in the phrase 'Communicat'st with dreams' links with Leontes's later remark to Hermione, intended as sarcasm but all too true, 'Your actions are my "dreams". | You had a bastard by Polixenes, | And I but dreamed it' (3.2.81–3).

Leontes lives in his own world of grotesque and obscene imaginings, a world in which there is 'no barricado for a [woman's] belly', which 'will let in and out the enemy | With bag and baggage', in which every gesture is bound to be misinterpreted, leading him inexorably down the vertiginous spiral of paranoia into

> Is whispering nothing?
> Is leaning cheek to cheek? Is meeting noses?
> Kissing with inside lip? Stopping the career
> Of laughter with a sigh? – a note infallible
> Of breaking honesty. Horsing foot on foot?
> Skulking in corners? Wishing clocks more swift,
> Hours minutes, noon midnight? And all eyes
> Blind with the pin and web but theirs, theirs only,
> That would unseen be wicked? Is this nothing?
> Why then the world and all that's in't is nothing,
> The covering sky is nothing, Bohemia nothing,
> My wife is nothing, nor nothing have these nothings
> If this be nothing.
>
> (1.2.286–98)

The manifest imbalance of Leontes's state of mind induces detachment rather than involvement, pointed within the play by the incredulity of his cupbearer Camillo and the more active ridicule of the courtier Antigonus and his strong-minded wife Paulina; they channel off some of the audience's reactions as normal spectators, helping to prevent the story from reaching tragic dimensions rather as the presence of Beatrice and Benedick in the church scene of *Much Ado About Nothing* prevents that scene from overbalancing the play. Paulina indeed acts as an embodiment of Leontes's conscience, rebuking him in his folly, impressing on him almost to excess the need for penitence, consoling him in his contrition, and guiding him in his actions when at the end he puts himself entirely in her hands. It is a splendid role, as powerful in its representation of forthright good sense as that of Emilia in *Othello*.

The contrast of innocence with experience, and the regenerative potential of a younger generation, are particularly prominent in this play. In the opening scenes the innocence of childhood is movingly presented through both recollection and direct presentation. Polixenes recalls the time when he and Leontes were

> Two lads that thought there was no more behind
> But such a day tomorrow as today,
> And to be boy eternal,
>
> (1.2.64–6)

a time when they 'changed | Innocence for innocence' and 'knew not the doctrine of ill-doing, nor dreamed | That any did'. And directly before us we see Leontes playing with his young son, Mamillius, who has already been described in the opening conversation as 'a gentleman of the greatest promise that ever came into my note . . . one that, indeed, physics the subject, makes old hearts fresh'. Polixenes, too, has a young son who is, he says,

> all my exercise, my mirth, my matter;
> Now my sworn friend, and now mine enemy;
> My parasite, my soldier, statesman, all.
> He makes a July's day short as December,
> And with his varying childness cures in me
> Thoughts that would thick my blood.
>
> (1.2.167–72)

The illness that afflicts Mamillius bears a symbolical relationship to his father's growing mental sickness, even though Leontes ascribes it (accurately in one sense) to 'the dishonour of his mother' (2.3.13), and the destructive power of Leontes's jealousy is confirmed in the scene of Hermione's trial for adultery when, immediately following Leontes's blasphemous denial of the message from the oracle declaring her innocent, news arrives that the boy, 'with mere conceit and fear |

Of the Queen's speed, is gone'. Just as, in *King Lear*, Gloucester's false view of his sons is cured on – we might almost say by – his blinding, so here the shock of the boy's death instantly brings Leontes to his senses:

> Apollo's angry, and the heavens themselves
> Do strike at my injustice.
>
> (3.2.145–6)

Another blow falls instantly as Hermione sinks to the ground, seemingly dead.

The stylization of the action here is appropriate to tragicomedy; the blatancy of the dramatic artifice checks involvement and leads our minds forward to what is to come. Shakespeare skilfully guides us into the idealized pastoralism of the middle section of his play, shifting the dramatic focus from the near-tragedy we have been witnessing to the entirely different perspective of the Bohemian scenes by presenting the terrible (and improbable) subsequent events: the abandonment in a raging storm of Leontes's infant daughter Perdita – the lost one – on the sea-coast of Bohemia along with the deaths of Paulina's husband Antigonus, who carries her there, and of the entire crew of the ship on which they have travelled, through the eyes of the comically uninvolved Clown and with the help of the notorious bear that chases and devours Antigonus – '*Exit pursued by a bear*' is the stage direction. This is necessary so that the penitent Leontes has no means of finding his daughter; one of the theatrical pleasures of seeing the play is the variety of ways in which the bear can be staged. Terry Hands, whose 1986 RSC production it pervaded throughout, made it only the central one among a number of bear images that came to symbolize the powers of irrational violence.

Sixteen years have to pass before Perdita grows to marriageable age. Long gaps of time are inconvenient to dramatists. Influenced perhaps by Greene's motto, *Temporis Filia Veritas* – Truth, the daughter of time – printed on the title-page of *Pandosto*, Shakespeare solves the problem in *The Winter's Tale* both by giving time a prominent place in the play's structure of ideas and by bringing him on stage in personified form as a Chorus to cover the 'wide gap' of time between the two parts of the play. As we have seen, the opening scene includes a poetic invocation of childhood illusions of timelessness; Polixenes, speaking of his son, had referred to his capacity to annihilate the effects of time – 'He makes a July's day short as December'; now this same son, grown to early manhood, woos Perdita, without knowing that she is a princess, in terms that magically suggest that her beauty, and his love for her, can suspend the passage of time:

> What you do
> Still betters what is done. When you speak, sweet,
> I'd have you do it ever; when you sing,
> I'd have you buy and sell so, so give alms,
> Pray so; and for the ord'ring your affairs,
> To sing them too. When you do dance, I wish you
> A wave o'th' sea, that you might ever do
> Nothing but that, move still, still so,
> And own no other function.
>
> (4.4.135–43)

The lines have an incantatory rhythmic function, created partly by the repetition of syntactic patterns – 'When you speak'/'When you sing'/ 'When you do dance' – and of individual words – 'you' occurs eight times, 'so' four times, 'still' three times, 'sing' twice. In part these repetitions create a rhythmic dynamic which presses the mind forward, but one of the most striking and original effects of the lines is the way in which, imitating rhythmically the swaying motion of the dance in the image of the 'wave o'th' sea', they create simultaneously an impression of movement and of stillness which is itself characteristic of a wave, retaining its shape even as the elements that constitute it are in continual motion, in a subtle wordplay that draws on the two contrasting meanings of the repeated word 'still', both 'continual' and 'motionless'. The sense of timelessness that this creates represents the ideal quality of Florizel's love and also links with the complex chain of imagery representing time as both destroyer and redeemer.

When we move back from Bohemia to Sicily for the play's concluding episodes we see time offering opportunities for repentance and redemption: though Leontes has performed 'A saint-like sorrow', he persists in penitence, intensely conscious of the wrong he did his wife and of its consequences:

> Whilst I remember
> Her and her virtues I cannot forget
> My blemishes in them, and so still think of
> The wrong I did myself, which was so much
> That heirless it hath made my kingdom, and
> Destroyed the sweet'st companion that e'er man
> Bred his hopes out of.
>
> (5.1.6–12)

With terrible intensity he remembers her and her beauty; her eyes were 'Stars, stars, | And all eyes else dead coals'. Ultimately a sense of renewal is created by the fact that the son and daughter of the estranged kings bring about their parents' reconciliation by their marriage.

If time is no less important among the ideas of this play than it is in, for instance, the sonnets, or *As You Like It*, or *Troilus and Cressida*, so also is another of the stock themes of Elizabethan literature, the relationship between art and nature; and just as Time makes a personal appearance, so also this theme is brought to the surface in a passage of unusually abstract discussion between Perdita and Polixenes in the sheep-shearing scene. Perdita scorns to grow 'carnations and streaked gillivors' in her 'rustic garden' because she has heard that 'There is an art which in their piedness shares | With great creating nature'. Somewhat sophistically, Polixenes argues that nature makes the skill that makes such grafting possible:

> So over that art
> Which you say adds to nature is an art
> That nature makes. You see, sweet maid, we marry
> A gentler scion to the wildest stock,
> And make conceive a bark of baser kind
> By bud of nobler race. This is an art
> Which does mend nature – change it rather; but
> The art itself is nature.
>
> (4.4.90–7)

The relevance of his remarks to the actual dramatic situation is apparent, and it is ironically complicated: Perdita herself is, so far as Polixenes knows, of wilder stock, which in theory should mean that he would be happy for her to marry his 'gentler' – more nobly born – son; but we are soon to see his fury at the suggestion. At the same time, Perdita is in fact of noble blood, but has been brought up close to the soil: so, like the flowers she scorns, she is a product of both art and nature.

Having stated this theme in the abstract, Shakespeare invites us to see its relevance to other parts of the story. The chastity of the young lovers, and the sexual continence of Leontes, all subduing natural instincts by the exercise of self-will, is a part of it; it lies behind the comedy of the assumption of gentility on the part of Perdita's substitute father, the Old Shepherd, and his son when, learning of her true origins, they declare they have been 'gentlemen born' 'any time these four hours'; it may be paralleled by the sophisticated artistry of roguery by which the tinker Autolycus, that 'snapper-up of uncon-sidered trifles', deceives the natural simplicity of the rustics; and the last scene forms an almost allegorical presentation of Polixenes's argument.

It is at the end of the play that Shakespeare departs most radically from his source. There, Hermione has truly died. Here, in an episode whose daring improbability could be justified only by a purpose beyond mere truth to life, we are asked to believe that she did not really die when Leontes thought she did, but that, by some amazing contrivance, she has not merely been kept alive though concealed for sixteen years not far from her husband's court, her whereabouts known only to one woman – who presumably had to trot across to her with parcels of food several times a day – but that she now consents to pretend to be a statue of herself, in the presence not only of the husband whom she has not seen for sixteen years but also of the daughter snatched from her as a baby, so that Paulina can stage-manage her resurrection. Shakespeare very rarely springs surprises such as this upon his audience. The only real parallel for it is the revelation in *The Comedy of Errors* that the Abbess who appears in the final scene is the wife who, Egeon thought, had been drowned in the storm that separated him from his twin sons and their servants.

Judged by realistic standards, the episode in *The Winter's Tale* is absurd, justifying Mrs Lennox's criticism: 'The novel has nothing in it half so low and improbable as this contrivance of the statue.' But by this stage in the play we know that we are not watching realistic drama, and if we have accepted the conventions in which the play is written, and responded to its poetry of both language and action, we shall experience this scene as the inevitable if unexpected conclusion of all that has gone before. Paulina presents the supposed statue as the product of art, the 'carver's excellence', and seeing it Leontes feels that the stone rebukes him 'For being more stone than it'; its majesty moves him to renewed expressions of penitence, and both Camillo and Polixenes declare that his long sorrow has fully expiated his sins:

CAMILLO My lord, your sorrow was too sore laid on,
    Which sixteen winters cannot blow away,
    So many summers dry. Scarce any joy
    Did ever so long live; no sorrow
    But killed itself much sooner.

                                 (5.3.49–53)

He is ripe for regeneration; the mere sight of the supposed statue has the same effect on him as Marina's music and speech had upon Pericles; the winter in his soul had been eroded by the arrival and recognition of Perdita, as welcome to him 'As is the spring to th' earth' (5.1.151), and now he is capable of the faith that Paulina demands as the price for the miracle of making the statue live.

The long wait before the statue moves, which has proved troublesome to many readers, is unfailing in its hold upon audiences. The effect is partly physical: knowing, or guessing, that this is an actor not a statue that we see, we hold our breaths along with that of the performer; and at the moment when Hermione starts into life, when the art that has made the statue is revealed indeed to have been nature, we, like Hermione, start to breathe again. This is another scene of resurrection, like that of Thaisa in *Pericles*, because there is a sense in which Hermione *has* been dead and is now being restored to the world; the same is true too of Leontes, ready to re-enter the world after his long withdrawal in penitence.

Leontes's realization that Hermione lives is one of those moments of silence in which Shakespeare in a sense leaves everything to the actor, yet in another sense has done everything for him. 'Silence is the perfect'st herald of joy', says Claudio in *Much Ado About Nothing*, and here (as in a similar scene in Euripides's *Alcestis*) husband and wife do not address each other; but there must surely be, as the First Gentleman has said of the reunion of Leontes and Camillo, 'speech in their dumbness, language in their very gesture'. So it was, at least, when Macready played the scene to the Hermione of Helena Faucit, who recalled:

> At first he stood speechless, as if turned to stone; his face with an awe-struck look upon it. . . . Thus absorbed in wonder, he remained until Paulina said, 'Nay, present your hand.'
> Tremblingly he advanced, and touched gently the hand held out to him. Then, what a cry came with, 'O, she's warm!' It is impossible to describe Mr Macready here. He was Leontes' very self! His passionate joy at finding Hermione really alive seemed beyond control. Now he was prostrate at her feet, then enfolding her in his arms. I had a slight veil or covering over my head and neck, supposed to make the statue look older. This fell off in an instant. The hair, which came unbound, and fell upon my shoulders, was reverently kissed and caressed. The whole change was so sudden, so overwhelming that I suppose I cried out hysterically, for he whispered to me, 'Don't be frightened, my

child! Don't be frightened! Control yourself!' All this went on
during a tumult of applause that sounded like a storm of hail. . . .
It was such a comfort to me, as well as true to natural feeling,
that Shakespeare gives Hermione no words to say to Leontes, but
leaves her to assure him of her joy and forgiveness by look and
manner only.[6]

That passage speaks eloquently of the methods of Victorian
actors, of the behaviour of their audiences, and of what both of them
sought and found in Shakespeare's play. More recent productions
have been less rapturous in their presentation of the reunion. Peter
Hall perhaps went too far in suggesting that reconciliation was still no
more than tentative, but an elegiac tone is appropriate to the suffering
we have witnessed; there is joy in the scene, but it is pregnant with
sorrow:

> in the very temple of delight
> Veiled melancholy has her sovereign shrine.[7]

Deep emotions have been stirred and will not be satisfied by a
conventionally cheerful ending.

I remember the first night of a production in which, earlier in the
play, Autolycus had sung a particularly catchy song. At curtain call,
after the first rounds of applause, he tried to strike it up again with
other members of the cast, but it fell completely flat. It might have
worked at the end of one of the romantic comedies whose final scenes
stress the restoration of the social order, of which the dance or feast is
the appropriate symbol. Here there are no macrocosmic implications.
Emphasis is placed not on the group but on individuals whose
suffering we have closely followed; the focus is upon a few figures in
their newly poised adjustments to each other, stressing the importance
of human relationships as bulwarks against the forces of disaster –
storm and tempest, both external and internal. There is sobriety as
Leontes in his closing lines suggests how each may heal the wounds
'Performed in this great gap of time since first we were dissevered'.
The emphasis is not on the young lovers but on the older generation;
we are reminded that Antigonus is dead, that, though Hermione has
been restored to Leontes, he has 'in vain said many a prayer upon' her
grave, and that he needs pardon from both Polixenes and Hermione.
The individuals must salvage what they can.

★

Whereas in *The Winter's Tale* a single story gave Shakespeare the framework for his play, for *Cymbeline* he himself devised an intricate tale from a wide range of sources whose variety is indicative of the eclectic nature of this highly original and often puzzling work. It is almost as if, in order to demonstrate the hospitality of the romance genre, he were deliberately weaving together in one play strands from different areas of his reading that he had previously drawn on for works in other dramatic kinds.

In part this is an English history play, deriving from Holinshed's *Chronicles* and other accounts that had formed the basis of Shakespeare's earlier histories. The title and setting come from the reign of the legendary King Cymbeline, or Cunobelinus, said to have reigned from 33 BC till shortly after the birth of Christ. The play relates to the Roman histories in that Cymbeline, trying to throw off the yoke of Roman domination, is in dispute with Rome about the need to pay tribute money; though Shakespeare does not make direct use of Plutarch, the figure of Julius Caesar, Britain's recent conqueror, looms large.

There are also many links with the romance tradition that had fed Shakespeare's imagination in his earlier comedies. Drawing probably on an old play of unknown authorship, *The Rare Triumphs of Love and Fortune*, acted in 1582, Shakespeare gives Cymbeline a daughter, Innogen,[8] and a wicked second queen with a loutish, vicious son, Cloten, whom she wishes to see on the throne in her husband's place. Cymbeline, disapproving of his daughter's marriage to 'a poor but worthy gentleman', Posthumus Leonatus, banishes him. Innogen's disguise as a boy on her way to Milford Haven, where she hopes to be reunited with her husband, recalls the disguised heroines of the romantic comedies. The strand of plot showing the placing and outcome of a wager that Posthumus, who has fled to Rome (and apparently acquired considerable wealth on the journey), lays on his wife's chastity is indebted, directly or indirectly, to Boccaccio's *Decameron*, which had also provided the story of *All's Well that Ends Well*. Another old play, *Sir Clyomon and Clamydes*, printed in 1599, may have suggested the bizarre scene in which Innogen mistakes Cloten's headless body for that of Posthumus; and Holinshed's *History of Scotland*, which Shakespeare had used for *Macbeth*, supplied the episode in which Cymbeline's two sons, Guiderius and Arviragus, who, like other royal offspring in these plays, have been separated from their father soon after birth, defeat the entire Roman army helped only by the old man, Belarius, who has brought them up far from the potentially corrupting influences of civilization, in the wilds of Wales.

The plot that Shakespeare contrives out of these disparate elements is clearly not designed to convey an impression of truth to ordinary life, and his manner of telling it draws attention to the play's artifice rather than attempting to conceal it. This has not always been understood; in fact a survey of both the criticism and the performance history of *Cymbeline* may justify the glimmerings of belief in the possibility of progress in understanding and criticism of the arts. The opening scene, in which one anonymous gentleman feeds another with questions in order to permit the exposition of the play's initial situation, was once quoted in an anthology of humorous writing as an example of unconscious comedy, and more generally the play's implausibilities have incurred the scorn of rationalist critics such as Samuel Johnson and Bernard Shaw. Johnson notoriously complained that 'To remark the folly of the fiction, the absurdity of the conduct, the confusion of the names and manners of different times and the impossibility of the events in any system of life, were to waste criticism upon unresisting imbecility, upon faults too evident for detection, and too gross for aggravation'.[9] Shaw's main criticisms of the play come in a review of Henry Irving's production of 1896 which is so eloquent a masterpiece of polemical prose that one does not need to take seriously what he says about Shakespeare to enjoy reading it.

Calling *Cymbeline* 'for the most part stagey trash of the lowest melodramatic order, in parts abominably written, throughout intellectually vulgar, and judged in point of thought by modern intellectual standards, vulgar, foolish, offensive, indecent, and exasperating beyond all tolerance', Shaw works himself up to the pitch of indignation that produces his most devastating attack on Shakespeare:

> With the single exception of Homer, there is no eminent writer, not even Sir Walter Scott, whom I can despise so entirely as I despise Shakespear when I measure my mind against his. The intensity of my impatience with him occasionally reaches such a pitch, that it would positively be a relief to me to dig him up and throw stones at him, knowing as I do how incapable he and his worshippers are of understanding any less obvious form of indignity.

That he goes on to say 'I pity the man who cannot enjoy Shakespear' does not palliate the obtuseness of some, at least, of his remarks about *Cymbeline*. He is judging it, as he later admits, by the standards of 'the modern theatre, where a direct illusion of reality is aimed at', standards which are manifestly inappropriate.[10]

It is not necessary to be a total bardolater (a word which, incidentally, Shaw invented) to claim that Shakespeare could distinguish between a probable and an improbable fiction, or that he knew when he was following convention and when he was flouting it. In the opening scenes of some plays, such as *Othello* – which starts in mid-conversation – he does aim at a 'direct illusion of reality'; the manifest implausibility of the expository opening of *Cymbeline*, like that of *As You Like It* (with which *Cymbeline* has many other points of contact), proclaims this from the start as a play that will operate in as self-conscious a mode of artifice as Sidney's *Arcadia* or Spenser's *The Faerie Queene*, and that will exercise the same kind of appeal to the baroque sensibility as do those works.

In *Cymbeline* Shakespeare takes to an extreme the technique of juxtaposition of opposites that characterizes the late plays in general. The plot's oppositions are both national and personal: Britain and Rome are in conflict, and many of the characters are at enmity with one another. And even more than *King Lear* the play is populated by antithetical characters. Some, such as Innogen, Posthumus's servant Pisanio, Belarius, and those children of nature Arviragus and Guiderius, are paragons of virtue; others, including Cloten and the Queen, are 'Too bad for bad report' (1.1.17). Giacomo, who wagers that he can seduce Innogen, is initially the conventional Italianate villain who – like Oliver in *As You Like It* – undergoes a sudden conversion to virtue when it suits the plot that he should do so. Posthumus moves from virtue to debasement brought on by Giacomo's deception and back to virtue again. Some of the characters, like villains in a Victorian melodrama – or indeed like Iago in *Othello* – conceal their villainy from most of those around them though not from the audience: only after his queen is dead does Cymbeline learn that she married him for rank and 'Abhorred' his 'person'; his reaction makes explicit the theme of the deceptiveness of appearances:

> Mine eyes
> Were not in fault, for she was beautiful;
> Mine ears that heard her flattery, nor my heart
> That thought her like her seeming. It had been vicious
> To have mistrusted her.
>
> (5.6.62–6)

Whereas the Queen seems virtuous but is villainous, Posthumus (like Othello) is mistaken to believe that his wife's appearance of chastity is a delusion. False seeming extends to physical disguise: Innogen, Posthumus, and Cloten are all disguised for part of the action; others – Arviragus and Guiderius – are unaware of their own true identity.

The play's frank acknowledgement, and its exploitation for comic purposes, of its stylization of character portrayal can be observed within the structure of individual scenes such as that in which we first meet Cloten (1.2), where his two attendant lords comment upon his folly in ironical asides, or that in which the Queen talks with a Doctor about drugs that are to play an important part in the play's action (1.5). It opens in prettiness as she instructs her ladies-in-waiting to gather flowers; their exit almost immediately subsequent to their entry is itself likely to seem comic. The Doctor expresses suspicion of the Queen's motives for requiring 'most poisonous compounds, | Which are the movers of a languishing death, | But though slow, deadly'. Not taken in by her protestations that she does it in the interests of pure science, he, like Cloten's servants, makes behind-the-hand utterances to the audience, saying 'I do suspect you, madam', 'I do not like her', and confiding that because of his suspicions he has given her merely sleep-inducing drugs such as those that caused the appearance of death in Juliet; thus 'She is fooled | With a most false effect, and I the truer | So to be false with her'. After her conversation with Pisanio in which she 'accidentally' drops the box containing the drugs, giving it to Pisanio with the pretence that it contains valuable medicines in the hope that it will bring about his, and perhaps Innogen's, death, she finally, in a return to prettiness, welcomes back her ladies with their 'violets, cowslips, and primroses'. The scene has no more psychological verisimilitude than an episode from *Snow White*, which it resembles, but its faux-naïvety is sophisticated rather than simple-minded. Its method is echoed in inverted form in the subsequent scene (2.3) in which Cloten arranges for a song to be sung before Innogen's room, in which, instead of prettiness enveloping evil, the dirty talk of Cloten to his lords – 'If you can penetrate her with your fingering, so; we'll try with tongue too' – both precedes and follows the exquisite serenade 'Hark, hark, the lark at heaven's gate sings', which also invokes the flower imagery that features so largely in this play.

The artificialities of the play's early scenes prepare us for the overt theatricalism as well as the potential absurdity of another episode which juxtaposes the ideal with the vicious, that in which, after Innogen has fallen asleep praying for protection from 'fairies and the

tempters of the night' while reading Ovid's tale of the rape of
Philomela, the lid of the trunk supposedly containing valuable
purchases made by Giacomo as gifts for the Emperor rises and
Giacomo emerges to seek evidence that will make plausible his claim
that he has seduced Innogen. After the courtly involution of much of
the play's earlier language the limpidity of the writing here helps to
create a riveting effect. The scene teeters on the brink of the ridiculous,
but is saved from it by the lyrical beauty of the portrayal of Innogen as
sleep overtakes her, and by the concentration that Shakespeare evokes
by technical means closely resembling those he had used in *Julius
Caesar* to prepare for the appearance of Caesar's ghost to Brutus. Like
Brutus, Innogen reads in preparation for sleep; she too has a taper
burning beside her. Shakespeare narrows the focus of the audience's
attention on the centre of the stage, preparing for the moments of
silence that must precede the slow opening of the lid of the trunk –
another box that contains poison.

In realistic terms it is as absurd that Giacomo should be able to utter
aloud his description of the sleeping Innogen, and of the room in
which she lies, that he should be able to slip her bracelet off her arm
and take observation of the mole on her breast, all without awaking
her, as that, in *Titus Andronicus*, Marcus should utter his long Ovidian
description of the raped and mutilated Lavinia without thinking of the
need to seek help for her; but incredulity is dissipated by the mesmeric
quality of the writing:

> The crickets sing, and man's o'er-laboured sense
> Repairs itself by rest. Our Tarquin thus
> Did softly press the rushes ere he wakened
> The chastity he wounded. Cytherea,
> How bravely thou becom'st thy bed! Fresh lily,
> And whiter than the sheets! That I might touch,
> But kiss, one kiss! Rubies unparagoned,
> How dearly they do't! 'Tis her breathing that
> Perfumes the chamber thus. The flame o'th' taper
> Bows toward her, and would underpeep her lids,
> To see th'enclosèd lights, now canopied
> Under these windows, white and azure-laced
> With blue of heaven's own tinct.
>
> (2.2.11–23)

The threat of rape hovers over the scene, in Giacomo's obvious sexual
attraction to Innogen and in the allusion here to Tarquin and later to

'The tale of Tereus' (who raped Philomela), classical references which relate the episode to literary tradition rather than to real life. But the threat is averted as Giacomo turns from contemplating Innogen to making notes on the contents of her chamber.

The play's oppositions reach their climax in the scene in which the play's main embodiment of evil, Cloten, enters the preserve of its embodiments of natural virtue, Belarius and the lost boys. Innogen had declared that she valued Cloten less than her husband's 'meanest garment'; now, dressed out of a perverted instinct in those very garments, and thus indistinguishable from Posthumus from the neck downwards, Cloten has come to Wales with the intention of murdering Posthumus and raping Innogen. But when he is unwise enough to insult and challenge the boys Arviragus cheerfully chops off his head and sends it floating down the river. Innogen too has – like Rosalind in *As You Like It* – disguised herself in male clothing for the journey to Milford Haven, where she hopes to meet Posthumus, and having come upon Belarius and her long-lost brothers and discovered a natural affinity with them without knowing who they are, has been housekeeping for them in their cave, even making them alphabet soup ('He cut our roots in characters').

Feeling ill, she swallows the drugs given by the Doctor to the Queen, and falls into a death-like slumber. Arviragus's entry carrying her apparently dead body is heralded by mysterious 'solemn music' played on an 'ingenious instrument' that has not sounded since the death of the woman the boys were brought up to think of as their mother. The stage direction '*Enter from the cave Arviragus with Innogen, dead, bearing her in his arms*' resembles that for Lear's entry with the body of Cordelia, but here the episode is treated with the sweetness of pathos rather than the intensity of tragic suffering. Comparing her to a bird that has died, and to a lily, the boys promise to sweeten her grave with flowers, and preparatory to laying the body in the earth they speak the dirge that continues so often to give consolation at funerals and memorial services:

> Fear no more the heat o'th' sun,
>   Nor the furious winter's rages,
> Thou thy worldly task hast done,
>   Home art gone and ta'en thy wages.
> Golden lads and girls all must,
> As chimney sweepers, come to dust . . .
>
> (4.2.259 ff.)

Innogen's body is unharmed, Arviragus found her 'smiling as some
fly had tickled slumber, | Not as death's dart being laughed at'; but
Cloten also has died, and his headless trunk is carried on and laid
beside her. The virtue of Innogen is juxtaposed with the vice of
Cloten; and there is a similar contrast in the spectacle of their bodies,
hers all beauty, his headless and, in the most powerful production I
have seen, with the veins of the neck hanging out and oozing blood.
The contrast is pointed by Innogen's words on awaking and seeing the
body:

> O gods and goddesses!
> These flowers are like the pleasures of the world,
> This bloody man the care on't.
>
> (4.2.297–9)

Few speeches present so many problems to the performer as this, and
as so often in this play it is difficult to strike the right balance – or to
know whether there is a right balance – between reactions of horror
and laughter. It is horrific that a woman should awake beside a
headless corpse, especially of a man she believes to be her husband,
and the pity of the situation is enhanced by her fears, by her hope that
she dreams, and by her prayer for heavenly pity:

> Good faith,
> I tremble still with fear; but if there be
> Yet left in heaven as small a drop of pity
> As a wren's eye, feared gods, a part of it!

But there is obvious theatrical contrivance in the fact that this is not her
husband but her worst enemy dressed in her husband's clothes, there
is detaching irony in her mistaken deduction that Posthumus has been
murdered by the faithful Pisanio, and the baldness of the language in
which she expresses her horror may strike the spectator as absurd
rather than as moving:

> O Posthumus, alas,
> Where is thy head? Where's that? Ay me, where's that?
> Pisanio might have killed thee at the heart
> And left thy head on.

The scene ends, after Innogen, her face smeared with blood from the
corpse, has been come upon by Lucius, leader of the Roman army, in a

final juxtaposition of the pretty and the grotesque as Lucius declares that he and his comrades will 'Find out the prettiest daisied plot we can' as burying place for the headless body.

If this scene, as in an allegorical painting, represents simultaneously both 'the pleasures of the world' and 'the care on't' (to use the words that Innogen speaks over Cloten's flower-strewn corpse), the final scene, in its long unfolding one after the other of a series of seemingly miraculous resolutions of the complications and oppositions that the play's action has produced, might be said rather to represent the entry of the repentant and virtuous characters to heaven itself. And as in a Last Judgement, it is presided over by a radiant god. The episode in the play that is farthest of all from seeking to create an illusion of reality is the dream-vision that Posthumus experiences after his penitence for having tried to have Innogen murdered – though he still does not know that she is innocent – followed by his heroic and self-sacrificing dedication to the British cause in spite of having returned to his native shores as a member of the Roman army. His aim, he says, is 'To shame the guise o'th' world' and to 'begin | The fashion – less without and more within'. The miraculous nature of the engagement in which the Britons have won the day as a result of the heroism of Belarius and the two boys is emphasized – "Tis thought the old man and his sons were angels' – and Posthumus happily accepts imprisonment as a prelude to the death that he desires as expiation for his sins. As he falls asleep we witness his dream in which his father, mother, and brothers plead with Jupiter to forgive him and rebuke Jupiter for allowing Giacomo 'To taint his nobler heart and brain | With needless jealousy'.

Climactically, we witness too, in an episode in which Shakespeare makes exceptional demands on his theatre's technical resources, Jupiter's descent '*in thunder and lightning, sitting upon an eagle*' and his throwing of a thunderbolt (in Shakespeare's theatre, fireworks strung along a wire), and hear his stern address to the ghosts, claiming that what he has done was ultimately for Posthumus's advantage:

> He shall be lord of Lady Innogen,
> And happier much by his affliction made.
>
> (5.5.201–2)

The artificial mode and incantatory verbal style of this episode, with its archaic diction and its old-fashioned verse forms, sets it off even from the rest of a play that never lacks artifice; to many critics it has proved distasteful, and it has often been regarded as a spurious interpolation. But it has obvious affinities with similar episodes preceding the resolutions of earlier plays, such as the appearance of Hymen in *As You Like It* or of Diana in *Pericles*, its diction and content are intimately related to the rest of the play, and theatrically it can be not only moving and impressive in itself but also, by lifting the action on to a plane of the ideal, an apt prologue to the multiple denouements of the final scene, in which all disguises are removed, all identities made known, and all misunderstandings resolved.

This is another scene whose tone is difficult to gauge accurately. Wonder is dominant as revelation follows upon revelation, and the play's revelling in its own implausibility may well arouse laughter, encouraged by lines such as 'Does the world go round?' and 'New matter still' from Cymbeline, or from the Doctor 'I left out one thing which the Queen confessed', or Guiderius's unashamed account of how he killed Cloten – 'I cut off's head, | And am right glad he is not standing here to tell this tale of mine.' Cymbeline himself is at the receiving end of many of the scene's surprises, and the way he responds will guide the audience's reactions; a director who wishes to encourage amusement will cause him to seem increasingly, and comically, bewildered, perhaps literally reeling with increasing astonishment, whereas a director who prefers to treat the scene more seriously will have him listening soberly and intently with increasing awe. Either approach is justifiable, but a response that allows mingled emotions may seem more characteristically Shakespearian, and perhaps truer to the way the scene is written.

One of the books that may well have influenced Shakespeare as he wrote *Cymbeline* is the ancient Greek romantic tale *Aethiopica*, by Heliodorus, believed to date from the third century AD, which had been translated into English by Thomas Underdowne as *An Ethiopian History* and published in 1569. Many incidents in the story anticipate episodes in *Cymbeline*; more importantly, perhaps, a passage describing the rejoicing at the satisfactory conclusion of events provides an apt description of the tone that Shakespeare sought in his closing scene. The gods' will, we are told, was that all

> should fall out wonderfully, as in a comedy. Surely they made very contrary things agree, and joined sorrow and mirth, tears and laughter, together, and turned fearful and terrible things into a joyful banquet in the end; many that wept began to laugh, and such as were sorrowful to rejoice, when they found that they sought not for, and lost that they hoped to find; and to be short,

the cruel slaughters which were looked for every moment were turned into holy sacrifice.

They 'made very contrary things agree': in the last scene of *Cymbeline*, as so often in the late plays, contraries are resolved. Failing initially to recognize Innogen, Posthumus 'strikes her down' as she approaches him, provoking from Pisanio the rebuke 'O my lord Posthumus, | You ne'er killed Innogen till now. Help, help!'; Cymbeline's reaction is 'If this be so, the gods do mean to strike me | To death with mortal joy', recalling Pericles's words on recognizing *his* daughter:

> Give me a gash, put me to present pain,
> Lest this great sea of joys rushing upon me
> O'erbear the shores of my mortality.
>
> (*Pericles*, 21.179–81)

The resolution of discord into harmony, of enmity into reconciliation through penitence and forgiveness, is more dominant here than in any other of Shakespeare's plays; it may well, as has been suggested,[11] have reminded Shakespeare's original audiences both that the reign of King Cymbeline spanned the time of universal peace – the *pax Romana* – during which Jesus Christ was born in Bethlehem, and that their current king, James I, who liked to be known as Jacobus Pacificus, prided himself especially on his achievements as a peacemaker who had brought about the union of the British isles. 'Pardon's the word to all', says Cymbeline, who has magnanimously agreed to pay tribute to Rome in spite of being the victor; and in the play's closing lines he celebrates the achievement of peace and unity with promises of 'holy sacrifice' to the gods and especially to Jupiter, who has brought it all to pass:

> Laud we the gods,
> And let our crookèd smokes climb to their nostrils
> From our blest altars. Publish we this peace
> To all our subjects. Set we forward, let
> A Roman and a British ensign wave
> Friendly together. So through Lud's town march,
> And in the temple of great Jupiter
> Our peace we'll ratify, seal it with feasts.
> Set on there. Never was a war did cease,
> Ere bloody hands were washed, with such a peace.

*

If *Cymbeline* may justly be criticized as having too much plot, *The Tempest* is equally open to the accusation of having too little; indeed a French critic unkindly suggested that 'Shakespeare finally succeeded in preserving the unity of time only by eliminating action altogether'. The fact that he seems to have made up the story – such as it is – for himself, along with the obviously symbolic nature of the action, may suggest that the play reflects peculiarly personal concerns, though as usual Shakespeare's imagination was fed by much reading: in classical literature, especially Ovid's *Metamorphoses* and the *Aeneid* of Virgil; in modern writings, including Florio's translation of essays by Montaigne; and in accounts of contemporary voyages. He seems particularly to draw on accounts of an expedition of nine ships that took 500 colonists from Plymouth to Virginia which set sail in May 1609, and in which their flagship was wrecked on the coast of the Bermudas. Accounts of the voyage trickled back to England and circulated in manuscript; the last written that Shakespeare seems to have read is a letter by William Strachey dated 15 July 1610, so probably he wrote the play during the later part of 1610 or in 1611. The King's Men acted it at Whitehall before their patron, James I, on 1 November 1611; presumably it went down well since it was also chosen for performance during the ceremonies for the marriage of James's daughter, Princess Elizabeth, to the Elector Palatine during the winter of 1612–13.

In narrative content *The Tempest* has many points of contact with the other late plays – shipwrecks, a child abandoned (here along with her father) to the winds and waves, relatives both parted from and at odds with one another, a kingly father parted from a son whom he mistakenly believes to be dead, a handsome and virtuous young hero and a beautiful and pure young heroine who fall in love with each other, a story in which the supernatural plays a part and deities appear on stage, which contrasts the experience of an older genera-tion with the innocence of a younger, which spans a wide geo-graphical area and a great gap of time, and which works towards reunion, reconciliation, and the happy conclusion of the love-affair. If the story were laid out sequentially, it would seem wholly typical of the romance genre. But in form *The Tempest* is completely different from the other late plays, because here Shakespeare has chosen to represent only the ending of the story, concentrating its action into a small space and a few hours. The only other Shakespeare play that employs this neo-classical structure is one written early in his career, *The Comedy of Errors*; in that play the father-figure, Egeon, is present only in the framework, whereas Prospero is at the centre of *The Tempest*.

It is the tension resulting from the combination of romantic material with classical form that gives this play its peculiar dynamic. The sea-voyages and land-travels of *Pericles, Cymbeline*, and *The Winter's Tale* here can be told only in retrospect, or at most symbolized by the wanderings of the shipwrecked men around the island. Again we are conscious of the importance of time, but instead of being moved from a present which in the later acts of the play becomes the past, we are throughout made conscious of the past in the present. The 'wide gap' of time in which we imagined the coming to maturity of Marina and Perdita has here become 'the dark backward and abyss of time' into which Miranda gazes with her father. Memory plays a large part in the play; we have to be told, and so the characters have to recall, what happened in the part of the story that is not represented; they are often bidden to remember the past, and our minds move with theirs so that, paradoxically enough, we are more consistently and deeply conscious of the effects of time here than in plays in which a wider time-span is directly represented.

By sacrificing the large dimensions of time and space common in romance, Shakespeare gains in concentration. The play is less dispersed and diffused than its companions. Nevertheless, something is lost too. The romancer, typically telling a story in which little attention is paid to motive, to the sequence of cause and effect, depends much on time, chance, or fortune (sometimes represented as an active god-figure) to render plausible those turns of action or changes of character for which no explanation is given. In *Cymbeline*, for instance, Giacomo's sudden last-act penitence goes psycho-logically uninvestigated but is the more easily accepted in that we last saw him some time ago in a different country. The story of *The Tempest* demands similar changes. Alonso, King of Naples, has to be seen in penitence for his usurpation of Prospero's dukedom and his transfer of power to Prospero's brother, Antonio, and the penitence shown to be the direct consequence of his experiences during the few hours he spends on the island. Shakespeare can, and to some extent does, hint that the Alonso we see at the beginning of the action is not as objectionable as he had been twelve years before, but the actual process of conversion has to take place within the play's brief time-span.

This is made convincing primarily by being shown as the result of Prospero's conscious purpose; in a more typical romance story, chance would have caused the shipwreck that puts his enemies at his mercy. In this play, though fortune plays a part – and Shakespeare is most subtle in his constant shifting of responsibility – it is Prospero himself who by his 'art' brings about the shipwreck. He is partly dependent on fortune, partly master of it. At times it is difficult to distinguish him from a supernatural controlling force. In a sense he is the 'god of this great vast' on whom Pericles calls. He has superhuman powers, yet remains human. He is both god and man, a worker of miracles who finally accepts the full burden of humanity. He combines the functions of such human figures as the Duke in *Measure for Measure* or even a malevolent intriguer such as Iago in *Othello*, on the one hand, with a supernatural figure such as Oberon in *A Midsummer Night's Dream* or the Jupiter of *Cymbeline*, on the other. It is partly by creating the wholly superhuman Ariel to act as the semi-independent agent of Prospero's will that Shakespeare is able to keep Prospero human – perhaps the most remarkable technical feat of the play.

As the controlling agent of the play in which he has his being, Prospero himself resembles the narrator of a romance story. This is true not merely of the second scene, in which he tells Miranda of her childhood in what is surely one of the longest expository narrations in all drama, a sequence which, beautifully written though it is, requires much of both actor and audience, but also of the methods by which he exercises his power. Frequently and deliberately Prospero tries to create a sense of awe, mystery, and wonder in the minds of those he aims to influence. His use of music – generally through Ariel – is part of this. There is perhaps no other play of Shakespeare's in which music plays so important a part; no wonder it has influenced and inspired so many composers, from Robert Johnson, lutenist to the King's Men, whose setting of two of the songs survives, to Vaughan Williams and Michael Tippett. (None of the many operatic versions has had much success; one of the most frustratingly unwritten masterpieces of music is the opera based on the play that Mozart was contemplating at the time of his death.)

Important too is Ariel's tricksiness, such as his appearance to the mariners causing them to feel 'a fever of the mad', and the living drollery that reminds Gonzalo of the romantic travellers' tales – like those told by Othello to Desdemona – that he had heard in his childhood. It is after the wonder induced by the appearance of the *'strange shapes, bringing in a banquet'* that Ariel makes his great speech of accusation against the courtiers beginning 'You are three men of sin', in which his voice is indistinguishable from that of Prospero; and in the last scene Prospero remarks:

> I perceive these lords
> At this encounter do so much admire
> That they devour their reason, and scarce think
> Their eyes do offices of truth, these words
> Are natural breath. But howsoe'er you have
> Been jostled from your senses, know for certain
> That I am Prospero . . .
>
> (5.1.155–61)

To jostle them from their senses has been part of his aim; his art, like that of many artists, is intended to change the lives of those who experience it; but not all are susceptible to change. The cynical Antonio and Sebastian deny the wonder expressed by the perhaps overcredulous old Gonzalo just as in *King Lear* Edmond denies his father's belief in portents and omens.

If Prospero resembles a spinner of romance tales, his daughter is even more clearly the ideal audience for such tales. Belarius (in *Cymbeline*), speaking of Guiderius, describes such a person:

> When on my three-foot stool I sit and tell
> The warlike feats I have done, his spirits fly out
> Into my story: say 'Thus mine enemy fell,
> And thus I set my foot on 's neck', even then
> The princely blood flows in his cheek, he sweats,
> Strains his young nerves, and puts himself in posture
> That acts my words.
>
> (3.3.89–95)

Miranda too has all the open-mindedness, the willingness to be impressed, the capacity for wonder, that a story-teller could desire. She is all sympathy and eagerness to believe the best:

> O, I have sufferèd
> With those that I saw suffer! A brave vessel,
> Who had, no doubt, some noble creature in her,
> Dashed all to pieces!
>
> (1.2.5–8)

Her first sight of Alonso's son, Ferdinand, arouses similar awe:

> I might call him
> A thing divine, for nothing natural
> I ever saw so noble.
>
>   (1.2.420–2)

And the climax comes in the last scene as Miranda looks up from her game of chess and sees the assembled group:

> O wonder!
> How many goodly creatures are there here!
> How beauteous mankind is! O brave new world
> That has such people in't!
>
>   (5.1.184–7)

By this time we know a number of these people rather well, and Miranda's innocence has a deep pathos, all the more pointed by Prospero's quiet comment, ''Tis new to thee.' But though Prospero's words provide an implied criticism of Miranda's attitude, they do nothing to destroy it. Shakespeare can show the coexistence of opposed attitudes, making us aware of the tension between them but not compelling us to decide in favour of one or the other. Miranda's naïve innocence and Prospero's mature wisdom are both part of the truth; to counterpoint one against the other is to create a harmony that more than doubles the effect of each alone.

Although *The Tempest* is the shortest of Shakespeare's plays except for *The Comedy of Errors*, he manages to cram a remarkable amount into it. He does so not by the multiplication of incident, the sheer length of many of its predecessors, but rather by an extraordinary multiplicity of suggestiveness, by his power of creating a structure which looks kaleidoscopically different from every angle – his myriad-mindedness, as Coleridge put it.

The enchanted island reverberates with sounds hinting at tunes that never appear fully formed. We can follow one strand through the work, but only by shutting our ears and eyes to the others. It invites consideration on a range of levels. Partly this is a result of the resonances of the verse, which often takes us far beyond the immediate situation.

Intimately connected is the fact that the characters – as often in the late plays – tend to be representative rather than individual. They are comparatively little distinguished by variety of style. Miranda is not a Viola, a Rosalind, or an Innogen. But though she may lack their vibrantly immediate impact, she gains in representativeness. Being less of a particular place and time, she becomes more of all time and everywhere.

In this context actions more easily take on a symbolical value. It is not necessary to go outside the play, for instance, to see Ferdinand's log-carrying as an expression of an idea that crops up at many points. In ordinary life it would be no great hardship for a healthy young man to spend a few hours carrying firewood; but any hint of this attitude in performance is ruinous. (Directors' attitudes to the play may be gauged by the quantity and apparent weight he is required to carry at any one time.) His task must appear as one of the complex of actions and statements connected with the idea of control: a complex that begins in the opening scene where the voyaging noblemen are seen powerless against the force of (as it seems) nature; which is further abumbrated in Prospero's control over nature, over Ariel, and over Caliban, in Caliban's failure to achieve self-control in his attempted rape of Miranda, in the falsely based power that Stefano and Trinculo achieve over Caliban, in their joint attempt to overcome Prospero's authority, paralleling Sebastian's and Antonio's plot to kill Alonso (which itself parallels Antonio's and Alonso's earlier usurpation of Prospero), in Prospero's ability to conjure up the masque (a peaceful counterpart to the tempest that he conjures up at the play's opening), and in the explicit themes of the masque itself (too often obscured by the wrong sort of spectacle or by music that does not foreground the words), which are clearly related to the sexual self-control that Prospero regards as so important in his future son-in-law, and finally in Prospero's ultimate renunciation of power. By a variety of juxtapositions, hints, and poetic devices, Shakespeare makes his romance story a carrier of what might be regarded as a scheme of ideas on a philosophical topic.

And he even introduces contemporary matters. It is reasonable to see in the play a whole set of correspondences to what for its original audience was a burning question of the day: the matter of colonization. It is no accident that among the play's few accepted minor sources are pamphlets on voyaging. There is little explicit reference to the topic; but there is enough for us to be sure that it was present in Shakespeare's consciousness. Caliban complains against Prospero's enslavement of him; and there is justice in his complaint. We are shown the totally irreconcilable situation that arises when civilizations clash. It is parallel to the situation of Shylock and Portia; and though we cannot but feel that Shylock and Caliban have the worse of the argument, yet we feel too some of the anguish involved in a complex moral impasse. To admit the relevance of colonization to the play is not, however, to endorse exclusive concentration on this idea in either criticism or production. Prospero is, after all, a colonizer only upon compulsion; and to focus too intently upon one of the play's systems of ideas, while it may provide a welcome grounding in specificity of its symbolism, risks reducing its multiplicity of suggestiveness.

While the unreality of *The Tempest* contributes towards the play's high suggestive power, it would be false to suggest that the total effect is unreal. The first scene is written in prose so colloquial and vivid that with only minor changes it could stand in a television script. But the opening lines of the next scene suspend reality as we learn that the storm was the product of Prospero's art, and for the remainder of the play the alternation and balance between the palpably unreal and the illusion of reality is maintained. The romance is toughened by a strain of anti-romance. The unrealistic idealism of Gonzalo, especially in his version of an ideal commonwealth (2.1.149–74), is countered by the callous cynicism of Antonio and Sebastian – just as Autolycus adds astringency to the pastoral scenes of *The Winter's Tale*. The virtue of Ferdinand and Miranda is not taken for granted; it is thrown into relief by our knowledge that Caliban has tried to rape Miranda, by his suggestions that the drunken Stefano should make Miranda his queen, and by the care with which Prospero guards the lovers' virtue.

Even Prospero's own virtue is not without its strains. A crucial point in the interpretation of the role comes when he can say: 'At this hour | Lies at my mercy all mine enemies.' The spirit Ariel declares that if Prospero could see them he would feel sorry for them:

> ARIEL   Your charm so strongly works 'em
>   That if you now beheld them your affections
>   Would become tender.
> PROSPERO   Dost thou think so, spirit?
> ARIEL Mine would, sir, were I human.
> PROSPERO   And mine shall.
>   Hast thou, which art but air, a touch, a feeling
>   Of their afflictions, and shall not myself,
>   One of their kind, that relish all as sharply
>   Passion as they, be kindlier moved than thou art?
>   Though with their high wrongs I am struck to th' quick,
>   Yet with my nobler reason 'gainst my fury
>   Do I take part. The rarer action is
>   In virtue than in vengeance.
>
> (5.1.17–28)

The question that faces the play's interpreters is whether from the start Prospero acted with the benevolent aim of bringing his enemies to a truer knowledge of themselves and then forgiving them, or whether, at the opposite extreme, he acted with the intention rather of seeking a vengeance from which he is deflected only by surprised acknowledgement of Ariel's sympathy for them. Traditionally he has been portrayed as an essentially benevolent figure, but in recent years – as in Peter Hall's 1988 production at the National Theatre in which Michael Bryant was an exceptionally irascible Prospero – the harsher elements in his behaviour, not only to his enemies of the past but also to Ariel, Caliban, and even Ferdinand and Miranda, have been emphasized. In such interpretations it is logical to play the interchange with Ariel as the resolution of an inner crisis that brings about a profound change. My own view is that the style of the passage is not anguished enough to bear this interpretation, that it suggests meditation rather than crisis; Prospero is not an inverted Macbeth, overcoming temptation as Macbeth gives in to it; nevertheless we are reminded that he might have taken vengeance, that the travellers are in fact his enemies. Prospero does not bear his responsibilities lightly; he is one in the long line of Shakespeare's worried rulers, extending as far back as Henry VI, for whom the burden of power is greater than its rewards.

In *The Tempest* vicissitudes such as are commonly undergone by inhabitants of the world of romance come to be seen, not so much as random happenings that they survive by the help of fortune, but as events designed to test and, during the course of the action, to define them. The play has exceptional moral seriousness. It is a romance that contains an inbuilt criticism of romance: not a rejection of it, but an appreciation both of its glories and of its limitations. Romance is associated with all that brings man nearer to Ariel than to Caliban. Responsiveness to nature and to art, the capacity for wonder, the ability to sympathize with those that suffer, the desire to shape experience in accordance with an imaginative and moral vision, the value of an attitude to life that denies cynicism even to the extent of creating a somewhat naïve credulity such as Gonzalo's: all these are included.

When art guides nature, when the civilizing forces of self-control are dominant, then Gonzalo's vision may be realized – a vision that looks forward to the masque in which Prospero conjures up goddesses 'A contract of true love to celebrate', heading off Venus and Cupid, who might tempt to wantonness

> this man and maid,
> Whose vows are that no bed-right shall be paid
> Till Hymen's torch be lighted.

Married chastity will bring its rewards:

> Earth's increase, and foison plenty,
> Barns and garners never empty,
> Vines with clust'ring branches growing,
> Plants with goodly burden bowing;
> Spring come to you at the farthest,
> In the very end of harvest.
> Scarcity and want shall shun you,
> Ceres' blessing so is on you.
>
> (4.1.95–7, 110–17)

This is indeed 'a most majestic vision', fittingly celebrated in the form of a masque-like performance enacted by the spirits over whom Prospero has power.

The early seventeenth century was the great age of the masque; nothing could have been more suitable as an image of the results that man can achieve by the exercise of mind and imagination. The masque was at once a symbol of power and wealth, frequently used as such in the Jacobean game of power politics, and also of the highest achievements of civilization, in which the arts of music, dancing, painting, acting, and poetry combined in entertainments whose splendour was enhanced by their folly. Many thousands of pounds were lavished upon a single evening's entertainment by those who could not command unpaid spirits to enact their fancies. So the masque was an apt symbol too of the vanity of human greatness. The glittering bubble is easily pricked. The visions of a Prospero are at the mercy of the Calibans of this world. Power that can create can also destroy, and so, when Prospero remembers the evil being plotted against him – 'I had forgot that foul conspiracy | Of the beast Caliban and his confederates | Against my life' – the vision vanishes leaving not a rack behind. Prospero's famous reaction – 'Our revels now are ended . . .' – is one of acceptance rather than of mourning. Though he is momentarily angered, he controls himself and consoles Ferdinand. The dream is recognized for what it is, but is allowed the reality that belongs even to a dream, or to any product of the imagination – a play, poem, or romance.

The ending of *The Tempest* disappoints those who ask for a full romantic climax. It is true that Prospero's forgiveness, though nominally extended to all, lacks warmth when he speaks to his brother Antonio:

> For you, most wicked sir, whom to call brother
> Would even infect my mouth, I do forgive
> Thy rankest fault.
>
> (5.1.132–4)

But perhaps we should have the right to be disappointed by this only if Prospero had been presented as wholly superhuman. Since Antonio is not shown as penitent, it is not easy to see why Prospero should be expected so soon to show warmth towards the man who has behaved to him somewhat as Macbeth had to Duncan. *The Tempest* is austere, and its final moments are muted; but it is not harsh in total effect. Antonio's impenitence is balanced by Alonso's contrition; Prospero's world-weary emotional exhaustion by Gonzalo's ebullient recognition of the good that has come out of these events, and also, in the younger generation, by the happy conclusion of the love-affair of Ferdinand and Miranda. If Caliban remains in bondage, he is at least temporarily the wiser for his folly; and after Prospero has taken care to ensure that the royal party will have 'calm seas, auspicious gales | And sail so expeditious that shall catch | Your royal fleet far off', he finally frees Ariel to the elements. One might even see a touch of humour in this reversal of the play's opening situation, in which Ariel's help had been harnessed to ensure that the royal party should have anything but calm seas.

There is paradox in the fact that a play so much concerned with control and restraint should end in liberty, but it is a Christian paradox – 'in whose service is perfect freedom' – and one that Shakespeare frequently echoes. Ariel, who has done the services required of him, is set free; all the travellers are liberated from the island to which they came against their will; finally Prospero himself, freed from the responsibilities of exerting his power, appeals to the audience to free him from the stage.

> Now I want
> Spirits to enforce, art to enchant;
> And my ending is despair
> Unless I be relieved by prayer,
> Which pierces so, that it assaults
> Mercy itself, and frees all faults.

As you from crimes would pardoned be,
Let your indulgence set me free.

In the Epilogue, as in other comedies by Shakespeare, the play melts into reality, the ordinary man shows through the actor's costume as the pageant fades; he is doomed to despair unless the audience grants him its prayers ('To prayers, to prayers!' the mariners had cried in the opening scene), and he appeals to them to do so in words that echo the best known of all Christian prayers.

We have no reason to believe that Shakespeare knew that *The Tempest* would be the last play he would write without a collaborator. It is no doubt sentimental to read Prospero's 'Our revels now are ended . . .' as the playwright's farewell to his art. And yet . . . Prospero functions in the play as a ruler, a magician, a father, a teacher, a moralist, but also as an artist, the controller of the action of a play, the conjuror up of a vision that derives from the traditions of literature, a figure who, at whatever stage of the dramatist's career the play had been written, would inevitably have borne some relationship to the author himself. And more than any other of Shakespeare's plays except perhaps *A Midsummer Night's Dream*, *The Tempest* concerns itself with those human achievements that result from control of the imagination, producing works of art which have at their strongest a power of transfiguration, a fresh revelation of the wonder of creation –'O brave new world!' – but which depend for their power entirely upon the sympathetic imagination. *The Tempest* at its first performance might have held its audience spellbound, might have worked on their imaginations as Prospero works on the imaginations of those who inhabit the world of the play; or it might have been hooted off the stage. Prospero's prayer is a real one, and through it we can hear the voice not only of Shakespeare but of all who work in the kingdom of the mind.

Notes to Chapter Fifteen

1 An interesting account of the attempts of several different directors to arrive at a workable acting text which realized the possibilities inherent in the Quarto rather than freely adapting it, is given by Roger Warren in chapter 5 of his book, *Staging Shakespeare's Late Plays* (Oxford, 1990).

2 It is for these reasons that the Oxford *Complete Works* offers a

reconstructed text in the modern-spelling edition while reprinting the Quarto letter for letter in the original-spelling edition.

3 'The Character of a Chambermaid' (1615), in *The Works of Thomas Overbury*, ed. E.F. Rimbault (1856; repr. 1890), p. 102.

4 J.I.M. Stewart, *Character and Motive in Shakespeare* (1949; repr. 1965), p. 35.

5 Roger Warren, *Staging Shakespeare's Late Plays* (1990), p. 102.

6 Helena Faucit, *On Some of Shakespeare's Female Characters* (new and enlarged edition, 1891), pp. 389–90.

7 John Keats, 'Ode on Melancholy'.

8 Although she is called Imogen in the Folio, there are good reasons to believe that this is a misprint: *Textual Companion*, p. 604.

9 *Samuel Johnson on Shakespeare*, p. 235.

10 *Shaw on Shakespeare*, pp. 49, 52.

11 By Emrys Jones, in 'Stuart Cymbeline', *Essays in Criticism* 11 (1961); reprinted in *Shakespeare's Later Comedies*, ed. D.J. Palmer (Harmondsworth, Mx, 1971).

SIXTEEN

A Lost Play Based on *Don Quixote*, One Last English History, and a Tragicomedy of Ancient Athens:

Cardenio, Henry the Eighth, or All Is True, and *The Two Noble Kinsmen*

Although *The Tempest* is not Shakespeare's last play, it may well be the last on which he worked without the help of a collaborator. Why this should be we don't know. Certainly his style was becoming more involuted; maybe he had lost interest in writing for the popular theatre, but went on for a while mainly to help a younger colleague. Maybe his fellows dissuaded him from continuing to write on his own: not to put too fine a point upon it, they may have eased him into retirement. Or there may have been external circumstances of which no trace survives. He was only in his late forties, but may have had an illness. He appears to have gone on working until a couple of years before he died, but not with his earlier fecundity. And one play of which he was probably part-author is lost. On 20 May 1613 the Privy Council authorized payment to John Heminges, as leader of the King's Men, for the presentation at court of six plays, one listed as *Cardenno*, and on 9 July of the same year Heminges received £6 13s 4d for his company's performance of a play 'called *Cardenna*' before the ambassador of the Duke of Savoy.

The name of the play resembles that of a character, Cardenio, in Part One of Cervantes's *Don Quixote*, which had appeared in an English translation in the previous year. The likelihood that the King's Men's play dramatized episodes from the novel is increased by an entry in the Stationers' Register for 9 September 1653 of a batch of plays including '*The History of Cardenio*, by Mr Fletcher and Shakespeare'. Though this entry must be looked on with suspicion, there is no reason to suppose that Humphrey Moseley, who made it, should have invented this distinctive title, and it is too close to the recorded facts of 1613 to be dismissed out of hand. It forms part of the evidence that after writing *The Tempest* Shakespeare gave up independent playwriting and wrote only in collaboration with his younger colleague, John Fletcher, born in 1579.

Although no play called *Cardenio* survives, in 1728 Lewis Theobald (whose edition of Shakespeare's plays was to appear five years later) published a play based on the story of Cardenio and called *Double Falsehood, or The Distrest Lovers* which he said he had 'revised and adapted' from one 'written originally by W. Shakespeare'; it had recently had a successful production at Drury Lane and was to receive a number of later performances. It is a tragicomedy with motifs – particularly a disguised heroine wronged by her lover and the reuniting and reconciliation of parents with children – that resemble those of Shakespeare's late plays, though the dialogue does not seem conspicuously Shakespearian. Theobald himself said that some of his contemporaries thought the style of the original play was Fletcher's not Shakespeare's, and it is perfectly possible that he based *Double Falsehood* on the play performed by the King's Men in 1613 and ascribed in 1653 to Fletcher and Shakespeare. Although Theobald claimed to own several manuscripts of an original play by Shakespeare, when he edited the complete works he included only the plays of the First Folio, not even adding *Pericles* and *The Two Noble Kinsmen* although he believed both of them to be partly by Shakespeare. It would be exciting if we could find one of these manuscripts, but in 1770 a newspaper stated that 'the original manuscript' on which *Double Falsehood* was based was 'treasured up in the Museum of Covent Garden Playhouse'; the theatre and its library were destroyed by fire in 1808.[1] For the present, and perhaps for ever, *Double Falsehood* is the nearest we can come to *Cardenio*. Though it is a perfectly performable tragicomedy, it exerts little appeal in its own right.

Fire was an even greater hazard to the thatched buildings of Shakespeare's time than in Georgian London, and on the afternoon of 29 June 1613 it struck a terrible blow to the King's Men: the Globe Theatre burned to the ground during a performance of a play written (at least in part) by Shakespeare himself. It was a newsworthy event, and happily numerous contemporary accounts survive, making this the most circumstantially recorded performance of any of the plays.[2] Most of the accounts refer to the play that was being acted when the fire started; some speak of it simply as a play about Henry VIII, but the title cited by the only three actually to give it a name differs from that under which it appears in the First Folio. None, unfortunately, says who wrote it.

One account was written by hand in an almanac by one Matthew Page: his entry for the date of the fire (but not necessarily written on this day) reads: 'The Globe on the Bankside was burned down to the ground by shooting of a chamber; they played *All Is True.*'

Three days after the fire Sir Henry Wotton, a distinguished poet, diplomat, and translator who had already served as ambassador to Venice and was to end his career as provost of Eton College, wrote about it in greater and more picturesque detail in a letter addressed to his nephew Sir Edmund Bacon:

> I will entertain you at the present with what hath happened this week at the Bankside. The King's players had a new play called *All Is True*, representing some principal pieces of the reign of Henry VIII, which was set forth with many extraordinary circumstances of pomp and majesty, even to the matting of the stage; the Knights of the Order, with their Georges and Garter, the Guards with their embroidered coats and the like, sufficient in truth within a while to make greatness very familiar, if not ridiculous. Now, King Henry making a masque at the Cardinal Wolsey's house, and certain chambers being shot off at his entry, some of the paper or other stuff wherewith one of them was stopped did light on the thatch, where being thought at first but an idle smoke, and their eyes more attentive to the show, it kindled inwardly and ran round like a train, consuming within less than an hour the whole house to the very grounds. This was the fatal period of that virtuous fabric, wherein yet nothing did perish but wood and straw and a few forsaken cloaks; only one man had his breeches set on fire, that would perhaps have broiled him if he had not by the benefit of a provident wit put it out with bottle ale.

If Wotton was not himself present at the Globe he must have talked to someone who was, and his letter is valuable not only for the information about the fire but for what he says about the staging of the play before the thatch began to burn. Interesting too is his aristocratic reluctance to see the trappings of greatness displayed on the public stage.

Another letter written two days later, by a young London merchant, Henry Bluett, adds to knowledge of the event:

On Tuesday last there was acted at the Globe a new play called *All Is True* which had been acted not passing two or three times before; there came many people to see it, in so much that the house was very full and as the play was almost ended the house was fired with shooting off a chamber which was stopped with tow which was blown up into the thatch of the house and so burned down to the ground. But the people escaped all without hurt except one man who was scalded with the fire by adventuring in to save a child which otherwise had been burnt.[3]

There is a discrepancy here from Wotton's account in that the masque comes towards the end of the first act of the play, not close to its conclusion; the stage direction preceding Henry's entry reads '*Chambers discharged*', so Wotton seems more likely to be right, Bluett to be dependent on hearsay. Both agree that the play was new, and Bluett's statement that it had 'been acted not passing two or three times before' gives more precision to this dating. And the concurrence of all three documents (two of which – those by Page and Bluett – were not discovered until the 1980s) demonstrates beyond all reasonable doubt that its first audiences knew the play as *All Is True*, not as *The Famous History of the Life of King Henry the Eighth*, the title under which it appeared in the First Folio, presumably in line with a consistent policy of naming all the plays about English history by the names of the kings most prominent in each of them.

Thomas Lorkin, writing the day after the fire (and referring to 'the play of Henry VIII'), remarked that it 'consumed the whole house' in 'less than two hours', but everyone agrees that there were no serious casualties even though, as John Chamberlain wrote, there were only 'two narrow doors to get out'; and judging by the amount of manuscript material that was available to those who put together the First Folio, it seems likely either that most of the players' papers, including prompt books, were not kept in the theatre, or that they were able to save them.

Additional evidence that *All Is True* was the play's original title comes from its use as the refrain of a lively eight-stanza ballad which is probably one of two entered in the Stationers' Register the day after the fire; neither survives in print, but one of them, known from an early manuscript copy, offers a vivid if unsophisticated description of the event ('Condye' is presumably Condell, and the 'drumheads' were the skins of the drums used by the theatre musicians):

Out run the knights, out run the lords,
    And there was great ado;
Some lost their hats, and some their swords,
    Then out run Burbage too;
The reprobates, though drunk on Monday,
Prayed for the fool and Henry Condye.
    O sorrow, pitiful sorrow,
        And yet all this is true.

The periwigs and drumheads fry
    Like to a butter firkin;
A woeful burning did betide
    To many a good buff jerkin.
Then with swoll'n eyes, like drunken Fleming's,
Distressèd stood old stuttering Heminges.
    O sorrow, etc.

No shower his rain did there down force
    In all that sunshine weather
To save that great renownèd house,
    Nor thou, O alehouse, neither.
Had it begun below, sans doubt,
Their wives for fear had pissed it out.
    O sorrow, etc.[4]

The ballad-maker offered the actors practical advice: that they use any money they might otherwise have spent on whoring in saving up to buy tiles, not thatch, for the Globe's successor; and indeed the second Globe, in use within a year, was tiled, whether or not as a result of self-restraint on the part of the actors. It was in this building, in 1628, that the then Duke of Buckingham, James I's favourite, Charles Villiers, commissioned the only other performance of the play recorded before the closing of the theatres in 1642; he took a party of guests, but stayed only until his namesake had left the stage for execution, early in the second act.

Wotton's remark that the play whose performance was halted by the fire represented 'some principal pieces of the reign of Henry VIII, which was set forth with many extraordinary circumstances of pomp and majesty' prefigured much of the interest that the play has had for later ages. It has been valued primarily for its presentation of significant episodes in the lives of King Henry, Cardinal Wolsey, Queen Katherine, and to a lesser extent the Duke of Buckingham, for the opportunities it gives to the performers of these roles, and for the theatricalism of its portrayal of pomp and circumstance and of regal spectacle in, especially, the defence of Katherine, the coronation of Anne Boleyn, and the climactic baptism of the future Queen Elizabeth I.

The spectacular episodes are described in exceptionally lengthy stage directions calling for an unusual number of performers: the first requires (as well as musicians who may be off stage) twenty-three actors who must all be on stage at the same time; the second, in addition to the two Gentlemen who '*comment on the procession as it passes over the stage*', eighteen actors along with on-stage trumpeters and choristers and 'certain ladies or countesses'; and the final scene opens with a procession calling for on-stage trumpeters and sixteen adult actors (one of them 'bearing the child Elizabeth richly habited in a mantle') and also requires the presence of King Henry and his guard (probably plural). These processions call too for elaborate royal and ecclesiastical costumes and for impressive props – for the trial, for instance, 'short silver wands', 'the purse containing the great seal and a cardinal's hat', two silver crosses, a silver mace, 'two great silver pillars', 'the sword and mace', a throne under a cloth of state, other seats, and various hand properties. If these directions (largely based on Holinshed) were put into practice, presentation of the play must have severely taxed the wardrobe master and the property department of the King's Men as well as its actors. Katherine's defence would have had particular resonances if it had been played in the Blackfriars, because the chamber occupied by the theatre was the very one in which the hearing had taken place.

For all the play's spectacular qualities, its emotional range is comparatively narrow. Like most of the histories written early in Shakespeare's career, it is composed almost entirely in verse; but unlike those plays – even *Richard the Second*, to which it is closest in style – it has no violent action, no on-stage deaths, and little comedy; indeed, the Prologue's opening words are

> I come no more to make you laugh. Things now
> That bear a weighty and a serious brow,
> Sad, high, and working, full of state and woe –
> Such noble scenes as draw the eye to flow
> We now present.

Emphasizing that the play will present 'truth', he draws attention too to the exemplary nature of the events it portrays:

> Think ye see
> The very persons of our noble story
> As they were living; think you see them great,
> And followed with the general throng and sweat
> Of thousand friends; then, in a moment, see
> How soon this mightiness meets misery.

This thematic statement is very much borne out by the play that follows. In this play we do not so much participate in the making of history as contemplate it with a sense of knowing what is to come. This is moral history, a formalized presentation of the rise and fall of greatness, a selective arrangement of incidents and episodes manipulating the historical sources in the interests of a moral and poetic design.

The very first scene presents a splendid and quintessentially late-Shakespearian vision – easier to read than to hear, and not particularly easy to read – of what the Duke of Norfolk calls 'earthly glory' in his description of the meeting of Henry VIII and the King of France at the Field of the Cloth of Gold as a prelude to the downfall of the Duke of Buckingham, who has no sooner declared he will denounce Wolsey's self-seeking to the King than he is arrested at Wolsey's instigation and carried off to the Tower where he will be executed.

As soon as Buckingham has made his eloquent if implausibly over-pious last addresses to 'the common people', seeking their prayers 'as the long divorce of steel falls' on him, the two anonymous Gentlemen who do much to stitch the play together come forward to tell us of 'A buzzing of a separation | Between the King and Katherine', setting off a second wave of action in which we see the rise of Anne Boleyn in the King's affections at the expense of Queen Katherine; overarching these events is the malignant power of Cardinal Wolsey, but his sway over Henry is challenged by the growing influence with the King of Anne and to a lesser extent of Cranmer, and Wolsey's overweening opposition to them, stated with formulaic simplicity (3.2.95–105), leads predictably and speedily to his downfall, which he foresees in lines which, though they are eloquent, take an outsider's view of his fate, as if he were writing a poem about it:

> Nay then, farewell.
> I have touched the highest point of all my greatness,
> And from that full meridian of my glory
> I haste now to my setting. I shall fall

> Like a bright exhalation in the evening,
> And no man see me more.
>
> (3.2.223–8)

He faces death more nobly than he has lived, mourned by his follower Thomas Cromwell, whom he foresees the King will advance but whom he advises to shun ambition and to avoid his own errors:

> O Cromwell, Cromwell,
> Had I but served my God with half the zeal
> I served my King, He would not in mine age
> Have left me naked to mine enemies.
>
> (3.2.455–8)

Wolsey's extended expressions of penitence and regret following his fall are part of the play's conscious patterning, and lead to retrospective evaluations of him from Katherine and her servant Griffith which serve also to remind the audience of the achievements by which he was remembered when the play was first performed; again, the pietistic, evaluative historian seems to take precedence over the dramatist.

Katherine has an even more elaborate and morally elegiac scene of farewell to life, complete with an angelic dream-vision (a little like those in *Pericles* and *Cymbeline*), than Buckingham and Wolsey, commending to Henry's 'goodness | The model of our chaste loves, his young daughter' Mary Tudor, although we have already heard a forecast that from the King's union with Anne Boleyn 'may proceed a gem | To lighten all this isle' (2.3.78–9). In the play's closing scenes we hear of the birth of this gem, the future Queen Elizabeth I; Henry's disappointment at her sex is played down, though the Old Lady who brings him the news (and obtusely says at first that the child is a boy) is clearly disappointed that she receives no more than one hundred marks as a reward; we also see Cranmer escape committal to the Tower only as a result of the King's intervention.

The climax is Cranmer's baptism of the baby princess in a speech of prophecy which, rather like the closing speech of *Richard the Third* – spoken by Henry VIII's father – extends the time-scheme beyond the events portrayed, through the intervening years, and up to the time of the play's original performance by looking forward to the peace and prosperity that England will enjoy as a consequence of the royal person we see before us. In *Richard the Third* the prophecy seems artistically justified because it comes as the logical and hard-won conclusion to the momentous events not only of the play we have been watching but of the three that preceded it. In *Henry the Eighth, or All Is True*, although Cranmer declares that none should think his words 'flattery, for they'll find 'em truth', it is liable to sound much more like a tacked-on and sycophantic eulogy not only of Queen Elizabeth – which perhaps we could accept as she was dead and more obviously deserved at least a measure of the fulsome praise she is accorded – but, less relevantly and less justly, of her successor, King James, patron of the company that performed the play at the Globe and, quite probably, before him at court. From the ashes of the phoenix Elizabeth, we are told, will arise

> another heir
> As great in admiration as herself,
> So shall she leave her blessèdness to one,
> When heaven shall call her from this cloud of darkness,
> Who from the sacred ashes of her honour
> Shall star-like rise as great in fame as she was,
> And so stand fixed. Peace, plenty, love, truth, terror,
> That were the servants to this chosen infant,
> Shall then be his, and, like a vine, grow to him.
> Wherever the bright sun of heaven shall shine,
> His honour and the greatness of his name
> Shall be, and make new nations. He shall flourish,
> And like a mountain cedar reach his branches
> To all the plains about him. Our children's children
> Shall see this, and bless heaven.

(5.4.41–55)

That is (as Celia says in *As You Like It*) 'laid on with a trowel'.

The structure of the play lays emphasis on set-pieces and on long, retrospective speeches, elegiac in tone, of self-defence and regret. There is little cut and thrust of dialogue, nor even any true introspection. Emotion is frequently generalized, and characterization suffers as a result. The verse is often excellent in its own right, but offers actors little basis in reality from which to build up their roles. The play has nevertheless an extensive stage history, but it has often been severely shortened to emphasize its opportunities for spectacle and to increase the importance of what are seen as the star roles, mainly Wolsey (one of Irving's best parts) and Katherine. But it has not appealed greatly to the post-war theatre, and although I have seen fine performances in it – Peggy Ashcroft's Katherine, for instance – I have never seen a production that made overall a convincing impression.

There is no external evidence that Shakespeare did not write the whole play, but doubts about its integrity go back to Malone in 1778; the first serious attempt to prove that Fletcher was a part-author came from James Spedding (at Tennyson's suggestion) in 1850. His views have been generally, but not universally, accepted; some scholars still regard Shakespeare as its sole author, some would add Fletcher's regular collaborator, Francis Beaumont, to the equation. The evidence for collaboration comes from language and style; some of it is highly technical, some more impressionistic: as Gary Taylor writes, 'The scenes assignable to Shakespeare display consistently the kinds of grammatical muscularity characteristic of his late style . . . those assignable to Beaumont or Fletcher do not, demonstrating instead the verbal ease and digestibility for which those writers were most famed in their own era and most criticized in ours.'[5] My own opinion is that this is a collaborative play and that Fletcher is one of the collaborators, but that the authors worked closely enough together to achieve at least a superficial unity of tone for most of the play. On the other hand the opening scene reads to me like pure Shakespeare, the epilogue pure Fletcher. Collaboration does not of itself imply inferiority; Fletcher was a highly successful author in his own time and some of his plays are still effectively revived; but it can diminish individuality, and this play does not seem to me to represent either author at his best. To Fletcher, I am happy to say, is generally assigned the eulogy of James I.

The last play with which Shakespeare is associated is *The Two Noble Kinsmen*. Like *Pericles*, this was not included in the First Folio. It had to wait for publication until 1634, when it was stated to have been written 'by the memorable worthies of their time, Mr John Fletcher, and Mr William Shakespeare'. There is no good reason to doubt this ascription: many plays of the time did not appear in print until long after they were written, and the compilers of the Folio may have omitted this one because they knew that much of it was by Fletcher, while including the play about Henry VIII in order to complete the history cycle. Or Fletcher may have withheld it.

The belief that *The Two Noble Kinsmen* is the last play that Shakespeare had anything to do with derives partly from its style but more firmly from the fact that the morris dance in Act 3, Scene 5 contains characters who also appear in Francis Beaumont's *Masque of the Inner Temple and Gray's Inn* which was performed before James I on

20 February 1613. Their dance went down well with the King, who called for an encore, and it seems likely that his players – some of whom probably took part in the masque – decided to exploit its success by incorporating part of it in a play written soon afterwards, in the last year of Shakespeare's playwriting life. The speaker of the Prologue refers to 'our losses', which may allude to the burning of the Globe on 29 June.

The play itself is a tragicomedy of a kind that became fashionable and popular during the last years of the first decade of the seventeenth century. It is related in style and content to Shakespeare's romances and to tragicomedies written by Fletcher with Francis Beaumont, also for the King's Men. Like *Pericles*, it derives from a medieval tale – this time by Chaucer – and is Grecian in setting. As in all Shakespeare's late plays, the supernatural looms large in both action and language, and is associated with ritualistic action and spectacular stage effects; the appearance of gods in *Pericles* and *Cymbeline*, the trick table and the masque in *The Tempest*, the supposed statue in *The Winter's Tale*, and the dream-vision in *Henry the Eighth, or All Is True*, have their principal counterparts here in the emblematic signs at the altars of Mars, Venus, and Diana in the last act, which also require trick properties, indicated by directions such as '*Here music is heard; doves are seen to flutter*', '*Here the hind vanishes under the altar, and in the place ascends a rose tree, having one rose upon it*', and '*Here is heard a sudden twang of instruments, and the rose falls from the tree.*' Characteristic of Fletcher are the theatrically effective, if psychologically implausible, reversals of behaviour resulting from the conflicting demands of love and friendship witnessed in Palamon and Arcite (the kinsmen of the play's title), and the tender if sentimental exploitation of nostalgia and pathos as in the reminiscences of the kinsmen and the madness of the anonymous Jailer's Daughter.

The individual styles of the two collaborators are easier to discern in *The Two Noble Kinsmen* than in *All Is True*, and the most characteristically Shakespearian passages were greatly admired by, especially, certain Romantic critics. Thomas de Quincey described the first and the last acts as 'in point of composition . . . perhaps the most superb work in the language' which 'would have been the most gorgeous rhetoric, had they not happened to be something far better'; less rhapsodically and more analytically, Charles Lamb had attempted a distinction between the two dramatists' styles: Fletcher's 'ideas moved slow; his versification, though sweet, is tedious, it stops every moment; he lays line upon line, making up one after the other, adding image to image so deliberately that we see where they join: Shakspeare mingles every thing, he runs line into line, embarrasses sentences and metaphors; before one idea has burst its shell, another is hatched and clamorous for disclosure'.[6] This Shakespearian complexity may be seen, for instance, in the speech in which one of the Three Queens, widows of kings killed in the siege of Thebes, addresses Hippolyta in the opening scene:

> Honoured Hippolyta,
> Most dreaded Amazonian, that hast slain
> The scythe-tusked boar, that with thy arm, as strong
> As it is white, wast near to make the male
> To thy sex captive, but that this, thy lord –
> Born to uphold creation in that honour
> First nature styled it in – shrunk thee into
> The bound thou wast o'erflowing, at once subduing
> Thy force and thy affection; soldieress,
> That equally canst poise sternness with pity,
> Whom now I know hast much more power on him
> Than ever he had on thee, who ow'st his strength,
> And his love too, who is a servant for
> The tenor of thy speech; dear glass of ladies,
> Bid him that we, whom flaming war doth scorch,
> Under the shadow of his sword may cool us.
> Require him he advance it o'er our heads.
> Speak't in a woman's key, like such a woman
> As any of us three. Weep ere you fail.
> Lend us a knee:
> But touch the ground for us no longer time
> Than a dove's motion when the head's plucked off.
> Tell him, if he i'th' blood-sized field lay swoll'n,
> Showing the sun his teeth, grinning at the moon,
> What you would do.

> (1.1.77–101)

The complex rhetoric of the speech, with its sixteen-line first sentence, tortuous in construction, piling subordinate clauses one on top of another, some in apposition, some subordinate to others, with its qualifying and parenthetical clauses, its figurative language, its mixture of concrete and abstract expressions, its coined compounds ('scythe-tusked' and, later, 'blood-sized'), its invented word ('soldieress', not previously recorded), its inversions and ellipses and elisions, its run-on verse lines and feminine endings, and the grotesque

imagery of the concluding lines, amounts almost to a parody of
Shakespeare's late style, making no concessions to either the speaker
or the hearer; and the bizarre image used to convey the brevity of the
time that Hippolyta should kneel – 'no longer time | Than a dove's
motion when the head's plucked off' – has a surreal quality, almost a
madness about it, like certain images in *Cymbeline*, as, for example,
that in which Belarius contrasts the low entrance to his cave with 'the
gates of monarchs', which 'Are arched so high that giants may jet
[strut] through | And keep their impious turbans on' (3.3.4–7), or that
in which Arviragus, expressing the love 'without reason' that he feels
for the disguised Innogen, declares, 'The bier at door | And a demand
who is't shall die, I'd say | "My father, not this youth" ' (4.2.22–4).
Such strange analogies surely derive from the same, possibly
disturbed, imagination.[7]

More characteristic of Fletcher in its evenness of style, its relatively
greater ease of comprehension, and its unforced eloquence is, for
instance, Arcite's refusal to plead for mercy to Theseus:

>   Where this man calls me traitor
> Let me say thus much – if in love be treason,
> In service of so excellent a beauty,
> As I love most, and in that faith will perish,
> As I have brought my life here to confirm it,
> As I have served her truest, worthiest,
> As I dare kill this cousin that denies it,
> So let me be most traitor and ye please me.
> For scorning thy edict, Duke, ask that lady
> Why she is fair, and why her eyes command me
> Stay here to love her, and if she say, 'Traitor',
> I am a villain fit to lie unburied.
>
>   (3.6.160–71)

There are then discrepancies of style within the play, and even of
subject-matter: in the second scene, ascribed to Shakespeare, for
example, the kinsmen deplore the moral laxity of Thebes, determining to leave the court of that 'most unbounded tyrant' their uncle
Creon, whereas in the opening scene of the second act, believed to
have been written by Fletcher, they talk of their 'noble country,
Thebes' with a nostalgia that seems at odds with their former
condemnation of its faults.

Nevertheless there are thematic links within the overall structure of
the play that suggest a high degree of collaboration in its planning.

Like *A Midsummer Night's Dream*, *The Two Noble Kinsmen* is based on Chaucer's 'Knight's Tale', but whereas the earlier play leads up to the marriage of Theseus and Hippolyta, the later one starts with it, and centres on the tale of the rivalry of the kinsmen, Palamon and Arcite, for the hand of Hippolyta's sister, Emilia. The play is deeply concerned with friendship, with love, with tensions resulting from the conflicting demands of friendship and love, and with marriage. And it is full of erotic tension, apparent in the mutual affection of the kinsmen, resolved into heterosexual love by the appearance of Emilia, and in Emilia's psychological problems, with her beautifully expressed nostalgic attachment to her dead childhood friend Flavina, and her deep-seated reluctance to forswear her devotion to Diana, goddess of chastity.

An invented episode in the first act seems designed to emphasize the theme of friendship: Theseus's friend, Pirithous, takes his farewell of Hippolyta and Emilia, provoking from Hippolyta an admiring account of the 'knot of love' between the two men; it is this that moves Emilia to talk of her childhood love for Flavina, who died when they were both eleven:

> The flower that I would pluck
> And put between my breasts – O then but beginning
> To swell about the blossom – she would long
> Till she had such another, and commit it
> To the like innocent cradle, where, phoenix-like,
> They died in perfume. On my head no toy
> But was her pattern. Her affections – pretty,
> Though happily her careless wear – I followed
> For my most serious decking. Had mine ear
> Stol'n some new air, or at adventure hummed one,
> From musical coinage, why, it was a note
> Whereon her spirits would sojourn – rather dwell on –
> And sing it in her slumbers. This rehearsal –
> Which, seely innocence wots well, comes in
> Like old emportment's bastard – has this end:
> That the true love 'tween maid and maid may be
> More than in sex dividual.
>
>   (1.3.66–82)

Emilia is sure she will never love a man; Hippolyta is sceptical.

No less intense, and sexually ambivalent, is the friendship between Palamon and Arcite; 'We are', says Arcite, 'an endless mine to one another: | We are one another's wife, ever begetting | New births of love' (2.2.79–81), and they sustain an antiphon of mutual admiration and expressions of love eternal which with calculated, and very Fletcherian, irony reaches its climax – 'after death our spirits shall be led on | To those that love eternally' – at the very moment that Emilia comes within view. Palamon is the first to see her – and will later, rather childishly, lay claim to her on this account ('I saw her first' [2.2.163]); both of them fall instantly in love with her, and within seconds are quarrelling over her. Their rivalry in love forms the backbone of the play, and leads to some effective episodes exploiting the tension between their enduring affection for each other and their rivalry in love, episodes such as that in which they reminisce nostalgically, and somewhat bawdily, about their previous girl-friends, reverting to a state of enmity as they recall Emilia (3.3), and another in which, while tenderly helping each other to arm for the duel they are to fight for Emilia's sake, they recall past exploits and express mutual affection and admiration (3.6). Theseus interrupts their duel and condemns them to death, but after Hippolyta, Emilia, and Pirithous have pleaded for them he relents and ordains that they shall take part in a combat in which Emilia will be the prize but the loser will be condemned to death.

Though Emilia is reconciled to the thought that she must marry, she is at a loss to choose between her suitors, and distressed that one of them must die. Preparations for the combat are elaborate, with lengthy speeches from Arcite to Mars, from Palamon to Venus, and from Emilia to Diana. Emilia refuses to watch the tournament, doubtless because theatrically it is more easily represented as taking place within earshot but out of sight. At first she hears that Palamon is winning, but finally Arcite enters victorious, and they plight their troth. The end of the story is both dramatic and expressive of the continuing magnanimity within rivalry of the kinsmen. As loser, Palamon prepares for death, nobly rejoicing at Emilia's forthcoming marriage. His head is on the block, and his knights are ready to follow him in death, when a messenger rushes in to stay the execution. Pirithous follows with news that Arcite has been thrown and mortally injured by the all-black horse that Emilia gave him: he is 'such a vessel . . . that floats but for | The surge that next approaches'. Arcite is carried in, cedes Emilia to his friend, and dies. Theseus rounds off the play with reflections on the paradoxes of Fortune: 'the conquered triumphs, | The victor has the loss.' For a day or two they will mourn for Arcite, then 'smile with Palamon'. Men must accept their destinies, feel 'thankful | For that which is', and not dispute with the gods in matters 'That are above our question'.

Alongside this courtly, elevated, and idealized portrayal of chivalric love and friendship, with its subtext of sexual inhibition, the dramatists run the linked story of the uninhibited but thwarted love for Palamon of the unnamed Jailer's Daughter. As Palamon and Arcite, in the prison, have fallen in love at first sight with Emilia, so has the Daughter with Palamon; but whereas Emilia is determined (at first) to preserve her virginity, the Daughter is desperate with desire to lose hers, as she reveals in a splendidly actable soliloquy:

> Fairer spoken
> Was never gentleman. When I come in
> To bring him water in a morning, first
> He bows his noble body, then salutes me, thus:
> 'Fair, gentle maid, good morrow. May thy goodness
> Get thee a happy husband.' Once he kissed me –
> I loved my lips the better ten days after.
> Would he would do so every day! He grieves much,
> And me as much to see his misery.
> What should I do to make him know I love him?
> For I would fain enjoy him.
>
> (2.4.20–30)

Although she succeeds in expressing her devotion to Palamon by releasing him from prison, and declares her love to him, his unresponsiveness eventually drives her lyrically mad in a style that owes much to the Ophelia of *Hamlet* with an odd reminiscence of *Antony and Cleopatra* in her words 'in the next world will Dido see Palamon, and then will she be out of love with Aeneas'. She inhabits a society with far freer attitudes to sex than that of the main plot, one in which rustics (who owe something to those of *A Midsummer Night's Dream*) dance for the Duke's entertainment a morris that has obvious reference to fertility rites, and in which a Doctor can propose that her Wooer, whom she has ignored for Palamon, should impersonate him in an attempt to restore her sanity, and sleep with her if she asks him; the device works, to their mutual satisfaction:

WOOER   Come, sweet, we'll go to dinner,
    And then we'll play at cards.
JAILER'S DAUGHTER   And shall we kiss too?

WOOER A hundred times.
JAILER'S DAUGHTER   And twenty.
WOOER   Ay, and twenty.
JAILER'S DAUGHTER And then we'll sleep together.
DOCTOR (*to the Wooer*)   Take her offer.
WOOER (*to the Jailer's Daughter*)
    Yes, marry, will we.
JAILER'S DAUGHTER   But you shall not hurt me.
WOOER I will not, sweet.
JAILER'S DAUGHTER   If you do, love, I'll cry. *Exeunt*
                                              (5.4.108–13)

In the last scene Palamon, preparing to die, learns that she is 'well restored, | And to be married shortly'; with chivalrous generosity, he and his knights donate their purses to swell her dowry.

The Two Noble Kinsmen has suffered as a result of its omission from the First Folio. For centuries it was regarded as part of the Beaumont and Fletcher canon, not of Shakespeare's; its first appearance in an edition of Shakespeare's collected works was among the 'Doubtful Plays' in Charles Knight's *Pictorial Edition* of 1839–41, and since then it has only sporadically been accounted as part of the canon, being omitted from such influential editions as the Globe, the Pelican, the Alexander, and the Arden. Partly, no doubt, for this reason it has also been neglected in the theatre. An adaptation by William Davenant called *The Rivals* (in which the Jailer's Daughter succeeds in marrying Palamon) was played with success in the 1660s, but the first recorded revival of the original play was at the Old Vic in 1928, and although I saw a university production in the open air at Stratford in 1959, it did not achieve professional performance there until 1986, when it was selected as the opening play for the Swan Theatre, where it was directed by Barry Kyle. No doubt the smaller theatre was chosen in part because the play was unlikely to draw the large audiences necessary to fill the main house, but it may have been appropriate to the way the play is written, since the title-page of the first edition says it had been performed at the Blackfriars, without mentioning the Globe.

    In the Swan production, as in many of the others, both amateur and professional, that the play has received, there was no doubt that the most appealing role in a play that is unusually rich in women's parts was that of the Jailer's Daughter, touchingly and amusingly played by Imogen Stubbs with an exciting combination of innocence and eroticism. A reviewer of the Old Vic revival in 1928 found that 'So long as we kept to madwomen, rustics, gaolers, school-masters and doctors, it was all right. But the moment we ascended the social ladder and mingled with Queens, lords, knights, and friends of knights, the general tone ascended also to the rarefied atmosphere of aristocratic obscurity'; that is an understandable if somewhat philistine reaction. The Shakespearian rhetoric of the first and last acts (described by the Swan director, Barry Kyle, as 'clotted') has often been abbreviated, but the elaborate ceremonies and rituals of these parts of the play can be both impressive and moving, and the success in performance of the more obviously Fletcherian scenes, especially those between Palamon and Arcite, suggests that collaboration with Shakespeare brought the best out of Fletcher. But the real success of the Swan production was to demonstrate the play's overall unity of conception, clinched by causing the final image to be a visual confrontation of Emilia and the Jailer's Daughter, one at each side of the stage.

If we have writ our annals true, *The Two Noble Kinsmen* was Shakespeare's last work for the theatre. Our only other record of him as a writer in 1613 is as the deviser of an impresa for Francis Manners, sixth Earl of Rutland, for the tilt on the King's Accession Day, 24 March – probably before the play was written. The account book of the Earl's steward records the payment 'to Mr Shakspeare in gold about my Lorde's impreso, xliiij^s'; Richard Burbage, artist as well as actor, received the same sum 'for paynting and making yt'. Shakespeare had demonstrated his ability at this kind of thing in a tournament scene in *Pericles*; perhaps Rutland had seen the play.

As I have said, we don't know why Shakespeare stopped writing; nor, except for a few records of activities centred mainly on Stratford, do we know how he occupied his time for the remaining couple of years of his life. Nicholas Rowe's version may seem too like one of the last-act visions of Shakespeare's own plays to be true, but is at least worth quoting as what might have been: 'The latter part of his life was spent, as all men of good sense will wish theirs may be, in ease, retirement, and the conversation of his friends.'

Notes to Chapter Sixteen

1 Brean S. Hammond, 'Theobald's *Double Falsehood*: An "Agreeable Cheat"?', *Notes and Queries* 229 (1984), pp. 2–3.
2 Those accounts known up to 1923 are discussed by E.K. Chambers in *The Elizabethan Stage*, vol. 2, pp. 419–23; two more discovered in the 1980s are reproduced in the Oxford *Textual Companion*, p. 30.
3 Modernized from Maija Jansson Cole, 'A New Account of the Burning of the Globe', *Shakespeare Quarterly* 32 (1981), p. 352.
4 Modernized from the transcript by Peter Beal, 'The Burning of the Globe', *TLS*, 20 June 1986, pp. 689–90.
5 *Textual Companion*, p. 134.
6 De Quincey and Lamb are cited by E.M. Waith in his Oxford Shakespeare edition (Oxford, 1989), pp. 9–10.
7 The strangeness of the images in *Cymbeline* was pointed out to me long ago by the late Professor T.J.B. Spencer.

CONCLUSION

Shakespeare was not the only great dramatist of his time. He learned from many others, especially, early in his career, from John Lyly, Robert Greene, and Christopher Marlowe. Some of his contemporaries succeeded in ways that he did not attempt. Ben Jonson is the greater satirist, Thomas Middleton the more acute observer of contemporary life. Shakespeare is predominantly romantic in tone. Still, he is unique among his fellows for the range of his achievement, and this is, as I wrote in my opening chapter, one of the reasons for looking at his work as a whole.

The 'universality' of his appeal can be exaggerated. There are many people who haven't heard of him, or don't want to know about him – and not only in areas of the globe remote from England. Still, there is no question that he is the most enduringly popular dramatist there has ever been – or at least that, for whatever reasons, his plays have dominated attention to an exceptional degree. This popularity is sometimes accused of being a political construct; and it is true that the centrality of his plays in our educational system has given an artificial boost to his reputation. It's true too that an illusion of popularity has sometimes been created through vulgarization.

Yet Shakespeare can exert an instant appeal; responsible productions of his plays can entrance unsophisticated audiences, while on the other hand his work has proved profoundly and complexly meaningful to some of the best minds of many generations and nations. Partly this is because of his command over language, which I have tried to illustrate at various points in this book. But if his plays survive translation, this is also because of their structural qualities, the ways in which their plots are bodied forth in dramatic terms that do not depend entirely on words.

More important still is the fact that he so often grapples with fundamental issues that never cease to concern us: with love and hate, with wit and folly, with the waywardness of the sexual instinct, with relations between generations, with violence and tenderness, with problems of self-government and of national government, with our need to come to grips with the inevitability of death and our yearning to find meaning in existence. He is finally the most humane of writers, the one who most poignantly convinces us of his compassion for his fellow human beings, and it is for this that we value him most.

Index

Note: Works by Shakespeare appear under title; works by others under author's name